Jacques Derrida

Opening lines

Marian Hobson

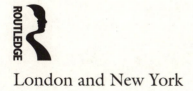

ROUTLEDGE

London and New York

First published 1998
by Routledge
11 New Fetter Lane, London EC4P 4EE

Simultaneously published in the USA and Canada
by Routledge
29 West 35th Street, New York, NY 10001
©1998 Marian Hobson

Typeset in Galliard by Routledge

Printed and bound in Great Britain by T.J. International Ltd, Padstow,
Cornwall

British Library Cataloguing in Publication Data
A catalogue record for this book is available from the British Library

Library of Congress Cataloging in Publication Data
Hobson, Marian.
  Jacques Derrida: opening lines / Marian Hobson.
    p.   cm. — (Critics of the twentieth century)
  Includes bibliographical references and index.
  1. Derrida, Jacques – Language. I. Title. II. Series: Critics of the
  twentieth century (London, England)
  B2430.D484H63   1998   98–13838
  194–dc21   CIP

ISBN 0–415–02197–9 (hbk)
ISBN 0–415–13786–1 (pbk)

Jacques Derrida

'Of the very many books on Derrida that have already appeared, Marian Hobson's must surely count as one of the most challenging and the most stimulating. Her own text interacts with those which she discusses in ways that are truly illuminating of both – not least in the very fact and nature of their interaction. Hobson displays a remarkable sense for the main deeply underlying themes of the philosophical-cum-literary tradition within and through which Derrida is working, themes which continue to work themselves out in his – and indeed her – writing.'

Alan Montefiore, Emeritus Fellow of Balliol College, Oxford

'In this exceptionally sophisticated book, Marian Hobson has done what no other book to date on Derrida has done: to explore the relation of argument to the mode of writing. By exhibiting the patterns of organizations, filaments of construction, micromovements, circuits of argumentation, which constitute the undercurrent of his writings from which, like the tips of icebergs, Derrida's coinages of individual terms, positions, and determined arguments, including "deconstruction", emerge to be thematized, Hobson succeeds in demonstrating the rigor of Derrida's work, more precisely, the unheard kind of consistency that characterizes it. Above all, this superb study on the question of language in Derrida, and Derrida's language, by emphasizing his writerly strategy of sketching links, reinforcing connections between words, themes, arguments, and providing for extensions into other texts, shows Derrida's work to stage incalculable possibilities of connection from whence future commentaries are allowed to proceed.'

Rodolphe Gasché, Eugenio Donato Professor of Comparative Literature, State University of New York at Buffalo

Marian Hobson is Professor of French at the University of London, Queen Mary and Westfield College. She is the author of *The Object of Art* (1982) and co-editor of *Reappraisals of Rousseau* (1980) and *Rousseau et le dix-huitième siècle* (1993).

Critics of the Twentieth Century

General Editor: Christopher Norris
University of Wales, Cardiff

For AB, JB, MGC, KE, JK, MJ, MNJ, RP, SP, AS, MW.

Contents

Acknowledgements

A debtor may not always be conscious of debts contracted. I have tried to record what I owe in footnotes and references, but I am aware of being a great deal more endebted than can easily be flagged, both to the writings and to the conversation of Geoff Bennington, Rodolphe Gasché, Chris Johnson and Sam Weber. Without Peggy Kamuf's generosity in reading several draft chapters and in responding to queries, this book might still be on the word processor. Terence Cave, Alan Montefiore and Margaret Whitford, each with a variety of dour kindness, helped me clarify the argument at certain important points; I owe a great deal to their patience. I owe thanks to Chris Norris, the editor of the series, for commissioning what was in the first stages of its composition a very different book, and for helping the finished manuscript through its last stages. At various points, I have been very grateful for comments or advice on problems I encountered from Tom Baldwin, Nick Denyer and Simon Glendinning. Sidney Allen has over a long period supplied me with philological detail which would have taken a long time to constitute unaided. I am grateful to Marianne Ronflé-Nadaud for her help in locating and in translating some of the quotations, and in constructing the bibliography. Finally, the book would not exist in a final form without Rodney Laing, Nick Higgins, and the NCCU at Addenbrooke's Hospital, Cambridge; nor without a group of friends, whose unsentimental visits, whose chatter over, across, round and at me when comatose, kept the unconscious on the move and body and soul together. The book is dedicated to them.

As a writer Derrida is both productive and difficult. This creates material and psychological difficulties in writing about his work. The library of Trinity College, Cambridge has made some matters of bibliography a great deal easier than they might otherwise have been, and I owe thanks. I am enormously grateful to the French Department of the Johns Hopkins University for the visiting professorship which allowed me the time I needed to finish the book. Writing in a case like this, where attempting to get things right is more than a matter of rectitude (in itself quite important enough) because the object of study can read and react, is a strange enterprise. The work studied is in the public domain, but has a live connection back to the private concerns of its author. I am grateful to my book's subject for an approval of the project which remained general and forebearing of further enquiry.

Abbreviations

The edition referred to appears under the date and title in the bibliography; italicized abbreviations refer to the translation (see under the original edition for details of the translation).

Derrida

AF	*Archéologie du frivole*, 1973
Aff	*Affranchissement du transfert et de la lettre*, 1982b
ALT	*Altérités*, Derrida and Labarrière, 1986b
AP	*Apories*, 1996
'At this very moment'	'At this very moment in this work here I am', 1991, see *Psyché*, 1987b
Beehive	'Women in the beehive', 1984b
CP	*La Carte postale: de Socrate à Freud et au-delà*, 1980
D	*La Dissémination*, 1972a
D	*Dissemination*, 1981
DP	*Du droit à la philosophie*, 1990c
DT	*Donner le temps*, 1991a
ED	*L'Ecriture et la différence*, 1967b
'Entre crochets'	'Entre crochets', 1976a
EO	*Ear of the Other*, 1988, see *L'Oreille de l'autre*, 1982a
Epérons	*Epérons: les styles de Nietzsche*, 1976b
Force	*Force de loi*, 1994
Force	*Force of Law*, 1992
G	*De la grammatologie*, 1967a
G	*Of Grammatology*, 1974
Genèse	*Le Problème de la genèse dans la philosophie de Husserl*, 1990b
Glas	*Glas*, 1974 (trans. 1986)
GT	*Given Time*, 1992, see *Donner le temps*, 1991a
'Inventions'	'Psyché: Inventions of the Other', 1989, see *Psyché*, 1987b
JA	'Ja, ou le faux-bond', 1977

LI	*Limited Inc.*, 1990
LI	*Limited Inc.*, 1988
M	*Marges de la philosophie*, 1972b
M	*Margins of Philosophy*, 1982
MC	'Mes chances', 1983a
MC	'My chances', 1984
NA	'No apocalypse', 1982, see *Psyché*, 1987b
OA	*L'Oreille de l'autre*, 1982a
OG	*Introduction à 'L'Origine de la géométrie' de Husserl*, 1962
OG	*Edmund Husserl's 'Origin of Geometry': An Introduction*, 1978
Oto	*Otobiographies: l'enseignement de Nietzsche et la politique du nom propre*, 1984c
Oto	'Declarations of independence', 1986 (part trans. of *Otobiographies*, 1984c)
P	*Positions*, 1972c
P	*Positions*, 1981
Par	*Parages*, 1986a
PC	*The Post Card: From Socrates to Freud and Beyond*, 1987, see *La Carte postale*, 1980
Pré	'Préjugés', 1985
Psy	*Psyché: inventions de l'autre*, 1987b
RB	'The deaths of Roland Barthes', 1988, see *Psyché*, 1987b
'Sending'	'Sending: on representation', see *Psyché*, 1987b
SéP	*Signeponge/Signsponge*, 1984a
SM	*Spectres de Marx*, 1993b
SM	*Specters of Marx*, 1994
SP	*Speech and Phenomena*, 1973, see *La Voix et le phénomène*, 1967c
Spurs	*Epérons*, 1976b
Title	'Title (to be specified)', 1981 (part trans. of *Parages*, 1986a)
Truth	*Truth in Painting*, 1987, see *La Vérité en peinture*, 1978
TWFJ	'Two words for Joyce', 1984, see *Ulysse gramophone*, 1987c
UG	*Ulysse gramophone*, 1987c
UG	'Ulysses Gramophone: Hear Say Yes in Joyce', 1988, see *Ulysse gramophone*, 1987c
VEP	*La Vérité en peinture*, 1978
VP	*La Voix et le phénomène*, 1967c
WD	*Writing and Difference*, 1978, see *L'Ecriture et la différence*, 1967b

Heidegger

BP	*Basic Problems*, 1982, see *Die Grundprobleme der Phänomenologie*, 1975

BT   *Being and Time*, 1967, see *Sein und Zeit*, 1979
BW   *Basic Writings*, 1977, see *Was ist Metaphysik?*, 1986
GA   *Gesamtausgabe*, 1978
ID   *Identität und Differenz*, 1957
IM   *Introduction to Metaphysics*, 1987, see *Einführung in die Metaphysik*, 1966
KPM   *Kant and the Problem of Metaphysics*, see *Kant und das Problem der Metaphysik*, 1929b
MFL   *Metaphysical Foundations of Logic*, 1984, see *Metaphysische Anfangsgründe der Logik*, 1978
SD   *Zur Sache des Denkens*, 1969
SZ   *Sein und Zeit*, 1979 [1927]
VA   *Vorträge und Aufsätze*, 1985
WG   *Vom Wesen des Grundes*, 1929a
WM   *Was ist Metaphysik?*, 1986 [1929]
ZSF   *Zur Seinsfrage*, 1956

Dummett

FOP   *Frege and Other Philosophers*, 1996 [1991]
FPL   *Frege: The Philosophy of Language*, 1973
IFP   *The Interpretation of Frege's Philosophy*, 1981

Hegel

PG   *Phänomenologie des Geistes*, 1973 [1807]
PS   *Philosophy of Spirit*, 1977

Kant

KRV   *Kritik der reinen Vernunft*, 1781 [2nd edn 1787]

Blanchot

EI   *Entretien infini*, 1969

Introduction

Language matters

A new science, which is wholly isolated and the only one of its kind, may be approached with the prejudice that it can be judged by means of the supposed knowledge that one already possesses, even though it is the reality of this very knowledge which must first be wholly doubted. To do this only produces the belief that what is seen on all sides is what was already known before, perhaps because the terms sound rather familiar. Yet everything must seem extremely distorted, nonsensical and like gibberish, because it is not the thoughts of the author that are being taken as the basis, but only one's own way of thinking, which by long habit has become second nature.

(Kant 1783)

Jacques Derrida is known still as a controversial and difficult philosopher, though his first work was published thirty-five years ago. Part of this reputation may be occasioned by the very extent of the interest his work has aroused: not just in philosophy or literary criticism, but in related academic disciplines – law (Derrida 1994), logic (Priest 1995) – and in others apparently farther removed. The extent of this influence is neglected by those who quite commonly say that it is principally literary critics who have adapted to and adopted his work.

But the undeniable interest students of literature have taken in his work can throw light on the nature of the arguments Derrida mounts. The present book will claim that writing in Derrida's work (including the fact that it is writing in French) sometimes induces an organization of ideas which affects their import. If I make this claim in terms of 'writing' it is no doubt due to an important article by Richard Rorty (1978). However, the claim is I hope not just a repetition of his: it is not based on a macro-historical distinction between two sorts of philosophy. On the contrary, it is a claim with subjacent implications about what sort of factors are in play in the construction of an argument, any argument, whatever natural and national language it is written in. The putting together of arguments, even in a scientific tradition, is affected by the particular scientific tradition and the particular language, national and cultural, it is occurring in. This is so even where the scientific problem tackled is anchored to an apparently concrete and straightforward problem in the world, as anyone reflecting on the different ways motorway engineers in Italy and the United Kingdom address the building of bridges might agree.

Now it is true that Derrida has experimented more widely than many philosophers with the forms he has used: *Envois*, 'a kind of novel', published in *The Post Card*, what one might be tempted to call multi-voiced dialogues; typographically as well as intellectually adventurous essay forms like *Glas* (Derrida has called it a 'Menippean satire'). But in a way that is harder to bring out, and also more crucial to their import, Derrida's works, like imaginative writing, seem at least occasionally to set up their own rules about how they will expose their subject. The reader has to adjust to a variety of factors: vocabulary, size of segment relevant to the argument the text is making, rhythm of exposition, tone. What the present book takes more and more as its centre is the relation of argument to mode of writing: it is claiming that to a degree, at any rate, the import of an argument made can be modified not just by its words, but by other factors, like the structure induced on it by the order in which it is advanced, and repetition. The reader has to work out what the relevant factors for understanding the argument are.

To argue this involves making the claim that language is freighted in ways that we cannot oversee and control. That imaginative writing lives from this excess is obvious; one usually assumes that it is not important in more straightforward language. The question then becomes, what is meant by more or less straightforward? How can that more or less be measured? Perhaps one way is through translatability between different natural languages. When the particularities of a natural language play a role in the sense of a segment of prose, when they are not easily translatable, though they can be explained by commentary, then the argument at work is more than lexical. This does not mean that the language used is incommensurable with any other, that the work cannot be discussed, but it does imply that there are elements active which move beyond the senses of the words bound into the sentences. Derrida writes in French, and this ought not to be effaced by any commentary – not merely are some of the works hard to translate (one at least, 'Pas', probably untranslatable), but even when they can be quite readily rendered into another language, they exploit the resources of French in a way that feeds into the meaning. It is for this reason that when Derrida is cited in this book, both the original and translations are given.

Another measure might be summarizability. Here the way the particular language is used by a writer, though explainable, needs commentary. While the possibility of making a précis of a piece of reasoning may be a test of its clarity, of its consistency, of its strength and, I fear many would argue, of its importance, to understand why it may not be possible to summarize without residue a sufficiently complex argument is to understand how we may learn things through language that we did not already know. Derrida's writing is designed at some points to allow for what is new, or difficult, to emerge. It also engenders a kind of awareness in its reader of this. In that this new element is understood, it has been expressed in the sentence(s) in which it emerged. At this kind of moment, the relation between thought and language is seamless. Knowing what thought is expressed, is understanding a sentence expressing the thought; it is not identifying the thought as if it pre-existed, and had been merely encoded. It is in this way that there may be effects in Derrida's argument which are not lexicalized, but arise from the suite of meanings in the sentences. They can be indicated afterwards (as this book tries to do) but are undoubtedly active before the awareness. This book's subtitle points to this sense of the opening out of his work's meaning.

Can this be called 'style'? I think not. Traditionally style has been opposed to 'content', which is exactly the divorce Derrida's mode of writing may at points be held to work against. The following book attempts to show that there is in his writing a very coherent putting in place at an implicit level, of structures, which can carry the problems and paradoxes thematized and discussed overtly.

Derrida's writing, it will be claimed, makes possible a particular rigour, one formed by the dense connectedness of the language of his books over time. This connectedness is of several different sorts. His originality has meant that thematizable terms, terms he offers for thematization, have been peeled off from their context and become widespread far from his work. Now if this is probably the way new terms always come into circulation, and a homage to their power to disrupt the circumstances in which they appear, it nonetheless has thrust forward an excessively lexical view of the matter. Words like 'différance' and 'deconstruction', having been almost like named islands for a time, show signs now of disappearing back into the ocean of everyday speech.[1] In Derrida's text, these represented for its readers something akin to points of accumulation of an argument, places where it was possible to bring complexity together into a word and hence raise as a theme. They have been the subject of much of the writing about Derrida, and in this book they will be referred to as 'lexemes'.

Although they are the best known, they are only one kind of distinctive feature in his texts. There are others, operations of a larger scale, longer strings, forming circuits of argument, or what I shall occasionally call 'micrologies'. These resist isolation because they have no lexical membrane round them separating them from their context, but as we shall see in Chapter 3, they recur. It is these circuits which perhaps provide most strongly the sense that there is orderly development from the earliest to the latest in Derrida's work, for they offer connection forward and back without the sense of development being one of pre-planned and pre-imposed order.

Finally, there are still wider patterns of concern – what is called here a syntax, a repeated form of articulation of one element of Derrida's discourse, one philosophical problem, with another. It is with these that I begin.

The book proceeds in a loosely chronological fashion. Chapter 1 starts from Derrida's first works to argue that among the articulating patterns in his writings, to which he constantly returns, namely what I call the syntax, are the relation between the empirical and the transcendental, and some of the paradoxes of infinity. Chapter 2 turns to the variety and multiplicity of his lexemes. It links this to the question of conditions of possibility as a definition of the

transcendental, and relates what has to be called the subversion of that definition in the phrase Derrida uses repeatedly, 'conditions of possibility and of
impossibility', to the proliferation of the lexemes as well as to other duplicating
strategies of writing: quotation and irony. Chapter 3 suggests that the repetition
of circuits of argument in Derrida's texts points to singularities which are each
unintuitable, each different, but which function in our thought by the relation
of negotiation and rupture of negotiation which they impose. They appear to
be shadowy entities which exhibit the shape of the paradoxes with which they
are connected. They are described as inducing a relation with themselves which
does not stall in paradox, but which can move on. In Chapter 4, the negatives
are explored which in the work allow this movement forward, a movement of
the idea being presented which is only partly conceptualized. The final chapter
examines how Derrida's writing develops a brand of consistency by the way
arguments relate to each other through what has to be called a kind of contiguity.

That the work is difficult, intellectually and linguistically, can hardly be
denied. One way of dealing with this difficulty is not to deny it, but to argue
that it is familiar. I have used the epigraph from Kant's *Prolegomena* because it
protests about something similar. England and France have amusingly different
tacks in the same tactic here. The term Derrida gave currency to, 'deconstruction', is sometimes treated derivationally, as after all equivalent, I have heard it
said, to 'analysis' (*analuein*, to loosen, undo). And French philosophers have
been heard to say that his way of writing is 'just' an 'explication de texte', the
detailed textual commentary which has been a pedagogical method in France
since at least the late nineteenth century. 'Deconstruction', like its master, can
then be ordered back to its home, as what has, after all, always been done. But
to my mind, there is a good deal of work still left to do to establish what his
arguments are, and how they work.

He is, for my money, an important writer as well as an important philosopher,[2] with the consequence that to read his work in translation is to be
distanced from some of its most thought-provoking implications. Yet his work
is not tied to the theatre of the French language, nor indeed to the French
'scene' as one might have expected from this quality. On the contrary, there is a
fundamental linguistic 'exogamy': his writing always refers to the language of
what he is working on, in the language in which it was written, and beyond this
is a tendency, unassuming but decided, to follow – one might almost say mime –
its rhythms and phrase structures.

Where for an English or American philosopher it makes sense to speak of
'improving' arguments, Derrida will not separate them from the words in which
they are expressed; they are localized with writer, chapter and verse, they cannot
be prised out of their linguistic and historical location. A comparison with
Kripke's work on Wittgenstein is instructive. He starts at the beginning of his
book to treat the private language argument as inhering in a well defined
manner in Wittgenstein's text, and finds that he cannot do so, that he is actually
engaging with a concept instituted by philosophical discussion, and thus with a

philosophical institution (Kripke 1982). Nevertheless, and although he admits his urging of a Wittgensteinian problem towards his own concerns, he still speaks of both as if they can be somehow floated free from their moorings in the respective texts. The energy of his book comes in fact from the excitement of doing this: 'the present paper should be thought of as expounding neither "Wittgenstein's" argument nor "Kripke's"; rather Wittgenstein's argument as it struck Kripke, as it presented a problem for him' (Kripke 1982: 5). Derrida on the contrary has an almost forensic drive to lead arguments back to their point of textual attachment, not to separate their style or their rhetoric from what they argue, nor their force from their sense. This book will argue in its final chapter that writing in Derrida's work might seem to operate as a 'subjectless transcendental field', yet it cannot, or can do so only imperfectly, for it is also rooted in space and time, in particular languages. At any point, writing – Derrida's writing – is a matter of experience, of event and location. He writes most often of precise passages of text, precise authors. In the location and event, he experiences or experiments with writing. Writing is a theme, but it is also what is at work – and this itself has been thematized by Derrida. His writings move between his own working and the text he is working on, in open-ended overlappings.

Yet more is going on in any writing than is thematized, set into words like molten lead into type. This much has always been agreed about 'literature' – there the histories of the elements of the particular language, its vocabulary, syntax and rhythm, have always been allowed to be in play, and indeed its future development too. What is implicit in the words, and the sentences or paragraphs they form, is as much at work in the text as their explicit dictionary meanings and their 'claims', to use the current term of analytic philosophy. In fact, almost this much is true of any writing – scientific writings too carry threads and fronds back to the magma in which they came together. Derrida's writing points to this inexplicit cargo (and in that way, as it used to be pointed out, deconstruction is like psychoanalysis). But his own writing also functions with that inexplicit. What is exciting about this functioning is that it is connected with the argument of the text.

Coherence is one of the targets of this book. In Derrida's writings, the incompleteness and the inconsistency (I am using these terms here as translations of *dissémination* and *dérive*, but in doing that am momentarily begging one of the questions that this book is posing) at work in thought never provide dominating concepts. There is not a pathology of what goes wrong with language, nor repeated diagrams of its skids. Instead, as I have tried to suggest with the terms *lexemes*, *circuits of argument* and *syntax*, there is a structuring of argument which is not purely thematic. This book is following certain possibilities of articulation, certain webs of relationships and lattices of concern. It makes no attempt to cover everything that Derrida has written. It also leaves aside certain ways of classifying his work – as a move into ethics, for instance. It does not review more than is strictly necessary for understanding its argument – the 'philosophemes' that have developed round 'presence' or 'différance' for instance – not because they are not important, but because there are some excellent books which do so (Staten 1984; Bennington and Derrida 1991; Johnson 1993, 1997) and because it seemed opportune to strike out in a different direction, one where 'force' and 'meaning' may not be sat on opposite sides of an intellectual compass.

1 Histories and transcendentals

On the one hand, in demonstrating a rigorous correlation between the determinations of the object and the procedures of the 'consciousness' which aims at them or which receives evidence from them, phenomenology has made thinking familiar with the idea that there is an empirical and transcendental relation, or, better, that it is intentionality which maintains the empirical and transcendental in a highly structured relation, an alliance which is essentially modern, that is, explosive. From this will come the result that the empirical is never empirical through itself: there is no experience or truth which can of itself claim to be in itself knowledge or truth, and from this there comes also the result that the 'transcendental' is not to be found localised anywhere: not in the consciousness, which is always outside itself, nor in the so-called natural reality of things (which has always to be suspended or reduced) but rather in the emergence of a network of relations which don't unify, which don't identify, but which maintain at a distance what is in relation, and make of this distance, reunderstood as a form of otherness, a new power of determination.

(Blanchot, *Entretien infini*, 375)

This chapter examines what is a persistent but relatively unrecognized site of investigation in Derrida's earlier writings: the relation between genesis and structure (to borrow the title of one of his earlier articles), or between the empirical (matters of event and act) and the transcendental (defined, for the moment, as those structures which form our mode of knowing what we know). In the above epigraph, taken from an article first published in 1967, the novelist and critic Maurice Blanchot throws a sharp – and retrospective – light on these concerns. Blanchot here points to the way in which a striking feature of phenomenology, namely its 'explosive' combination of the empirical with the transcendental, was carried over into structuralism.[1]

Derrida examined the problem posed to phenomenology by history in his thesis (1953–4, but only published in 1990) with reference to a whole sweep of texts by the founder of the phenomenological movement, the philosopher Edmund Husserl; then concentrated on one late text, in his introduction to his translation of Husserl's *Origin of Geometry* (1962).[2] The relation between empirical genesis and structures which might be thought of as transcendental, that is, structures which are built in to the way we think the world (a question which might be thought of as that of the relation between history and mathematics, or indeed philosophy) is not just a theme in these earlier writings of Derrida, nor just the object of a reflexive investigation on Derrida's part in regard to the structure and history of that theme in Husserl. It is an example of what my introduction has called a Derridean 'syntax': a form of argument which is articulated by philosophical terms acting in relation to their distribution, that is, as functions rather than as lexemes, and which, as does syntax, conveys a form of meaning which is not lexical, but structural. The piece of 'syntax' studied in this chapter articulates philosophy with history of philosophy; it articulates a set of problems considered as a system and separable from their historical circumstance, with history as a complex succession of interdependent effects, events, or moments; or it sets off different values of 'transcendence' (according to the context he is working in, Husserlian or Heideggerian and occasionally Kantian, as will be explained in the context) against 'history'.

Now phenomenology as a movement sought to get beyond mere facts of experience, to forms of experience and to structures of consciousness and of the 'living present' which would be general and essential. To Husserl, mathematics seemed the purest example of such essences. Yet maths clearly has an empirical genesis; it has a history; its concepts do change and develop. In such disciplines as geometry (and, one might add, philosophy), the intellectual structure of investigations appears to develop through time and yet have to be thought of as a stable component in the activity of reason; there are constructions or discoveries which are made in the empirical course of the development of the discipline, but which appear also to constitute part of the fundamental and permanent structure of thought. The present chapter argues that this can be examined in the early work of Derrida by means of the syntax which contrasts 'empirical' and 'transcendental'. I am not claiming that there is in his writings a use of associated oppositions which might each induce the same partition on his work. One cannot even align the patterns this chapter is picking out as sets of oppositions in his work (they cannot be all ranged in complementary pairs). But there is a constant way of articulating the questions he is concerned with in this earlier work which is not thematized as a conclusion in the work; it acts more like a load-bearing formation, a way of thinking the questions. It is for this reason I have called it a 'syntax'. This 'syntax' has been on occasions acknowledged by Derrida quite explicitly (he says, for instance, of his own work on the word 'idea', that he refuses to choose between 'perfectly closed systematic structures' and a 'transcendental history of philosophy' [M, 304; *M*, 255], that is between viewing a system internally, so that its elements relate primarily to each other, and, on the other hand, moving beyond the patterns of specific systems, and constructing a history which works at a different level). However, these remarks have not hitherto been followed up; this piece of 'syntax' itself is not especially salient, and has hitherto escaped notice. The point of the first part of this chapter is to show that this 'syntax' bears, structurally and tacitly, on what has appeared so far to readers to be the fully thematized and overt content of these works of Derrida.

In his writings on Husserl, Derrida gradually foregrounded the intervention of the infinite in the former's argument. He laid bare the three areas in which this intervention is apparent: time, relation with others (intersubjectivity) and language. The introduction of the infinite by Husserl into his account of our apprehension of the world, which is necessarily finite, engenders aporias in these areas, that is, problems which have no way out. The question has been for Derrida of how to investigate these without, on the one hand, repeating Husserl's gesture of phenomenological and transcendental reduction (that is, the 'bracketing' or disconnecting of our mental activity from its engagement with the world of fact, which is rife with presuppositions) and, on the other, without abandoning Husserl's rigour, by turning to empiricism or relying on happenstance. The syntax of these aporias also runs through Derrida's work, from early to late.

Writing and difference

Sketching out the foreground: 'writing', 'difference' and 'deconstruction'

In 1967, Derrida published three books: *Writing and Difference*, *Of Grammatology*, and *Speech and Phenomena*. Their arguments brought him notoriety by their power and innovation: the terms 'writing' and 'difference' were given specific stamps by these works; 'deconstruction' was new. They have been much studied, because they are in the foreground of what are conceptually very dense texts. They are not the object of this study, but must be sketched because they form part of the surface sense under which functions the 'syntax' of the relation between the empirical and the transcendental, and that of the aporias.

Difference is a term which, without being a logical operation, acts as a negative.[3] Partial and provisional, it does not radicalize heterogeneity (as terms like Other and Otherness do); it allows for a complex set of distinctions, without opposition. But *difference* does not merely allow multi-placed distinction, it seems each time localized (unlike the Sartrean *néant*); each time it is used, it seems to require an answer to the question 'different to what?'. It is a relational term, even if it is frequently used with those relations unmentioned or cut off. These two implications, conservation of heterogeneity and localization, may be why Deleuze, for instance, followed his discussion of 'difference' and 'transcendental empiricism' (1968: 80) with an enthusiastic account of a linguistic plethora, recommending a creation of concepts (in a manner similar to Paul Feyerabend). For it might seem to follow that each context required a new and local coinage, each distinction a distinctive linguistic marking. Certainly Derrida and, for instance, Julia Kristeva develop their writing and in turn mark their contemporaries' writing. There is a jubilant but specific inventiveness, or sometimes an appropriation and thus disappropriation of terms used by others (*supplément* for instance, developed from Rousseau, or, less certainly and noticeably, *trace* and *écart* [gap]). Such terms in Derrida's use have a kind of *sotto voce* quotation (see Chapter 2) and are active through a particular charge which they have received. *Difference* was perhaps the most powerful of such terms; it enabled the thinking of gender and ethnic difference as a distinctiveness which did not merely imply binary opposition, and thus became a structuring force in the theorizing of sexual and racial inequality. Hence no doubt, when reasons need seeking beyond the great quality of the intellectual work involved, the forceful effect of French theory, the influence of Derrida, Foucault, Kristeva, Lyotard and Lacan, in the United States since the late 1960s.

With the word 'difference', Derrida brought together the ontological difference of Heidegger and the semiotic difference of Saussure. It was from the ontological difference, the distinction between Being and beings, that, Heidegger had said in the twenties, something like an understanding of being became possible (MFL, 151–2);[4] we only know beings in their different modes of existence, never being. But what then is the generality and unity of the term 'being'? Being itself 'is' not. This difference between being and beings is 'turned into the factical' (WG; GA vol. 9, 134–5)[5] by our transcendence (see below). It is by our transcendence, our going beyond ourselves, that there are individuated beings for us. Saussurean *differentiation* is what gives rise to meaning within language: in language there are only differences, there are no positive terms (Saussure 1985: 166; 1972: 116); units of sound, like units of meaning in an actual language, are isolated by a diacritical process; they exist by differentiation from the rest of the language. Meaning thus rests on the analysis of the non-coincidence of a given fragment of language with the rest (1985: 163; 1972: 116). In both these lineages of 'difference', however distinct they are, it is through a process of distinction or differentiation that there arises the 'factical' or the unit of meaning, that is, something to work with at all.

However, in an article on Freud first published in 1966, ('Freud and the Scene of Writing'), 'différance' picks up a vowel change only legible, not audible. In discussing the Freudian unconscious and its strange temporality, Derrida shows that Freud's model of a relation between the unconscious and the conscious is not merely or always that of the translation into consciousness of a message which was pre-existing but unavailable in the unconscious. 'Difference' is overlaid with the sense of deferral (*différer* also has this meaning in French). In the quite ordinary verb 'to defer', the time when something might have occurred is not the same as the time when it did occur; the occurrence seems then somehow to exist as a possibility before it happens. Especially if this is also a process of differentiation, then these times cannot be thought of as points of time, as moments, and the process cannot be one of linear succession, but must be a more complex overlapping. In this article, both life and meaning are being thought, not as elements already possible, though to be modified by supervening time (ED, 302; *WD*, 203), not even as arising from a differential grid, but as a trace or passage.[6] (A pointer to the next chapter: in such a way of thinking, the possible exists not as an object but as a mode, Fine's 'modal actualism' (Prior and Fine 1977: 117).)

'Writing', 'écriture' (a word often associated with Barthes and with his *Writing Degree Zero* of 1953, a kind of *year zero* for structuralist criticism), made possible a discussion of style without aestheticizing connotations. With its meaning of 'handwriting' it also allowed a reference both to the material and to the praxis of writing to be incorporated into notions of composition, with no necessity of any reference to literature, nor to the author nor the individual work.[7] At the time of Derrida's triple publication, linguistics appeared to be the intellectually dominant non-scientific discipline (though Chomsky's work was not well known in France at that time) and Derrida's work might have appeared at first to be a development of semiology.[8] Writing, he might seem to be claiming, is a better model for sign systems than language, that is, spoken language. And this indeed is how his work was read. But what Derrida terms 'writing' or 'trace' is never merely letter forms, gestures of handwriting, or any kind of material vehicle. And further, Derrida gives historical and ethical purchase to his claims about writing. He makes of it more than merely a widening of what is meant by sign, and builds into it an account of why this has not been recognized, of why writing, as he claims, should have been held to be secondary to the spoken language. He calls this weighting of sound 'phonocentrism'. The term was a neologism and is worth considering: it extends patterns of arguments associated with culture and the much more familiar 'ethnocentrism' and suggests, by its very coinage, that philosophical positions about writing may be deeply embedded in our thinking, and that they may suffer similar structural skewing, initiated by what acts as the centre (*ethnos* or *phone*). (The linguistic baptism, the use of neologism by which Derrida induces this effect, must be noted here and will be discussed later in the book.) 'Phonocentrism' also raises the question of where what is being said about 'sound-centredness' is being said from.

'Phonocentrism' could then be read as a pointing to a neglect of a material factor in all language: whether sounds, scratches or transfer of electronic impulse. But there is with Derrida no corresponding 'graphocentrism' – we do not have an endorsement of matter (as against abstract form, or against vivifying spirit) but on the contrary a movement to undo that very opposition. Derrida's history of 'writing' suggests that the distinction between sound and writing is part of the whole philosophical distinction, derived from the Greeks, between intelligible and sensible. So that the inferiority impressed on writing was one way of subordinating matter to spirit, or at least to the bodiless vibration of sound (G, 24; G, 13). Sound, the voice speaking, is supposed to be *present*, whereas the whole point of writing is to supplement presence, to be what we have recourse to when the speaker is not present, or when we fear our own absent-mindedness. Derrida suggests that the development of phonetic writing, historically later than ideograms or hieroglyphs, was one way of marking the subordination of writing to speaking.

Phonetic writing moreover implied, says Derrida, a specific and linear time structure, an arrangement of temporal flux into a sequential array of atom-like particles, the globular 'now' (G, 128; *G*, 86). The paradoxes of time (time is both movement and things in succession), explored since Zeno, have tended to be collapsed into their second term, succession. This allows linear analysis and has come to dominate scientific thought. But the paradoxes cannot be eliminated, and they stretch and flaw the ideas of linear time and linear writing – a moment of time, however minutely analysed, appears a bundle of events difficult to separate; a distinctive feature in linguistics, however minutely analysed, is a collection of features whose separation seems only possible in reference to other points in time. However, Derrida does not make the problematic limits of the linear conception of time merely an effect of atemporal paradox. There is in *Of Grammatology* a kind of internal history of writing, and an account of where and how that history can be written: the division of that history into stages relies, it is implied, on an underlying conception that historical epochs can be determined by the unity of certain of their elements (cf. G, 117; *G*, 79), and that this unity can simultaneously be understood and undermined when a point has been reached from which the unity can be perceived.[9] It is when you see an epoch as some sort of whole that you can move out of it.

'Phonocentrism', the binary distinction between speech and writing, argues Derrida, is thus not innocent and equipolar but is a hierarchy, where traditionally speech is held to be both superior to and more fundamental than writing. But, against this, what of the *scripta manent* tradition of interpretation of writing, where its value is to persist even when the voice may be lost? It is here that Derrida's undermining of the distinctions sensible/intelligible, writing/speech begins. The idea of 'trace', though linked more clearly with writing, in fact underlies both. It is ultimately not opposed to speech, but subtends it as a root or generic (the latter equivalence will need adjusting later). Derrida will argue here, as elsewhere, two points: one, that it may be prudent to move upstream, logically and historically, to the root from which the distinction between writing and speech branches; and two, that the favouring of one pole historically has crystallized contexts and weighted not just speech over writing, but a whole set of concepts which have been twinned and opposed – man over woman, for instance, or white over black. One might well object to this and say that power has always accompanied writing; Derrida will, as we shall see, answer that such an accompanying power is each time empirical, an effect of historical context, and not a universal structure built into writing.[10]

Why introduce this tension to what might have been a much more uniform exposition of paired concepts in the history of philosophy? Why group it round the hierarchized opposition of writing/speech? The opposition of speech to writing, and the privileging of writing in the history of philosophy, which Derrida illustrates again and again from diverse quarters – Saussure, the Copenhagen school of linguistics, Lévi-Strauss, Rousseau, the later work of Plato – is related but not identical to the much more familiar form/matter distinction. But, as has already been indicated, instead of a simple binary distinction, Derrida in fact either exhibits explicitly or works with implicitly an array of satellite distinctions: signifier/signified, body/mind, passive/active. He does not present these as a completable repertoire of possibilities, and it therefore cannot mark out logical and philosophical space into a grid (a repertoire symbolized, he says, by the book which can be closed and whose possibility is only established by virtue of the preceding totality of meanings to which the book can refer). As with speech and writing, each set of oppositions claims to be a pair, but is in fact a hierarchy; each is out of kilter, and for each one Derrida will show what are the consequences of this disparity. But they are interlinked both in the way they arise for Derrida through his work on Husserl and Heidegger, and in their relation to 'writing'. For 'writing', as the next section will try to show, allows overlapping relations between active and passive, recording and recorded, and, finally, a different kind of temporality, to be thought. Such temporality has direction, as time obviously has, but is not linear.

A detour round 'writing'

Derrida takes 'writing', 'trace', 'inscription' as the unmetaphorical locus of a relation to the history of philosophy. But this constellation of terms also has the advantage that by and of itself it works to undo the distinction between form and content, being both theme and medium for the theme (discussion of writing is done in writing). The terms bring with them, as has been suggested earlier, the possibility of a non-linear temporality; they also render inseparable the understanding of something and that thing itself. In regard to the central concern of this chapter, they make possible a negotiation of the apparent opposition between genesis and structure. To bear this out, I now consider two other examples, in other domains, of the idea of writing, and the term 'trace'.

The first is a piece of work in the theory of biogenetics, exactly contemporary to Derrida's first publications, which will serve to indicate clearly some of the conceptual problems with which the idea of writing enables one to engage. H. H. Pattee published work in the 1960s on the origins of life, relating the problem to the problem of measurement in quantum mechanics, where, notoriously, the observed and the observer cannot be divorced. Pattee's articles are concerned with the relation between inorganic structure and the genesis of living organisms. They use the notion of writing to conceptualize the overlapping relations of structure of possibility, that is, of 'initial conditions' on the one hand, and of genesis and development on the other. Pattee suggested that the difference between living and inert matter (namely the former's collective behaviour in the course of time) might be properly expressed in terms of keeping and writing records:

> In biological terminology we describe the recording process as the accumulation of genetic information by natural selection. But this accumulation is now apparent only in highly evolved cells in complex ecosystems. The origin of life problem is to explain how this record accumulation began and why it can survive the universal tendency towards loss of records which

occurs in non-living matter. . . . Symbols and records have existed since life existed. . . . Writing symbols is the preservation in space of time-dependent activity.

(Pattee 1971: 310–12).[11]

Writing in this speculation on the origin of living matter is used precisely because it prevents a conflation of distinctions: the distinction between the commenting system doing the observation or measurement and what is commented on cannot be assimilated to the distinction between human mind and physical matter. 'Writing' allows the idea of selecting and preserving information through time to be thought without implying intention or purpose, and without separating writer and written-on, or agent and acted-on. The usual thinking of the relation of active to passive, as source and result, or creator and created, cannot function. Further, writing allows a paradoxical chronology to causality. The 'pure origin' of life cannot be located, not because it involves infinite regress, but because the effect, that is, the ability to make records, seems to act as cause. In Pattee's work, archive and recording appear out of the 'equations of constraint', that is, the relations which adapt the coordinates of the system in order to preserve its momentum. The archival process of living matter involves, Pattee suggests, a selective freezing-out of degrees of freedom by a pattern of constraints which are not back-traceable to original conditions, and thus not reversible. Such a pattern of constraints must be 'inherently statistical in its structure and dissipative in its operation' because of its irreversibility (*ibid*.: 314). The conception of a record, an archive which writes/is written, which is both effect and cause of measuring and of differentiation, has led Derrida and Pattee to interestingly similar conclusions: writing as irreversible temporal process, which upsets in its origins the active/passive distinction, and thus disturbs causality as a consecutive temporal sequence of action on separately definable elements; writing as involving constraints of selection, which entail corresponding dissemination. It is as if a thinking through of 'writing' enables a dissolving or displacing of the conceptual difficulties underlying 'genesis', 'structure' and the difference between life and non-living.

Likewise, it is as if a thinking through of 'trace' enables understanding and what is understood to be brought together, dispensing with the conception of objective truth-values which can be determined independently of our knowledge or means of knowledge. Michael Dummett's work, as we shall see, because of its roots in intuitionism, throws a particularly sharp light on some of the concerns of this book. In his (arm's-length) construction of a verificationist view of the truth of some statement made now about the past, 'trace' expresses the complex chronology necessary if we do without a realist notion of truth. A realist notion of truth suggests that it makes sense to speak of truth even if we do not in practice know how to decide the truth of a statement in all circumstances.[12] For the realist, in Kantian fashion, argues that where we cannot recognize a particular statement's truth, it could be recognized by a Being whose powers are like ours, but sufficiently extended. A verificationist would argue against this that there will be undecidable sentences for which, though we might come across, so to speak, the recognition of their truth and falsity in certain situations, we have no idea what we would need to find out to be able to get to that recognition where we are aware that we do not have it. But sentences in the past tense impose a strange temporality on the verificationist:

> A previous observation can serve as conclusively establishing the truth of a past-tense sentence only in so far as it is known to have been made, e.g. remembered; so, from a verificationist point of view, it is not the past observation itself, but the present memory (or other trace) of its having been made which constitutes the verification of the assertion.
>
> (FPL, 469)

Derrida could not be called a 'verificationist' without enormous misprision; yet where a timeless system of truth-values existing independently of our knowledge (that is, realism) is abandoned, the problems of knowing things about the past lead to an overlapping of the known and the means of knowing, and an idea to play the role of the 'trace' is needed.

'Deconstruction' as an articulation of philosophy and history of philosophy

It has been often acknowledged that there is, in *Of Grammatology*, a setting of the history of writing into a history of philosophy. The history of philosophy Derrida is working with in this text has been taken to be part of the programme of the 1960s: part of the 'movement out of structuralism' in micro terms and out of metaphysics in a large-scale perspective. But it has not often been acknowledged that in *Of Grammatology* there is a complication of this programme which goes beyond the evident problems: where do we stand to make such a move; how is such a move possible when we are using language deep-dyed in the philosophical metaphysical tradition to effect such a move? When his arguments are looked at closely, Derrida is avoiding two opposed but twinned intellectual tacks: that of treating Husserl and Heidegger's work as specific systems, which may be considered for themselves or as operating within quite specific linguistic and intellectual contexts; and that of treating their work only suprahistorically, that is, in a perspective which engages with the ideas separated from their anchorage in a context. The following section will attempt to show how he does this. We shall see that the contrast just drawn is a variety of that between histories and transcendentals on which this chapter is based.

The end of metaphysics, or rather its destruction, was called for by Heidegger (the title of Section 6 of Heidegger's *Being and Time* is 'The task of a destruction of the history of ontology'[13]). Heidegger's *Destruktion* is not a jumping out from tradition by what he calls 'vicious relativism', by what we should call historicism, which would see each phase as a given historical stage. Instead, it is a working through of the limits of past formulations.[14] There is to be a *working back* through traditional concepts of being and time to 'reawaken the question of Being' (*BT*, 49). One can see here how in the word 'deconstruction' that Derrida began to apply to what he was doing, the double prefixes *de* and *con* do indeed suggest a temporal working back through traditional concepts, one that is more fraught though less violent. But might not the term be seen in structuralist perspective? Does the *de* apply to the *con*, or do they simultaneously gesture in different though not opposed directions? In this instability between the *de* and the *con*, it is clear that there is a movement out of structuralism, and its grid of equivalent binary distinctions. (The question of logical grid in the latter possibility, of the effect of time on process in the former, are in fact the problems of this chapter.)

What can such a movement be, and from where can it be charted? Self-location is in some ways characteristic of French intellectual activity towards the end of the 1960s. Both Sollers and Kristeva, for instance, produce instant mini-histories of 'western thought' at points in their work, proclaiming that times are changing at the very moment of writing. They were right – the Chinese Cultural revolution, the barricades of *mai '68*, the fall of de Gaulle, all were contemporary. This tone is neither intellectually nor ethically frivolous: the historian of science Georges Canguilhem, and then Michel Foucault, produced models for an intellectual history of epochs riven asunder by radical discontinuities, which supply tension but also ethical direction to their narration. Kristeva's endeavour for instance is to strive to see the period with the maximum of distance, to be on the edge of her own intellectual system; this process of self-localization is self-referential but not self-satisfied; it creates an undertow of pathos, as of being on the edge of a promised land.[15] This possibility, which in Kristeva's case is related to her socio-poetic concept of the role of the artist, is better thought of in more logical terms, in Derrida's case, as a kind of 'cosmic exile', to borrow Putnam's phrase. Derrida calls it in some of his earlier texts 'le point exorbitant': in a way to be discussed later in this chapter, it is the point at which history and logic, genesis and structure, meet. In the particular question that concerns us here, Derrida speaks of wishing to attain 'le point d'une certaine extériorité par rapport à la totalité de l'époque logocentrique' ('the point of a certain exteriority in relation to the totality of the age of logocentrism') (G, 231; *G*, 161), the point that gives the leverage to make of deconstruction not just timeless logical system but also event. There is here an exorbitance which allows a historical epoch to appear, and to be seen as a unit, a totality.

Now Derrida has voiced suspicion of the cant intention to jump free at one bound from traditional metaphysics (cf. P, 63–5; *P*, 47–50); his work constantly shows that it is not possible to crawl out from under the whole net of actual language, the language of one's own time and place, even if that 'point of a certain exteriority' may be attainable. At the same time, he does, rightly in my view, claim to have moved away from, to have moved on from, the underlying assumptions of much traditional philosophic discourse. Much of his work takes the very nature and possibility of such a move as one of its chief problems.

Many of his earlier writings are concerned explicitly, if not always centrally, with what it means for an intellectual system to change, and how changes that occur in such a system are related to a kind of turbulence, a perturbing effect exercised by what is not taken up into the system either through oversight or ignorance or because it has been designated as 'outside' or 'other'. There is no simple exteriority, no clearly designated external perspective, be it even that of a tangential point for Derrida. No system is closed off from its context, there is always interchange and permeability, however slight. (In fact, this disarraying of the opposition between inside and outside is source and effect of one of the most striking effects of his writing, his irony.) Structure and genesis, as synchronic system and process of development through developing contexts, are always in interaction.

The question then is, what is the position from where the unity of an epoch can be understood? (In Derrida's work on Descartes, we shall see that the exorbitance becomes a kind of excess, and the totality, a formation more general than the unity of an epoch.) In *Of Grammatology*, Derrida makes of that position not a point[16] but a process: deconstruction. He articulates Husserl's idea of living present and Heidegger's question of being with developments in linguistics. The elements of this articulation have often been recounted: Derrida argues that the privileging of the spoken word, and the experience of the effacement of the signifier in the voice which hears itself, generate in philosophy the idea of an ideality whose expression is completely transparent, whose meaning is immediately present. This ideality is part of 'the history of truth' and cannot be stepped outside of so easily (G, 34; *G*, 20), but it is a 'trap'. Such a wordless meaning, unsymbolized and inarticulated, has been thought by analogy, as an extension of human powers towards the divine.[17] (As such, it is unavailable, and the nature of truth has to be rethought.) In the ultimate stage of this process of philosophy, in Heidegger, it is the word (as unit) which composes the unity of the signified and signifier in the voice. Such an experience is experience of being, is taken for granted in every language and is a precondition of Heidegger's question of being. It might seem, then, that with experience of being we reach a changeless stratum precomprehended and underlying every articulation performed by the actual languages, which are of course radically different among themselves (G, 34; *G*, 20). (This leads on the one hand to the question of linguistic relativity and on the other to the question of what transcends language, to the problem of whether there can be such a stratum lying under every actual language – this will be discussed in Chapter 5. It is here that we dip, so to speak, into some of the most difficult areas of this part of Derrida's work: the question of the units of our thinking, and the nature of their existence if separately considered from actual linguistic embodiment.) It has to be said, says Derrida, that Heidegger never made a 'trans-epochal' sense out of the word 'being', one that could be torn from historical linguistic systems, specific languages, specific words. So that the relation between transcendentals and history as specific linguistic location is not one where transhistorical senses are encoded into actual words and phrases, nor on the other hand one where senses in actual languages are relative and incommensurable.

The question of the sense of being is part of the complex relation Derrida is building at this point in *Of Grammatology* between his own work and Heidegger's 'history of being'. Heidegger had called Nietzsche 'the last metaphysician', remaining one even in his 'hammering of metaphysics'. Derrida will turn against Heidegger arguments which the latter had used against Nietzsche. He edges into this process with verbs in the conditional (one of the grammatical functions of which in French is to report speech), and a set of plurals, summarized as 'les concepts d'*interprétation*, de *perspective*, d'*évaluation*, de *différence*, et tous les motifs "empiristes" ou non-philosophiques' (G, 31) ('the concepts of *interpretation, perspective, evaluation, difference*, and all the "empiricist" or non-philosophical motifs') (*G*, 19). It is through such concepts, says Derrida, that Nietzsche 'might have' made writing independent of meaning as truth anchored in *logos*, discourse, reason, the Divine Understanding, that is as truth existing regardless of whether we have the means to know it.[18] Meaning, on the contrary, would then be constituted by writing. These are empiricist motifs, we are told, which, because they always have represented metaphysics' own incoherence, are, when read in a certain way, not empirical naiveties at all. They merely are such if read from within philosophy, but that is, according to Nietzsche himself, badly read. So that Nietzsche's discourse, if read in a certain way, cannot be made part of the search for a pre-metaphysical origin, nor for 'the question of being'. In fact, it is Heidegger, who with this question is still metaphysically guiding his history of being by something external to the stages of being – the *primum signatum*, a kind of transcendental signified, that is, earlier than any category and any linguistic determination, a 'voice of Being' (G, 33; *G*, 20). For Heidegger, it is in the voice of consciousness and conscience, speaking to the self, that the signifier, the linguistic shell of what is signified, is effaced. The signified in this still, small voice is both spontaneously produced and universally available – it rises from the resources of the self and is also open to others. It is in this exteriority at the heart of interiority that Derrida will show paradox and instability to lie.

But yet again, and against Nietzsche, Heidegger, says Derrida, points to a rupture between what he calls 'voice of being' and sound, *phonè*, between originary sense of being and the word, between the call of being and articulated sound. Heidegger at the same time confirms and sets in doubt a group of fundamental metaphors; his position in relation to phonocentrism (or, in a shift of terminology, logocentrism) and the metaphysics of presence is ambiguous. In a circuit of argument which resumes the end of Derrida's introduction to *Origin of Geometry*, and extends its account of history, Heidegger's ambiguity is said in *Of Grammatology* to be part of a path or passage from the taking of the 'sense of being' as a transhistorical value, as a changeless thread running through history, even if hidden by history, towards an attitude where it is at each moment located in history, in intellectual transit and is then historical. This transition, from 'sense of being' to that of the difference between Being and beings, is then relayed out implicitly to Derrida's own extension of that difference beyond origin, so that the phrase 'originary differance' will no longer signify. Yet by this path we have not arrived, says Derrida, at the production of something which can act as a transcendental for Heidegger, but at the question of what produced transcendentality at all (G, 38; *G*, 23).

Derrida's 'yes and no' attitude to Heidegger needs two preliminary comments, which will be developed later. First the balancing of Heidegger against Nietzsche is what Derrida will call reinscription, and is the second moment of deconstruction. It is not merely a use of the rhetorical form 'tu quoque',[19] though it is that. It is also a recognition of a 'hesitation' necessary in any attempt to move beyond current thought structures, a 'trembling' located in post-Hegelian philosophy, in a passage out of Hegelianism, Derrida suggests. Such movements are always both simultaneously inside and outside the systems they are working on: 'Les mouvements de déconstruction ne sollicitent pas les structures du dehors. Ils ne sont possibles et efficaces, ils n'ajustent leurs coups, qu'en habitant ces structures' (G, 39) ('The movements of deconstruction do not destroy structures from the outside. They are not possible and effective, nor can they take accurate aim, except by inhabiting those structures') (*G*, 24). A propos Nietzsche and Heidegger, and at this point, Derrida denies that this 'trembling', these failures of thinkers to be coherent according to the criteria they themselves have set up, are mere incoherences. They are not just unmastered consequences of their own ideas nor even unexpected resistances on the part of what they are moving against. More logically fundamental problems are emerging at this point, indicated by Derrida's use of his 'lexemes' (in this section of *Of Grammatology*, 'différance' and 'trace'). These problems produce tremors for, like terrestrial fault lines, they represent points of articulation, where the difficulties associated with thinking the relation of a structure to a genesis show up even as they are articulated. And Derrida is not merely commenting on the difficulties – he is moving them on. For the arguments Derrida examines are embodied; he doesn't lift them from their textual and linguistic moorings; this is the reason for the unexpected relation his work has to the texts he uses, being neither commentary from an external point of purchase, which might seem to command, nor an internal explication and reiteration which might seem merely to reduplicate. Derrida's work, we have said, is localized in time and in writers. So that deconstruction is not a free-floating method, nor a theory which can be practised or applied; it is a process through positions which are not subsumed but altered by the passage. It has often been forgotten that Derrida's deconstruction is set within a history of philosophy.

But this 'reinscription' of Heidegger in Nietzsche and Nietzsche in Heidegger is set in a journey through Husserl's transcendental phenomenology (which the latter defined explicitly 'not as a science of facts, but as a science of essential Being' [Husserl 1931: introduction]). The journey is necessary, says Derrida, to get beyond the transcendental which yet protects the rear of the argument from 'naive objectivism' (G, 90; *G*, 61).[20] 'Transcendentality' and transcendental arguments are thus both used and questioned by Derrida. They come with a declaration of origin as it were (one reason no doubt for Derrida's frequent use of the conditional, the tense in French, we have said, for reported speech as well as for tentative statement). The 'transcendental' referred to here in *Of Grammatology* is Husserl's, and is not, at this stage in Derrida's argument, given a global meaning. Yet it is not relativized, given a merely historical location, either. What is being investigated here is 'ce qui constitue notre histoire et . . . ce qui a produit la transcendentalité elle-même' (G, 38) ('what constitutes our history and what produced transcendentality itself') (*G*, 23). A positivist tradition would produce a 'history of the idea of the transcendental'. Husserl (see below) strove at the end of his life to work out the 'powerful structural a priori proper to [history]',[21] that is, a transcendental history. Derrida will weave between these approaches: coming after Husserl, he seems to imply here, can allow a position which is rigorous, non-transcendental without being not transcendental. What might this claim mean?

Deconstruction and empiricism

It has just been shown that this double gesture is the point of imbrication of deconstruction in the history of philosophy as Derrida develops it (he uses the term 'déconstituer' [G, 35]). To understand it, and its simultaneous use and questioning of transcendental arguments, there needs to be consideration of the process by which Derrida distinguishes his work from structuralism. For the gesture gives rise to what might seem to be 'empiricist' motifs, just such as were attributed to Nietzsche at one stage in Derrida's deconstruction of Heidegger's relation to Nietzsche.

Structuralism operates with a grid of binary distinctions. The first article of *Writing and Difference*, on the structuralist critic Jean Rousset's book *Forme et signification* (1962), argues that structuralism is a kind of formalism, one form of argument (the other is historicism) against which Derrida is writing, and in opposition to which he develops the syntax of his arguments. He courteously criticizes in Rousset's study of forms the neglect of an 'internal genetics' of a work of art or literature. 'Form and signification', the title of Rousset's book, is better thought of as 'force and signification' (the title of his own article, and another single-letter permutation). Rousset has been neglectful of the tensions and of the disproportions internal to a work, which cannot be squared off into the polar opposites with which structuralism works. For structuralism operates with and within closure, locating even the pathological accident as resolvable according to rule and thus still part of the structure.[22] As with mathematical closure, any combination of elements in the set produces an element which remains within the set. And, as with mathematical closure, it is this which is a necessary though not sufficient condition for rigour and consistency. One of the principal conditions of consistency in mathematical logic as in natural logic is related to working within a field of possibilities which has been closed off.[23] Now the contesting of the possibility of closure is indeed one part of the way Derrida's work has shown up the restrictive assumptions, the models of discourse which secure our bases of argument and agreed modes of coherence, but which are often hidden. It has just been pointed out that Derrida substituted the words 'hesitation' and 'trembling' for what a philosopher in a different tradition might have called incoherence. In this way, he introduced time into an atemporal logical fix. But though 'closure' may be used to point to the place from which the unity of a historical epoch may be discerned, and thus undermined (see above; and Critchley 1992), Derrida explicitly uses the term also to trace out structures of argument in the logical sense, in relation to closed sets. For it will be shown at the end of this chapter that his first published work, in which Husserl's use of a type of infinite set is foregrounded, has filamentary roots through Husserl to some of the great investigations of logical and mathematical consistency of the 1920s and 30s. Hence, no doubt, the aporetic feel, so to speak, which this work of Derrida has.

One of the consequences of tampering with closure is an extreme sense of the fragility of distinctions, and this has long been noticed in his work. Derrida, in an article of 1966 ('Structure, sign, and play in the discourse of the human sciences', in *WD*) sketches a brief history of this totalizing or this closure. (Significantly, it was the work by which he was first known in the United States, the first translated into English.) To totalize in its prestructuralist version was, says Derrida, to find a centre 'qui, à pouvoir être aussi bien dehors que dedans, reçoit indifféremment le nom d'origine ou de fin, d'*archè* ou de *telos*' (ED, 410) ('which, because it can be either inside or outside, can also indifferently be called the origin or end, *arche* or *telos*') (*WD*, 279). Elsewhere, this is amplified but also reduced to an invariant presence: 'On pourrait montrer que tous les noms de fondement, du principe ou du centre ont toujours désigné l'invariant d'une présence (*eidos, archè, telos, energeia, ousia* (essence, existence, substance, sujet) *aletheia*, transcendentalité, conscience Dieu, homme etc.)' (ED, 411) ('It could be shown that all the names related to fundamentals, to principles, or to the center have always designated an invariable presence – *eidos, arche, telos, energeia, ousia* (essence, existence, substance, subject) *aletheia*, transcendentality, consciousness, God, man, and so forth') (*WD*, 279–80).[24] Neither exploring back to the origin, to the arche, nor forward to the end, or *telos* (as in eighteenth-century arguments about world order, end and origins are symmetrical) can guarantee the whole. The usual safeguards of rigour: closure, that is the possibility of sealing off the context of relevance; telos and origin, that is the possibility of constructing a series of verifiable steps in argument; the relation between the centre and the circumference and thus the opposition between important and unimportant or serious and frivolous, all seem endangered.

Moreover, in psychological and not logical terms, the possibility that the human subject might guarantee consistency by overseeing, by spanning discourse, so to speak, is contested. (This is not the only argument of Derrida which has traditional links with scepticism's exposition of the frailty of human reason and memory, as it has also been the basis for the search by thinkers such as Leibniz for the 'blind calculus', a formalism which could unfold mechanically once set in motion.) Even the Freudian unconscious, which might seem to supply foundations and base, albeit unreachable, cannot be so treated:

> Que le présent en général ne soit pas originaire mais reconstitué, qu'il ne soit pas la forme absolue, pleinement vivante et constituante de l'expéri-ence, qu'il n'y ait pas de pureté du présent vivant, tel est le thème, formidable pour l'histoire de la métaphysique, que Freud nous appelle à penser.
>
> (ED, 314)

> That the present in general is not primal but, rather, reconstituted, that it is not the absolute, wholly living form which constitutes experience, that there is no purity of the living present – such is the theme, formidable for the history of metaphysics, which Freud . . . would have us pursue.
>
> (*WD*, 212, trans. mod.)

For the present not to be present, for this to be thinkable, the locus in time assigned to cause and effect has to be changed: 'effects' can precede causes which are reconstituted afterwards, in German 'nachträglich'.[25] What to a linear and punctual view of time is a non-sense, becomes in fact clearer if the uncon-scious is not to be merely a 'has been conscious'.[26]

> Le texte n'est pas pensable dans la forme, originaire ou modifiée, de la présence. Le texte inconscient est déjà tissé de traces pures, de différences, où s'unissent le sens et la force, texte nulle part présent, constitué d'archives qui sont toujours déjà des transcriptions.
>
> (ED, 314)

> The text is not conceivable in an originary or modified form of presence. The unconscious text is already a weave of pure traces, differences in which meaning and force inscribe themselves – a text nowhere present, consisting of archives which are *always already* transcriptions.
>
> (*WD*, 211, trans. mod.)

Concepts spring from differentiated forces, not from invariants; from pushes and pulls, not from themes and psychic objects. Instead of psychic object there is Freudian 'Bahnung' ('trace'), a path like the traces left by nuclear particles in a cloud chamber; there is *différance*.

Derrida seems then to be vulnerable to a version of traditional arguments against scepticism. Traditional criticism of scepticism argued that it used discourse to denounce the coherence of discourse, and that it could not do so coherently (a version of the 'tu quoque'). For Derrida to find an invariant, pres-ence, under or within such varieties of philosophical concepts as the list above (p.21), seems itself to be an invariant. Has not Derrida invariably found an invariant, and is he not accordingly subject to his own arguments?

Again, one might think that a traditional filiation between scepticism and empiricism shows in another example, where Derrida begins to undermine one of the philosophically most rigorous attempts to isolate what in language is capable of 'pure' meaning, that of Husserl. This is defined by the latter as 'the single, self-identical intentional unity set over against the dispersed multiplicity of actual and possible experiences of speakers and thinkers' (Husserl 1970: I, 327). It is in the process of examining Husserl's attitude to language in his first *Logical Investigations* that Derrida shows that conscious intention is insufficient to guarantee coherence. The function of indication, which is not controllable by intention, is set by Husserl against the expressive function, related to intending to mean (the French expression 'vouloir dire' brings both together). Yet indication can never be excised; in spite of Husserl's efforts, it is entwined into the very possibility of language. (Derrida throws light on the historical tradition of analysis of the will within which Husserl is working [VP, 36–7; *SP*, 33–4].) What we say can always be treated as an involuntary gesture as well as a meaning-filled expression of intention, and Husserl's own discussion involuntarily reveals this. Indication is linked to those 'actual and possible experiences of speakers' which Husserl in the quotation above is striving to reduce because they both carry 'valeurs d'existence mondaine, de naturalité, de sensibilité, d'empiricité, d'association etc.'(VP, 40) ('The elements of wordly existence, of what is natural or empirical, of sensibility, of association, etc.') (*SP*, 37). The string of genitives by which Derrida suggests the complexity of the different 'values' being aligned nevertheless finds its 'last unity', he says, in 'non-presence'.

Derrida's work sketched in this way, and it often has been, seems then to unsettle our discourse by showing its reliance on ideas of presence and of identity immediately grasped as actual presence. It appears thus to reveal the fuzziness of what seemed established intellectual forms, to show up the instability of distinctions; it also seems to show in the particular case of Husserl that what he was struggling to reduce was precisely such fuzziness, which he associated with empirical life, and finally with non-presence, lack of consciousness, lack of intention. It is as if Husserl were struggling against both empirical methods and empirical facts (he is at the same time close to and far removed from Hume, cf. Mall 1973). But Husserl is not alone in his struggle to reduce the empirical. Derrida takes to task both the anthropologist Claude Lévi-Strauss and, as we shall see later, the philosopher Emmanuel Levinas, for leanings to empiricism. Lévi-Strauss' awareness of the way in which his work could be seen as idiosyncratic resulted in his account of the *bricoleur* or 'do-it-yourself man'. It is related to the distinction between a 'scientific' and an 'empirical' discourse. The open-ended attitude of the do-it-yourself man comes about because he inherits tools, because he adapts already given tools derived from various origins to the task in hand (ED, 418; *WD*, 285). Lévi-Strauss had contrasted him with the engineer, but Derrida undermines the distinction. He deconstructs it and shows that for it to be viable, the engineer would have to invent each time his own tools, or, in the case of the anthropologist, his own language. It seems then that Lévi-Strauss conserves 'comme instrument ce dont il critique la valeur de vérité' (ED, 417) ('as an instrument something whose truth value he criticizes') (*WD*, 284). If Husserl strives and fails to reduce 'mondanity', that is, empirical life, if he strives and fails to reach a totally self-sustaining rigour, Lévi-Strauss on the other hand, in settling for that failure, seen as a necessary incompleteness and falsifiability, settles also for staying with the less-than-rigorous. Of Lévi-Strauss it is said: 'L'empirisme serait le genre dont ces fautes seraient toujours les espèces' (ED, 421) ('Empiricism would be the genus of which these faults would always be the species') (*WD*, 288).

At this point in the article, we are all, by the very nature of language, 'bricoleurs'; the very existence of the 'engineer' is impossible, and the weakness applies to us all. The bricoleur is incoherent, an incoherence related by Derrida to empiricism, but so are we all: we can none of us justify our thinking from the ground up – 'La seule faiblesse du bricolage – mais à ce titre, n'est-elle pas irrémédiable? – c'est de ne pouvoir se justifier de part en part en son propre discours' (G, 200) ('The only weakness of *bricolage* – but, seen as a weakness is it not irremediable? – is a total inability to justify itself in its own discourse') (*G*, 138). We seem, then, to have reached an impasse. From this kind of argument, Derrida's work has been considered as a brilliant and rigorous exhibition of the fuzziness, of the crankiness in our intellectual systems (unrecognized systems as well as conscious ones), of slipperiness in our concepts. But it seems to follow, then, that any attempt either to construct a rigorous system or to exit from metaphysics seems to be condemned to be a version of the Liar paradox, the metaphysical discourse which says that all metaphysical discourse is vitiated, and as has been said, this is an account often given of Derrida's work.

Such a view makes of paradox an atemporal structure, as Derrida does not. This chapter has already suggested that Derrida always embeds philosophical positions in a pathway which is not a chain of causes and effects, but which provides points from which the positions become perceptible. The viewer and the viewed are interlinked, not distinct. So that, except in a very few articles, Derrida's own argument is each time local, each time applied to work within a context, work which connects to his own. This book will argue that paradox is not in Derrida's work a framework which stalls arguments as of right, transcendental right. On the contrary, it is a form of intertextuality. For paradox is disabling only in an oppositional and stationary structure; intellectual history is not such: '[elle] ne constit[uait] pas un système donné, une sorte de table anhistorique et foncièrement homogène, mais un espace dissymétrique et hiérarchisant, traversé par des forces et travaillé dans sa clôture par le dehors qu'il refoule' (D, 11) ('[it] never constituted a *given* system, a sort of ahistorical, thoroughly homogeneous table, but rather a dissymetric, hierarchically ordered space whose closure is constantly being traversed by the forces, and worked by the exteriority, that it represses') (*D*, 5). Our intellectual horizon, in that it is historical, is always a localized skewed field. Against a harmonized and simplifying account of intellectual systems, Derrida sets a plurality of ethically loaded, historically located structures (ethics and epistemics are not watertight compartments). The implications for consistency of such a claim and such a way of writing will be discussed in Chapter 5.

Derrida, to summarize, sets up contradiction as tensions active in a textual-historical context. Take the article on Lévi-Strauss. The latter's resignation to slippage and lack of coherence accepts that closure is impossible, and thus that the elements to be considered cannot be totalized. But Derrida argues that this acceptance can be of two sorts, both being found in Lévi-Strauss. Empiricism is the first variety: it refuses totalization, closure, and thus rigour, because the infinite richness of the real cannot be caught by a finite human consciousness or discourse. In the second variety, totalization is refused in the sense that it is useless: Lévi-Strauss' syntax of myth allows an infinity of substitutions to operate within a finite corpus: a game [jeu] which is infinite because it has no centre which can organize the substitutions (ED, 423; WD, 289).[27] Faced with this latter lack of a centre which might delimit and structure, there are two possible reactions: a nostalgic search for an origin which is outside the play of substitutions on the one hand, and on the other an affirmation of the play, and thus the passing beyond the epoch of humanism which is defined by that nostalgic search. To these possibilities could be attached the names of Rousseau and Nietzsche, and these are the two current interpretations (at the date of the article) of interpretation (ED, 427; WD, 292). The article has often been taken as privileging the Nietzschean reaction (it is true that the account of it is more enthusiastic), and has led to talk of 'free play of the signifier' in connection with Derrida. In fact the text explicitly refuses such a choice (ED, 428; WD, 293). For the later disruption of the possibility of totalization has already in the earlier part of the article been situated historically – it is the moment of structuralist and linguistic penetration into modes of thought. The centreless structure is compared by Derrida to language, and in Derrida's speculative history this is the moment when the thought came that there was no centre, that the absence of central origin or transcendental signifier makes possible a never ending play and passage of meaning.[28] Such passages of meaning cannot just be affirmed, as the bricoleur affirmed his use of tools without concern for their provenance or *ad hoc* nature. Such a moment must have as its tissue the 'critical work' which preceded it, if it is not to collapse into incoherence; it must have relation to its historical context in order to go beyond it, but this implies in turn, we are told, that this history, that is, metaphysics, is still active in the very language that is used. This article ends with a plea for a different kind of history. Lévi-Strauss had broken with that history where a becoming is imposed to order events, but his structuralist history still takes the form of catastrophic lurches, *ruptures*, from one structure to another (ED, 426; WD, 291). In the last paragraph of the article, the relation between genesis and structure, through the question of the history of that relation, is once more evoked.

Deconstruction is in fact a recognition of cursus, of history within which, but also with which, we think (it is not something that just happens by natural development). It is this cursus, *parcours* or passage, which enables rigour. But it also makes consistency in the sense of water-tightness impossible. The rest of this book will attempt to suggest that part of Derrida's work can be gradually understood as putting in place possibilities of consistency. These are not a guarantee – for loss, inconsistency, are formally essential, they are not accidents which come after, but are part of what it is to think, part of the history of thinking in the widest sense. Derrida builds up a coherence, not by developing rules for it but by establishing connections, contacts, links and extensions.

Empiricism and transcendentality

The question of empiricism arose in a twofold way in my preceding section: first, in its relation to what Husserl was aiming to excise in meaning, empirical 'values', which could not, Derrida argued, be just stripped out of ideal meaning; second, in its being used to articulate the nature of the incoherence admitted by Lévi-Strauss. So that arguments associated historically with empiricism appear at this point to be both accepted and to be criticized for falling short. Yet we saw earlier that Derrida implied, in *Of Grammatology*, that coming after Husserl could allow a position which is rigorous, non-transcendental without being not transcendental. In the part of that text my argument is concentrating on, we have arrived, in the company of Heidegger, says Derrida, not at the production of something which can act as a transcendental, but at the question of how transcendentality was produced (G, 38; *G*, 23). How is it then that Derrida both uses and questions both empirical and transcendental arguments?

Now it was for neglect of the historical nature of his own tools that Lévi-Strauss was gently reproached. History, and the history of metaphysics, is in that article, as elsewhere in Derrida's work, not thought of as a medium in which things just are, which is outside and which pre-exists the object of study. It is worked into language, so that it is through language that its workings must be revealed and understood. Hence Derrida brings forward as strategies of deconstruction *paleonymy* and *neonymy*. The first is a formation recalling what was discussed à propos the bricoleur, where an old signifier brings with it archaisms into a changed context. *Neonymy* where a sudden linguistic coinage, sometimes deliberately baroque and shocking in Derrida's own case ('double invagination chiasmatique' for instance), warns that what is said is unlikely to be assimilable to anything but itself. Derrida's extreme attention to the status of his own lexis makes of it something which both reveals and works on language even as his language operates. (As in a quotation, there is the sense of the expression and the sense of that expression as quotation.) *Paleonymy* and *neonymy* work together; they both warn how any fragment of thought is locally incised in its own language, and in its own history, but is also incised by being worked on and picked out. Terms bring with them their own history, *paleonymy*, but when worked on also point to other histories which are forming, and which may be marked by new coinages, *neonymy*. Reference to time, reference to others, are integral to language.

It is here that the question of transcendentality as raised so far in relation to

Of Grammatology may move on a stage. Derrida shows this through a working back to the 'common possibility' (G, 68; *G*, 46) of all systems of meaning: the idea of the 'instituted trace'. The phrase arises in Derrida's argument in the following way. He recalls how Saussure developed the theory of the 'arbitrariness of the sign',[29] where there is no 'natural' relation of resemblance between meaning and word: convention, collective habit, underpin every means of expression. Yet the implication of some of Saussure's remarks on the written word is that it is somehow even less natural than the spoken word. Writing, or at least phonetic writing, may try to indicate the word's pronunciation, but in doing this, says Saussure, it actually affects speech, it exercises a tyranny over speech, in spite of its dependence on it (G, 53; see G, 45–6; *G*, 29–30). Derrida is here investigating as he does elsewhere, à propos Saussure, the gestures of inferiorization, of expulsion, by which writing has been pushed to the 'outside'. For all individual signs are arbitrary, and the graphic sign is not different in this respect from a phonic one. Both phonic and graphic signs, even where pictural and cratylic, that is onomatopoeic, must be instituted. The opposition natural/cultural has the function in our thought of getting history started by disengaging culture from its opposite, nature – but such an opposition is unsustainable, Derrida argues. Things are rather the other way round: it is the notion of writing, with the values of the 'irrational' or the veiling of the vision of language (both in Saussure 1985: 51; 1972: 29) which makes possible the notion of 'arbitrariness of the sign'. If this concept, instead of being one of the poles of the nature/culture opposition, is thought of as prior, upstream as it were, of the distinction, if it is thought of as 'instituted trace' (the nature of this 'priority' will be examined in the next chapter), then it marks, as we shall see directly, the imbrication of the non-living, of absence, and of reference to the other, in what has been taken, by Saussure and by others, to be living presence, self-present and natural.

It is the trace which allows into the structure of meaning reference, but also change; which allows of meaning by retaining differentiation within what is a relaying structure (and delaying, see above): 'On ne peut penser la trace instituée sans penser la rétention de la différence dans une structure de renvoi où la différence apparaît *comme telle* et permet ainsi une certaine liberté de variation entre les termes pleins' (G, 68) ('The instituted trace cannot be thought without thinking the retention of difference within a structure of reference where difference appears *as such* and thus permits a certain liberty of variations among the full terms') (*G*, 46–7). Derrida has here moved upstream, from a compelling demonstration that a non-contradictory distribution among signs of the binary opposition natural/arbitrary is impossible, to *différence* as the differential matrix from which phonemes and concepts are determined. Saussure had allowed that '*Arbitraire* et *différentiel* sont deux qualités corrélatives' (Saussure 1985: 166, quoted G, 77 note) ('*Arbitrary* and *differential* are two correlative qualities') (Saussure 1972: 118, quoted *G*, 52 note 18). Derrida explicitly does not remain within the Saussurian net of differences, however. *Différence* and *trace* lead back to an ontological root, for in the synthesis which is meaning, where only differences, not 'positive terms' are being synthesized, there is 'announced', he says, the completely other, which is by definition never attained, always absent, which can only announce itself by dissimulating itself (G, 69; *G*, 47). The *trace*, like Heideggerian Being, hides and reveals: both make possible diacritical difference, but not in any stable fashion, so that it has to be constantly reworked.[30]

The way in which difference refers out in the 'instituted' trace is very soon further explicated:

> La structure générale de la trace immotivée fait communiquer dans la même possibilité et sans qu'on puisse les séparer autrement que par abstraction, la structure du rapport à l'autre, le mouvement de la temporalisation et le langage comme écriture.
>
> (G, 69)

> The general structure of the unmotivated trace connects within the same possibility, and they cannot be separated except by abstraction, the structure of the relationship with the other, the movement of temporalization, and language as writing.
>
> (*G*, 47)

Relation to the other, temporalization, and language as writing, come together in this difference. Or, using language which marks in an important way the non-empirical referent of the terms, and makes of them the products of an 'arche-synthesis': 'L'archi-écriture, mouvement de la différance, archi-synthèse irréductible, ouvrant à la fois, dans une seule et même possibilité, la temporalisation, le rapport à l'autre, et le langage' (G, 88) ('arche-writing, movement of differance, irreducible arche-synthesis, opening in one and the same possibility, temporalization as well as relationship with the other and language') (*G*, 60). Language just is relation to others (there can be no private language, confined by its essence to one speaker); and it just is the possibility of inscription, for 'ni des idées ni des sons ne pre-existeraient au système linguistique' (Saussure 1985: 155) ('neither ideas nor sounds would pre-exist the linguistic system') (Saussure 1972: 166), and these mean in turn existence in relation to time.

All these, temporalization, relation to the other, language, are opened by an 'arche-synthesis', which Derrida's own language flags, by his use of the prefix 'arche', as some kind of transcendental, that is, as shaping the essence of our experience, rather than being experienced as such. In that, they represent, as we shall see, a quite specific development of elements in the later Husserl's work (elements which can be related to Heidegger: in this way, once more, Derrida's work at this point is philosophy *and* history of philosophy). In this collocation, rather sudden in the argument of *Of Grammatology*, they all refer to the necessarily absent: they are all, time, language, and the other, intentions of the infinite, as we shall see, and are necessarily intuitionless, for the infinite cannot be the object of intuition. (A man or woman is finite; they cannot therefore apprehend the infinite immediately in a self-evident way through intuition; intentions, as developed by Husserl, and in the vocabulary that he adopted, are object-directed acts of thought: one can direct one's thought to the infinite, but it is not obvious how it may be made self-evidently present in its totality.) They are transcendental in the Kantian sense: 'condition de tout système linguistique' (G, 88) ('the condition of all linguistic systems') (*G*, 60) and in the Husserlian sense of eidetic, that is essential, not factual. At this point in my argument, a problem to be discussed later must be flagged: how much weight can be put on this 'transcendentality'? For the uncertainty of their scope, their lexical mutability – in close succession, we have 'archi-écriture', 'archi-synthèse', 'archi-trace' – makes one uncertain, and this uncertainty is certainly increased by the rhetorical question put by Derrida himself in an interview: 'N'ai je pas inlassablement répété . . . que la trace n'était ni un fondement ni une origine' (P, 71) ('have I not indefatigably repeated . . . that the trace is neither a ground, nor a foundation, nor an origin') (*P*, 52). (Derrida has also called such lexemes 'quasi-transcendentals'[31] but discussion of the sense of that 'quasi' must be deferred to Chapter 2).

Here, I need to recall that it is against the threat of a 'naive objectivism', and against the recourse to the *ad hoc*, to the merely empirical (G, 89; *G*, 60) (the 'irremediable fault' of the do-it-yourself man) that Derrida in *Of Grammatology* has allowed himself transcendental arguments, indicated by the prefix 'archi'. This pattern, which, it has been shown above, is also used of Heidegger's relation to Nietzsche, is a deconstructive one. But it is a pattern of argument that refers to its own history, to its cursus; it is not just a 'tu quoque', for then it would be only a trivial turning of the argument's tables, in this case against himself. It is a concern to move beyond structural oppositions, particularly the Husserlian one between empirical and transcendental arguments, to a situation where the history of the problem's discussion has altered the ground of the discussion. Lévi-Strauss' neglect of the history of his own terms is infra-transcendental. On the other hand, it should be possible to move beyond the Husserlian transcendental criticism, and it is the wake of this movement, its cursus, which allows a new sort of rigour beyond the 'either/or' of the choice we seemed enfolded in (and which produced the accusations of scepticism against Derrida's work). At this point in *Of Grammatology* Derrida suggests a 'crossing-out' of the value of transcendentality after it has made its necessity felt (G, 90; *G*, 61). But there must be a deliberate incorporation of contradictory possibilities within the term 'trace' to provide a reminder of this cursus. If 'trace' is not to be the empirical mark left by some presence which has disappeared, then the concepts of 'trace originaire' and 'archi-trace' are needed, which in Derrida's formulation as it is being developed in these passages is paradoxical: 'Et pourtant, nous savons que ce concept détruit son nom et que, si tout commence par la trace, il n'y a surtout pas de trace originaire' (G, 90) ('Yet we know that that concept destroys its name and that, if all begins with the trace, there is above all no originary trace') (*G*, 61). This points forward to the instability of such later Derridean coinages as *pharmakon* and *hymen*, an instability built into the word through its contradictory senses, and must remind us that contradiction comes about not just in a logical operation, but through historical location, through different inherited strands of discourse rubbing up against each other.

Derrida is then splicing together phenomenological, transcendental and historical methods. But the whole question of the relation between *structure* and *genesis*, between formalism and historicism, between Platonism and constructivism can be seen to shape his discussions of poets and philosophers in *Of Grammatology* and *Writing and Difference*.[32]

Writing and universal conditions

Derrida, we have seen, had in the first article of *Writing and Difference* worried at a structuralist critic's formalism, at his lack of attention to the forces of development internal to the literary works investigated. In another article in that volume and in *Of Grammatology*, Derrida turns to a kind of mirror image of structuralism, which he occasionally refers to as historicism: the making of what is a universal condition, a condition of possibility, into an empirical event.

When Saussure made writing secondary, he was repeating a gesture of separation between nature and culture whose function is to make historicity secondary, to make of the beginning of history an event in nature (G, 90; G, 61). For *Of Grammatology*, the opposition between nature and culture was given its modern form by Rousseau. In showing this, Derrida goes through an apparent detour, the consideration of a particular section from the autobiography of Lévi-Strauss. Among a Brazilian tribe, the Nambikwara, it is forbidden to reveal a proper name. Nevertheless, a little girl revealed a proper name to the anthropologist. Now this might appear to be a contradiction of the thesis Derrida has been developing: there would be a proper name, a localization which is unique, and an 'end station' which anchors language in nature through that name, even if it were then effaced and subject to prohibition. Against this, Derrida argues that the prohibition only makes sense because the proper name is not unique. Developing Levinas' thought at this point, he argues that the act of naming is not creation but classification, it is a suspension of any absolute appeal to the interlocutor, an overriding of absolute singularity,[33] which cannot be both spoken and respected because language immediately makes it common property: 'Penser l'unique dans le système, l'y inscrire, tel est le geste de l'archi-écriture, archiviolence, perte du propre, de la proximité absolue de la présence à soi, perte en vérité de ce qui n'a jamais eu lieu' (G, 164) ('To think the unique *within* the system, to inscribe it there, such is the gesture of the arche-writing: arche-violence, loss of the proper, of absolute proximity, of self-presence, in truth the loss of what has never taken place') (G, 112). So that prohibiting the revelation of personal names is not the fundamental violence, but a secondary violence: one which by protecting and separating, in fact by instituting morals, tried to make good the first violence.[34] This first violence is that of inscription considered, as the word 'archi-écriture' warns us, as a transcendental, a condition of possibility of there being relation to the other through language at all. Thus the violation of the secret, in which the personal names were revealed to the anthropologist, is a third violence, this time empirical, not necessary – it can happen or it may not happen.

This unfolding of violence is given a more questioned status in work on Levinas and Foucault published in *Writing and Difference* but related to this account of Lévi-Strauss. In all three cases Derrida separates with great care 'historical' or 'empirical' event and a situation which is in some sense beyond, or of a different category.

Lévi-Strauss in this episode with the Nambikwara had related writing to power: the anthropologist's use of writing as an aid to knowledge is by that very fact itself a use of writing as an aid to power.[35] Against this, Derrida argues that it is not writing in the wake of science, but writing in the larger sense – differentiation itself – which is connected with violence. For Lévi-Strauss, this episode shows that an empirical force has claimed universality and used it for particular purposes: 'L'universalité est toujours accaparée, comme force empirique, par une force empirique déterminée' (G, 192) ('Universality is always monopolized as empirical force by a determinate empirical force') (G, 132). In the argument as it develops, Lévi-Strauss takes the spread of literacy to be the tool of localized and particular political power, which is how literacy can be at once for him the secret of a caste and imposed on a proletariat. To this Derrida replies by answering the question: 'what does it mean to be subject to a law of universal form?' (a Kantian question, be it noted). Literacy here, like reason in Derrida's work on Foucault, is, as we shall see, a kind of universality and is not to be resolved into empirical events. Its spread does not involve subjection in any classical sense of 'empirical loss caused by actual event'. On the contrary, it is a condition, not conditioning: 'L'accès à l'écriture est la constitution d'un sujet libre dans le mouvement violent de son propre effacement et de son propre enchaînement' (G, 193) ('The access to writing is the constitution of a free subject in the violent movement of its own effacement and of its own bondage') (G, 132). Political violence latches on to this primary violence, it is not identical with it. Cultural violence comes after, and not before, the dividing, differentiating power inherent in writing-as-language. A global condemnation of writing in the narrow sense is thus as useless as a global approval. Beyond this point comes something much larger: all intellectual activity (science, professional writing, of which grammatology like ethnography are only parts) is constituted by the intersubjective violence that is inscription and classification. Now, the injection of such a word as violence into such a structure of thought may appear strange to a different philosophical tradition, all the stranger as Derrida rigorously prevents this intersubjective violence being smudged with political and thus empirical violence. Why then, one might ask, introduce such a term at all? Its result is that all of intellectual activity is shot through with ethical and not merely logical force. The insistence on the priority (logical and historical) of speech is a secondary violence against writing, an attempt to master an originary violence, which is the violence of classification, the violence of inscription. In a conflation of different categories of violence, a universal condition is being interpreted by Lévi-Strauss (and by Foucault, as we shall see) as historically local. Whereas any relation to the other which is less than infinitely respectful of Otherness and thus of absence, in other words any intersubjective relation at all, is violent in this primary sense.

Universal conditions and historicism

Both in its account of violence, and in its account of the way in which universality is bent into being an empirical force at the service of empirical force, what Derrida says of Lévi-Strauss is structurally similar to the argument of his article on Foucault's *History of Madness* – it uses the same 'syntax'. Derrida argues that Foucault takes the violent exclusion of madness, when the mad were shut up in seventeenth-century France, as both an extra-temporal *partage* or separation and as a history occurrence.[36] Foucault presents reason as both a universal norm and as a specific, historically located one. Derrida preys on Foucault's argument, so to speak: it is Foucault who links exclusion of madness to the very possibility of history (ED, 67; WD, 42). But this then implies that the decision by which, according to Foucault, reason constitutes itself, turns madness out of subjectivity and makes of it an object, is not an event occurring in the seventeenth century but a condition: 'l'historicité elle-même, la condition du sens et du langage, la condition de la tradition du sens, la condition de l'oeuvre' (ED, 67) ('historicity itself, the condition of meaning and of language, the condition of the tradition of meaning, the condition of the work') (WD, 42), so that the seventeenth-century shutting-up of the mad of which Foucault speaks cannot be a model, but must be an instance, with its own particularities. Foucault, then, like Lévi-Strauss, has assigned a universal relationship to a particular event. ('A vrai dire, pour aller au fond des choses, il faudrait aborder directement pour elle-même la question du fait et du droit dans les rapports du Cogito et de la folie') (ED, 83) ('To go to the heart of the matter, one ought really to confront directly, in and of itself, the question of what is *de facto* and what *de jure* in the relations of the Cogito and madness') (WD, 53). For to write a history of reason, as Foucault claims he is doing, is to write the history of one of the *determinate forms* of reason, and this is not to be confused with 'the historicity of reason in general' (ED, 68; WD, 43). As Lévi-Strauss made of writing at once the secret of a priestly caste and an instrument for oppressing the proletariat, so Foucault argues simultaneously that the Greek logos is not identical with reason (and could thus have a relation to madness different from the one Foucault discerns for classical reason) *and* that Socrates had already, in classical Greece, organized the logos by dividing it into reason and its opposite. But either Socrates' dialectic is not 'reassuring', not a ploy to cast out darkness, but is upstream of that distinction; or else the (French) classical era's rejection of madness is not the first rejection of madness.

Derrida's strategy here consists once more in moving upstream to a position which is logically and ontologically prior, to a common root of sense and non-sense: 'le logos originaire en lequel *un* langage et *un* silence se partagent' (ED, 68) ('the original logos in which *a* language and *a* silence are divided from one another') (*WD*, 43). (The nature of this root will be examined in the next chapter.) Derrida is developing an argument about category distinctions and the necessity of distinguishing between *de jure* and *de facto* arguments. But instead of using that distinction to refuse work which does not make it, and thereby making a gesture of exclusion, a 'partage' which would probably reiterate the gesture of exclusion under discussion, he examines the ground of the opposition. His argument moves upstream historically (but also further up the decision tree). Reason, language, historicity are conjoint. Reason as historicity, he implies, is the condition of sense and of language (ED, 67; *WD*, 42). To get beyond reason is also to get beyond language and history. Madness as non-reason, like absolute singularity in the argument about the Nambikwara names, cannot be said without beginning its reintegration into reason in general. (And in an underpinning of the argument to be further examined below in Chapter 5 of this book, the common root of reason, as of language and historicity, is not a positive origin, but is derived from a wordless and non-historical negativity, 'le fonds non historique de l'histoire' ('the non-historical capital [basis] of history') where finally a non-classical dissociation of word and thought is made: 'Il s'agirait alors d'une négativité si négative qu'elle ne pourrait même plus se nommer ainsi' (ED, 55 note) ('It would be then a question of a negativity so negative that it could not even be called such any longer') (*WD*, 308.)

In the latter part of the article 'The Cogito and the history of madness', these objections, which are less objections than developments of the argument in a direction not allowed for by Foucault, are elaborated in relation to Descartes. Contrary to what Foucault's argument needs, madness is not the most serious form of doubt about our knowledge. Descartes in his search for unassailable certainty produces the dream as an exasperation of the hypothesized madness, and that position is then further hyperbolized by the hypothesis of the evil genius, where even ideas of intellectual origin, those of mathematics, are set in doubt. Behind this process of doubt is Descartes' confidence that language encases madness. This confidence is not merely local or *de facto*, not merely a product of Descartes' failure to go to the end of his own argument, and thus in this, not merely a product of a particular historical situation. Madness can only be evoked inside language and this is not a historical failure, on Descartes' or on anyone else's part; nor, without justifying a charge of historicism, can the whole of history be described as a mystification by reason, as is the implication of Foucault's book.[37] For Descartes uses 'theoretical fictions'. Fiction, as a kind of admission of possibility, is the only way of evoking madness from inside language without overpowering and enclosing it.[38]

Derrida, having suggested that there is a common root between logos and madness, suggests that upstream, historically earlier than these historically determinate forms of struggle between madness and reason, there is a point at which the project to think these forms, as relative to the common root of sense and nonsense, becomes possible. This point is immediately described by Derrida as the thinking of a totality of such determinate forms, by removing oneself from the totality: 'Il est le point où s'enracine le projet de penser la totalité en lui échappant' (ED, 86) ('It is the point at which the project of thinking this totality by escaping it is embedded') (*WD*, 56). (This point is related to the 'point exorbitant' met earlier in the chapter, where history and logic, genesis and structure, come together; it is the point that gives leverage for change.) To think these forms as determinate is to think a totality; to think of them as historically determinate is to think of infinity as a totality, as closed, that is, to think the positive infinite. The project Derrida is attributing to Descartes is like the project behind the realist notion of truth, discussed earlier, which relied on the totalizing or closure possible to the Divine intuition. In that it aims to escape from the historically determinate forms towards the infinite, which is towards the thought of God, Descartes' project is mad, and recognizes madness as that which is its own possibility, as that which makes it free. The project is described by Derrida as 'excess' of possible over real, and of right over fact, because Descartes means his argument to work *even if* in practice thinking the totality is unattainable: 'C'est pourquoi, en cet excès du possible, du droit et du sens sur le réel, le fait et l'étant, ce projet est fou, et reconnaît la folie comme sa liberté et sa propre possibilité' (ED, 87) ('This is why, by virtue of this excess of the possible, of right and of sense over the real, the factual, and the existent, this project is mad, and acknowledges madness as its liberty and its very possibility') (*WD*, 56, trans. mod.).

This point, the Cogito, which at the point of its thinking is extrafactual, is also the point at which both Descartes and Foucault are reinserted into history. Descartes is said by Foucault to pull madness and reason into determinate history. But Foucault is reiterating this gesture by neglecting the transcendental thrust of the Cogito, and only working it into historical location. When Derrida writes 'je dis que cette réduction à l'intra-mondanité est l'origine et le sens même de ce qu'on appelle la violence et rend ensuite possibles toutes les camisoles de force' (ED, 88) ('I say that this reduction to intraworldliness is the origin and very meaning of what is called violence, making possible all straitjackets') (*WD*, 57), his account gives to Foucault's text the same pattern – violence that is articulation – found in the argument on Lévi-Strauss rehearsed above. Descartes gives the Cogito a Divine Guarantor (thus neutralizing the Cogito's excess, its madness) and earlier in his text, but in the same movement, he lays down axioms. Foucault historicizes the Cogito by assimilating it to a localized historical reason. In both cases – the relevance to Foucault is left implicit – there is a kind of fall into localized or organized philosophical discourse, in Foucault's case one which led to an identification of the light of reason with normalization, in Descartes' case, to a reassurance against madness. The forcing of the hyperbole to re-enter the world – 'réduction à l'intra-mondanité', its reduction to historical determination – is violent,[39] just as, in the account of Lévi-Strauss, reduction to linguistic determination was the originary violence.

Derrida is radically reworking, against the grain of Foucault's thought, the distinction *de jure* and *de facto*, and is developing the relation between sanity and madness. In doing so, he goes beyond work of the 1960s on madness (Laing, Sollers) in the precision of the stages and distinctions he introduces. Philosophy, he says, must tack between the excess of such an hyperbole which moves beyond any totality (thus treating itself as an absolute) and the insertion into determinate historical structures. Here, speech becomes what will later be called a 'dear purchase': an originary violence against madness, a forcible integration of it into determinate structures, and yet an integration which is only valuable in its staying close to madness, in being able to speak of the violence it itself is (ED, 94; *WD*, 60–1). This hyperbole, this 'excess of opening', this 'ouverture absolue', which cancels relation, which is un-determined because beyond totality, is always caught, recuperated into an economy which moralizes reason and excludes madness (ED, 95; *WD*, 62). There is then an interchange between crisis and falling back, hyperbole and historical determinateness which is the movement of temporalization itself (ED, 94; *WD*, 60–1); it is only by the oppression of madness at each stage of the process that there can be finite thought and a history at all.

This movement of dialogue between excess or hyperbole and historical determinateness constitutes the historicity of philosophy without historicizing it. Derrida implicitly links his work here with the meditation (by him, but also by Kristeva and Foucault) on poetry and madness. Madness in its widest sense is linked by all of these with silence, and contrastingly with the violence that is speech: 'silence non pas déterminé, non pas imposé à ce moment plutôt qu'à tel autre, mais lié par essence à un coup de force, à un interdit qui ouvrent l'histoire et la parole' (ED, 84) ('not a determinate silence, imposed at one given moment rather than at any other, but a silence essentially linked to an act of force and a prohibition which open up history and speech') (*WD*, 54, trans. mod.). The long tradition of linking madness with prophets and poets is developed here so that speaking is a kind of forcing. Historical events, in general, like language, do not start as factual events against a background of nature and silence, but are wrung therefrom as from a condition of their own possibility. To use non-Derridean terms, they arise from a kind of *agon*, struggle, or with a word he does use, a rhythm, or, after Heidegger, from a *polemos* (war).

The 'syntax': transcendentals and historicity

Foucault, like Lévi-Strauss, made a transcendental condition into an empirical event. This smudging of distinctions of right and distinctions of fact is a variety of historicism. They turned a 'transcendental and preethical violence' (ED, 188; *WD*, 128) into determinate forms of reason or ethics. Descartes and Foucault violently reduced the excess, the hyperbolic doubt, to historically local axioms. ('Hyperbolic' doubt is a technical term here for the excessive doubt of the Cartesian procedure.) They led, in one case, to a reassurance through the proof of God 'that he exists' and the recovery of the beliefs which had been put into brackets or inverted commas in Descartes' process of doubt; or in Foucault's case, to a consciously historical interpretation which is then repressive of the whole process of excess-and-fall-into-determination. The 'human sciences', anthropology for instance, have historicized this violence, made of it a historical or political event when it rather belongs to transcendental historicity (ED, 189 note; *WD*, 129 note 46). Violence and discourse are coeval in history, they do not occur at a point within history.

So to begin to get at the relation between the transcendental and history indicated by Derrida, in a way that tries to show the 'syntax' at work under the detail of each of his articles, the question of language needs further examination. As the article ('Violence and metaphysics') on Levinas makes plain, no discourse can escape from this necessary violence (though Derrida here acknowledges the strangeness of the term, and enters the caveat here: 'à supposer . . . qu'il y ait quelque sens à parler de violence pré-éthique' (ED, 188) ('supposing . . . that it is somehow meaningful to speak of preethical violence') (*WD*, 128). Derrida urges against Levinas that the imbrication of discourse and violence is transcendental in Husserl's sense, since Derrida says it is revealed by analysis of essence, 'eidetico-transcendental' (ED, 189); violence is the origin of meaning and discourse, a condition of the human as finite being, so that in order to understand or even to perceive, a person must determine, separate, and thus render partial: 'c'est la violence comme origine du sens et du discours dans le règne de la finitude' (ED, 189) ('it is violence as the origin of meaning and of discourse in the reign of finitude') (*WD*, 129).

Against Levinas' demand for absolute respect for the other in its otherness, Derrida urges that to speak of the other as other cannot, by its very nature, be done elsewhere than from the other's 'appearance for me'; in that way, it has to make the other subsidiary to my viewpoint – and thus does not conserve it respectfully in its otherness (ED, 188; *WD*, 128). Playing Levinas against Hegel, Husserl and Heidegger, Derrida shows how the structures allowed to speech and to appearance for me are similar: the very movement of appearance, that is, of phenomenalization, follows the path attributed to the other and thus to speech (compare *Of Grammatology*'s linking of other, discourse and temporalization). To appear, like to speak, is to detach/be detached from the inchoate: 'La guerre [*polemos*] est donc congénitale à la phénoménalité, elle est le surgissement même de la parole et de l'apparaître' (ED, 190) ('War, therefore, is congenital to phenomenality, is the very emergence of speech and of appearing') (*WD*, 129). Derrida in this way links Levinas with Hegel against Levinas' will; the other can only appear as such in its relation to the same, and that is the originary violence. To speak, as we saw in Derrida's paragraphs on Lévi-Strauss, was violently to make determinate against the hyperbolic, the wordless excess. But discourse then acquires a second degree of violence by trying to recuperate, to make good the negativity of the *polemos*, the determination that inaugurated it. This secondary violence is the only way to avoid 'le rien ou le non-sens purs' (ED, 191) ('nothingness or pure non-sense') (*WD*, 130), a non-sense whose philosophical counterpart, in this text, is nihilism. To deny that this secondary violence cannot be reduced or done away with, is to land in a worse violence, a kind of pre-Kantian dogmatism, which simply does not pose in any way the question of a human's finite nature (ED, 191; *WD*, 130).

'Altérité', 'otherness', for Levinas has an ethical function which affords an answer to this problem. By maintaining otherness, it is guaranteed in the most radical way possible that the other cannot be brought into the power of the same. Husserl on the contrary, did just that; in the fifth *Cartesian Meditation*, he treated the other as an intentional modification of the ego, but in so doing, says Derrida, he at least accounted for the way in which what cannot be got at, the other, still can appear to the 'I'. Levinas refuses this as an encroaching on the other. Now the other is indeed and in principle unreachable, but not just through our 'merely medical' failure to have the infinite time necessary to explore it, as is the case with things. It has a further unreachability, a strong one, so to speak: 'you' cannot appear to me as deictic origin, 'you' as centre of your indexicality as such, can never, in a way that will need further commentary in the second part of this chapter, become an object of my intuition. How things look from your point of view is in principle never wholly available to me. (We saw earlier that language, time and relation to the other, are intentionless intuitions: in that they partake of infinity, they cannot be made self-evidently present to me as a whole.) But then Levinas should never even speak of the infinitely other; yet he does in fact (ED, 183; *WD*, 125). He cannot justify his own language (the extent to which this article extends the work on Lévi-Strauss is clear here). Such a discrepancy is typical of empiricism, says Derrida, it is a protestation 'against the concept' (ED, 224; *WD*, 151). It is a dream of 'heterological' thought, thought other than discourse, a 'pure thought of pure difference'. Traditional empiricism unconsciously, Levinas consciously, separate thought and language, protecting the other and its difference from language and from assimilation through language. But attention to the individual and the particular is only possible through language, and language, as we have seen, is violent, in that it is at once generalizing and classifying: in a phrase added to the original article 'La violence apparaît avec l'*articulation*' (ED, 219) ('Violence appears with *articulation*') (*WD*, 147–8). To accept this incoherence, by which Levinas *speaks* of the infinitely other which is the origin of language and thus beyond language, is to neglect the *a priori* and the transcendental horizons of language (ED, 224; *WD*, 151). Language preempts otherness, drawing back into the same, failing to respect difference, but this is the price of relating to the other, of speaking, at all.

Now Levinas dismisses this violence of language as historical and secondary. It is not the originary gift of language to the other, which is beyond being, that is, *epekeina tes ousias*, and thus, in the philosophical tradition, the positive or absolute infinite. Being beyond historical determination, it is transhistorical. Against Heidegger, for whom the ontological difference, the gap between Being and beings, opens history by opening otherness,[40] Levinas wished to make the relation to other beings primordial; but he has stamped a precedence existing in fact onto a transcendental relation:

Cette 'préséance' [ontologique ou transcendantale] ne contredit pas plus qu'elle ne confirme la précession ontique ou factuelle. Il s'ensuit que l'être, étant toujours *en fait* déjà déterminé comme étant et n'étant rien hors de lui, il est toujours déjà dissimulé. La phrase de Levinas – préexistence du rapport à l'étant – est la formule même de cette occultation initiale.

(ED, 212)

This 'priority' no more contradicts than it confirms ontic or factual precedence. It follows that Being, since it is always, in fact, determined as an existent and is nothing outside the existent, is always dissimulated. Levinas's phrase – the preexistence of the relation to the existent – is the very formula of this initial concealment.

(*WD*, 144)

A determination which specifies thereby reveals 'l'étant'. But in doing so, it also veils or hides Being. This is the very (and very Heideggerian) condition of history (ED, 213; *WD*, 144). Once more, it seems, a new relation between the transcendental and the factual, *de jure* and *de facto*, is being worked out through discussion of Levinas' criticism of Heideggerian being.

Levinas, like Foucault and Lévi-Strauss, has printed over a transcendental relation with a factual one. Their gestures are historicist ones. But how is the relation to be rethought if historicism is rejected? Derrida elsewhere agreed that the arguments Husserl mounted against historicism (in his case, Dilthey's or Hegel's historicism) were valid, but not the platform from which he did it, which was that of a teleological history of reason (P, 79–80 note; *P*, 105 note 32). But if history is not told from the point of view of conditions treated as facts (historicism) nor from the point of view of an end to be reached (teleology), how is a sceptical relativism to be avoided, how is a 'transcendental historicity' (Derrida's words) to be constructed?

This question induces a pattern already discussed above, one that is a recurrent circuit of argument in these texts of Derrida: a totality can be seen because there has been a hyperbolic move to exceed it. Derrida, as has been shown, argues of philosophical discourse in 'The Cogito and the history of madness' that its history is the history of exits, of moments of excess over totality, which are followed by relapses into history. Likewise, against Levinas, Derrida makes of history 'le mouvement même de la transcendance, de l'excès sur la totalité sans lequel aucune totalité n'apparaîtrait' (ED, 173) ('the very movement of transcendence, of the excess over the totality without which no totality would appear') (*WD*, 117); cf. in a different article: 'réduction transcendentale ... l'acte libre de la question qui s'arrache à la totalité de ce qui la précède pour pouvoir accéder à cette totalité et en particulier à son historicité et à son passé' (ED, 251) ('transcendental reduction ... the free act of the question, which frees itself from the totality of what precedes it in order to be able to gain access to this totality, particularly to its historicity and its past')

(*WD*, 167). Thinking in relation to a system is working through it without relativizing it, but is also exceeding it. Philosophy just is the history of such exits into 'cosmic exile', and such history is then a process of transcending which allows a totality to appear.

Here the various glosses I have made so far, as they are needed, on the term 'transcendental', must be pulled together. In Kantian writing, 'transcendental' referred to the nature and conditions of the *a priori* in experience, what was part of the shape of experience without itself being empirical. Husserl takes this in a developed sense. Things transcend our perceptions of them, in that they are over against our perception, not in it; that is what makes it always possible for us to perceive more, to try to fix our perceptions and make them clearer. So that the different ways we see things, the different perspectives in our perceptions, are an essential part of this clarifying process, not an accidental weakness of human constitution (Husserl 1931: §149). The mind stands beyond – not in the world, but as a subject for which this world has meaning and being. Here, 'transcendental' applies not, as with Kant, to conditions of possibility, but implies that the 'I' is the concrete source and place of every *a priori* or essential piece of knowledge.[41] Heidegger in his commentary on Kant had put that transcendentality in relation to what he argued was the central datum with which Kant was working – that experience precisely was given, that we are receptive of the world as well as active, that built into our experience was our own passivity, our limits, our finitude, our own death. This he developed further in ways relevant to Derrida's use. Transcendence in such texts as *Vom Wesen des Grundes* (*The Essence of Reasons*) is *Dasein*'s[42] transcendence (*Überschwung*), a literalization of the Latin roots, a climbing beyond. It is this climbing beyond which is the ground of being able to allow the ontological difference to be manifested through fact, 'in dem die ontologische Differenz faktisch wird' (GA, vol. 9, 134–5, previously quoted), i.e. whereby phenomena can appear to *Dasein*'s receptiveness.[43] Derrida is allowing to lie side-by-side as it were the Cartesian cogito, Husserlian transcendentality and Heideggerian *Überschwung*, and relating them to historical determinateness, to a movement which lets that determinateness appear by moving out of it, transcending it, being of a different category, of a different level.

In these different articles, 'transcendental' then hooks into a different philosophical context each time, but it is the case that a link between these is made, and not just by following those philosophers' use of the same word. It is here that the question, of the weight to be put on the 'transcendental' in these earlier texts of Derrida, deferred above, must be further considered. First, though the term when it is used is worked into a philosophical context, this is not a historicized position (though my account of it may well be). 'Transcendental' is thoroughly active in the philosophical history of philosophy which is being worked through by these Derridean texts. The point of the argument about Nietzsche and Heidegger, as he develops it, is that it is not a fall into empirical ways, nor does it just ignore the rigour which Husserl made possible. The 'transcendental' historicity, we shall see in the next section, has made possible a movement beyond the 'transcendental'. This is, at one level, a historical statement, about the relation between Husserl and Heidegger. As Derrida (OG, 169 note; *OG,* 151 note 184) and then Tugendhat (1965: 255) have argued, and as we shall see, it is from working beyond the Husserlian transcendental phenomenology that Heidegger can approach 'pure facticity' in a way that does not objectify the fact but grounds it in a more originary intersubjective history, one without, because prior to, preconstituted subject and object.

But at another level, the statement is not only a statement about the history of philosophy. For it implies ultimately an overlapping relation between the historical event or set of events, and the 'transcendental'. Here, Derrida seems to me to extend the notion of 'transcendental' (through the history of the word, Kantian, Husserlian, Heideggerian), in a way that recalls an interpretation of Wittgenstein's late work by Bernard Williams in the direction of a position which is constructivist (and which would thus have roots in intuitionism). We have seen that a non-realist account of truth maintains that where we do not know in practice how to decide the truth of a statement in all circumstances, we cannot with good sense speak of 'truth'. Non-realism when mapped by Dummett reinterprets truth conditions as what justify our assertion of a sentence. Bernard Williams has pointed out that, in Wittgenstein's late work, if 'deciding the truth of a statement' is given the content not of truth conditions, but assertion conditions, then the decision as to what counts as basis for the assertion conditions is a matter of praxis. The decision need not be thought of as actual decision, indeed must not be if empirical idealism is to be avoided; but it has to be thought of as 'a decision to count certain conditions as adequate for assertion' in order for the assertion to be determinate in all cases. And that is a matter of human praxis. 'The point . . . is . . . in the thought that the determinacy of reality comes from what we have decided or are prepared to count as determinate' (Williams 1981: 163). The transcendental here 'shows itself in what we are and are not prepared to regard as sense', which is conditioned by historical process. We then leave behind, in this interpretation of the late work of Wittgenstein, the sense of historical implantation of the decision to treat the assertion conditions as adequate. They can indeed, after the decision, only be properly spoken of as not historically derived. They would then be conditions of possibility – transcendental, in the Kantian sense (in fact, at the end of the article, Williams inflects the Wittgensteinian position to which I am comparing Derrida's argument 'in the direction of a "transcendental idealism"'). The article throws an illuminating light on the work 'transcendental' is doing in the Derridean texts discussed above. Here, the passage and cursus through arguments, through Heidegger's on Nietzsche, and through Husserlian phenomenology to Heidegger, enables a relating of ideas of history and the transcendental to be taken up so that an opposition between the level of the event and something like the conditions of our thinking is no longer possible. The *de jure* and *de facto* distinction is at once respected and dissolved. (Williams makes of this a paradox: see pp. 41–2).

At this point, at the end of the first section of this first chapter, it is necessary once more to reflect on how Derrida conducts his argument, since the general thesis of this present book is concerned with what in his argument is not thematized, or not generally and inevitably turned into individual terms. So far, what has been picked out are not really themes, but patterns of organization. Derrida, it is important to realize, is not expounding the thought of the thinkers he works in and on, but testing it by developing it in other contexts of argument which may well work out its implications, but not only on its own ground. What he is doing in these difficult articles of *Writing and Difference* is to take up with great care strands of argument, which he relates in a precautionary way to the host texts, to Levinas, Lévi-Strauss, Rousset, Husserl or Foucault. Though Derrida is respecting the coherence of a thinker, he is not treating it as a sealed unit, but urging it towards other historically relevant texts, through the unveiling of patterns, through developments of vocabulary; urging it towards some kind of community for discussion, some exploring of communication between these texts. So that although it can be said, it just has been said, that Derrida is working between empiricism and transcendentality, history and closed structure, and as we shall see, constructivism and Platonism, these are not given possibilities, but currents in the texts he is working on and in. They localize the text, and Derrida's own work, by inclining them towards positions in the history of philosophy, which act as a kind of selvedge in Derrida's concerns. They are a kind of syntax and a powerful force of organization in the dense weave of a Derridean text. They cannot be aligned one on the other, but as a syntax they articulate, bringing together while holding separate, the threads in the history of philosophy with which his work at this period is woven.

But in the two extended texts on Husserl of this period, the relation between the transcendental and history is rooted logically and chronologically back into the paradoxes of the infinite, and into a set of aporias whose status needs to be discussed. By 'paradoxes of the infinite' I am referring to paradoxes where a short-circuit in reasoning, one that sometimes resembles a 'vicious circle', occurs because there is recourse to a set which is infinite, yet is treated as a totality, as a closable whole. The second part of this chapter will attempt to show how a syntax of argument associated with the aporias of the infinite occurs throughout certain of Derrida's writings.

The infinites

Williams' work on the later Wittgenstein discussed above suggested that for the latter, it is a historical 'decision' that makes what 'we are prepared to regard as sense' into a set of non-historical conditions for the assertion of an utterance, that is, makes of it something transcendental. What in the relation between Husserl and Heidegger, developed by Derrida as by Tugendhat, is a working through and beyond Husserlian transcendentality to that facticity which might seem to be pre-transcendental without being empirical, is developed into paradox by the Williams article discussed above. Williams also mentions, without in this article taking it farther,[44] what is a crucial problem forming another piece of 'syntax' in Derrida's work. That problem is the infinite, or rather, in the context in which Williams is working in this article, the problem of achieving a finite set of assertion conditions in all circumstances: to achieve the determinate in utterances is in potential conflict with the infinite sequences in which what is being determined might be inserted. Now we saw that in the articles on Foucault or Levinas, there was presented an alternation between totalizing the world in its infinity, and falling back into historical determinateness. 'Infinity' in the work of Derrida being discussed in this chapter, in the forms in which it has been traditionally distinguished, the actual and the potential infinite, acts as articulator and organizer of what might be called the space of a whole set of arguments.

The two infinites

The movement discerned in the articles on Foucault or Levinas, of moving towards an absolute, exceeding the world, seeing it as a totality by transcending it, unifying it momentarily into a totality and thus causing determinateness (and hence rigour) to appear, was in rhythmed interchange with a falling back into determinateness, into historical localization.[45] After this movement to the absolute, rigour becomes localized rigour. To neglect the first phase, Derrida implies, is to historicize (Foucault, Lévi-Strauss). To neglect the second is to reject history (Levinas). But, as we have seen, Derrida claims that Levinas, in speaking of, that is relating, the other as absolute (where relation has been dissolved), fails to account for his own procedures (like Lévi-Strauss and the bricoleur, he is then empirical). In unacknowledged self-description of his own predatory alertness, Derrida speaks of a vigilance which is

> une violence choisie comme la moindre violence pour une philosophie qui prend l'histoire, c'est à dire, la finitude, au sérieux; philosophie qui se sait *historique* de part en part (en un sens qui ne tolère ni la totalité finie ni l'infinité positive) et qui se sait, comme le dit en un autre sens Levinas, *économie.*
>
> (ED, 172)

> a violence chosen as the least violence by a philosophy which takes history, that is finitude, seriously; a philosophy aware of itself as *historical* in each of its aspects (in a sense which tolerates neither finite totality, nor positive infinity), and aware of itself, as Levinas says in another sense, as *economy.*
>
> (*WD*, 117)

Here, the historical awareness refuses both finite totality (the reproach Levinas made against history was that it views everything as finite totality) and positive infinity (totalized infinity). This rejection of alternatives is repeated elsewhere in the same article:

Il faudrait peut-être montrer, comme nous le suggérions plus haut, que l'histoire est impossible, n'a pas de sens dans la totalité finie, qu'elle est impossible et n'a pas de sens dans l'infinité positive et actuelle; et qu'elle se tient dans la différence entre la totalité et l'infini, qu'elle est précisément ce que Levinas appelle transcendance et eschatologie.

(ED, 180)

Perhaps one would have to show, as was suggested above, that history is impossible, meaningless, in the finite totality, and that it is impossible, meaningless, in the positive and actual infinity; that history keeps to the difference between totality and infinity, and that history precisely is that which Levinas calls transcendence and eschatology.

(*WD*, 123)

The rejection of alternatives is also repeated, in different terms, in the article on Foucault:

L'historicité propre de la philosophie a son lieu et se constitue dans ce passage, dans ce dialogue entre l'hyperbole et la structure finie, entre l'excès sur la totalité et la totalité close, dans la différence entre l'histoire et l'historicité.

(ED, 94)

The historicity proper to philosophy is located and constituted in the transition, the dialogue between hyperbole and the finite structure, between that which exceeds the totality and the closed totality, in the difference between history and historicity.

(*WD*, 60)

From these quotations, it becomes clear that these poles of finite totality and positive infinity (or, perhaps, finite structure and hyperbole), in the form 'neither/nor', define for Derrida the space for history – and for language as well. But they are abbreviated references, pedagogical and traditional references, building articulations with philosophers and philosophical themes which are beyond as well as in Levinas. In much twentieth-century philosophy and in work on the foundations of mathematics, the relation between 'totality' and 'infinity' has been the persistent but fissile site of philosophical distinctions made and kinds of limitations proposed. In the texts of Derrida here considered, the two kinds of infinity form part of another piece of 'syntax' which organizes and articulates the argument.

Epekeina tes ousias, 'beyond Being', the abode of the Good for Plato, can act to destroy for Levinas what in ontology (Heidegger) or phenomenology (Husserl) does not respect the otherness of the other. Derrida, like Levinas, links this to positive or actual infinity, which is opposed to negative infinity, in a workhorse opposition perhaps more familiar in French tradition than in the

English. Positive infinity has traditionally been defined as that infinity which is always absolutely more, unrelatably other; it is self-sufficient, in some sense given as a completed whole, though evidently not conceptualizable, since it is infinite. Negative or potential infinity is an infinity of process, in the sense that it never stops – as in the infinite set of natural numbers, given any determinate number, however large, there is always another, the set is never closed. Levinas, going against philosophical tradition, makes of the other not the *heteron* (that which is other), but the *epekeina tes ousias*, the positive infinite. Later in this section, the historical function that has been assigned to thought of the positive infinite will be explored (assigned for instance by Derrida in ED, 222; *WD*, 149). For many philosophers, from Aristotle to Poincaré, it has been the dangerous infinity; in Derrida's descriptions it often has a dramatic edge: it is 'excès vers le non-déterminé, vers le Rien ou l'Infini d'un excès débordant la totalité de ce qu'on peut penser' (ED, 87) ('an excess in the direction of the non-determinate, Nothingness or Infinity, an excess which overflows the totality of that which can be thought') (*WD*, 57, trans. mod.); or it is the curious penumbra evoked in Derrida's introduction to *Origin of Geometry*, no longer the field for phenomenological activity 'mais la source à jamais nocturne de la lumière elle-même' (OG, 150) ('but the forever nocturnal source of the light itself') (*OG*, 137). Levinas, argues Derrida, makes use of the positive infinite to ensure that the otherness of the other is respected.

To protect the other, a person must be absolutely beyond relation, unspeakable of, not classifiable and reducible by language. For ethical reasons, for the best of reasons, Levinas has impatiently jumped over the interminable navigation through location and determinateness imposed by language and by history. But 'L'Infini positif (Dieu) si ces mots ont un sens, ne peut être infiniment Autre' (ED, 168) ('The positive Infinity (God) – if these words are meaningful – cannot be infinitely Other') (*WD*, 114). By making of the infinitely other the positive infinite, Levinas has excised from it its negativity, its work (the reference is to Hegel's 'work of the negative'); he has refused the infinite as indefinite, that which is merely not finite (ED, 168; *WD*, 114). And yet, suggests Derrida, it is this indefinite, 'in a deep sense, originary finitude', which escapes from the python that is Hegelian dialectic, where the other is worked through till it is *aufgehoben*, subsumed, and reduced by mediation. Against Levinas' positive infinite, Derrida suggests that the negative infinite respects the other:

> que l'infinité de l'horizon husserlien ait la forme de l'ouverture in-définie, qu'il s'offre sans fin possible à la négativité de la constitution (du travail d'objectivation), n'est-ce pas ce qui le garde le plus sûrement contre toute totalisation, contre l'illusion de la présence immédiate d'un infini de plénitude où l'autre devient tout à coup introuvable?
>
> (ED, 177)

That the infinity of the Husserlian horizon has the form of an indefinite opening, and that it offers itself without any possible end to the negativity of constitution (of the work of objectification) – does this not certainly protect it most securely from all totalization, from the illusion of the immediate presence of a plenitudinous infinity in which the other suddenly becomes unfindable?

(*WD*, 121)

Kant had related the positive infinite to illusion, though not in the way Derrida does in the preceding quotation. Descartes in his *Méditations métaphysiques* had earlier been concerned to define the divine as an actual infinite, and not as the negative infinite, that is as consisting of finite acts of accretion, indefinitely pursued.[46] The idea of God was not merely a negative view of the limited, an indefinite string of negated attributes for instance, the not-finite, and thus merely potentially infinite, but on the contrary, actual. Now Kant argued that such an actual infinite was not, as some thought, contradictory, merely unattainable. God might perceive an infinitely large expanse, say, as a whole, in his intuition, without the need to go through successive steps and the need to assume the steps continuing in infinite time. In his untying of the antinomies of reason, Kant shows that reason demands an unconditioned, absolute totality (KRV, A409, B436) as a ground for the synthesis of the conditioned (KRV, A322, B379); but the understanding, which does the donkey work for cognition, cannot attain such a totality, no experience being unconditioned (KRV, A326, B383). For the finite human mind, the unconditioned is not attainable, but only approachable by successive steps; the use of the unconditioned in argument leads to antinomies, or paradox. The illusion diagnosed here is crucial for the whole thrust of the present book: it is that our need for connection in our concepts is turned into an objective necessity in the world of things (KRV, A297, B353); like perceptual illusion, it can be understood but cannot be done away with. The principle of totality 'can only be *set as a task*' (KRV, A508, B536); and the principle of reason is a rule, not telling us what the unconditioned is like but only forbidding us to bring the movement to the infinite to a close by treating what we arrive at as unconditioned. It cannot be used to construct, to constitute experience, but only to regulate. In thus regulating, it functions as a Kantian Idea. Yet Kant suggests that this idea of necessary unity may be useful, indeed 'the indispensable condition' for moral ends (KRV, A329, B386).[47] The next section will discuss Derrida's account of the role played by the Kantian Ideas in Husserl's late work.

The powerful syntax that the negative and positive infinites form in Derrida's own writing will be further explored in Chapter 3. The point here is to show their operation in his account of Husserl's conception of the history of geometry. History for Husserl, it was said above, must like all human experience have a 'powerful structural *a priori*': the aim of his philosophy was to get beyond mere facts of experience and the worldly present to *forms* of experience prior to facticity, the 'eidetic structures' of consciousness, of the 'living present'. From his first writing, and from the *Logical Investigations* (1900), Husserl opposed both empiricism and historicism: phenomenology was 'to have as its exclusive concern experiences seizable and analysable in the pure generality of their essence, not experiences empirically perceived and treated as real facts' (Husserl 1970: 249). With Husserl as with Descartes, mathematics seems the purest example of such essences. Geometry or mathematics in general seem to make possible ideal repeatability of thought without the interference of language except as pure meaning. Yet maths clearly has a history, its concepts clearly do develop. It raises particularly acutely the question of the relation between the anchorage in historical fact of the development of a mode of thought and the intellectual development of its object as constituted by the thinking. It has an empirical origin, as discoveries and as decisions about those discoveries, and yet it is transcendental in what it becomes for us. The question then is, how is this polarity to be thought? Is the empirical origin of a mathematical discovery not after all merely the discovery of a structure which exists timelessly, and which therefore transcends human praxis? This is the account of mathematics which is called 'Platonist'. Or, as was suggested at the end of the first part of this chapter by means of Williams' interpretation of the later Wittgenstein, is it that an empirical development in mathematics becomes, by human decision, transcendental in a certain way, that is, part of the structures which form our mode of knowing what we know, and thus not empirical at all? It was suggested above that the relation Derrida constructs between Husserl and Heidegger, and between the historical cursus of thought and the thought of transcendentality, constitutes a kind of feedback loop where, after Husserlian work on the transcendental, it becomes possible to move to a position where empirical and transcendental are not opposed in a traditional way.

We shall see directly that it is through exploration of the way Husserl uses Kantian Ideas that an understanding of Husserlian historicity is elaborated by Derrida; and, in the subsequent section, through examination of the use Husserl makes of a distinction between infinity in idea and the idea of infinity, we shall see that Derrida develops further the relation between the empirical and the transcendental, by elaborating the connection between Heidegger and Husserl.

Husserl's Kantian Ideas and historicity

Derrida (Genèse, 39 note, 99) picks out four realms in which Husserl makes use of the Kantian Idea[48] to avoid empiricism and to guarantee the transcendental. It implies a connected whole: of logic, of experience, of 'life world' and, finally, of process of development of mathematical concepts. Every experience in space or time is in a horizon which is both limitless and in a sense given, ensuring the possibility of exploration out from the experience fixed on which is both harmonious and endless (Husserl 1931: §143). In *Ideas*, it is the 'Idea in the Kantian sense' which explains how the stream of experience is given as a unity, when precisely what would make of it a unity, the 'adequate'(§83) determination of its content, is unobtainable, since that content is infinite. Derrida in *Origin of Geometry* shows how the Kantian Idea, in Husserl's account of mathematical origins, acts as structural determination of what is undetermined, providing a possibility of unifying future experience which is always virtual but always there. Husserl has developed concretely what remained rather abstract in Kant; he has done that by making the *a priori* and teleology coincide (OG, 123; *OG*, 117).[49] For the formal structures of the idea of infinity are at the same time always there and yet constituting a project which develops towards an end.

The Husserlian manuscripts, says Derrida, develop the Idea, this infinite aim or Telos, into Logos and into God: the Idea is a direction which is both in history and above history. It is at this point in Derrida's argument that the possibility is evoked of a historicity which could cut loose from telos. Husserl has moved beyond the division between actual infinity which then falls (*dérive*) into history and the indefinite infinity which has to work through history, Derrida implies. But the going-upstream of that division has not made of the Idea some transhistorical Absolute. Instead, like all ideality, like language, it is something which exists throughout historicity only because it is an infinite *process* of determination. This process, in a pattern now familiar to us, causes the fact or history to appear by moving to an absolute, by exceeding it (OG, 164–5; *OG*, 149). The telos and origin have both been caught up by Husserl into what is now a movement; the Absolute for this late Husserl can be nowhere else but in the movement of history itself – '*L'Absolu est le Passage*' (OG, 165) ('the *Absolute is Passage*') (*OG*, 149). (The peculiar relation of infinity to finitude in the Idea, the crucial impossibility of turning it into a theme, and the way Derrida develops this, will be discussed in the next section.) Husserl seems to have shown that a historicity can be thought which is neither purely empirical history nor merely a historicized rationalism. From the point of such a historicity, both origin and telos of the development of geometry seem to disappear in the movement of geometry's history, yet this movement is not historicized. It might seem that this is transcendental historicity.

It is at this point in the introduction to *Origin of Geometry* that Derrida articulates Heidegger with Husserl, and 'infinite historicity' with facticity. It is at this point that the question 'What is a fact?' can be asked, and at this point that the thinking of facticity has become possible, facticity[50] meaning not brute fact over and against which one positions oneself, but a concrete way of being in the world, or being delivered up to the world. Husserl has led us to the onto-logical question ('Is there and why is there historical facticity?', OG, 167; *OG*, 150) since it is phenomenology which alone has faced the eventuality of a loss of meaning in its exploration of the possibility of pure meaning and pure history. Heidegger comes after Husserl, and a taking-seriously of facticity is not a return to precritical philosophy and empiricism. But then there can only be retreat. Ontology may ask the question as of right; any answer, says Derrida, will be phenomenological. Husserl comes after Heidegger, and the method which seemed to be a propaedeutic can only be continued. It is interminable: 'Seule elle [la phénoménologie] peut faire apparaître l'historicité infinie, c'est-à-dire le discours et la dialecticité infinie comme la possibilité pure et l'essence même de l'Etre en manifestation' (OG, 170) ('For phenomenology alone can make infinite historicity appear: i.e., infinite discourse and infinite dialecticalness as the pure possibility and the very essence of Being in manifestation') (*OG*, 152).

Husserlian phenomenology is what preserves Heideggerian facticity from empiricism; the development of philosophy from Husserl to Heidegger is not then accidental, but 'after' in a sense beyond mere chronology. It is as if, in Derrida's account, a Husserlian sediment has accrued to Heideggerian ontology and as if, matching Husserl's account of history, it can be developed or reactivated. Husserlian temporalization is a movement backwards and forwards, a tension between protention and retention, between anticipation and verification of experience. Husserlian tradition is a 'question back' to origins, to original insight or discovery whose sense was project, movement forward – so that neither the present as absolute nor the absolute origin is available; and phenomenological method, with its reduction which can never terminate, is awareness that Discourse is always behind-hand in relation to Being. The presence of being is infinite deferral.

> L'impossibilité de se reposer dans la maintenance simple d'un Présent Vivant, origine une et absolument absolue du Fait *et* du Droit, de l'Etre *et* du Sens, mais toujours autre dans son identité à soi-même, l'impuissance à s'enfermer dans l'indivision innocente de l'Absolu originaire parce qu'il n'est *présent* qu'en se *différant* sans relâche, cette impuissance et cette impossibilité se donnent en une conscience originaire et pure de la différence.
>
> (OG, 171)

> The impossibility of resting in a simple maintaining of living Present, the origin one and absolutely absolute of the Fact *and* of Right, of Being *and* of Sense, always other in its self-identity, the incapacity to close oneself in the innocent indivision of the originary Absolute, because it is only present in ceaselessly deferring itself, this impossibility and incapacity give themselves as a pure and originary consciousness of Difference.
>
> (*OG*, 153)

At this point, after Heidegger has been inscribed on Husserl and Husserl on Heidegger, 'difference' might have been thought to be a transcendental and the condition of possibility of history. But Derrida, in a paragraph whose syntax suggests a kind of swing of jubilation at the reaching of such a point, draws it back into a philosophical tradition. A hinted condition is reported, is a conditional. But from the effect of the French conditional tense, it becomes reported speech and surmise: 'Transcendentale serait la Différence' – difference might be, is said to be, transcendental (OG, 171; *OG*, 173). We are left with the historical moment of transcendental historicity, of passage between Heidegger and Husserl, even if one of 'exemplary signification'.

Infinity of and in Idea

But the Husserlian Idea points to paradox. The horizons of our temporal experience – what is just out of focus – are endless. The Kantian Idea allows a fundamental connectability of experience – determinable and open but never inconsistent (Husserl 1931: §83). But this connection, since it is infinite, is unobtainable. It cannot be thematized. As a totality, which might guarantee the connectability, that is, guarantee that nothing will come out at us from past or future and disrupt the connections, it cannot be intuited. Nevertheless, the very next sentence in §83 tells us it is 'intuitively graspable' 'in an intrinsically different way'. Later in *Ideas*, in §143, à propos perception, the fundamental inexhaustibility of the thing in finite perception is admitted, yet its complete givenness, Husserl says, is *prescribed* as a Kantian Idea, which as a kind of field regulates the thing's endless development in a set of perceptions ever more exact, though never inconsistent. This seems to pose the problem: how then does the infinite continuum of appearances appear in a finite act? We have to avoid 'an absurd finite infinity' (*ibid.*: §143). Yet Husserl suggests that the infinity of the continuum of appearances *can* be given in intuition. This appearing of what cannot in its essence appear, that is, the infinity of the continuum of appearances, has, Husserl suggests, a type of evidence all its own. It lies open to a type of insight which is unlike any other: 'The idea of an infinity essentially motivated is not itself an infinity; the insight that this infinity is intrinsically incapable of being given does not exclude, but rather demands the transparent givenness of the Idea of this infinity' (*ibid.*: §143, quoted OG, 153; *OG*, 139).[51] Infinity cannot be given in intuition, but the idea of infinity is not infinite, and can. The non-infinite idea of infinity is thus 'transparently given' as the intrinsic incapability of being given of the Idea. Derrida points out (disagreeing in this with Ricoeur) that Husserl separates intuition and intention, that is object-directed act of thought, not just in the non-essential case of an intuition which is not filled for accidental reasons, but in the case of the Idea: it cannot be given in intuition (it is infinite) yet its non-givenness is given, is formally determinate, thus finite. What is given then for Husserl is the possibility of connection without limits, determinability; that is, objectivity *per se* (OG, 153; *OG*, 139). In the Idea appears only the regulating possibility of appearing. This is an intuitionless intention, and contains within it, *Genèse* already suggested, negation and the necessity for an endless sequence of finite adjustments and mediations (Genèse, 170). Husserl, *Genèse* argued, had thus already in *Ideas*, that is, well before his late work on the origin of mathematics, introduced absence into the heart of what can be given in lived experience, though he had not yet begun to think through the consequences of this introduction.

The account in *Origin of Geometry* of how Husserl with the Kantian Idea steps round the problem of the infinite totality which cannot be given, by using the *form* of the infinite, which can be given, develops and modifies in an illuminating way the passage from *Genèse* already mentioned.[52] There it is an actual intuition of the indefinite, the negative infinite, which is the way round the difficulty for Husserl; there is concrete intuition of essential incompleteness (Genèse, 169). However, in the texts actually published in the 1960s, Derrida faces the 'contradiction' of the finite infinite, the particular structure of the paradox of thinking about the infinite, and the paradox of Husserlian objectivity.[53] The infinite is inaccessible to intuition, it cannot be given in intuition, and the intuition is empty, that is, it has no content. The givenness of that empty intuition is finite, and relates to its form; it is this that makes construction possible through patient and rigorous work. Each step of that construction is finite, and in it the absence of the intuition may be, indeed has to be, neglected.

This idea of the infinite has a striking structural relation to Derrida's account of the other, of language and of time in Husserl's thought; they are all intentions of the infinite which necessarily remain without intuitions. We have seen that they are brought together in *Of Grammatology*. The other, we have seen, cannot be an intuition of mine; what does appear is this impossibility of appearing (ED, 181–2; *WD*, 123). Likewise meaning in language: in these texts of Derrida, it is just the condition of its functioning at all that it can function without a fulfilling intuition. (And that to a further degree: its ideality, its univocity, is also an horizon, not an intuition. Of both, Husserl, says Derrida, makes Kantian Ideas (OG, 107; *OG*, 104).) Husserl's difficulties with the indexical 'I', noted by Jakobson,[54] involve a neglect of the necessary non-fulfilling of intention by intuition in language. 'I', when read or heard by another, signifies without intuition, and exhibits clearly the functioning of language in general – it signifies without necessarily being fulfilled by intuition. Though this is true of all language, writing illustrates it particularly clearly. That I can always be dead when 'I am alive' is read, that alive I can always write 'I am dead' and be understood, is no supervening accident: it is not a 'mere' fact but the condition of saying anything at all (VP, 107; *SP*, 95–6). Similarly, the indexical anchorings of the other lead to what can be intended but not intuited in its otherness – I cannot ever see or understand completely what things look like from another's point of view, their view can never be totalized by me. In the account Derrida gives of Husserl's Living Present, the strange knot that is the Kantian Idea is presented even more fully. The absolute present of experience as given, that Husserl searched for, can only appear as such if it appears as indefinite, prolongable in a unity of possible meaning which is limitless though connectable through the Kantian Idea. But then, says Derrida of Husserl, the finite mode of appearance of the indefinite is neglected; human finitude is not built into the account. This is tantamount to making of death a fact, not a condition, and thus extrinsic to the process. So in Husserl, it is the eliding of death which makes possible the thinking of this unity of possible meaning, but this unity can never itself appear, and be given. Further, this unity causes time itself to appear, though it never appears itself (OG, 150; *OG*, 137).

To sum up the argument of this second part of the chapter so far: the question of how to describe the genesis of reason's structures without making of them either something empirical, their development a matter of trial and error, or on the other hand fixed structures which just continue unchanging through time,[55] is resolved for Husserl by recourse to the Kantian Idea; yet he never builds the impossibility of intuiting infinity into his solution. The Kantian Idea prescribes regulated repetition into infinity: the connectability of experience is achieved, says Derrida, by importing the inaccessible intuition into the indefinite extension of its form which can be intuited and lived as the certain indefinite. That is, to elide death. But earlier, in the preceding section, Derrida was said to argue that the ontological question posed by Heidegger was possible because phenomenology had faced the eventuality of loss of meaning while investigating the ground of pure meaning. How can Husserl be at once accused of eliding death, which seems to wipe out meaning, and congratulated on facing the possibility that meaning might be erased from the experiences which constitute its source? It is Husserl's understanding of writing's role in the development of science which brought together these two stances. It is the embodiment in writing which makes meaning 'transcendental', in the sense of 'free from attachment to interpretation by any one particular empirical subjectivity', and thus enables scientific discoveries to be transmitted to later ages. Yet embodiment in writing also makes the sense being transmitted vulnerable to empirical accident, since the transmission itself can go wrong, and is subject to destruction, whether deliberate or as the effect of time. A piece of writing can be lost irremediably through war and through material degradation, and its sense can be lost through the passage of time and the failure of the traditions which could read it. Nevertheless, the writing-down of a scientific discovery is essential to its being cut free from the empirical circumstances of its production, to its existing as science in the first place. Husserl has made of the development of geometry something which is coeval with the possibility of accident, and the possibility of accident is part and parcel of the way in which a discovery in geometry is more than empirical, and more than the product of an individual subjectivity. It is important to see here, as we saw in the discussion of H. H. Pattee's work, that writing implies something wider than the use of a human graphic sign system; it means 'recording' as a bringing-together of conditions of possibility (the transcendental) and the question of genesis.

To develop this: if language is the bearer of this idealization, in that it is the objectification of truth, then a virtual intentionality must be there and accessible (OG, 91; *OG*, 94), although all actual writers/receivers may be absent (OG, 90; *OG*, 94). Even though mathematics is ideal, depending not at all on any actual language, its virtual intentionality can only be guarded by writing. Writing is what allows the transmission of mathematical knowledge, it 'reduces', in the phenomenological sense, the historical and specific circumstances of its discovery. But this necessity of embodiment in physical writing also means that meaning can be lost. (Husserl would, I think, ultimately argue that it cannot be lost entirely; the actual embodiment, the token, is still only one example of ideal meaning.) One can see why later, after *Origin of Geometry*, Derrida explores writing, since more than speech it is paradoxical in the required way. It may act for Husserl as the condition of idealization, of repeatability in the absence of either emitter or receiver, and has thus the required essential status. At the same time, it has to be a set of traces, a physical object, and as such is capable of being lost or destroyed; it thus cannot be essential.

Loss of meaning is possible for Husserl in another way, not through destruction but through equivocity, through a cultural and linguistic sedimentation whose layers impede access to the original meaning. But, argues Derrida, loss of meaning can equally occur through univocity, whose limit is sterile repetition (OG, 104; *OG*, 102). Language requires both equivocity and univocity: in ways explored by Rodolphe Gasché (1994a), Derrida argues both that Joycean equivocity could not function without a singleness of meaning (or it would be unintelligible) and that Husserl has to admit an irreducible equivocity in the very functioning of language, for the project of meaning is infinitely open; equivocity is a mark of every culture (OG, 106; *OG*, 103). These poles of language are not symmetric: univocity is inaccessible (for Husserl it is a Kantian Idea) but it is a condition of equivocity (itself a necessary part of empirical culture), not as some underlying substratum on which varieties of meaning may be built, but as a pole which unifies by causing what is equivocal to tend towards it.

The aporias of the infinite

Husserl argues in *Ideas* that intuition of the infinite is impossible, yet he neglects the finite mode of appearance of the infinite, as the indefinite. It is the indefinite, in the form of the Kantian Idea, which allows both the connected thinking of the infinite as process, and rigour in this connecting as an aim or telos. But the form of that idea of the infinite is itself finite. Husserl treats this finite as accident, when it is a condition. Now, at the end of *Speech and Phenomena*, Derrida quarries further the teleological structure of Husserl's system of 'essential distinctions' in his phenomenology, which is the source of his rigour. Achievement of the distinctions is always deferred. Husserl's entire work is devoted to showing that the factual can be sifted from the ideal, the empirical from the transcendental, through purification (the reductions, as he termed them, phenomenological, eidetic and then transcendental). Yet, at the same time, the role of the Kantian idea and Husserl's use of the indefinite implies, says Derrida, that he knew the distinctions were unavailable in the way he sought to make them. Out of this Derrida develops the 'following aporia': in fact the distinctions are never respected; and in the idea, they do not exist because in the idea the distinction between fact and right is abolished; that is, if the distinction between fact and right is abolished in the idea, then the set of distinctions which exist in right but not in fact are *ipso facto* not possible either in right, that is in the idea: 'leur possibilité est leur impossibilité' (VP, 113) ('their possibility is their impossibility') (*SP*, 101). (This aporetic feel, often signalled by the yoking of impossibility and possibility, occurs in much of Derrida's work.) The problem is induced by the infinite, where all cats are black.[56]

I need now to point to the site of the most persistent excavation round the infinite in this century. For it was precisely problems associated with the use of the actual or positive infinite in the set theory inaugurated by G. Cantor which triggered the crisis over the foundation of mathematics at the turn of the century. Cantor's work seemed to have consequences which dashed all hopes of a rigorous theory of infinite sets. He 'opened the paradise' of infinite numbers, but thereby opened what some of his contemporaries felt to be a Pandora's box, a box of paradoxes.[57] A paradox disturbs: its argument is of the form 'If X is true then it is false and *vice versa*', which suggests not just that X is very peculiar, but that it must be wrongly constructed, that it has been got wrong. But what if it is necessary, or necessarily so constructed? Cantor's development of a series of cardinal numbers for infinite sets illuminated the structure of number systems. It also led to such paradoxes. In one of his defences, Cantor claimed of the negative, potential, or syncategorematic infinite that it designated no *idea* but was merely a 'prosthetic representation' (*Hilfsvorstellung*) of our thought. The potential infinite is 'a finite, changeable quantity growing beyond all finite limits', whereas the actual infinite is 'a quantum which is constant, stable in itself, but like the other side of all finite quantities' (Cantor 1932: 373, my translation).

The problems which arose in the foundations of logic were in fact in large part connected with the problem of totalizing with infinite sets: for instance, talking about the set made up of all the sets in an infinite set (the 'power set' of an infinite set). Paradox seemed to be avoided if the class were disbarred from being a member of itself (for instance, 'concept' is both an element and a class in 'the class of concepts'): a higher order grouping can apply to a lower order one, but must not be reflexive, that is, applied to itself (so the 'concept of "the class of concepts"' is disbarred). Moreover, and interestingly in the perspective of the 'event' to be discussed in Chapter 3, it was accepted that there had to be a choice function, justified by a separate axiom, to set up the infinite set.[58] In particular, there were difficulties in moving from making a negative statement about all the members of an infinite set, to making a positive statement about one of its members (from 'not all Xs are Ys' to 'there is (at least) one X which is not Y), because such a statement involves assuming that every member of the set can be said to have the property or not, an inference based on the excluded middle. But since the set is infinite by definition, the statement is unverifiable, unless at least one X can be exhibited.

A result was that the school of intuitionism, which in the 1920s seemed closely connected with phenomenology, rejected both the excluded middle when used of infinite sets and the actual infinite. It insisted on mathematical procedures which are *constructive*, those whereby what is said to constitute a proof can actually be produced. (Notoriously, this cuts out a goodly part of classical mathematics, and all of Cantorism; classical mathematics of course admits constructive proofs, but it admits others as well.) Whereas 'Platonism' or 'realism' holds that mathematical objects, or rather statements about them, can be true and false independently of whether we have any means of knowing whether they are true of false. Gödel's works showed that when the founder of intuitionism, Brouwer, rejected the excluded middle, he was making an interpretation of this principle which amounted to making it claim that all mathematical problems were soluble (Kneale 1971: 680–1); in other words, to assuming that both the infinite and the unknown, that is in effect problems which have not been discovered, and may never be, can be squared up, so to speak, and to some extent preregulated.

One way of considering Derrida's work on Husserl is as a working out of the paradoxes of the infinite which are buried there and which surfaced through the debates and quarrels round intuitionism. Such problems, I argue, tensed and shaped the work of Husserl and even Heidegger.[59] Because Derrida is a very respectful, coherent and urgent reader of others, he picks up these tensions, and works on them. Thus his use of the word 'undecidable' in the *Origin of Geometry* is not a modish applying of a 1960s synonym for 'ambivalent': it is absolutely appropriate, tracking back to the 'Decision problem' of the late 1920s and to early 1930s' investigations into the foundations of mathematics, where methods were sought to determine in general whether a given logical schema was valid, and where it was shown by Church and others that there could be no such procedure for general logic.[60] (Gödel had, prior to this, exhibited 'formally undecidable sentences', sentences which were true, but not provable within any given version of formalized arithmetic.) Some of the questions to which Derrida returns again and again develop a Husserlian and Heideggerian heritage; but they have nodes of concern common to the more general logical reflection of their time: the problems associated with infinite sets; the nature of the development of logical thought (is it inventing in the sense of finding something there to be discovered, or is it a kind of construction?). In Derrida's work, these all point to the problem of the nature and consistency of limits. In that way, they abut on the question of human finitude.

We saw above that in *Origin of Geometry*, at the point of a crucial argument about Husserl's account of the non-empirical origins of mathematics, he was said by Derrida to have elided death. In that text, as in *Speech and Phenomena* (1973), death was that which is neglected by Husserl because the unity and connectability of experience are guaranteed by an infinite which cannot appear, cannot be intuited; the guarantee takes the form of form, the form of the regulated possibility of determinateness by which the finitude of each step is subtended and elided.[61] Death is made external to this process, it is made a fact, since the finite mode of appearance of the Kantian Idea is neglected by Husserl. (Once more, there is the pattern of fall from absolute infinity into determinateness.) This is further extended in a much more recent text, *Apories* (1996) – or rather, perhaps, note 89 about the infinite in *Genèse* is worked through, more recent Derridean work being pinned back into it, so to speak. In a section of *Apories*, which was the last section of the original lecture, the role of death in §50–53 of Heidegger's *Sein und Zeit* is examined. The 'aporia' of death is said to be one of the ways in which Heidegger keeps the limits he is working with from unravelling (AP, 87); but the aporia is also one which destabilizes such limits. For Heidegger, humankind alone can experience death. Death is the 'most proper possibility of Dasein ["being there"]'; it is what can always happen, what is always possible. Death is the 'possibility of the pure and simple impossibility of Dasein'. Heidegger, Derrida says, would not have accepted the taking of this aporia as one among others; for him, it is only Dasein (here Dasein appears as man, not animal) for whom death can appear. Death as the most proper possibility of Dasein must be resolutely assumed. But death is also the impossibility of Dasein's continued existence.[62] So death may be the possibility of the impossibility of Dasein, or (if it is to be resolutely assumed) the possibility of the appearing as such of the possibility of Dasein's own impossibility. Yet my death is unintuitable, and cannot appear as such. If it is the impossibility of this appearing which can appear as such as possible for Dasein, this is precisely the definition of the 'improper' relation to death, used by Heidegger to mark inauthentic forms of existence. Once more the unintuitable induces a structure imbricating possibility and impossibility, and once more a system of distinctions is rendered mobile and aporetic.[63]

History and absolute infinity

In all these texts, at the point where Derrida examines infinity and death, he evokes, in a way that is almost a piece of shorthand, the Hegelian criticism of Kant's refusal of the positive infinite: limits can only appear when they are exceeded, and the positive infinite is necessary for the negative infinite to appear. (It is possible to suggest a kind of premonition of limits which escapes this criticism – for instance, Wittgenstein's 'Feeling the world as a limited whole – it is this that is mystical' [1961: 149]). If Husserl recognizes the structure of the unending work of construction in the indefinity of the Kantian idea, he never brings that to the foreground of his meditations. Hegel in that way at least is more radical, says Derrida, for the Kantian indefinite is just a finitized infinite unless the absolute infinite is thought (VP, 114; SP, 101–2). Hegel argues that for something to be designated a limit is for it already to have been gone beyond – the limit is seen from both sides so to speak: 'For a determination, boundary is only determined as limit in opposition to its other as in opposition to its unlimitedness; the other of a limit is just the beyond of itself' (Peddle 1980: 113).[64] Otherwise, as was seen earlier, the unintuitable of the Kantian idea is elided by the form; for it to appear as such (for differance to appear), my death has to appear; the finite mode of appearance of the infinite has to appear. But at this point the comparison with the positive infinite makes death appear extrinsic. In *Speech and Phenomena*, where Derrida is recounting a kind of philosophic history, the paradox is stated: 'The appearing of infinite differance is finite'; which leads to the italicized '*infinite differance is finite*'. It is in this way that Hegelian absolute knowledge, the thinking of the positive infinite, provides a point from which history can be seen as a whole because there is a moving out of it. The Hegelian moment was what in the history of philosophy recognized the relation between exceeding a limit and knowing where it is.

After Hegel, a non-historicist history is made possible by his having engaged with the positive infinite. But the infinite, of whatever sort, is unintuitable. Husserl strove to explicate lived experience, not as empirical content of an individual life but as structures of consciousness. His is in the last resort an intuitionist theory of consciousness (VP, 100; *SP*, 90), where the possibility of bringing an object into intuition is what creates meaning. And yet Husserl, in his work on the question of the genesis of experience, had excavated three cases – time, the other (intersubjectivity), language – where the non-fulfilment of intuition does not merely happen, as an occasional accident. It is essential to the experience of language (as of intersubjectivity and of time) that intuition and intention do not coincide, and that the intuition may be indefinitely deferred. Husserl, in Derrida's analysis, used the Kantian Idea as a way of ensuring 'regulative possibility' and consistency of experience, but the possibility itself pointed to an aporia: that of the finite form of infinity (as absent, non-intuitable content). This aporia, however, is of a particular nature – in Derrida's thesis he called it 'dialectic', and there is at least one trace of the term in *Origin of Geometry* – it is, however, what might be better called the movement of *différance*. It has a curious dissymmetric form, already indicated in the thesis: the 'dialectic' within genesis, between absolute beginning and indefinite temporal context, between transcendence and immanence, is 'la possibilité d'une continuité de la continuité et de la discontinuité, d'une identité de l'identité et de l'altérité etc.' (Genèse, 8) ('the possibility of a continuity of continuity and discontinuity, of an identity of identity and otherness etc.') (trans. MRN). The next chapter will discuss this dissymmetry, and the question of possibility it is enfolded by.

This chapter has shown, contrary to much that has been written on Derrida, that there was in his first writings on Husserl a singularly consistent exploration of the question of history: the nature of the anchorage of philosophical questions in the time they appear; the nature of the genesis of such disciplines as geometry (or, one might add, philosophy) where the intellectual structures of geometrical investigation appear both to develop through time and to be stable components in the activity of reason; to be on the one hand either constructed or discovered in the course of the progress of mathematics, and yet on the other hand to be part of the fundamental structures of thought. In this exploration, which was at first clearly situated in the history of philosophy, and in a tracing of Husserl's struggles with the nature of genesis, Derrida gradually foregrounded what might be called the intervention of the infinite in Husserl's argument. Husserl had remained within an intuitionist theory of consciousness, in spite of his repeated discovery of areas where intuition did not merely not match the mind's intention, but necessarily could not ever match it. At four points in his development of phenomenology – in connection with the infinite development of logic, with the idea of an infinity of temporal experience, with the idea of the world as ground for the infinity of possible experience and then with the idea as teleological direction (Genèse, 39 note 12) – Husserl had recourse to the infinite in the shape of Kantian Ideas, separating intention and intuition (in an un-Kantian way). Derrida laid bare in Husserl's work the sites of this intervention: time, intersubjectivity and language. The question, then, was how to explore these sites without on the one hand repeating the Husserlian gesture of phenomenological and transcendental reduction, or on the other abandoning Husserl's rigour to turn to empiricism and mere happenstance. As we have seen, according to Derrida, the introduction of the infinite engenders aporia: Husserl's essential distinctions can only function at all if they function as non-essential, impure. Derrida here, we saw, begins to use varieties of a phrase which will recur in varied form throughout his work: 'leur possibilité est leur impossibilité' (VP, 113) ('Their possibility is their impossibility') (SP, 101); compare 'la condition de possibilité et une certaine impossibilité' (ED, 243) ('the condition of possibility and a certain impossibility') (WD, 163) of the transcendental opening of consciousness; and in the formulation to be discussed in the following chapter: 'La différance, disparition de la présence originaire, est *à la fois* la condition de possibilité et la condition d'impossibilité de la vérité' (D, 194) ('Differance, the disappearance of any originary presence, is *at once* the condition of possibility *and* the condition of impossibility of truth') (D, 168). The question raised urgently by such phrases, that of their relation to logic, and more generally of Derrida's relation to the language of logic, will only be discussed in the final chapter of this book. However, in the next chapter, they will be considered in relation to the problem of the transcendental in its relation to possibility. Kant had used the phrase 'conditions of possibility' of our experience, for example, in explaining the object of the transcendental deduction, that is 'the mode of our knowledge of objects in so far as this mode of knowledge is possible a priori' (KRV, A12, B26; A94, B126). The effect of these Derridean yokings of possibility and impossibility seems to be to short-circuit a transcendentality which might have created a homogeneous logical space for thought and text; as such, they seem to perturb the very distinctions and ground usual to thought. But we saw that though this paradox is focused in relation to Husserl's Kantian Ideas, it does also point to Heidegger's movement out of Husserl, and to the historical articulation of ontology with phenomenology. We shall further see in the next chapter that these short-circuits do more: they express the aporetic status of the possible when used as founding condition, and their investigation has an important history.

The aporias associated with the infinite are then part of the syntax of Derrida's thought, recurring throughout his writing in fact more readily than the other piece of 'syntax' discussed in the first part of this chapter, the treatment of histories and transcendentals in the earlier writings. This chapter has attempted to pick out how there are effects of argument which, though they are thematized, are also more covert, more implicit than a fully expressed theme. The next chapter will look at the way Derrida uses lexemes, and will attempt to argue that in spite of some highly characteristic words – 'deconstruction' and 'différance', for instance – which have become attached to his name in a way that is highly particular, it is in effect the multiplicity of such words, their replication, which is really striking in his mode of writing. The chapter will also look at other modes of replication which are not lexically based, but which certainly double the text: for example, quotation and irony.

2　Replications

> 'The one and the other' seems by this double division, at once unequal and ill-defined, yet in very ancient usage, to make allusion to the archaic necessity of an apparently binary reading (as if everything had to begin in twos).
>
> (Blanchot, *Le Pas au-delà*, 104)

The previous chapter suggested that Derrida's 'syntax' – the functioning induced on some of his arguments by patterns in the distribution of their elements – implicitly articulated a recent history of philosophy in terms of genesis and structure, or in terms of what my chapter title grouped as 'histories and transcendentals'. It suggested too that his texts of the early 1960s also brought to the surface a further piece of 'syntax', in operation at a more visible level, that of the 'impossible possibility' or the 'possibly impossible'. This further piece of syntax could take the form of an equation: 'Their [Husserl's essential distinctions] possibility is their impossibility' (VP, 113; SP, 101) or of an imbrication, as in 'This possibility of the impossibility' (AP, 127, quoting Heidegger). This piece of 'syntax' is related to the paradoxes of the infinite, and in the good deal of critical attention it has attracted it is often divorced both from its anchoring in Derrida's relation to the history of philosophy, that pointed to in the first part of my first chapter, and from its point of origin in Derrida's reading of Husserl. With the latter, in *Ideas* as in the very late texts, the Kantian Ideas guaranteed connectability of perception, or of experience in general. But the infinite which is drawn into the argument by Husserl's recourse to the Kantian Idea cannot be intuited. We have seen the consequence drawn from this by Derrida at the end of the preceding chapter: the rigour made possible by the recourse to the Idea is at the same time made impossible by the absence of intuition – of Husserl's essential distinctions Derrida says, as we have seen: 'Their possibility is their impossibility'(*SP*, 101). Derrida elsewhere brings together in similar conjunction the Kantian phrase, 'conditions of possibility', with his own phrase, 'conditions of impossibility'. Such paradoxical couplings seem to render doubtful any idea of a transcendentality which would, so to speak, make stable a space for thinking. I leave aside for the present the fact that this occurs at a specific point in the history of philosophy as thought through by Derrida. It is not a mere result of the sharpening of Husserlian perspectives into paradox. (This is parallel to what occurs in Wittgenstein's case, as explicated by Williams and discussed at the end of the preceding chapter, where the paradox surfaces at a point after Wittgenstein's encounter with intuitionism is alluded to. It does not figure merely as a tightening of opposing playful-oracular trends within Wittgenstein's argument.)

Now the same effect, that of both setting up and undermining a kind of transcendentality, may be thought to be brought about at the level of Derrida's lexemes. Already in the preceding chapter, it was shown that at the moment in *Of Grammatology* where the 'archi-synthesis' was evoked, and thus a transcendental level of analysis seemed to be reached by virtue of the language of 'archi' itself, this transcendentality was doubled in disquieting fashion by a multiplication of terms – 'archi-writing' and 'archi-trace'. The lexemes to which Derrida gives a characteristic timbre early on in his work are already multiple, and in the texts to be considered in this chapter (most published in the early 1970s) they proliferate in very startling fashion. Their odd status is often pointed to by their being borrowed coinages, sometimes indeed borrowed from another language. Now Derrida himself has called *différance, supplement*, and other terms, *parergon* for instance, 'quasi transcendentals'.[1] Derrida himself has said that they 'organize the theoretical space in a quasi-transcendental way' (LI, 231; *LI*, 127) and has pointed to the accusation of wilful perturbation of common sense and the laws of logic that such an 'organization of space has incurred'. The preceding chapter suggested that in the syntax of Derrida's arguments, transcendental and empirical were folded together so that they work not as concepts but as complex procedures active in the history of philosophy he is undertaking. One particular example of this was the way radical finitude (in Heideggerian ontology) and the rigorous tension given by an infinity of project in Husserlian phenomenology were imbricated to make possible for Derrida an attention to facticity which did not fall back into empiricism; such an attention might be thought to allow precisely for a way of working which is 'quasi-transcendental'. However, in the passage quoted immediately above, Derrida is not referring to this imbrication (called 'ultra-transcendental', for instance G, 90; *G*, 61), in other words, he is not referring to a piece of 'syntax' but rather taking up the way in which his work has struck his contemporaries, that is, particularly through its characteristic lexemes ('différance' being the most celebrated, and the most long-lived). This chapter will try to understand what might be meant by 'quasi-transcendental' when used of lexicalized items. It will become apparent that for this one needs to understand the kind of proliferation such terms undergo in his work.

The once-common summary of Derrida's work, 'that there is only the play of signifiers', that he argues that we are locked into an infinite spread of linguistic signs without end, neglects the way he writes. In particular, it neglects the differentiation that his highly individual lexemes display. They bear a textual index of their provenance, they carry with them effects emanating from their previous context; they resist classification, as we shall see (LI, 185; *LI*, 100), and while Derrida insists on their separability (LI, 182; *LI*, 97 and in other places) no one (yet) has compiled a list, picking them off and 'attributing' them to boxes like compositors used to do with type. So this chapter will not pick up the characteristic lexemes for exposition, which has been done before, and well done, but rather look at the contexts of their proliferation, and relate these to other, structural, forms of doubling which make appearance in the same texts: reflexivity, quotation, irony. It will focus on *Dissemination* (1972a) but will also refer to a group of articles on language: 'Signature event context' reprinted in *Margins of Philosophy*, the reply by the American philosopher J. Searle, and Derrida's response to that reply in *Limited Inc.* (Searle replied further in the guise of a book review.) The doubling, both semantic and syntactic, which operates at the level of theme through the proliferation of the lexemes and at the level of the mode of writing through irony, is pervasive at this moment in Derrida's work. It, like the lexemes, will be related at the end of this chapter to 'conditions of possibility' and their use in transcendental arguments. It is at this point that the two relations between possibility/impossibility, putting them edge to edge in paradox with 'and' or imbricating them with 'of', will be brought together.

Roots and the *a priori*

The articles in the collections published in 1972 develop, we shall see, the movement Derrida argued for when he went 'upstream' of the Foucauldian 'decision' or *partage* between madness and reason. This 'upstream' is developed in relation to Plato as a place where chronological and logical priority come together. But this upstream, it will be shown, is also a place where the characteristic Derridean lexemes seem to multiply and relay each other.

'Conditions of possibility' or 'structure of possibility' (M, 379; *M*, 318) have often been related to the *a priori*. *A priori* has a complicated recent history; but to start simply, it has often been treated in the history of philosophy as if it referred to timeless essences, which could be known regardless of individual and specific experience. Kant turned upside down his contemporaries' expectations about the *a priori*: instead of giving knowledge about objects, it could be shown to give knowledge about the nature of our understanding of objects. The term ('from the earlier') models logical precedence on chronological priority, perceived from a position which is later. So that what we recognize later is a possibility contained in the earlier: 'to cognize something a priori means to cognize it from its mere possibility'.[2] Now this appears indeed to make of the *a priori* something like the structural possibilities of our knowledge (this is the beginning of Heidegger's account in *The Basic Problems of Phenomenology*). It is worth noting here that there is a similar oscillation between structural and historical, or at least between the logical and chronological, which is pointed at by the Heideggerian phrase 'always already' adopted by Derrida,[3] one adverb implying permanence, whether through time or beyond time, of a happening prior to what is under discussion, the other implying position in relation to what is later.

The *a priori*, seen then as possibilities which are both earlier and structural, now must be linked to what Derrida at several different points calls 'the root'. The last chapter suggested that Derrida moves 'upstream' of a distinction or a polar opposition: that he moves to something both chronologically and ontologically prior, to a point which is before and above determinate contradictions. In the reinterpretation of the 'transcendental' that was being carried out in *Writing and Difference* it was said against Foucault:

> Il s'agit alors de faire retraite vers un point où toute contradiction *déterminée* sous la forme de telle structure historique de fait peut apparaître et apparaître comme relative à ce point zéro où le sens et le non-sens déterminés se rejoignent en leur origine commune.
>
> (ED, 86)

> It is therefore a question of drawing back toward a point at which all *determinate* contradictions, in the form of given, factual historical structures, can appear, and appear as relative to this zero point at which determinate meaning and nonmeaning come together in their common origin.
>
> (*WD*, 56, trans. mod.)

The *cogito* 'at its sharpest point' is also at the source from which reason and madness can become determinate and can be 'said', i.e. spoken of (ED, 91; WD, 58–9).

Now Derrida plays on the botanical and philological sense of 'root', to trace back how it brings forth what in the article on Descartes, following Foucault, is called the 'decision' or the *partage*. This separating out of the unseparated reason and madness, which is not only the enclosure of the mad, Foucault admits, but the very possibility of history, is an exhuming of

> le sol vierge et unitaire sur lequel a obscurément pris racine l'acte de décision qui lie et sépare raison et folie. Raison et folie à l'âge classique ont eu une racine commune. Mais cette racine commune, qui est un logos, ce fondement unitaire est beaucoup plus vieux que la période évoquée par Foucault. . . . Il doit y avoir une unité fondatrice . . . celle du logos, c'est à dire d'une raison; déjà historique certes. . . . C'est dans l'élément de cette raison archaïque que la discession, la dissension vont survenir comme une modification.
>
> (ED, 62–3)

> the virgin and unitary ground upon which the decisive act linking and separating madness and reason obscurely took root. The reason and madness of the classical age had a common root. But this common root, which is a logos, this unitary foundation is much more ancient than the medieval period . . . evoked by Foucault. . . . There must be a founding unity . . . the unity of a logos, that is, of a reason; an already historical reason

certainly. . . . It is within the element of this archaic reason that the dissection, the dissension, will present itself as a modification.

(*WD*, 39)

Derrida has used the term 'discession' which is not in dictionaries, and which I take to be a neological latinism meaning 'separation'. Likewise, in an article on the linguist Benveniste's treatment of the verb and concept 'to be', Derrida employs 'racine' (root) to describe how Aristotle takes analysis back to the common origin of the opposition 'language'/'thought' to ask what is categoriality in general (M, 218; *M*, 182). Another example: the philological relation, the linguistic source shared for instance by Husserl's *Anzeige* (index) and *hinzeigen* (expression) points, we are told, to the inextricable interlinking of involuntary and voluntary speech (VP, 24–5; *SP*, 23), and is called 'root'.[4] So that a linguistic connection is added to the suggestion that chronological priority may be stranded into logical priority. What are dialecticized by thinkers into opposites may be rooted in commonality; and to deconstruct may be precisely to move back to that larger branch from which they spring. (Derrida indeed speaks at one point of 'la racine nécessairement *une* de tout dilemme' (OG, 164) ('the necessarily *single* root of every dilemma') (*OG*, 148).

But is not such a root precisely the logical 'genus', which, in Aristotle, related the predicate of a sentence to the subject according to the group to which the latter belongs, and within which it was distinguished by its specific difference (*diaphora*)? Once more, the relation between history of philosophy and philosophy becomes apparent in Derrida's work. To push back to the root, to the larger filiation, is not, for him, to hierarchize distinctions into *genus* and *species* but to move back prior to them, to activate what is a medium in which those distinctions have not yet occurred. This medium is not, we are told, any mere mixture, any *coincidence of opposites* which, though they may have been separated out later, have always and forever been opposed to each other. It is a 'milieu'.[5] Already the retrospective implications of this are apparent: to do philosophy is inseparable, whether we will it or know it, from the history of philosophy; and to write history is to be driven by the way we grasp history, for our understanding of the prior is determined by what the prior has become.

The return to the root through the history of philosophy is one of the strategies of 'Plato's pharmacy' (1968). Derrida there relates Plato's condemnation of writing and his championing of speech in the *Phaedrus* to the institution of philosophy as a discipline and to the development of Platonism against the Sophists. In so doing, he himself looks very minutely at certain aspects of Plato's language. Now, though the rhetors who wrote before Plato had criticized writing as a fixing of what should be mobile, they still made of the *logos* (reason/discourse) a *pharmakon* (that is, a drug, whether medicine or poison, and precisely the term used by Plato of writing which he will oppose to *logos*):

En tant que *pharmakon*, le *logos* est à la fois bon et mauvais; il n'est pas commandé d'abord par le bien et la vérité. C'est seulement à l'intérieur de cette ambivalence et de cette indétermination mystérieuse du *logos* et lorsqu'elle aura été reconnue, que Gorgias *détermine* la vérité comme *monde*, structure ou ordre, ajointement (*kosmos*) du *logos*. Par là, il annonce sans doute le geste platonicien.

(D, 131)

As a *pharmakon*, *logos* is at once good and bad; it is not at the outset governed exclusively by goodness or truth. It is only within this ambivalence and this mysterious indetermination of *logos*, and after these have been recognized, that Gorgias *determines* truth as a *world*, a structure or order, the counterpart (*kosmos*) of *logos*. In so doing, he no doubt prefigures the Platonic gesture.

(*D*, 115)

It is in the light of the categories developed out of this logos (from the *decision*, to use the Foucauldian term), that by a kind of reflux, this logos itself might be called irrational. (Socrates himself had a daemon, the earlier article on Foucault reminded us – these articles, it becomes clear, are in part a history of the development of the idea of rationality.)[6] Derrida carefully traces the strands of the term *pharmakon*, meaning both drugs and magic, when, in Plato's dialogue the *Phaedrus*, with what might seem an instance of Socratic irony, it is applied to writing. Yet, in spite of the irony, Plato's underlying point is clear: ambiguity, empiricism, chance, operation by means of magic, effect through distance, are put on the side of writing, whereas clear necessity and well defined cause are not (D, 81; *D*, 72). But yet, and against the clarity of this underlying point, the term *pharmakon* does mean both drugs *and* medicine: it is at the root of effects and cannot be classified simply as good or bad. It opens the possibility of the decision and the separation of components, but itself, says Derrida, has no essence, no *eidos*: 'C'est plutôt le milieu antérieur dans lequel se produit la différenciation en général' (D, 144) ('It is rather the prior medium in which differentiation in general is produced') (*D*, 126). To sum up, this medium, if it is thought before the decision, is not a mixed medium; it is an element, a bearer, and in a daring prolongation into its future filiation in modern philosophy, it is said to be analogous to what much further downstream, round the Kantian decision, will be allowed to the transcendental imagination, which is neither sensible nor intelligible, neither passive nor active.[7]

So the Platonic decision 'which inaugurates logic' occurs within and against the ground of the *pharmakon*, the milieu in which identification and distinction become possible. Logic is then made possible by a separation historically operated within a medium which is not a mix of already separated elements. There is a historical gesture which inaugurates a structure – the *a priori* in the fullest sense.[8] Yet this medium, to which the translation of a Heideggerian term *réserve* [*Vorenthalt*] is also applied, cannot be homogeneous if the decision is to be possible: the logic which is our logic cuts into an earlier logic where the same is not the identical. (It may be that this play of same and identical is anchored in the play of time in Derrida's reading of the history of philosophy; see next chapter.) It is in this sense that the *pharmakon*[9] is both an instance of Platonic irony and the irony itself: 'le propre du *pharmakon* consiste en une certaine inconsistance, une certaine impropriété, cette non-identité à soi lui permettant toujours d'être contre soi retourné' (D, 136) ('the *pharmakon* properly consists in a certain inconsistency, a certain impropriety, this non-identity-with-itself always allowing it to be turned against itself') (*D*, 119). In other words, it lacks form or *eidos*. The *pharmakon*

> [constitue] le milieu dans lequel s'opposent les opposés, le mouvement et le jeu qui les rapportent l'un à l'autre. . . . C'est à partir de ce jeu ou de ce mouvement que les opposés ou les différents sont *arrêtés* par Platon. Le *pharmakon* est le mouvement, le lieu et le jeu (la production de) la différence. Il est la différance de la différence. Il tient en réserve, dans son ombre et sa veille indécises, les différents et les différends que la discrimination viendra y découper.
>
> (D, 145–6)

> constitutes the medium in which opposites are opposed, the movement and the play that links them among themselves. . . . It is on the basis of this play or movement that the opposites or differences are stopped by Plato. The *pharmakon* is the movement, the locus and the play: (the production of) difference. It is the differance of the difference. It holds in reserve, in its undecided shadow and vigil, the opposites and the differends that the process of discrimination will come to carve out.
>
> (*D*, 127)

Here, then, is an important example of proliferation among the lexemes. The ambivalence of the *pharmakon* becomes, we are told, the same and not the same as Derridean *différance*, said elsewhere to be the 'common root' of our workaday conceptual oppositions.[10] Note how in the quotation above, the operation described is also actually effected on the elements in Derrida's description, by what might have seemed quirks of conjunctions: 'le mouvement et le jeu' becomes later 'ce jeu *ou* [de] ce mouvement' to move back into the conjunctive 'et'. In its passing from *et* to *ou* and back, the phrase exhibits the very kind of instability in discrimination being presently analysed, for the copula passes over into a disjunction as the strands separate, and back as the focus changes to what was prior to the distinction. This distinction, Derrida suggests, has stabilized – it has become, in and since Plato, the excluded middle; the interstice has been divided up into binary terms which are mutually exclusive. In Plato's texts, the *pharmakon* as a medium, a middle, is also a *pharmakos* (a term actually used of Socrates), a human scapegoat, and must be ejected from the city.

By tracing the complexities of Plato's use of *pharmakon*, strictly speaking incompatible with the logic that he inaugurated, Derrida gets back upstream to that which precedes, which is older than the two contraries (D, 145; *D*, 127). Writing was a *pharmakon* for Plato. For writing is a kind of memorizing, and the values of poison or medicine attached to it are related to two forms of memory. They too have, as we shall see, a common root – repetition. In the 'medicine' what is repeated in memory is that which is intelligible, stabilizable form, *eidos*. In the 'poison', in the Sophists and their techniques, what is repeated can be absent, in the same way as in writing the originating meaning or intention, that is, the life, can be absent. In the first form of memory, the repetition gives access to some kind of ideal content, which is presented through its form; in the other form of memory, there is merely continuous replication: 'Ce qui se répète, c'est le répétant, l'imitant, le signifiant, le représentant' (D, 127) ('What is repeated is the repeater, the imitator, the signifier, the representative') (*D*, 111). All of these – repeater, imitator, signifier, representative – are repeated, but not by virtue of something in themselves; they make a constant reference to something else, that which they imitate, signify, represent. This kind of repetition folds over on itself, as we shall see. Socrates' dialectic, Derrida says, acts for the first sort of memory and against the second; its object is that which can be repeated as always the same (D, 140–1; *D*, 121) not the simulacrum, the false and empty imitation. Socrates' dialectic uses drugs to counteract poison.[11]

Now it is as if in this article, the *pharmakon* itself becomes a proliferating sign. This strange Janus, facing both ways, to poison and to medicine, is threaded by Derrida into a string of related terms. He takes them from Platonic texts: *pharmakeus* and *pharmakos* are cognate; he also points out other words whose relation is semantic – *goes* (magician) for instance, in relation to *pharmakeus* (poisoner, sorcerer). So far, Derrida is doing what a commentator attentive to language ought to do, showing up echoes and overtones, which echo to other tones. But he goes further; he weaves into these strings his own developing characteristic lexemes: *différance*, as we have just seen, and *supplement* (D, 193; *D*, 167). Their movement of instability between two meanings, their non-identity within the same word, signalled by the alteration of spelling in *différance*, is deliberately compared to the Platonic terms. Are they then to be treated as repetitions of these? The procedure whereby *pharmakon*, the root which branched out to cognate words, can relay but not replace *différance* or *trace*, means that one is not the genus of which all the others would be the species, says Derrida. There is no hierarchy prescribed for these terms, they are not arrayed in a single tree of meaning. In that case, *différance* is not the root from which they all branch and does not act as a key, as a rule to a series.

Here, the analogy between the way Derrida writes and what he is writing about seems to break down. If there were a common root, a historical *reserve*, out of which opposed senses of one term were discriminated, must there not be some relation between the terms he himself has thus related through this pattern of proliferation? What is the status of the stated similarity between *pharmakon*, *trace*, *différance* and, as we shall see, *iterability*? What is their relation to each other? A problem which has already been flagged more than once again becomes visible, one which will consistently and increasingly edge up to the surface in Derrida's work, the problem of connection itself. So far, the lack of relation between *pharmakon*, *trace* and *différance* is pointed to by the different location of each in the history of philosophy, the different point therein from out of which they are active, and to which we work back in order to understand. But they cannot themselves be put into an array, they do not seem to have a common form, *eidos*, nor concept. Each may be seen as the head of a filiatory line, by which they replicate, they engender doubles. The nature of their connection (and connection will increasingly be the theme of this book) will be discussed in the next section.

Writing and the 'fold'

The *pharmakon* is distinguished into medicine and poison out of a 'milieu' which was undifferentiated. But it has been mentioned above that writing was called *pharmakon* in the *Phaedrus*. We shall see now that writing is said by Derrida to 'exceed' (D, 118), but that the excess is one of constant replication, of constant repetition of the gesture by which the distinction was made in the first place.

Writing is a *pharmakon* in that it is a *supplement* to memory, a prosthesis, and is thus parasitic on that which it supplements. Plato draws out of it structural oppositions: true/false, essence/appearance, good/bad. These opposed pairs can partition the semantic field exhaustively and disjointedly; they can exclude the middle from which they sprang. But this partition is working on a system, writing, which is unstable. Its instability arises from the conflict between the two faces of repetition previously mentioned: writing can make possible *eidos*, truth, law or the episteme, dialectics, philosophy (D, 142; D, 124) by repeating itself as the same. In this sense, *eidos* is both the form and the content, because it is what is stable in repetition. But writing is also the series 'sophisté, menteries, archives, relations, récits, listes, notes, doubles' – which cannot, we are told, be subsumed one under another stably, but which add to each other in untidy fashion. Writing, the *pharmakon*, cannot be assigned only to the second of these series, as King Thamus in *Phaedrus* (274b–275b) does; but neither can it be stably placed under concepts which have developed out of it, which it has itself made possible: 'L'écriture comme *pharmakon* . . . ne se laisse pas subsumer sous des concepts qui à partir d'elle se décident' (D, 118) ('writing as a *pharmakon* . . . cannot be subsumed under concepts whose contours it draws') (*D*, 103) This is the *de jure* and *de facto* distinction invoked against Foucault, here no longer a timeless logical tool, but in fully fledged historical form. It is a distinction to which Derrida will return, for example in his important article on the linguist Benveniste in *Margins*. This excess of 'writing' (by speaking of 'excess', Derrida links it with the 'Cogito' article discussed in the preceding chapter) is not outside the series but is 'un *certain* déplacement de la série. Et un certain *repli* – nous le nommerons plus tard *remarque* – dans la série de l'opposition, voire dans sa dialectique' (D, 118) ('a *certain* displacement of the series. And a certain *folding back* – which will later be called a *re-mark* – of opposition within the series, or even within its dialectic') (*D*, 104). (In this quotation, the problem of iterability, of the relation between the same and the identical, is indicated by the prefix *re* of the terms introduced here, and marked as introductions by italicization. The phrase itself shows a process of extension through replication of a series – Derrida first brings up the couple 'repli'/'remarque', then relays what it governs through a genitive, 'of opposition', by the word 'dialectique').

There is a kind of generation by opposition in this double series of good writing and bad writing. There seems to be an unequal splitting: writing makes possible a distinction between *eidos*, that is, ideal repetition, and mere repetition, but their common root, in writing, engenders a new separation, and so on:

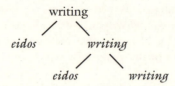

One node splits off in opposition but is not stable, so that the operation has to be continued. The account of this dynamic recurs throughout Derrida's writing, as we shall see. At this stage in my argument, it suffices to point out that it resembles dialectic but is not dialectic, for there is no subsumption, *Aufhebung*, *relève* [relief], as Derrida sometimes translates the German word, that is, remainderless synthesis of the two poles, but instead, replication of the splitting off. This movement has the same structure as the reply by Derrida in the *Origin of Geometry* to Cavaillès' critique of Husserl on the grounds of infinite recursion (that the structures of logic as they are constituted in turn need an infinite hierarchy of constituent consciousnesses). Derrida suggests against Cavaillès that dialectic and structure, history and genesis, activity and passivity are not assignable to a time before or after in relation to each other:

> Nous avons vu combien cette '*activité*' de la conscience était à la fois antérieure et postérieure à une passivité; que le mouvement de la temporalisation primordiale, ultime fondement de toute constitution, était dialectique de part en part; et que, comme le veut tout dialecticité authentique, il n'était que la dialectique de la dialectique – l'implication indéfinie, mutuelle et irréductible des protentions et des rétentions – avec la non-dialectique – l'identité absolue et concrète du présent Vivant, forme universelle de toute conscience.

(OG, 157–8)

We have seen how much this 'activity' of consciousness was both anterior and posterior to passivity; that the movement of primordial temporalization (the ultimate ground of all constitution) was dialectical through and through; and that (as every authentic dialectic makes happen) this movement was only the dialectic between the dialectical (the indefinite mutual and irreducible implication of protentions and retentions) and the non-dialectical (the absolute and concrete identity of the Living Present), the universal form of all consciousness.

(*OG*, 143, trans. mod.)[12]

This phrase 'the dialectic between the dialectical ... and the non-dialectical' picks up a passage in Derrida's thesis in which a series of opposed terms are conjoined in the same dissymetric fashion, a passage which leads to the suggestion that Husserl's 'absolute origin' is itself dialectic and secondary, so that the the very distinction between the Husserlian transcendental and the Husserlian worldly collapses.[13] Of this strange movement, where a division is replicated, but only on one side, so that it is dominated but not contained, Derrida here uses a perfectly ordinary phrase: 'il faudrait alors *plier* à d'étranges mouvements ce qu'on ne pourrait même plus appeler simplement la logique ou le discours' (*D*, 118) ('one would then have to *bend* into strange contortions what could no longer even simply be called logic or discourse') (*D*, 103). The fold, the *pli*, which this induces becomes a Derridean term – *pli* and its italics here representing what could be called his market in futures, his forward trading. It points forward to the *fold* in the article 'The double session', republished with 'Plato's pharmacy' in *Dissemination*, which develops Mallarmé's *pli* of the fan or *plié*, the dancing step. Now Heidegger's *Zwiefalt* is translated as *pli* [fold] in the French translation of *Vorträge und Aufsätze* (*Lectures and Essays*); it is the fold between Being and beings. 'Fold' is one more of the lexemes, the terms marked out by tone and by emphasis, which are active in the Derridean text, but also in a wider exchange (for example, Deleuze's *Le pli* and Merleau-Ponty's *Le visible et l'invisible*).

The suffix '-ble' of 'double' derives from 'plex', that is, 'fold' or 'pli'. 'Double' is both quantifier and mode of quantity. It says how many times, and, etymologically, at least, in what way how many times. It is because repetition – or replication – is itself complex, that this 'strange folding' of repetition comes about. Repetition, we have seen, has two faces, the *eidos*, 'le même, le clair, le stable, l'identifiable', but also 'mimêmes, icônes, phantasmes, simulacres'. This duality of repetition cannot be prised apart, in spite of all Plato's and later philosophers' efforts. The *eidos* springs from the same possibility as the phantasm.

This is a logical point, of the same ilk as J. L. Austin's showing that, for instance, 'real' and 'not real' 'take in each other's washing' philosophically. But it is also a historical point. Derrida is anchoring his analysis in the history of philosophy, by relating it to Plato's cave, and Heidegger's account of Plato's cave.

L'invisibilité absolue de l'origine du visible, du bien-soleil-père-capital, le dérobement à la forme de la présence ou de l'étantité, tout cet excès que Platon désigne comme *epekeina tes ousias* (au-delà de l'étantité ou de la présence) donne lieu, si l'on peut encore dire, à une structure de suppléance telle que toutes les présences seront les suppléments substitués à l'origine absente et que toutes les différences seront, dans le système de présences, l'effet irréductible de ce qui reste *epekeina tes ousias*.

(D, 193)

The absolute invisibility of the origin of the visible, of the good-sun-father-capital, the unattainment of presence or beingness in any form, the whole surplus Plato calls *epekeina tes ousias* (beyond beingness or presence), gives rise to a structure of replacements such that all presences will be supplements substituted for the absent origin, and all differences, within the system of presence, will be the irreducible effect of what remains *epekeina tes ousias*.

D, 167)

What appears can always become mere appearance, what stands in for what has appeared can always become mere icon. The instability between the appearing and the appearance, this constant supplementation, Derrida calls it, is occasioned 'if it may still be said' (omitted from the translation) by the excess that is always beyond: *epekeina tes ousias* ('beyond the essences' in Plato's work, the abode of the good). Derrida is here shaping and stretching the Platonic system by the distinction to which it itself gave birth, a distinction developed by Aristotle, and which has been a powerful current in the history of philosophy: the distinction referred to in the previous chapter, between the positive and the negative infinite. In an ambitious connecting through transference and through metaphor, Derrida extends the Platonic abode of the good beyond being, the sun, the positive infinite, to the father (through certain of Plato's modes of reference to Socrates) or capital (through a pun on 'bien' – wealth). All are that which is unattainable but which sets in motion indefinite supplementation, indefinite circulation. The absolute infinite, beyond being and essences, occasions indefinite approximation, interminable and negatively infinite.

Platonic dialectic supplements knowledge. But the double nature of repetition rivets dialectic to its inferiors, to the mimetic arts, to play, grammar and writing (D, 193; D, 167) So the division/decision between good and bad repetition can only continue, the asymmetric duplication gives rise to a process of supplementation. Now identity is usually, we often forget, a two-place relation. But when one of the two terms is itself replicated (as in the 'dialectic of dialectic and non-dialectic' discussed above), identity is insecure, constantly slipping. It is not that there is an identity which is then replicated, but that replication constitutes identity. This movement of identity (which is not the same as sameness) is thus immediately double, constituted by appearing as identity and truth. Since, by the very nature of appearance, what appears and its appearing slip apart, identity is destined to become un-true.

> La disparition de la vérité comme présence, le dérobement de l'origine présente de la présence est la condition de toute (manifestation de) vérité. . . . La différance, disparition de la présence originaire, est *à la fois* la condition de possibilité et la condition d'impossibilité de la vérité.
>
> (D, 194)

> The disappearance of truth as presence, the withdrawal of the present origin of presence, is the condition of all (manifestation of) truth. . . . Differance, the disappearance of any originary presence, is *at once* the condition of possibility *and* the condition of impossibility of truth.
>
> (*D*, 168 previously quoted)

We have arrived at the development and simultaneous short-circuiting of the Kantian 'condition of possibility' which will be discussed further later; for the moment, the paradoxical condition *différance* constitutes truth, for truth can only be shown if it disappears, if the appearing becomes the appearance.

Derrida here refers implicitly to Heidegger's account of the development of 'Plato's doctrine of truth' in his work of that name, but gently and radically alters its emphasis. The appearance of being at once splits into mere appearance and something behind or beyond, which is appearing:

> L'étant présent (*on*) dans sa vérité, dans la présence de son identité et l'identité de sa présence *se double* dès qu'il apparaît, dès qu'il se présente. *Il apparaît, dans son essence, comme* la possibilité de sa propre duplication. C'est-à-dire, en termes platoniciens, de sa non-vérité la plus propre, de sa pseudo-vérité réfléchie dans l'icône, le phantasme ou le simulacre.
>
> (D, 194)

> The being-present (*on*) in its truth, in the presence of its identity and in the identity of its presence is *doubled* as soon as it appears, as soon as it presents itself. *It appears, in its essence, as* the possibility of its own most proper non-truth, of its pseudo-truth reflected in the icon, the phantasm, or the simulacrum.
>
> (*D*, 168)

Both in the movement that is identity, and in the movement of presentation, of appearing, there is a necessary replication. But there is not what I would call Heidegger's catastrophism in these passages from Derrida. What Heidegger traced as a deviation from the original perception of the nature of truth as a kind of *parousia*, is not a process of fall for Derrida. It is much more like a kind of logical form of 'appearance', to use a term taken from a different philosophical tradition (cf. the just-quoted 'l'étant-présent (*on*). . . . *apparaît, dans son essence, comme* la possibilité de sa propre duplication', D, 194). The logical or formal sense of *a priori* comes together with its temporal sense. For Heidegger, appearing and appearance are part of a process; for Derrida the duplication is unstable, and thus constantly repeated (within *supplement*, and *différance*, and then in some measure between the lexemes). But this instability is not transcendental; it is not a condition of anything being there at all, it is formal, part of the logic of 'appearance'.

To sum up: this instability then reworks the asymmetry of the two sides of the duality *eidos*/writing, or the dialectic of dialectic and non-dialectic. It powers the constant duplication, since what one might call the parody of dialectic, the failed subsumption, calls for constant supplementation. The asymmetry I am explicating is a kind of surplus (*plus*, it 'exceeds', it is the descendent of the 'excess' of the earlier articles). In its functioning, it is outside the series as well as within it, it is the medium out of which the series can determine itself. The series, because of the particular folded repetition, can never stay still, the 'earlier' always has a representative in the polar opposites, which collapses the distinction back (D, 284; *D*, 252). And once more this analysis is enacted to some degree in the way Derrida writes. For likewise, in Derrida's own case, the system, the collection of lexemes, moves forward by plethora and proliferation, new terms develop – *différance* and *supplement*, then *pli* and *pharmakon* – and sometimes disappear (the nature of these terms is not simple; they are not the only repeated terms, merely the strangest either through their provenance or through the status accorded them by Derrida's writing). But there is no law to the series (D, 284; *D*, 252) controlling the elements' relation to each other.[14]

Doubles

The proliferation of lexemes has then no rule which rules the extension through assymetry of what appears. But it does take the form of an unstable duplication. This needs further comment.

The articles in *Dissemination* make double the way of writing and what is written about. They are themselves in fact divided into two – and one title, 'The double session', plays on this (and is itself double, in that it is a pun: 'La double séance' punning on 'la double science'). The article entitled 'Dissemination' starts up twice, by saying and then repeating 'cette fois enfin'. And there is an intellectual stake in this. 'The double session' brilliantly repeats the argument about repetition and about *eidos* traced in 'Plato's pharmacy', in recounting the fortunes of *mimesis* in the history of philosophy and aesthetics. The argument runs like this: as with Platonic memory, when the nature of being of the art work is evaluated, when it is measured ontologically in relation to a pre-existing work, art's existence could be either condoned, as different from and even improving on its model, or condemned, as derived and deviant, helplessly dependent on what it merely seeks to copy – worthless because a double. Imitation, mimesis, in both cases is subordinated to concepts of truth: in one case to truth of reference, as revelation, that is, *aletheia*, whereby *physis*, nature, must duplicate itself in phenomena, and the appearing is part of a cycle of showing and hiding – appearance is only appearance on what might be called the diastole of the movement; or, in the other case, to truth as a relation of *adæquatio*, where appearance can be measured up against what has appeared. Again, this is a dissymmetric duality, the tree structure already pointed to in the discussion of writing and *eidos* above, with one branch replicating the structure of the whole, since *adæquatio* is the stabilized systole of *aletheia*.

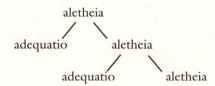

This logical 'machine' controls the history of the idea of imitation, Derrida says in a brief passage (D, 213; *D*, 187) – a note in fact – which characteristically throws sharp and illuminating light on the development of European aesthetics, as anyone familiar with seventeenth- and eighteenth-century theories of art will find. Derrida takes a little known text by Mallarmé, *Mimique*, which appears to insert itself in this history of aesthetics by claiming to imitate the Idea. This latter would then constitute some last resort, some ultimate guarantor, some stable peg on which imitations could model themselves in a relation of adequation, of adequate measuring up, to the Idea. Derrida's argument sets out to undermine this 'Hegelian' interpretation of Mallarmé. He claims that the Mime imitates nothing pre-existing, but is nonetheless imitating, imitating without a model. It is thus 'un double qui ne redouble aucun simple' (D, 234) ('a double that doubles no simple') (*D*, 206). In that sense, the Mallarméan text is presented as a doubling of Platonism or Hegelianism (D, 235; *D*, 207), for the Platonic *phantasma* becomes not a derivative of the *eidos*, a pale hanger-on of form, but simply all that there is. Mallarmé's work is ontologically effective, it disturbs the status of the abstract entities 'Livre' [Book], 'Esprit' [Spirit], 'Idée' [Idea], with which it appears to operate. These are in the Mallarméan text both Platonic ideas and non-beings (D, 236; *D*, 208). Derrida here is giving definition to the sense of disquiet Mallarmé's capital letters provoke in the reader, the double sense that they create, of undermining or emptying of being at the same time as positing. The 'matérialisme de l'idée' (D, 236) ('materialism of the idea') (*D*, 208) (Derrida borrows Hyppolite's phrase) short-circuits in paradox the relation holding between *eidos*–idea–form and content; we have, says Derrida, only a theatre of simulacra operating in what is a reversal of Plato's cave. In Plato's myth the prisoners were led to distinguish between reality and imitations. Here, the mime is imitating, but the imitated, the model, the ontologically more real in the structure of imitation, is not there. And in a difficult sentence, Derrida makes allusion once again to the positive infinite, *epekeina tes ousias*:

> L'idéalité de l'idée est ici, pour Mallarmé, le nom, encore métaphysique, encore nécessaire pour marquer le non-étant, le non-réel ou le non-présent; cette marque indique, fait allusion sans briser la glace vers l'au-delà de l'étantité, vers l'*epekeina tes ousias*, hymen (proximité et voile) entre le soleil de Platon et le lustre de Mallarmé.
>
> (D, 236)

> The ideality of the idea is here for Mallarmé the still metaphysical name that is still necessary in order to mark non-being, the non-real, the non-present. This mark points, or 'alludes without breaking the glass', to the beyond of beingness, toward the *epekeina tes ousias*, a hymen (a closeness and a veil) between Plato's sun and Mallarmé's lustre.
>
> (D, 208)

The sun is that which is beyond all measure, the positive infinite, with Mallarmé's chandelier (lustre) as a kind of negative reversal of that infinite (the article on Foucault referred to 'nothing or the infinite'), like Heideggerian Being, which is nothing outside beings. The point of non-junction, or of articulation between these infinites – we are not told further which – is a new paradoxical lexeme, *hymen*. Derrida develops *hymen* from the Mallarméan text, making it indicate both proximity and separation. So that in ways to be further determined, the different sites of the *reserve* or the medium, that is *pharmakon* and now *hymen*, are the relation and the difference between the two infinites.

Hymen, like *pharmakon*, and like *différance,* is double in meaning – both separating membrane and fusion in marriage. Like such terms, it seems to tempt one into making of it a key lexeme, a load-bearing term, in Derrida's work. The very lexical strangeness of the Derridean terms may have seemed to pick them out for this – it has certainly helped their success in spreading beyond discussion of his texts and into other contexts. But in fact, this success may have obscured how they actually function in the Derridean text – as the analysis in 'The double session' proceeds they are treated not as foci, but as junction points, from which meaning can pivot in lateral relation to what is around, sending out and being subject to ripples of insecurity in the surrounding text (in doing so they double some of the striking effects of Mallarméan syntax).

The syntactic rather than semantic function of these lexemes becomes evident at the fulcrum of Derrida's analysis, a correction made by Mallarmé. The poet, argues Derrida in a passage which will be more fully analysed later, introduces syntactic ambiguity in his text, whereby the relation between subject and object in the phrase is not stable – it can be read with apparent subject as object or *vice versa*, though not indeterminately – the possibilities are determinate.[15] 'La syntaxe [a] ménagé un effet de flottaison indéfinie entre deux possibles' (D, 254) ('The syntax at any rate has produced an effect of indefinite fluctuation between two possibilities') (*D*, 225). The Mallarméan phrase swings and moves between passive and active, and it is this, says Derrida, which generates in Mallarmé's text the proliferation of simulacra, so that it is impossible to be certain what is imitating what. But it is important to see that this liberation of simulacra in the Derridean working over of Mallarmé is not a free-for-all. Derrida connects the perturbing function, which liberates the simulacra, first with the positive infinite, then with the Platonic *epekeina tes ousias*, then with the Idea in Mallarmé (D, 236; *D*, 208). In the preceding chapter, the Kantian Idea seemed to make necessary a constant work of approximation; so here, in Mallarmé according to Derrida, the sun or *lustre* induces an infinite embedding of replications: 'La *Mimique* décrit une scène d'écriture dans une scéne d'écriture et ainsi sans fin' (D, 252) ('*Mimique* describes a scene of writing within a scene of writing and so on without end') (*D*, 223). This infinite embedding is given tension and rigour by the reference to the 'idea which is nothing' (*D*, 208), by the gesture to the *epekeina tes ousias* (this tension will be further explored in the next chapter).

Reflexivity as *mise en abyme*

The lexemes have then a syntactic function attributed explicitly to them. They seem to multiply in Derrida's text, but they also cause proliferation and doubling. In the next group of sections, it is this structure of doubling which will be examined.

Now mirrors create doubles. Interest in the way the work of art or literature refers to itself, and in the mirror as symbol for this, was current at the time Derrida wrote these articles; the process was usually referred to as *mise en abyme*, a heraldic term that Gide had used.[16] In literary theory, with the *mise en abyme* as a series of reflections or internally contained scale-models of the literary work, such doubles might give consistency and coherence to the literary or pictural work by encapsulating images which reflect the whole, by reinforcing and repeating it. The work was reflexive, it reflected itself, and contained that reflexion. There is a tradition of interpretation of Mallarmé which takes this approach. But Derrida refuses such an analysis. He is denying in 'The double session' that there is a 'system closed on itself', as it has to be if it encapsulates mirror images. The work on the contrary 'has' he says (the obligation is interesting) to be both open and closed, the mere fact that it is both in writing and about writing is not enough. The determination of self-reference and reference to other writing is to be done not just through the textual equivalent of mirror images, that is unit-like symbols, but through textual operations of quotation: by grafts, borrowings, incisions. (The open-ended *summum* of this will be Derrida's *Glas*; see p. 87.) A work will not then be a mirroring of mirroring through tidy embedding, but a palimpsest of excerpts, an overlapping stratification of quotations. This complexity of intertextual relations, which open out rather than embed, is exemplified by Mallarmé's own relation in his *Mimique* to the work by Paul Margueritte which precipitated his own text. Now, the last article in *Dissemination* relates *mise en abyme* to Philippe Sollers' practice in his novel *Nombres*. In this article, the cognates *greffe* (graft) and *graphein* (Greek, 'to write') enable a communication between writing and heterogenous extension which must be explored further (see Chapter 5) in a properly textual move away from the domination of the visual at work in the *mise en abyme*, the *idea* and the *theatre*.[17]

This movement away from contemporary (1960s) treatment of the *mise en abyme* is part of the subversion of phenomenological criticism that Derrida's text is operating. The diacriticism of Jean Pierre Richard, for instance, while insisting on plurality, was always concerned to disengage a set of themes, whose relation to each other was that each was a transformation of a central kernel. Subtending such literary criticism, implies Derrida, is the notion of the endless richness of the master work, which is in direct analogy with certain empirical theories of knowledge: the incomparably rich tissue of meanings in the work of literature is said to offer never-ending interpretation. As with Husserlian perception, the horizon of sense is one we can never master (D, 282; *D*, 250–1). Against Richard's *polysemy*, Derrida sets his own and Heidegger's *dissemination*, and refines and reworks the refusal of mastery that dissemination entails. It is now not a result of being *in* a horizon within which one can always move further. On the contrary, it arises from the skewing of this relation of part to whole: the horizon may and will become part of something else, so that there is no harmonious, Husserlian opening out of ever-greater perspectives one from within the other. There is no embedding of infinite horizons within perception, regulated by possible extension to the Kantian Idea, as there can be no summing of series in order to arrive at omnivalent themes. There is not a bijection with an enumerable symmetric correspondence of points between two sets, but instead an irregular and lateral folding back of text onto itself (D, 282; *D*, 250–1). Derrida is here using terms which have a possible mathematical sense (*recouvrement, sommation, limite*) to insist on the notion of an infinity which cannot be numbered, but which is yet not uncountable through a richness of meaning. We do not have the Husserlian limitless horizon, but instead the constructed effect of processes which are not observably present (perhaps something like the trace of a particle in the cloud chamber, D, 390; *D*, 350–1). As the possibility opposed to thematics, we have effects of themes: 'il n'y a pas de noyau thématique, seulement des effets de thèmes qui se donne pour la chose même ou le sens même' (D, 282) ('there is no such thing as a thematic nucleus, only theme *effects* that give themselves out to be the very thing or meaning of the text') (*D*, 250). In the earlier article on Plato's pharmacy, the *eidos* as appearing was inseparable from the appearances and the dissemination of appearances by which it appeared, and thus it was inseparable from deceptive copies; here the theme is a construction projected out from the actual textual instances which give rise to it, an effect. By calling it 'effect' Derrida makes it appear derived and somehow having less reality.

The *fold*, it was suggested above, might refer to the instability within 'writing', for instance, which gives rise to the unequal and reiterated duplication of writing and *eidos*. At this point, we must deal with the anchorage of the term in the Mallarméan text. In the detail of Derrida's account of Mallarmé, he does not only pick out the themes discerned by Richard and by phenomenological criticism, and the analogues of such themes (as fan, and then what opens and closes, the fold (*pli*), the page, the veil). He also shows how the very movement of the text between these elements is that of the fold: it is a folding of what seems like a separable theme back into the supporting structure. Derrida's account then goes beyond any gathering into a kernel of a multiplicity of themes, to show how the operation giving rise to the themes actually mimics them. The same is true of another kernel designated by Richard, the theme of 'white'. We can take this as an element. But as the blank page, and referred to as such by Mallarmé, it is also the matrix in which our work is going on, namely 'the transcendental space of inscription' (D, 285; *D*, 253). It is by being both operation and element, that 'white', like 'fold', is not an embedded series of themes, but rather what creates the effect of a series, causing agglomerations 'to be taken for' substances (D, 285; *D*, 254) (the similarity to materialist arguments about substance is striking). What is going on here is a skeining out by Derrida's commentary on Mallarmé of any once-and-for-all determinate distinction between theme and medium, and thus between active or distinguishing and passive or distinguished, that is, between subject and object.

The 'fold', both cursus and theme, is then an insistence on syntax as well as on semantics, on lateral relations as well as on the word-unit; an insistence on the syncategoreme, the articulating lexeme that needs completion, as well as on the categorematic term, the word which can be used by itself. It is part of an insistence that the uncircumscribable nature of meaning is not built out of richness, seen either as ever-extending horizons of signification, or as words infinitely assemblable as building blocks. It is built structurally, out of slippages and losses, out of graftings and cuttings. The infinity of language is not derived from the arraying of atomic words, but from the 'jeu d'articulations morcelant ce corps ou le réinscrivant aussi bien dans des séquences qu'il ne commande plus' (D, 287) ('play of articulations splitting up that body or re-inscribing it within sequences it can no longer control') (*D*, 255). In language, the word (the categoreme) misleads, for it seems to provide a key, the *passe-partout*. But 'white' and 'fold' are both words, units, and also operations on those units. The textual articulation, the *blanc* of the white page, the spacing that holds the words separate on the page,[18] is also a theme, as the Mallarméan syntax performing the 'fold' was also a theme: both fold on themselves, they are both operations and elements. It is this duality that short-circuits and prevents our abstracting out of the page a word that can stand as genus to the other lexemes, since each instance of the theme in fact stands *in* not merely for another instance but also for the operation. To sum up: Derrida here hitches his analysis to specifically Mallarméan terms, *blanc*, *pli*, *hymen*, as he had done earlier to Plato's *pharmakon* or indeed in a lexeme not studied here, Rousseau's *supplement*; they allow infinite addition (the system is open) by a doubling, a kind of cell division, a proliferation of stand-ins whose status is uncertain and whose fate is unassured.[19] But the paradoxical fold, or the blank, means that that infinity is not straightforward, it has a tangled nature, the doubles double back.

It is here that the lexematic proliferation and the asymmetric repetition, induced by the fold, need to be related to other forms of structural doubling. At points in this article, Derrida's writing both doubles, that is mimics, Mallarmé's, and enacts the doubling in his own writing. Consider, for instance, the phrase of summary taken from Mallarmé: 'Le livre, expansion totale de la lettre, doit d'elle tirer, directement, une mobilité et spacieux, par correspondances, instituer un jeu, on ne sait, qui confirme la fiction' ('The book, the total expansion of the letter, must draw from it, directly, a kind of mobility and, spacious, through correspondences, institute a play, one doesn't [quite] know, which confirms the fiction'). The commentary by Derrida which precedes this has traces of Mallarméan syntax and is marked by the proliferation of analyses:

> Cette chaîne ('fiction', 'hymen', 'spacieux' etc), elle-même spacieuse et mobile, *se prend*, mais pour la désorganiser, dans toute la machine ontologique. Elle en disloque toutes les oppositions, elle les entraîne dans un movement, leur imprime un jeu qui se propage sur toutes les pièces du texte, les déportant toujours plus ou moins régulièrement, avec des décalages, des inégalités de déplacement, des retards ou des accélérations brusques, des effets stratégiques d'insistance ou d'ellipse, mais inexorablement.
>
> (D, 266)

> This chain ('fiction', 'hymen', 'spacious', etc.), itself both spacious and mobile, *gets caught in*, but thereby disorganizes, the whole ontological machine. It dislocates all oppositions. It carries them off, impresses upon them a certain play that propagates itself through all the text's moving parts, constantly shifting them, setting them out of phase, more or less regularly, through unequal displacements, abrupt slowdowns or bursts of speed, strategic effects of insistence or ellipsis, but always inexorably.
>
> (*D*, 236)

Plurals, reduplication, phrases which catch themselves up: in the very way these sentences are written, all these seem to mime the proliferation that is being discussed.

Reflexivity and subjectivity

This doubling back, making unclear the distinction between imitating and imitated, is thus both thematized à propos Mallarmé through the 'fold', and also practised: the pivoting lexemes, the phrases which interchange grammatical subject and object, all these disrupt the opposition between passive and active, something that in this text means that the subject, that is the origin of the text, cannot be securely located (D, 254; *D*, 225). Now, traditionally, the mirror which doubles the person looking into it has been a figure of the subject, of consciousness reflecting on itself; but it has also been a symbol of illusion. We shall see now that Derrida implies that the Mallarméan mirror picks up both threads, to twist them into something which is altogether different from that antithesis. Indeed, in Derrida's article 'Dissemination', which works from the novel *Nombres* by Philippe Sollers, and which follows the article on Mallarmé in *Dissemination*, reflexivity in the text is neither complete nor unskewed. Nor is it so in the subject. In this article too, the harmonious insertion of mirror image into text, suggesting a stable periphery within which the textual reflexivity and unrefracted reflection for the subject can take place, that is, the *mise en abyme*, does not occur here.

In the article on *Nombres*, the subject is not a unit entity, an in-dividual in the literal sense of undivided. It is the scene of intersections, of complex competing forces, in a theatre which is that of language and writing itself. Derrida, in suggesting this, is subtextually writing against Sartre (as he also does in *Glas*). He works against the Sartrean idea of the act, and the linguistic act in particular, not by mention of Sartre's name, but by textual reference. He picks up echoes from Sartre's preface to Mallarmé (Sartre 1977 [1952]), as from the prefatory work which was drawn into *L'Idiot de la famille* (1971–2), where necessity can be created out of chance and the subject can be delivered from the random. Derrida counters, with inexplicit but clear reference:[20]

> celui qui dit *je* au présent, dans l'événement dit positif de son discours, ne saurait avoir que l'illusion de la maîtrise. Alors même qu'il croit conduire les opérations, à chaque instant et malgré lui sa place – l'ouverture au présent de quiconque croit pouvoir dire *je*, je pense, je suis, je vois, je sens je dis . . . est décidée par un coup de dés dont le hasard dévéloppe ensuite inexorable-ment la loi.
>
> (D, 330–1)

> he who says I in the present, in the so-called positive event constituted by his discourse, would be capable of only an illusion of mastery. At the very moment he thinks he is directing the operations, his place – the opening toward the present assumed by whoever believes himself capable of saying I, I think, I am, I see, I feel, I say . . . is . . . being decided by a throw of dice whose law will subsequently be developed inexorably by chance.
>
> (D, 298)

It is important to be precise about what is being claimed here. It is not that the subject is abolished. But through these references to Sartre's Mallarmé and, as we shall see, to Kant, Derrida is suggesting a much more shadowy and illu-sionary subject, one that is in Sollers' novel both constituted and 'deconstructed' (Derrida uses the term) by writing.[21]

First, a logical point. Although the article just quoted, 'Dissemination', from which the collection takes its title, goes further in what might be called Nietzschean gaiety than other of Derrida's texts, as we shall see, it can be thought of as a brilliant and funny working, indeed working over, of philosophical questions of existence, identity and meaning. In it, Derrida suggests that to take one side of a pair of opposed arguments is merely to remain within the same intellectual region, and is self-cancelling. (This point is undoubtedly made in relation to, and in a sense against, the *Tel Quel* group's materialist aesthetics – cf. D, 51; *D*, 43–4.) And indeed the arguments about the subject are reversible – if the 'subject' is a phantasm, an effect of the mirror, the mirror does still produce effects, they are there. To dissolve the idea of the subject is merely to enact the other pole of the assertion of the individual.

Derrida's article proceeds as if the Sollers novel is a strange machine for criticizing theories of the subject, by treating our consciousness as an effect of processes external and representing it. As in Brechtian criticism of stage illusion, we are told that in the Sollers' novel 'representation' is 'put on' by the 'old ghosts named author, reader, producer, machinist' (D, 329; *D*, 297). What might this consciousness as an 'effect' mean? Stanislas Lem (1971) in a 'book review' imagines a computer creation of a mental world, where the 'personoids' who inhabit it have no bodies but do have souls.

> This soul – to an outside observer who has a view into the machine world . . . appears as a 'coherent cloud of processes', as a functional aggregate with a kind of 'center' that can be isolated fairly precisely, i.e., delimited within the machine network.
>
> (Lem 1971: 498)

We seem to have from the Lem story the suggestion that such a view of 'soul' as effect of inscriptional computing processes is a kind of God's (or outside observer's) view of a Cartesian world. Indeed, in the same Derridean text, it is implied that we place ourselves at the apex of the cognitive as of the visual pyramid, at the point which seems to control the visual field, the point from which things in our visual field are present to us. But actually the visual field is in front of us, and moves with us.[22] Presence, as controlling subjectivity, is an illusion; however, as we shall see directly, it is not an illusion easily removed.

Lem, immediately after the cited passage about the 'personoid' soul, moves on in a brilliant excursus to suggest that all consciousness, whether human or computer-generated for 'personoids', is 'in its physical aspect an "informational standing wave", a certain dynamic invariant in a stream of incessant transformations' (*ibid.*: 499). This dynamic invariant is a compromise – from an engineering point of view, a semi-harmonizing of different imperfectly hierarchized brain functions of regulation; as different functions of control were added through evolution, the whole ought to have been 're-engineered', that is, old regulating functions abandoned and new ones redesigned; this of course was impossible. Consciousness, in this 'book review', arises out of conflicts of operation which are subject to 'arbitrational procedures'; and these never finally arbitrated conflicts are necessary, so that consciousness 'will not admit of any closure'; it is only a

plan for such a closure, for a total 'reconciliation' of the stubborn contradictions of the brain. It is, one might say, a mirror, whose task it is to reflect
other mirrors, which in turn reflect still others, and so on to infinity.

(Lem 1971: 500)

Now Derrida compares consciousness to the Kantian transcendental illusion
'which does not cease even after it has been detected', and one of the examples
of which is the illegitimate conclusion from the transcendental concept of the
subject, 'a bare consciousness which accompanies all concepts', to the absolute
unity of the subject itself.[23] In both Lem, and Derrida writing about Sollers,
consciousness is a paradoxical, constantly exfoliating entity.

Thus vigilance, says Derrida, may not dissolve the effects of presence; the
effects of self are polemically described as illusionistic phantoms: 'un *je* qui fait
partie à la fois du spectacle et de l'assistance et qui, un peu comme 'vous' assiste
à (subit) sa propre réinscription incessante et violente dans la machinerie arith-
métique' (D, 361) ('an "I" that is both part of the spectacle and part of the
audience; an "I" that, a bit like "you", attends (undergoes) its own incessant,
violent reinscription within the arithmetical machinery') (*D*, 325). As 'inscription' indicates, the question is the subject's relation to writing, which is
particularly complex in this novel. *Nombres*, it has already been suggested, both
exhibits illusion and dismantles it, rather as the computer imagined by Lem may
construct 'worlds' – individual subjectivities – but which by their very construction are revealed as having a limited validity even while for their 'personoid'
they are binding and absolute. But Sollers has written not just a novel showing
up the subject as textual effect. He has written a novel about the experience of
the subject as a textual effect from out of the words of a novel. However, even
this does not stabilize as a dichotomy between writing and experience of
writing. Since both the process of writing the experience of the subject as
writing, as being written, and the sense of an actual writing taking place as one
reads (the latter a common technique for creating the illusion of authorial presence) are part of the novel, they are also an illusion. They are an effect of
presence, not real presence – the opening into the presence of the experiencing
subject is only apparent.

There is then in this novel a proliferation of doubles (the sense of a process
of writing of the sense of process of writing of the sense . . .) which short-
circuits presentation because it is quartered into a similar series (the process of
writing the experience of the subject as writing) so that writing and being
written fold into each other. It is in this way, I believe, that Derrida's text can
argue that what we have is an existential judgment ('il y a'), there is writing; but
against Sartrean accounts of language, that writing is not fixable, however
dialectically, into a point of time where an act, that is, an act of enunciation,
might take place. Indeed, Sollers' novel, and Derrida's article, might be said to
be constructed in order to make this separation between act of writing and what
is written impossible to make cleanly (I shall return later to this point). The
contrast between act of enunciation and what is said, or the point of articulation

of a spatio-temporal set-up exterior to language and the statement made at that point, is rendered insecure. It is said by Derrida to be tainted with illusion:

> le 'il y a' de l'avoir lieu n'est au présent que dans l' 'illusion' de l'énoncé de l'énonciation. Contenu et acte de ce langage sont aussitôt ouverts sur l'autre-présent. Ce qui a lieu, ce qu'il y a c'est l'écriture, c'est à dire une machination dont le présent n'est plus qu'une toupie.
>
> (D, 345)

> This 'there is' of the 'taking place' is in the present only through the 'illusions' of statement or utterance. The content and act of this speech are immediately open upon the extrapresent. What takes place, what there is, is writing, i.e. a machination in which the present is no longer anything but a whirligig.
>
> (*D*, 311)

What takes place in a statement is illusion, it is made of centrifugal forces towards the not-present, whether past or future, and these create the illusion of the present like the illusory stability of the centre of a spinning top. The enunciating subject, like the present and the theme, is spun out as an effect of forces, rather than a unitary unifying point: it is 'a pure place of passage for operations of substitution' (D, 361, my translation).

We have seen that Derrida glosses Mallarmé's emendation of his own text (note 15 above) to make of it a hovering between two determinate readings of the syntax, one active, one passive. (This develops the Heideggerian analysis of Kant, where the transcendental imagination is at the root of and beyond the distinction between spontaneity and reception, between active and passive.) This syntactic hovering is attributed to a mirror, that is, to mimicry:

> Le Mime ne lit pas son rôle, il est aussi lu par lui. Du moins est-il à la fois lu et lisant, écrit et écrivant, entre les deux, dans le suspens de l'hymen, écran et miroir. Dès qu'on interpose un miroir quelque part, l'opposition simple de l'activité et de la passivité, comme du produire et du produit, ou encore de tous les participes présents et de tous les participes passés (imitant/imité, signifiant/signifié, structurant/structuré etc) devient impraticable.
>
> (D, 253)

> The Mime does not read his role; he is also read *by* it. Or at least he is both read and reading, written and writing, between the two, in the suspense of the hymen, at once screen and mirror. As soon as a mirror is interposed in some way, the simple opposition between activity and passivity, between production and the product, or between all concepts in -er and all concepts

in -ed (signifier/signified, imitator/imitated, structure/structured, etc.), becomes impracticable.

(*D*, 224)

Yet such a distinction between active and passive is necessary if a theme is to emerge fully, or if the enunciation is to result from the act of enunciation. Now Sollers' text, with its mirror effects and, as we shall see, its extensive quotation, makes thematization insecure. In work on the notion of fetish which will be examined in the next chapter, Derrida quotes Sollers quoting Marx on value,[24] to argue that the reification of value in actual object or in an intellectual object, a concept, is fetishism. Sollers with his textual theatre, where the distinction between passive and active ceases to be operable, insists Derrida, unpicks any thematics, any fetishism. (There are here signs of unflagged disagreements with Sollers' wife Julia Kristeva, for the article 'The double session' warns against ontologizing Mallarmé, whether towards mimesis or towards 'actuality, reality or even materiality' (D, 266; *D*, 235), and there is a warning in the preface, *Outwork*, that Kristeva's reliance on the value of materiality, which is what enables her to continue allegiance to materialism, is in fact a kind of idealism, in which matter or history or the real have become a last resort, a transcendental signifier [D, 51; *D*, 43–4].)

In Sollers' novel, mirror effects or, more broadly, reflexivity, do not merely derealize themes; they are used, says Derrida, to unsettle meta-language. A meta-discourse might try to set up a master-grid, which would reflect the structure of the object language; but Sollers renders the meta-discourse, that is, the commentary on the novel contained within the novel, impermanent by disorganizing pairs of values (true/false, high/low, inside/outside) so that their exclusive and complementary nature is insecure. On the contrary, they act, says Derrida, as if self-exclusive and enclose their opposite, in a paradoxical movement: 'Chaque terme capte l'autre et s'exclut de lui-même' (D, 351) ('Each term takes over the other and excludes itself from itself') (*D*, 315). The reflexivity of the meta-language cannot then be simple. Indeed, it is another kind of reflexivity and another kind of infinity – the part which is equal to the whole is only possible in infinite sets (for example, even though the set of the even numbers is contained by the set of the natural numbers, it has an infinite number of members, just like the set of the natural numbers, and the infinite is of the same sort – they have the same cardinal, they are called 'reflexive' and each can be contained by one of their own proper parts): 'Le monde comprend le miroir qui le capte et réciproquement' (D, 351) ('The world comprehends the mirror which captures it and vice versa') (*D*, 316).[25] The infinite cannot close in on itself – it is not clear whether it is contained or containing. In this novel, a meta-language which mirrors is unavailable.

To summarize: 'Dissémination' in a way continues and fills out the remark at the end of the introduction to *Origin of Geometry*: 'L'absolu est le passage' (OG, 165) ('The *Absolute is Passage*') (*OG*, 149) In Sollers' novel, 'the column', which by being at the centre of one of Sollers' diagrams might seem to focus themes of presence, to represent the copula 'is' but also to have 'phallic' significance, is declared to be: 'rien que le passage de la dissémination' (D, 391) ('nothing but the passage of dissemination') (*D*, 351) (the inverted commas are Derrida's). Units, whether word, subject or theme, tend to dissolution, they tend to disseminate. By which is meant, not that there is a unity which forms them and which is afterwards dispersed, but that from the first they are constructs, trace effects arising from shifting forces, liable to change. And the figure of this is the expression of the first person, available to one and all: '*Je* qui, pur lieu de *passage* livré aux opérations de substitution, n'est plus une singulière et irremplaçable existence, un sujet, une 'vie" (D, 361) ("'I" that, functioning as a pure place of passage for operations of substitution, is not some singular and irreplaceable existence, some subject of "life"') (*D*, 325, trans. mod.). The subject, in Derrida's text as in Sollers', does not so much arise out of writing as it *is* the place of writing.

Quotation

The mirror, said Derrida, made active and passive less separable: in Mallarmé's mime, what imitates what is far from clear. In Derrida's article 'Dissémination' that is textually the case, in some cases, by the very way it is written, in its relation to Sollers' novel, and by its use of quotation, as we shall see directly.

Derrida's article on, or rather perhaps from, *Nombres* continues his work on Mallarmé. Both articles were in fact written within the ambit of the *Tel Quel* group, and Derrida on Sollers, as in the Mallarmé article, pits dissemination against Richard's polysemy, the latter defined, as we have seen, as a complex of themes which can be located round a kernel – rather as Kristeva at more or less the same time contrasts the new novel and the new new novel, in a strife that could be called generational in both senses. But Derrida sets up a curious kind of relation to Sollers' novel (an underrated novel, in this reader's estimation) both respectful and leap-frogging, waving the novel through, so to speak, as well as going beyond it. 'Dissémination' is a term used by Sollers of a complex movement of self-loss and reassertion, but it is also a possible translation of the Heideggerian *Zerstreuung*.[26] The novel with its repetitive abstract structures, organized in groups of four, and its wild use of quotation is in a sense mimicked by Derrida's own mimicry of a 'présentation, commentaire, interprétation, compte-rendu, ou recensement' (D, 326) ('presentation, commentary, interpretation, review, account or inventory') (*D*, 294). Derrida quotes the novel *Nombres*, other works by Sollers, and other texts, as well as adopting some of the grammatical features of *Nombres* (use of the second person plural for instance). The two works begin to form a multiple intersecting entity, where commentary and commented on, citation and parody are hard to prise apart in the flow of the text, however separate they are in physical fact of publication. In this dual guise, we have the appearance of presentation, but not its *eidos*. What we are reading may always turn out to be a quotation. Such citation is an exacerbation of Derrida's way since *Origin of*

Geometry, where as has been said, *oratio obliqua*, the conditional which in French hovers between on the one hand the hypothetical or conditional, and on the other reported speech, had already served to render unstable the distinction between commentary and text commented on: 'Transcendentale serait la différence' (OG, 171) ('difference might be [is said to be] transcendental') (*OG*, 153) has already received attention, where the surprise that difference might act as a transcendental is undercut by the possibility that it is a report of Heidegger's relation to Husserl. This tentative 'writing over' means that what is said in the Derridean text is not presented to us; it is not there in the commonsensical way, the reader doesn't know where he or she is. And piling Ossa on Pelion, the quotes-within-quotes fragment the argument as far as it will go. Yet the result, Derrida's article, is tautly organized, it has numbered chapter headings which, like Sollers' novel, play with number theories; it has mysterious titles which suggest an ordering, orderly and implacable machine working against the apparent diffusion.

So that the quotations in 'Dissemination' develop the way in which Derrida treats Plato's *pharmakon* as a one-word quotation, carrying into its context of phrase bits of its past neighbourhoods. Such quotation is an insertion of the heterogeneous; it thus cannot be spread flat, like a mosaic, nor absorbed into the host, nor prevented from radiating back to the text from which it came. It is a kind of graft, an incision. Such grafts suggest an important trait in the texture of thinking: that the way we think, be it ever so cogent and careful, is one of seamed extension, a stitching forwards and backwards between items of different age and different provenance, and of which items the same could be said, *ad infinitum*. They also raise urgent questions about the status of what we are reading.

The doubling of irony

The quotation in these two articles, especially in 'Dissemination', makes the reader feel uncertain about the attribution of authorial provenance, about the authority in the text. This uncertainty is increased by what I am going to suggest is a form of irony. By this, I do not mean ironic in the sense of not serious.[27] It has already been suggested that 'The double session' in its work on doubles, in its quoting of Plato, 'idoles, icônes, mimèmes, phantasmes' (D, 212 note) ('idols, icons, likeness, semblances') (*D*, 186 note 14; *Sophist*, 241 d–e) seems to work in part as a brilliant ironization of philosophical themes. The double opposed meanings of such terms as *pharmakon* and *hymen* and their stratified provenance, Platonic or Mallarméan and Derridean, are a strident version of the puns in the same article, which of course mimic Mallarmé's own wordplay. But Derrida's writing develops an irony which is not pinned to terms, to words as units; indeed, at this point in 'The double session', to pin everything on the term *hymen* is said to be to fall into a trap (D, 249; D, 220). Derrida takes the second version of the Mallarmé text, where the word 'entre' makes an appearance, but reads it as double in meaning ('hymen . . . entre la perpétration et son souvenir'). Of this Derrida makes a pun between 'antre' (cave), in the context, the Platonic cave, and 'entre', 'between'. This causes a noun, and a preposition, a categoreme and a syncategoreme, a word that could be a theme, and one that is an expression of relationship, to replace each other. The effect is not semantic but syntactic: 'L'effet en est d'abord produit par la syntaxe qui dispose l' 'entre' de telle sorte que le suspens ne tienne plus qu'à la place et non au contenu des mots' (D, 249) ('It produces its effect first and foremost through the syntax, which disposes the *entre* in such a way that the suspense is due only to the placement and not to the content of words') (*D*, 220). And the effect is not just described, but enacted by Derrida in such a phrase as 'allusion perpétuelle au fond de l'entre qui n'a pas de fond' (D, 248) ('perpetual allusion being performed in the background of the *entre* that has no ground') (*D*, 219). In the prepositional expression, the interpretation moves, encouraged by the spelling, between 'entre'/'between' and 'antre'/'cave'; but to this there is added a slight shift, an Empsonian ripple which does not merely swing between the lexemes but between reading the first genitive as being governed by 'perpetual allusion' with the phrase 'au fond' as a concessive adverbial expression (i.e. 'the perpetual allusion, finally, of the between/cave which has no ground') and reading the 'au' as a preposition ('perpetual allusion to the between/cave'). Such phrases occur several times in Derrida's work, and the un-immediate, halting or trammelled nature of the double reading is common to them. Here the phrase pivots, and renders the phrases around it insecure. We do not move between two secure readings, but four; it is the multiplying which removes security, for each of the possibilities is quite determinate. Derrida mimics; he also doubles here the Mallarméan phrase which he set out to comment on.

I wish to argue that this doubling engenders irony, but not that for instance of Friedrich Schlegel's 'transcendental buffoonery', lifting itself up to soar over everything limited, nor that of Kierkegaard's Socrates, whose 'tunneling under existence' seemed to work towards an 'ironic totality'.[28] In spite of the connections made, rightly, to romantic irony,[29] there is an important difference: this ironic movement is not a change of level, but of current, as it were, like an electronic switching mechanism. There is what Derrida calls, as we have already seen, 'un effet de flottaison indéfinie entre deux possibles' (D, 254) ('an effect of indefinite fluctuation between two possibilities') (*D*, 225). This switching between different but determinate possibilities within relatively short segments of prose certainly has ironic effects, but ones that are syntactic, not related to a human mind with transcendental overview – or underview, in Kierkegaard's Socrates' case – however temporary and endlessly renewed that transcendental climbing up and beyond may be. On the contrary, they are ironic effects which derive from syntactic units joining together in unstable ways.[30]

Nevertheless, such irony certainly operates by doubling the meaning between these pivoting phrases. Irony has always been said to undercut by suggesting something else beyond its words. In 'Dissemination', there is also related effect by doubling, that of parody. There is a sense of talking to Sollers and Kristeva through the quotations, the number games, the respectful mimicry as a way of avoiding the genre of academic commentary. For insistent quotation is uncommonly like parody. The montage of quotations in 'Dissemination' gives what is quoted a status at the same time privileged and uncertain. This mode of writing is developed in the strange and difficult work *Glas* (1974). Discussing it, Derrida speaks of 'farce' (both stuffing and farce), of Menippean satire, that is, the grafting together of several genres[31] – what in telecommunications is known as cross-talk. *Glas* is constructed round two columns of text, in different type-faces. The first column is a commentary on Hegel, and his attitude to the family and to Judaism. The second is on Genet, petty crook, long-term prison resident and poet. The two columns can be read independently; though they do 'cross-talk', they cut across each other in ways unpredictable by the reader. Each column contains very extended quotations; beyond that, into each column are let 'hanging paragraphs' of commentary or quotation. The complexity of quota-tion and gap, column and inset, is compounded by the fact that at least two of the 'host' texts in *Glas*, Hegel's *The Philosophy of Right* and Genet's 'Ce qui est resté d'un Rembrandt déchiré en petits carrés bien réguliers et foutu aux chiottes' were themselves printed as two texts, Hegel's with a running commentary beneath, and Genet's in two columns in different fonts. Now if *Glas* is an arcane and highly original work, it is certainly not the wilful form it has sometime been taken for. Indeed, it has been pointed out that it is related to the rabbinic tradi-tion of commentary. It has been argued that its textual set-up puts into practice the eighteenth-century game of 'cross-reading', reading across columns of newsprint instead of down (see the *Oxford English Dictionary* article of that name[32]), which was imitated by the German aphorist Lichtenberg and which links up with collage techniques used both in painting and in poetry in the twentieth century.[33] One way of reading it is indeed as a parody of the Hegelian resolution of contraries, the *Aufhebung*: a parody in part working through the very way the text is set out, in opposed columns, *Glas* deliberately short-circuits any sense of completion. The biographical opposites, Hegel and Genet, are crossed from column to column but these contraries are not resolved. Lengthwise the text opens and closes in mid-sentence. In it the parodistic possi-bilities of quotation are worked out with great brilliance and a kind of sardonic brio.

'Dissemination' goes less far. It does not always separate off quotations by marks or italics, nor always fuss over them with imperatives such as 'ne vous éloignez plus de l'ellipse' (D, 396) ('you shall no longer stray very far from the elliptical') (D, 356) which could represent the writer's marginal note to the self or an admonition to the reader. The mimicry – Derrida uses 'vous' as does Sollers in the passages in his novel marked at their beginning with '4' – merges into allusion. So that the ceremonious placing in inverted commas of a text come from somewhere else runs into unlocalizable parroting which may be excess of humility or may be ironic distance. The locus of responsibility for bearing meaning has been disturbed: we cannot undo the statements and assign functional indices to them, as speech which is 'direct', 'oblique', 'doubly oblique', etc. If the complexity is less than *Glas*', it is still formidable. The conditional of reported speech, quotation and ironic mimicry all replicate in destabilizing fashion. But what are the implications of constantly holding up statements in inverted commas, or pincers, so to speak?

Indirect speech

Derrida has here not just located, but exploited, a major instance of the slippery nature of natural languages. It is indeed, as already mentioned, a common misapprehension about Derrida's work that he encourages what has been called, though not by him, the 'free play of the signifier'. 'Dissemination' might indeed seem to go furthest down that road, for example in a statement like 'Il n'y a plus ici aucune profondeur de sens' (D, 389) ('Here there is no longer any depth of meaning') (*D*, 350). For meaning as depth, the article implies, is derived from an 'is' which designates essence, which makes of the text something immobile created by themes. Whereas, against this, the 'is' in Sollers' novel is one of formalized substitution. Polythematicism, such as that of the critic Jean-Pierre Richard, implies Derrida, works within a horizon, created by a total reading, a closing-off of the context of determinations: 'horizon d'une parousie finale du sens enfin déchiffré, révélé, devenu présent dans la richesse rassemblée de ses déterminations' ('horizon of the final parousia of a meaning at last deciphered, revealed, made present in the rich collection of its determinations'). Whereas,

> Les *Nombres*, en tant que nombres, n'ont aucun sens . . . n'ont aucun contenu présent ou signifié. *A fortiori* aucun référent absolu. . . . Plus précisément, le moment du sens présent, leur 'contenu' n'est qu'un effet de surface, la réflexion déformée de l'écriture sur le quatrième panneau dans lequel vous tombez sans cesse, fascinés par l'apparaître, le sens, la conscience, la présence en général.
>
> (D, 389–90)

> *Numbers*, as numbers have no meaning . . . no present or signified content. And, *a fortiori*, no absolute referent. . . . More precisely, the moment of present meaning, of 'content', is only a surface effect, the distorted reflection of the writing on the fourth panel, into which you keep falling, fascinated by appearance, meaning, consciousness, presence in general.
>
> (*D*, 350–1)

Such statements have been mobilized against Derrida himself and taken as straightforward denials of sense. Yet it is not clear how far they are specifically 'about' Sollers' novel, how far generalizable. The article might be a discussion of *Nombres* as a 'new "new novel"', as one working against polythematicism as 'The double session' worked against Richard's polysemy. The slightly breathless style, the use of 'vous' in Derrida's text as in Sollers', implies indirect speech, or at least imputed speech, which appears to report Sollers' sense. Thinking about this apparent reporting is helped by Dummett's treatment of the Fregean distinction between sense and reference, and the problems of its application in *oratio obliqua*, to which I shall now turn.

Indirect speech, like intensional statement, has always seemed especially resistant to the principle of extensionality; that is, resistant (along with certain forms of modality) to the Leibnizian rule that those things are the same which can be substituted for each other without changing the truth of the whole statement, *salva veritate*. In both indirect speech and intensional statement, the way the object in the statement is considered cannot be translated out of the phrase without loss: the standard example here is that of Oedipus' wish to kill the haughty stranger, which was not a wish to kill his father, though the stranger was in fact his father (Kneale 1971: 609). One of the ways of preserving the principle of extensionality, which guarantees homogeneity and substitutability in language, is to work with the distinction between 'use' and 'mention', to indicate the difference between using a word and pointing to the actual word as a reference. 'Mention', then, in principle, is supposed to mark off a word or statement by inverted commas, and such a statement is in fact treated in such an analysis by some philosophers as if it were a collection of symbols rather than an articulation of senses. The use of inverted commas here is then a prophylactic. But intensional statements even thus treated cannot be acceptably translated; any translation or rewording relies on treating the statements inside the inverted commas as being used as well as mentioned – precisely, both as designating what would be the ordinary sense of the phrase and using it (*ibid.*: 607). Derrida's complex and apparently over-liberal use of inverted commas (or italics, for that matter) seems to be making the same point.

Dummett's interpretation starts from the fact that meaning for Frege is not merely associating something in the world with a word or expression; specification of reference does not exhaust meaning. The linguistic expression picks out the thing in the world (which doesn't have to be an item, an object, but is extra-linguistic), doing so by means of its own sense – the sense is the route to the referent (IFP, 46). Reference here is a kind of terminal, not necessarily pre-existing, which is arrived at by the route of the sense. Now, in direct speech, two expressions having the same reference may be substituted for each other without changing the truth value of the sentence (if something can be truly said of the referent with one expression, it can be so using the other). But this is not true of indirect speech, which thus seems to constitute an area where the principle of extensionality (whereby if two terms are equivalent and a predicate can be attached to one, then it can be attached to the other) does not hold. Frege developed his distinction between sense and reference to give an account of the way different senses may have the same reference – his famous example is the fact that 'the evening star' and 'the morning star' both refer to the planet Venus – and thus how, when that is discovered, we really learn something about non-linguistic as well as linguistic matters.[34] The problem is then to know what the reference of a phrase in reported speech is. Frege argues that it is in fact its sense that, as Dummett puts it, what we are picking out to refer to in such speech is in fact the route by which we would get to the referent in direct speech, the aspect under which it is being considered. So reported speech refers not to an 'object' or 'state of affairs' in the world, but to the sense of the expression, and Frege in fact called 'indirect sense' the sense of the expression in reported speech, distinct from that in direct speech (IFP, 89).

From this it might seem that with double reported speech (*X* said that *Y* said that . . .) we would need an indexed hierarchy of indirect senses of indirect senses of expressions. But Dummett's work on Frege has moved the distinction in a different direction, by making an expression in reported speech have the same sense as in direct speech but a different referent – its ordinary sense. In other words, within indirect speech the same expression gives both sense and reference. And an expression in double *oratio obliqua* has the same sense as single *oratio obliqua* and as direct speech but its referent is the single *oratio obliqua*'s sense, and the latter's referent is the piece of direct speech's sense (FPL, 268–9). The infinite embedding of indirect sense in indirect sense, which Frege seemed to call for, is thus avoided. But there is more. In this account of reported speech, and since 'no sense can be given save as the sense of some particular expression', an expression in indirect speech has a covert (or overt) reference to an expression whose sense it refers to, 'stands for' in direct speech (IFP, 91). An expression in indirect speech thus refers to the sense of that expression in direct speech as well as bearing the sense in the indirect speech. But it is the same expression which refers to the sense and bears it. The expression in indirect speech in some way refers to itself.[35] Dummett's extremely subtle analysis throws light on what is going on in Derrida's text. That it should do so is not surprising, given their common if attenuated roots in intuitionism. The constant, almost obsessive attention Derrida pays to the status of his linguistic expressions is obvious but difficult to get hold of beyond that general remark. Dummett's work enables a kind of purchase on Derrida's use of indirect speech (whether with the conditional as reporting tense, or in oblique quotation, which he employs a great deal). That imbricated expressions in some way refer to themselves; that the sense of the same expression in direct and indirect speech may remain the same but the reference in indirect speech refers not to a state of affairs but to that sense (whether in direct or indirect speech, since they are the same); all these give some shading to a particular feature of Derrida's writing and of his philosophic interests: its insistent linguistic attention to the aspects under which any subject is considered, its strong sense of the striated modalities in any language use.

There is a further complication, to be discussed in the final chapter: we cannot understand a sense without the means of expressing it; but two expressions may have the same sense. Derrida's use of indirect speech seems to me to extend or play on this analysis by having as an important feature an insecurity: the senses, direct and indirect, are the same, but the expressions might not be.[36] The actual expression in indirect speech in some way foregrounds itself, not by way of its component words *qua* words, but in that any substitution for the expression is insecure, and understanding this is what it is to understand indirect speech.

Now, works like *Glas* and 'Dissemination' use direct speech, quotation and indirect speech in a way that makes them hard, if not impossible, to prise apart. Indeed, 'Dissemination' claims that Sollers' novel, like Mallarmé's poetry, causes us to witness a generalized placing of inverted commas round the literary text, doubling it, so to speak, turning it into 'a simulacrum' (D, 323; *D*, 291).[37] Use and mention are not separated cleanly. Moreover, there is nothing in Derrida's article 'Dissemination', for example, which guarantees that we know where we have got to on the scale of quotation – we may be reading reported speech, and reported speech within reported speech without knowing it. (There is a long literary tradition for this: compare, for instance, the main character's defence of obscene language in *Jacques le fataliste*, by Diderot, which turns out to be a verbatim quotation from the more respectable writer Michel de Montaigne.) Indeed its implications go far beyond, and are much more interesting than, any injection of doubt as to which voice is speaking, as to the locus of the bearer of the act of enunciation. For the texts become complex layerings of commentary, where precisely the aspect under which the phrase is being considered is being pointed to, and the expression designates its sense as well as bears it. But that sense is also the indirect sense and indirect reference of the expression we are reading, though the expression may or may not coincide with expressions used by Sollers, which expressions accordingly may or may not be absent to intuition.

Now these possibilities are indeterminable but they are determinate. Already in 1971, Derrida made clear that he is in no way suggesting that we do without the distinction between sense and reference, and argues that what is needed is a different determination of their effects.[38] What in his earlier work was a critique of historicism, which he made without recourse to stable or eternal values, becomes, as we shall see, especially in the altercation with the philosopher John Searle, precisely a search for such a determination. By 'effect', Derrida seems to imply that sense, or ideality, is short-hand for formations which are integrated in a more diffuse set-up.

It looks as if for Derrida no use of a word, no phrase, can be cleanly distinguished from quotation. His ideas of *neonymy* and *paleonymy*, previously discussed, suggest this – words are held to drag with them a nimbus from their former contexts. Dummett's analysis of Frege in dealing with indexicality and *oratio obliqua* shows that the latter is operating with two views of sense, one as a mode of presentation, and one as a major component of conventional significance (what a speaker must know about the expression to determine its referent) (IFP, 103).[39] (The term in traditional logic for devices pointing to the different modes of presentation was *reduplicatio*, one version of the subject of this chapter, and reduplication is an essential device in Derrida's writing.[40]) For Derrida, it is as if the sense of a word is indeed precisely its former contexts; but these cannot form such conventional significance, for they cannot be totalized into a protocol which regulates their use completely. As if in some infinite dictionary, when the word is combined into an expression, it also tends to stand for, to refer to those senses from other contexts. That at least would be true, it seems to me, of some of the strange formations in his own writing – *pharmakon*, *différance*, for instance, which by their strangeness, their italics, are like quotations. This suggestion is also confirmed by the strange circulation of vocabulary between his work and that of some of his contemporaries, already mentioned à propos Deleuze. It is interesting in this respect to note how much, in Derrida's work, even the unit of significance is constantly changing. The very construction of some of his articles might seem to confirm this – for example, 'The double session' with its strange changes in the rhythm of argument, and thus in the reader's sense of the size and nature of the elements being placed in it. So that the reader who picks out the types of duplication in the practice of quotation, or the pivoting phrases, or the indirect speech, needs also to pick out the doubling which is going on at an even more general level in the text.

Parody of/and philosophy

Statements in 'Dissemination' are flying over, based on, indeed partially replicating, a novel which deliberately sets up chains of meaning which are only partial and incomplete, and which, Derrida implies, in a kind of parody of the novel's frenzy, plethorize sense (D, 405; *D*, 364–5). But nevertheless, as we have seen above, the novel in its systematic construction as well as in its themes, suggests the taking over by a machine of psychic activity and writing, so that the proliferation seems to be mechanically generated and not the result of any deeper 'spontaneity' or 'creativity'. Indeed, this thematization in the novel of the psychic activity of writing could itself be the machine. The novel could be describing itself. But in that case we would have merely moved up a notch in the process of description of the process, from plethora to automatic generation, neither of which allows for conscious and full control of the process. More and more as one reads Derrida's article, the account of sense, the account of subjectivity, appear as an unflagged, or hardly flagged, critique of Sartre, and have to be read in that context. This has already been suggested above, where we saw that Derrida called the 'taking place', which implies a present moment of an utterance or an uttering, an 'illusion' (a necessary one, but still, see above) since both utterance or uttering are open to non-presence, to what is unintuitable. So that the idea of act as something which takes place in the world and is assumed by a consciousness at the moment of action is an illusion also. Later in 'Dissemination', consciousness itself is in constant exfoliation, constantly moving and disturbing that totalizing which creates meaning for subjectivity, and which is an illusion of consciousness (D, 405; *D*, 364–5).

Now Sartre had countenanced the possibility that the truth about a 'person' might be plural, but had argued that his work on Flaubert would establish connections and 'profound homogeneity'. (Once more, it becomes clear that at stake in all this is the very nature and possibility of connection itself; a question which must be left until the final chapter of this book.) This Derrida contests. He contests it in part through the nature of language, for repetition of the 'same' words in different contexts, though it is what makes language possible, yet makes stable identity of those words impossible. And, contrarily, since identity is a two-place function, not the same as sameness, it is only through repetition that identity can be possible, that we can say that something *is* something (identity is not sameness, for you learn something from an identity). For the unique cannot be classified, cannot be known: 'L'unique – ce qui ne se répète pas – n'a pas d'unité puisqu'il ne se répète pas. . . . L'unique est donc l'apeiron' (D, 405) ('The unique – that which is not repeated – has no unity since it is not repeated. . . . The unique is thus the *apeiron*') (D, 365). Earlier, in *Origin of Geometry*, the 'pure facticité existentielle comme singularité sauvage' ('pure existential [existentielle] factuality as wild singularity') had been called the *apeiron*, that is the limitless, the infinite (OG, 169 note; *OG*, 151 note 184). Sartre constitutes the individual kernel as that which is unrepeatably singular and as that which threatens repeatability, which is excluded from the generation of meaning because meaning implies generality and thus repeatability (I follow the interpretation of Frank (1983: 461, 555) in which Frank relates the Sartrean individual to Derrida's *différance*; see below).

In *Dissemination* then there is a covert criticism of Sartre's 'universel singulier'. Sartre, we have seen, denies that his investigations on Flaubert might have as final result merely disparate layers of experience irreducible one to the other, or that Flaubert's experience might be irremediably heterogeneous. On the contrary, there will be a final whole which makes such irreducibility merely an appearance. A human is never an individual, but a 'universel singulier' created out of reciprocal totalizations: 'Totalisé et, par là même, universalisé par son époque, il la retotalise en se reproduisant en elle comme singularité. Universel par l'universalité de l'histoire humaine, singulier par la singularité universalisante de ses projets' ('Totalized and thus universalized by his epoch, he retotalizes it in reproducing himself in it by the universalizing singularity of his projects') (Sartre 1971: 7, my translation). Derrida uses a cryptic reference to Sartre, and a phrase which is syntactically unstable, to undo this account: 'Singulier pluriel qu'aucune origine singulière n'aura jamais précédé' (D, 337) ('It is a singular plural, which no single origin will ever have preceded') (D, 304). The syntactic instability, by engendering a hesitation between which term might be adjective and which noun, between the singular as strange plural or as plural singularity, and placing this at the head of a denial that any term can be the origin, for all terms are plural, enacts a criticism both of Sartre's notion of 'totalization' and of the idea of person who is performing and focusing such a closure.

In the interest of retaining the (human) subject of an action and an action occurring at a definite moment, Manfred Frank has here performed a symptomatic massaging of the Derridean text. He attempts to identify 'singulier pluriel' with *différance*, as an *element* which resists classification.[41] Then, through the Greek *idios* played on in Sartre's title to his work on Flaubert

L'Idiot de la famille . . . – the proper, the particular to one, and the private – Frank develops Sartre's *universel singulier* towards his own concept of the *individual*. And thus in a gesture which other critics of Derrida have performed before him,[42] he links the individual with *différance* (both, he says, are conditions of possibility for the permanence of social and symbolic orders; both form the foundations of these by a movement of retreat from them; both are pure negatednesses with no core of self-identity (Frank 1983: 464). The individual is for Frank what is unrepeatable. Thus *différance* like 'individuality' can perform the task Frank really wants it to perform, which is to safeguard the integrity of the person, and the ideas of irreducibility and freedom.

With this manoeuvre, Frank points to a site of controversy for critics of Derrida's work, the problem of the (human) subject. In an attempt to forge or force a link with existentialist ethics, Frank, in my view the only critic to have discussed this in depth, suggests, following Sartre, that the individual (in the neuter) is the non-meaningful element excluded from the 'signifiying arsenal' of language and culture. It is this exclusion, and the way it makes of the individual as excluded that which is not even itself, since it is not stabilizable into what may be repeated in orderly fashion, in a universal set of relations, in language, which explains how the order of the general and the basis in ideas of that order are constituted at all (Frank 1983: 463–4). (The individual almost becomes in his description a Mephistophelian 'spirit which always negates'.) But Frank also maintains, using additional material not published in the *Course in General Linguistics*, that Saussure made of the distinguishing of unities in discourse an active process, and of *parole*, the engenderer of change in language, the product of individual activity. Frank maintains against 'Dissemination' that sense derives from acts of interpretation; the mark is only a system of relationships, on which meaning must then be conferred (ultimately by an active individual human), when all's done it is nothing without the interpreter and his or her act. Like Sartre in his reaction to a psychoanalyst's tape (Sartre 1972), Frank insists that language is not a process, but a giving of meaning at a point of time through an act. The 'individual', however negatively described, becomes thus much more like the traditional concept of the subject.

Fundamental here is the problem of what kind of entity a term like 'individual' or 'différance' designates. This problem comes to a head with the interpretation of Derrida's *restance*, which will be discussed in the next sections. The nature of the problem will however be mentioned here, because *restance* encapsulates clearly the questions often raised by Derrida's characteristic lexemes. It is indicative that where Frank summarizes a very difficult page and defines *restance*'s purpose in Derrida's argument as the 'minimal identity' of a sign necessary for it to function (LI, 104–5; Frank 1983: 552), the page actually says that *restance* is 'linked to the minimal possibility of *remark* – remark being, quickly and for our purposes, re-use. Now Derrida insists that the identity of a sign is always divided. A 'minimal identity' is not possible, then, in the sense of 'identity' to which the adjective 'minimal' could be attached.[43] The problem thus becomes, how this is to be thought. Frank defines this as two possibilities: either make of *restance non-présente* and other formulations a minimal identity, or deny even momentary signification, which is to deny meaning and is absurd (Frank 1983: 549). But since Derrida repeats many times in 'Limited Inc *a b c . . .*' (1977) his insistence on the divided identity, the alteration in the very heart of the repetition, the first Frankian option is not consonant with the text. Rather than turn immediately to Frank's second option, there seem to be two other possibilities: either argue that the paradoxical formulation is like a piece of intellectual sticking plaster, introduced when the argument is coming to a halt in contradiction; or follow through what it means. If the latter path is taken, *restance* cannot be thought of as an element or entity; the two parts of the 'paradoxical' *restance non-présente* have to be taken together. I shall show in the next chapter that ultimately it is the structure of the moment of time that is at stake here for Derrida. To sum up, whereas Frank is taking 'identity' as a minimal element (just as he wishes to relate 'différance' to 'individual', which however negatively defined by him is still an element), I shall argue later that *restance* is the name for a paradoxical structuring in the possibility of meaning itself.

But first, the very distinction between active and passive is being resited, reworked by Derrida. As will be shown, the very notion of pre-existing subjectivities, which can then act on objects, is queered or queried – what is happening is not the destruction of the subject, but its deconstruction. Against Sartre he will urge: 'Un langage a précédé ma présence à moi-même' (D, 378) ('My own presence to myself has been preceded by a language') (D, 340); like Lacan, for Derrida subjectivity is dependent on, that is arises out of, language. But language is not thereby merely constraining, with the human user passively determined by it. No more is the user actively interpreting passive data. Rather, determining and being determined, active and passive, mingle as they do in the Greek middle voice. Derrida fully exploits the possibilities available through French reflexive verbs; he plays with their power in French to hover between the passive and the active, to suggest a kind of textual reflexivity which is not that of the mirror: 'Les *Nombres* s'énumèrent, s'écrivent et se lisent' (D, 322) ('These *Numbers* enumerate themselves, write themselves, read themselves') (D, 290). And if Sollers is teasingly reminded (through his family name, Joyaux, which he does not use to sign his books) that no authorship of a traditional sort, anyway, can be claimed for the novel (D, 365; D, 328–9), immediately there is a re-propriation for this expropriation: 'la puissance d'expropriation ne se produit jamais comme telle mais dans l'altération des effets de propriété' (D, 368) ('the power of expropriation never produces itself as such but only arises through an alteration of the effects of property') (D, 331). A new voice arises, not that of the author, but one where rhythm can provide a no-longer-personal subjectivity (D, 369–70; D, 331–2).

There is, then, in this article, a two-way irony. Philosophical themes: existence, the nature of meaning, the subject, are brought to bear on the explication of a novel which itself makes out of these very themes illusions; but the very 'arithmetical machinery' (*D*, 325) of the novel is also being revved up, and perhaps slightly overheated into parody. Out of this come sketches for what might be meant by 'meaning', by 'text', by 'subject', which are more fragile and impermanent than those of tradition, and where, above all, they are resultants of process and not kernels or elements. They have a status which is not that of building block, however small, or negatively defined, but of non-lasting operation. But if one tries to think this through, the question of what there is for one to be able to talk of an operation at all is tricky. If the processes keep changing, so must the resultants, and the only unity will be that of language. Derrida, we have seen, puts forward the term *restance*, glossed as 'minimal possibility' for a sign's re-use. The final sections of this chapter will try to address the question of what might be meant by this minimal possibility, of why it is defined as a possibility rather than an actual entity, and how this relates to the structure of doubling which has been the theme of this chapter.

The modality of quotation

To start by returning to the problem of quotation and indirect speech: expressions within reported speech are in several crucial ways like expressions of modality, that is, phrases which begin with 'it is necessary that . . . ' or 'it is possible that . . . ' or equivalent. Both make statements about propositions ('he said that *P*', 'it is possible that *P*') and they both seem to constitute threats to the principle of extensionality. And both, as will be seen later, can be apparently infinitely doubled – 'it is possible that it is necessary that *X*' is a well formed sentence, just as is 'he said that he said that he said . . . '. It has been suggested above that one of the functions of indirect speech in Derrida is to foreground the problematic relation between mode of presentation, referent and expression. It is from such a position that Derrida voices suspicion of the notion of code, no doubt because of the implied binarism it carries with it (original/encoded), but also because it may mislead us about the nature of meaning. In a 1971 conference on communication, Derrida read a paper ('Signature event context', in *Margins of Philosophy*, 1972b; trans. 1982) which explicitly broke away from semiotic models. It argued that communication can always fail, that no code is unbreakable (both in the sense of failing to observe it, and in the sense of deciphering it). In the last two sections he illustrated this by discussing the particular rhythm adopted by the English philosopher J. L. Austin in his development of an account of 'how to do things with words'.[44] Austin had pointed out that many utterances are more than statements – they are what he called 'performatives': social actions, of promising, naming, cursing; but, says Derrida, he had difficulties in enumerating and then legislating for the way in which such acts may go wrong – for example, because we are not the right person to do the act, because we are quoting, or because we are of unsound mind. Austin needed to define the context of the pronouncement exhaustively; he needed to insist on the sincerity of the illocutor (to be sure, for example, of disallowing promises made with no intention to keep them); he needed to exclude quotation. None of this is possible absolutely in practice, for many utterances of performatives include complicated motives related to their situation which go beyond the communication of an order or a wish or whatever. Derrida argues that that impossibility should be taken into account.

John Searle (1977), who in his own work had taken Austin's searching (in both senses, probing and open-ended) discussion and tightened it, replied to the article from a base within Anglo-Saxon linguistic philosophy, but apparently without any preparation in the base from which Derrida had written, nor any sign of consciousness indeed that it might be different to his own. (The condescension in the tone of the reply, which has often been adopted by later debaters of the same persuasion, is thus rendered particularly irritating.) Derrida's attitude to Austin is much more complex than Searle realizes: he wonders why Austin, who had spoken of the 'fetish [the opposition] truth/false, and the fetish value/fact', who, he says, is closer to Nietzsche than one would expect, and who recognizes the continuous risk of failure in the performative act, yet immediately, by aiming at an ideal regulation, cordons off this risk and makes it accidental. Searle picks out four main points of disagreement: Derrida has failed to understand the token/type distinction, which is what allows for the iterability (*itérabilité*) they both agree is inherent in language; he has confused iterability with permanence; he has not understood intentionality, or Searle's version of it; he has misunderstood the kind of exclusion zone Austin placed around failed performatives.

But Searle's reply is handicapped by the fact that he himself has not grasped the status of writing in Derrida's argument – he replies by insisting that writing and speech are similar, which is exactly Derrida's point. So much so, indeed, that Derrida is arguing that the possibility of writing's performance in the absence of any empirical emitter (or indeed receiver), far from being a peculiarity of writing, is a constituting feature of sign systems. But not a necessary one – in the answer to Searle, Derrida will have to deepen his argument round the question of this possibility because Searle, generalizing what he takes to be Derrida's point, objects that absence of emitter or receiver is not necessary in writing (I can write a note to myself). The disagreement between them in fact turns on a modal problem, as we shall see, that of the relation of 'necessary' to 'always possibly not'.[45]

Both are agreed, as Derrida points out in his reply 'Limited Inc *a b c . . .*' (1977), where the ink has not in fact been spared, that iterability is in some way essential to language. Searle argues that Derrida has, in his notion of writing, confused permanence with iterability: the fact that, like any system of representation, writing can be repeated, has nothing to do with its permanence. What is at stake between them is the question of generality of idealization.[46] For Derrida, all discourse is marked by 'iterability' in that, however deeply embedded in the context or processes of its circumstances of production, it is repeatable in other circumstances applicable elsewhere. This follows from his work on Husserl's *Origin of Geometry*, and needs to be briefly expounded in order to understand both how Derrida follows Husserl and goes beyond him.

Derrida shows how Husserl strove to develop the thought of a geometrical truth independent of the particular culture and particular languages in which it had arisen, accessible to future mathematicians not belonging to that culture, and repeatable by them. This independence, however, turned out to be also transcendental dependence, because if it is to be objective, the truth needs the possibility of language in general, and it is writing which will allow this object-ivity to be absolute. Writing is the prime example of 'communication sur le mode virtuel' (OG, 186) ('communication become virtual') (*OG*, 164), when the originator may be dead and the receptor unavailable. In other words, the purity of possibility is raised a degree. It is at this point that Derrida quotes Hyppolite on the possibility of a subject-less transcendental field, out of which the subject could be constituted, and remarks that writing constitutes such a field (OG, 84–5; *OG*, 88) (see Chapter 5). It is exactly this possibility which is objectivity, argues Derrida. This possibility of functioning for a transcendental subject *in general* is the same as being able to do without any actual writer or reader. So that in *Origin of Geometry*, as in 'Signature event context', Derrida suggests that the very value of transcendentality, and thus the correlative tran-scendental subjectivity, are made possible by writing functioning as a transcendental field ('La valeur ou l' "effet" de transcendantalité se lie néces-sairement à la possibilité de l'écriture') (M, 375) ('The value or effect of transcendentality is linked necessarily to the possibility of writing') (*M*, 316).[47] Now Husserl in *Origin of Geometry* translated by Derrida says that mathematics is not 'spatio-temporally individualized') (OG, 180; *OG*, 160–1). Yet a geomet-rical object is discovered by one or more spatio-temporally individual minds: how then does it become the kind of ideal entity unique to mathematics, identi-cally repeatable through the ages, when for example tools, or 'works of architecture' (Husserl's example here is a strange one), exist as multiples?[48] It is through 'linguistic incarnation' that geometry becomes intrapersonal, for when formulated in language it is formulated for others. It becomes part of the 'communauté d'intropathie et [la] communauté de langage' (OG, 185) ('a community of empathy and of language') (*OG*, 163), which enables this geometrical ideality to be communicated as objectively valid, and it is writing as an opening to others, in time as well as space, which 'perfectly constitutes' this objectivity.

But such an objectivity is nevertheless constituted by a language, which is not ideal but actual, which is spatio-temporally located: how can this be 'reduced', and pure ideality made possible? Through each geometer reaching back beyond the reiterated formations that constitute the geometrical tradition and reactivating the original intentions of the geometrizing. Such language and such writing free the sense of the mathematical discovery from the circum-stances of its origin; they make it historical purely and not contingently – that is as a matter of its essence, not of accident – by making it virtual, that is, available in the absence of the discoverer. The access they afford is in fact the possibility of repeating the original insight – the productive activity of repeating the theorem matches the memory of the theorem as produced by others, and the evidence of their identity is obtained. Iterability then is the very foundation of meaning for Husserl: it guarantees that 'mondanity' – the formula's attachment to specific language, time, and place – will be stripped away, reduced, and ideality achieved.[49] But through the ineradicable reference to community and the subjectivity of others, to language, writing and time, Husserl, as was shown in the previous chapter, has also allowed that the intuition which might fill the intention is not there. The question debated with Searle is what that 'not there' might mean.

As has been said, for Derrida in 'Signature, event, context', there is possible absence of both empirical originator and receiver; and this possible absence of empirical source and terminus in language is precisely what has been meant by the transcendental, constituting the constraining *a priori* conditions, the very possibility of objectification (M, 375; *M*, 315–16). This is why there cannot be a private language; language just is the possibility of repetition and thus decoding, of transference of a word or phrase out of one context and into another whose intentional field is hitherto unrelated. Searle uses the 'token/type' distinction, of Anglo-Saxon philosophy to disagree: the iterability for him is possible for a quite different reason, because of the stable form, the type, which is instantiated many times over by the token. However, his use of the token/type distinction, and of the idea that any linguistic act-token is programmed by conventions, produces no account of change in meaning, since while rules govern speech acts, linking type to token, there seems no way within the account for a reverse movement, for token acts to change rules, though they undoubtedly do. For that to happen, the token act has to be retrospectively treated as type, its deviation retrospectively cancelled. For Searle defines rule-governed behaviour as that in which deviations are recognized to be 'somehow wrong or defective' (Searle 1969: 42).

Iterability in Derrida's article is a process which is one of change – he points out that 'iter', again, and 'alter', other, are philologically related. To be repeatable is to be alterable, which is why it is incorrect to say that Derrida confuses permanence and iterability. How may this be argued?

First, iterability means that meaning cannot be merely context-bound. For Searle (1969: 45) meaning is a matter of convention as well as intention, of the application of context-rules as well as linguistic rules. These rules are in fact conditions and determine speech acts.[50] But for Derrida, no context can be 'a protocol of a code' (M, 376; *M*, 316).[51] Language is segmental, constituted by spacing, and, he argues, these segments can always be re-sited in another context far from the originating context and thus, in Searlean terms, from the rule-conventions which governed their original use. Quotation becomes an extreme case of what any language utterance does – recontextualize (providing quotation is seen as working with both use and mention, so that a mentioned expression may also be used).[52] The ability to stand free of originating context as of originator simply *is* what makes linguistic signs, spoken or written. The separation of token and type implies, however, that what stands free is of a different category, a repeatable form, not an embodied example. It is at this point of the argument, as he asks whether this disembodiment is possible, that Derrida uses the word *restance*, which Searle took to mean 'permanence', but which is a neologism, coined from the present participle of *rester*, and referring to *reste* (remainder) without being identical with it (in this sense it relates to and relays the term *trace*). It is the 'minimal possibility', says Derrida, of re-using a sign (LI, 105; *LI*, 53) (not 'minimal identity', see above).

Does it serve, then, like 'type' or like Saussure's *langue* to explain how within the empirical diversity (of idiosyncratic pronunciation or usage) we recognize a word? It may perform something of the same function, but only in a loose sense. As a minimal and limited idealization (LI, 120; *LI*, 61), *restance* does not refer to the category of a 'type' because it makes possible 'identity and difference at the same time' (LI, 105; *LI*, 53). Once more we have the radical reworking of the *eidos*, as seen throughout this chapter in different guises:

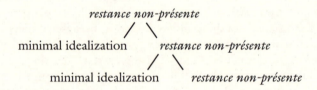

Of *iterability* we are told that it cannot be the genus for which quotation or other phenomena are the species (LI, 85; *LI*, 100), as *différance* could not be for *pharmakon*. The 'restance non-présente', as Derrida calls it, and as we have seen above, appears paradoxical, for while it is 'a minimal idealization', it is not to be a form, a type, or any stable entity – the very possibility of recontextualizing, or of fictionalizing, Derrida says, renders stability of essence impossible. Its implication of both identity and difference is not just a fact – that any instance of repetition is a different instance from the preceding one, even if the instances are 'identical' (which is structurally a two-place relation). The very notion, we will see, cuts across the distinctions, that between fact and relation, and that between contingency and permanence. It does this because at the basis of the possibility of an item or element, of fact as of relation, is temporality. The possibility of there being a 'restance' is the possibility already explored by Derrida (G, 92; *G*, 63) of the 'originary synthesis' being 'retention dans l'unité minimale de l'expérience temporelle'; any point in time is a relation, created out of a temporal crossing over between protentions, movement into the future, and retentions, referrings back into the past.[53] This synthesis, this 'minimal unity of temporal experience' will be further explored in the next chapter.

Reiterated modalities

This idealization without *eidos* is formed, then, in the crossings of temporality, making of each point at the crossing of past and future a relation between the different and the same; the *restance*, like the moment, is the relation of being both the same and different which is the basis of time (LI, 120; *LI*, 61). Now, the process where what he has called *restance* emerges, that is, *iterability*, has a similar structure, by virtue of its relation to possibility. For Husserl (and Searle) idealization is an intentional unity. Derrida, however, explores the 'able' of *iterable*, to argue that language in its repetition never guarantees fulfilled intention – on the contrary, the fact that it is always possible that the original intention is lost, or not fulfilled in being repeated, is part of the structure of language, and has to be built into any account of it (as the *restance* was *non-présente*). Derrida's argument turns in fact on the interpretation of this 'always possibly not'. The possibility of the intention in meaning not being fulfilled is no accident (LI, 96; *LI*, 48). Possibility of absence, he says, is not a negative of presence (and thus discountable). 'Always possibly not present' is analysed implicitly by Derrida as 'necessarily possibly not', in a reiteration, a replication of modalities which cannot be left aside. The possibility of absence is structural, a necessary part of the analysis of iterability – it cannot be side-stepped as an accident that might never happen. The 'accidental infelicity' cannot be waved aside in the interest of idealization – idealization just is that possibility, since it is because a linguistic sign can be used in a different context that it is a sign at all.

This movement back to a common root, this movement upstream prior to the 'decision' (here between 'serious' and 'non-serious' illocutionary act or between successful performative and performative flawed through accidental infelicity) we have met before. The *racine*, the root of iterability, is double and cannot be simplified without cost (indeed, without prompting a search for motives (LI, 168; *LI*, 90). The double root – iterability as a basis for identity/iterability as a proliferating ragged set of duals – is a repeat and a relay of the double form, the double memory discussed earlier in the chapter. And in that the double root makes possible, it helps to explain the phrase 'always already' – if the factical appears out of the virtual, then the 'virtual' is in one sense already there. It becomes clearer now why doubles should appear. There is no absolute beginning for an event, cut off from what precedes. So that a clear distinction between what happens and what does not happen becomes difficult:[54] 'Ce qui rend possible la possibilité (éventuelle), c'est ce qui la fait arriver avant même qu'elle n'arrive comme événement au sens courant' (LI, 113) ('What makes the (eventual) possibility possible is what makes it happen even before it happens as an actual event (in the standard sense)') (*LI*, 57).[55] But this is immediately equated to what prevents any event happening fully. In some sense the possible occurs as a possibility before occurring as an event, and as an event is never fully actualized. A sharp distinction between act and set of enabling circumstances for the act is rendered difficult by such an argument. What is there and what is not there, in the ordinary sense, are not complementary sets. (Hence Derrida's interest in ghosts, thought of not as some kind of objects, but as traces like *restes*. This might be compared to the modal logician A. N. Prior's resistance to not-yet, or indeed, under one model, to ceased-to-be existent objects, Prior 1957: 30–1.)

But Derrida speaks of 'the general space of their possibility' (M, 390; *M*, 327) where the usual elements in speech act theory (intentions, performative, event) are *not* opposed to their contraries in the sense of excluding them, but presuppose the possibility of lack of intention, and failure of act 'in dissymmetric fashion'. Such an opposition should rather be embedded in what Derrida on several occasions in *Limited Inc.* calls 'structural possibility'. (LI, 96, 112; *LI*, 48, 57).[56] An integration of such possibility will have paradoxical results, Derrida has already agreed (D, 194; *D*, 167–8).

Having spoken of the suffix 'able', the 'iter' of 'iterability' needs reexamination. For Searle, this is part of the 'recursiveness' of language; a rule or code applied to the linguistic phenomena means that the identity of units from one occasion to another is guaranteed. But Derrida puts this in doubt.[57] Recursivity for him is not a machine, for iteration implies identity and difference. If words were merely identical tokens of the same type, would it make sense, for example, to enquire so narrowly into their use as both philosophers and literary critics do? To which is added the differential relation of each term to the other elements in the language. So the element, the unit of discourse, is a differential structure. How then do we identify anything at all (if we do not have at our disposal the distinction token/type)? By a limit process: 'restance minimale (comme une idéalisation minimale quoique limitée) pour que l'identité même soit répétable et identifiable *dans*, *à travers*, et même *en vue de* l'altération' (LI, 105) ('a minimal remainder (as well as a minimum of idealization) in order that the identity of the *selfsame* be repeatable and identifiable *in*, *through*, and even *in view of* its alteration') (*LI*, 53). It is precisely this minimalization which makes language possible, as we have seen, and it is writing, the 'graphème', which most clearly points to this characteristic. The never-closed identity of the element which provides sense makes a route to the referent, but the reference in the world and to things is never completed.

> Parce que la structure même de la marque (par exemple le minimum d'itérabilité requise) interdit l'hypothèse de l'idéalisation, à savoir l'adéquation d'un *meaning* à lui même ... l'itérabilité permet l'idéalisation, donc une certaine identité répétable, indépendante des événements factuels dans leur multiplicité – mais elle limite l'idéalisation qu'elle permet, elle l'*entame*.
>
> (LI, 119–20)

> Rather, the very structure of the mark (for example, the minimum of iterability it requires) excludes the hypothesis of idealization, that is, the adequation of a meaning to itself ... iterability makes possible idealization – and thus, a certain identity in repetition that is independent of the multiplicity of factual events – while at the same time limiting the idealization it makes possible: *broaching* and *breaching* it at once.
>
> (*LI*, 61)

It is not a convention of repetition: the minimal idealization which allows repetition is exactly what allows change and all the uses called 'parasitical' by Austin. I understand this as implying that the identity is (at least) a two-place relation: it is undermined as it is made, and this double movement structures the field of meaning, it does not take place within it.

This double movement is the 'structural possibility' that mishap may occur[58] which cuts across boundaries of necessity and possibility, essence and accidence, chance and necessity: but what does this 'structural' possibility mean? (Likewise his argument over intention, which is *not* that intention is eliminable, in spite of what is frequently said about his thought, but that it is never completely fulfilled, that it is structurally unfilled.) Derrida speaks of law, eidetic law, here: intention is always put aside (*écartée*): 'Si cet écart est sa possibilité, il n'attend pas, il ne lui survient pas comme un accident ici ou là. L'intention est *a priori* . . . différante' (LI, 111) ('If this remove is its condition of possibility, it is not an eventuality, something that befalls it here and there, by accident. Intention is *a priori* . . . *différante*') (*LI*, 56). As we have seen, 'always possible' is here equivalent to 'necessarily possible' or '*a priori* possible'. Now to say that something is possible means that something may not happen, with the time controlled by the indeterminate verb. Likewise, to say that something may not happen is to admit that it may; the point of difficulty occurs with the tense of the statement about the possibility, not the succeeding clause. 'It is always possible' that something may/may not happen does not imply anything about the time occurrence or non-occurrence of the happening; it is a statement about the nature of the possibility.

Does this make the possibility of 'mishap' or 'failure' a condition of possibility of successful performance? And what could condition of possibility imply? Derrida denies that 'iterability' is a 'condition transcendentale de possibilité' (LI, 185) ('a transcendental condition of possibility') (*LI*, 100). But yet he speaks of 'la structure de possibilité de cet énoncé' (M, 379) ('the structure of possibility of this statement') (*M*, 318), for which quotation and other phenomena would be conditioned effects. He also warns, having used the word 'law' of the structure he is describing: 'Cela ne veut pas dire que cette loi ait elle-même la simplicité du principe logique ou transcendental. On ne peut même pas parler à son sujet de fondement ou de radicalité, dans le sens philosophique traditionnel' (LI, 171) ('Which does not amount to saying that this law has the simplicity of a logical or transcendental principle. One cannot even speak of it being fundamental or radical in the traditional philosophical sense') (*LI*, 92). This is because the law is double, both limiting and permitting idealization. Yet the 'pharmakon' was a root, even if it was double, though not double in the sense of mixed, already separate, parts. After the 'decision' which occurs through but not totally within the Platonic works, *pharmakon* was assigned to one of the prongs of the double root. But, warns Derrida, 'une racine double ne peut jouer le rôle de radicalité philosophique' (LI, 171) ('twofold roots cannot play the role of philosophical radicality') (*LI*, 92). Any concept (aspiring 'upwards towards the foundations', in Austin's terms) must have its pretentions checked. Derrida has here replicated the root; here in *Limited Inc.*, the double root roots the possible.

Now the possible here, Derrida agrees with Searle, is the 'standing possibility': 'a meaningful sentence is just a standing possibility of the corresponding (intentional-)speech act', says Searle. But this possible must be taken into account, not left, precisely, standing. It is a possibility, what can turn up; but it is also, *qua* possiblity, necessary or *a priori*; it always can turn up. Though *a priori* in the temporal sense, it is not transcendental in the usual sense. The possible absence of emitter and receiver is, says Derrida, a 'condition of positive possibility of the mark, the condition of its functioning' (LI, 99; *LI*, 49).

But the discussion of iterability moves one stage further: we have seen that it limits the idealization that it permits. It is a possibility for idealization, then, but it is also what renders pure idealization impossible. It is the condition without which no meaning can be, yes, but with which it can never be complete. It is 'structurally divided and differing [différante]' (LI, 135; *LI*, 70); its structure, the structure of temporalization (LI, 120; *LI*, 61) as will be shown in the next chapter. Now *différance* was such in 'Plato's pharmacy': it was condition both of possibility and of impossibility of truth: 'Il [l'étant-présent] n'est ce qu'il est, identique et identique à soi, unique, qu'en *s'ajoutant* la possibilité d'être *répété* comme tel' (D, 194) ('[It] is not what it is, identical and identical to itself, unique, unless it *adds to itself* the possibility of being *repeated* as such so that it is "à la fois la condition de possibilité et la condition d'impossibilité de la vérité", *at once* the condition of possibility *and* the condition of impossibility of truth') (D, 168). The phrase 'condition of possibility' had been part of Kant's explanation of how a synthesis of appearances was possible and had functioned in terms of *a priori* principles of the form of experience, which gave rules, making the interconnection of experience possible through a 'completely interconnected (possible) consciousness' (KRV, A156–7, B195–6). To this phrase, Derrida often tacks its opposite: condition of impossibility. The importance of the implication of this phrase in relation to the philosophical tradition to which it belongs, its disruption of the possibility of any type of connection that rests on a possibility of unity and totality, will be discussed further in the last chapter. But in *Limited Inc.* the phrase 'condition of possibility and impossibility' does not seem to appear. It is the *necessity* of the possibility of failure of idealization, or of absence of the receiver, which is examined: a reiteration of modalities rather than their conjunction. ('Necessarily possibly not' may be rephrased as 'impossibly not {possibly not}'.) That this 'always/necessarily possibly not' represents a problem for theories is not denied, though the problem, Derrida implies, is rather one of un-limiting them by recognizing the limits they have adopted. There needs to be an incorporating into their structure of an awareness of their limits. Reiterating the modality, moving from 'possibly not' treated as a column in a truth table to an 'always possibly not' which embeds the 'possibly not' in a second-level structure is not a conjunction of opposites. The equation of the 'necessity of possibility' of a proposition and its 'possibility' is refused.[59]

The idea that there may be a necessary structure which embeds a possibly-not is not contradictory, though intuitively slightly dizzying (even more so if the embedding is continued, so that there are possibly necessarily possibles). We have returned to one part of the aporia with which the last chapter closed. In *Apories* Derrida picks up the different formulations with which Heidegger relates death and impossibility. Dasein can be identified as what it is because there is a closure of a field of investigation, operated on three levels: that of type of problem, that of humanity's concerns ('anthropological') and that of concept (AP, 78). Derrida argues that it is death that holds these three closures together in these sections of *Sein und Zeit*: anthropology can close off its field of problems for investigation only if the concept of death is given to it by the existential analytic of Dasein (AP, 85). Death or our relation to it is what makes possible for Heidegger questions about conditions of possibility – so it founds the search for foundations. But it is also what unsettles such demarcations, argues Derrida, it is at once constituting and outside the jurisdiction of what it constitutes: 'Un "la-vie-la-mort" qui ne tombe plus sous le cas de ce qu'il rend possible' (AP, 87) ('A "Life/death" which is no longer under the regime of what it makes possible') (my translation); as the *pharmakon* opened the possibility of oppositions (good/bad, true/false, essence/appearance) which did not contain it (D, 118; D, 103). Here relation to death has been subsumed in a strange and non-Heideggerian phrase, encapsulating as opposed the terms of the relation 'life/death'.[60] It is the underivable character of death for Heidegger that makes him opt for finitude as the primordial character of Dasein. Yet Derrida's contradiction encapsulated in the phrase 'life/death' points to what in Heidegger, within the same set of phrases, is ambiguous. Derrida's phrase, its juxtaposition and use of the slash, syntactically lodges aporia in the potentiality for being that is death for Dasein, a potentiality Heidegger says to be without relation, absolute – *unbezüglich*.

There follows Derrida's analysis of the reiterated modalities with which Heidegger describes death for Dasein: 'Death is the possibility of the absolute [*schlechthinnig*] impossibility of Dasein' (SZ, 250; BT, 294); but then also in terms of 'understanding [this possibility] as *the possibility of the impossibility of any existence at all*' (SZ, 262; BT, 307). The most proper potentiality for Dasein, death is the possibility of the impossibility of relating to anything. The expressions, Derrida points out, tremble between a contradiction between possible and impossible, that must be endured, and the reiteration of modalities: the sense that death, the unique case, is where the impossible may possibly appear as such for Dasein, the only creature capable of this appearance, the only creature capable of truth and non-truth. The movement between contradiction of possible and impossible and their embedded reiteration make what is defining of Dasein. (This part of *Apories* extends the last pages of *Speech and Phenomena*, by working over its thinking of death both as what makes possible the appearance to finite being of indefinite differance and as empirical accident.)

But Derrida does not stop this pattern at the second reiteration: he asks what difference there is between the possibility of the appearing as such of the possibility of an impossibility, and the impossibility of appearing as such of the possibility of an impossibility (AP, 131). This reiteration makes insecure the conditions of possibility which the uniqueness of Dasein's relation to death was founding, but not it seems to me by adjoining, in the same dimension so to speak, the equivalent of 'conditions of impossibility'. The interference is multipolar, the embedded levels loop disturbingly between the logic of appearance, of possibility, and of the implications of the phrase 'as such'. What indeed is the difference between the possibility of the appearing as such of the possibility of the impossibility of Dasein existing . . . and the impossibility of the appearing of the possibility . . . ; for if the impossibility of existing can be possible for Dasein, then it is an impossibility appearing as such, that is, too close for comfort to that disappearance of a relation to death which is the mark of inauthentic being. And with this the relation to death which marked off Dasein from other creatures is made unreliable as a frontier, and itself is plunged into an empirical historical tradition, that of the fall, and into the reinscription of theological motifs into Heideggerian philosophy, however startlingly different the latter is from the tradition.

This chapter has sought to show the radical reworking of the notion of form, of *eidos*, that goes on in this part of Derrida's work. Derrida is quite clear about the effects of this: it prevents an accident being (nothing but) an accident; for even if in fact it never happens or only happens once, the possibility of its occurring, or being repeated, is an essential part of the structure which will give an account of meaning (LI, 96; *LI*, 19–20). 'Repetition', 'iterability', 'pharmakon', 'difference', 'writing', are the root, the medium, into which it is folded. These lexemes in their different ways point to a circuit of argument, which is an aporia. They make possible what at the same time they make impossible. But there is more. If *différance*, *pharmakon*, and above all *death* are part of what Derrida at different points in his works refers to as 'a more powerful logic' or 'a different logic' (AP, 87), a claim which will be considered again in the final chapter, they are part of an argument which does not rest with contradiction of an equipoised pair of opposites, of conditions of possibility and impossibility. The simple if paradoxical closure so suggested cannot take place, because the reiteration of modalities is not stopped at any one point. But neither are they strictly imbricated like Russian dolls. The aporia is multilayered: it is, as the title of Derrida's recent work suggests, aporias.

The next chapter will again take up the question of *restance*. We have a 'minimal idealization' necessary for iterability and meaning, yet one paradoxical in its being a 'non-present remainder'. The present chapter has suggested that this paradox is not cheaply bought, as critics sometimes imply, but summarizes the structure of reiterated possibility, the 'always- [i.e. necessarily-] possibly-not-fulfilled intention' at work in meaning, not just because receiver or emitter need not be there, but because there are always structural 'commitments to meaning' (the phrase is Tom Baldwin's[61]) with any statement which reaches out into the future, as they do back into the past, before it was made. The matrix of this 'always possibly not' is then time.

3 Strange attractors
Singularities

What attracts us has already granted us arrival.[1]

Circuits of argument

The preceding chapter showed that Derrida's characteristic lexemes, *pharmakon* or *différance*, for instance, are not just multiple, but can be said to multiply, and that their proliferation takes a particular form. Their status is that of entities between the empirical and the transcendental, in that they organize 'theoretical space' in a 'quasi-transcendental way', as Derrida and others have said (LI, 231; *LI*, 127). This status seems to make a set of distinctions at once possible and impossible: possible, as conditions of possibility and conditions for rigour; impossible, in that the distinctions are not unexceptionable, they can always possibly not work, and that is no accident but a condition of possibility too. The novel imbrication of facticity and the transcendental, discussed in Chapter 1 in connection with Derrida's relation to the history of philosophy, is thus in Chapter 2 of this book related to a pattern of reiterated modalities, where 'it is always possible that not . . . ', where a misunderstanding, for instance, is not an accident supervening on the norm of communication but is part of the 'structure of possibility' of iterability and thus of meaning. This 'structure of possibility' is itself implied by a structure of temporalization, of relation to time (LI, 120; *LI*, 62), which will be the subject of the third section of this chapter.

The structure of temporalization in *Limited Inc.* underlies *restance*, the 'minimal idealization' necessary to meaning, which, as we shall see, has the paradoxical structure of the temporal moment. In the possibility of repetition, which is at the basis of using language at all, lie both identity and difference, says Derrida. Rather than thinking any linguistic element as already there and then employed later, it is necessary to think it as divided *a priori* by its being able to be used elsewhere, at other times. Its identity is one of differential relation with other elements; it has no preset kernel of meaning of its own, but works through commitments of meaning which the past continually imposes and which arise from what will be the future's effect. It is here that a difficult problem occurs, which is the subject of this chapter, though it was flagged in the preceding one. What is the nature of this *restance*? If Derrida's paradoxical formulation of such minimal idealization is taken seriously, then it seems to share features of a trace effect, to have a certain essential spectrality.

We saw in the preceding chapter that this spectrality which arises in some of Derrida's analyses has sometimes been privileged by critics. In that chapter, it was shown that the structure of some of Derrida's most characteristic lexemes is that of a root which is in fact an original replication – they are multiple and multiply. However, when Derrida has been read by critics, that replication, that original folding, has sometimes been neglected and collapsed back onto one branch of the root. As a result, many critics have taken as primary that Derrida who analyses in the etymological sense, who dissolves certainties of opinion, and who renders permeable the distinctions with which they are framed, who in Nietzschean mode reveals conceptual entities – themes, subjects – as structures which are 'theme effects', and thus both dependent and in some sense 'less real'. And it is true that Derrida, as the preceding chapter showed, in 'Dissemination' relates these conceptual entities, in particular the idea of subjectivity or the 'I', to what in Kantian philosophy is called transcendental illusion. Being aware of them does not cause their disappearance, nor allow mastery of them, and their status is not what is normally meant by 'illusion', for the illusion is structural.

In this present chapter, conceptual entities which have traditionally been used to mark this 'lesser reality', for instance 'fetish' and 'phantasm', will be compared to *restance*. Although all three are linked by Derrida to contradictions, *restance* alone – and it is alone, for it appears in 'Limited Inc *a b c . . .*' and not much beyond – seems not to function as a semantic accretion which is used to set in doubt what it labels. The product not so much of the conjunction of 'possibility and impossibility' as of their imbricated reiteration ('the possibility of impossibility'), *restance* becomes like the limit of a particular kind of mathematical process, which is usable under certain precautions and limitations, but itself unattainable. *Of Grammatology*'s 'originary synthesis' of the 'minimal unity of temporal experience' has become a vanishing point.

In this chapter we shall see that a series of formations arise in Derrida's texts which have a similar structure. They are not marked in the text by such highly characterized lexemes as those that formed the subject of the first part of the preceding chapter. On the contrary, they emerge in shadowy fashion from circuits of argument, as I have named them, which repeat each other from context to context or which at least resemble each other very strikingly. These circuits of argument are each time concerned with the singular; they also each time involve words like 'negotiate', 'address' and 'compose'. The circuits are put in place by repetition of vocabulary, and they all cause something, a formation which is off-limits and out of frame, to negotiate with or compose with a process of infinite approximation. In that way, they seem to enact processes which it is tempting to associate with the positive and negative infinite that were discussed in the first chapter of this book.

A detour about language

I need to emphasize at this point that I am looking each time and quite specifically at the language which Derrida uses round these formations – this is not a general argument about any concept which may have a distinctive linguistic timbre in his work (and, indeed, I believe it would be inapplicable, in his work up to date, anyway, to some of what I have called the lexemes). But it is this kind of programme, or circuit of argument, which helps understand what is going on in certain texts of Derrida besides the readily apparent and straightforward arguments which are also there. They operate as *micrologies*, at the level of the phrase, not the article or book.

At this point, too, the plot of the preceding chapter should be related in a preliminary way to Derrida's way of writing. 'Plato's pharmacy', in its unfolding of Plato's usage of the term *pharmakon* made of it a 'root', an 'original medium', a 'réserve' (D, 112; *D*, 99), prior to a division into exclusive and disjoint terms: logos/madness, poison/medicine. This 'réserve' was not merely prior, it was an excess over, it was always more than, any possible 'decision' which might bring about separation or determination into simple opposites, into positive and negative, rational and irrational. So the Greek *pharmakon* of Plato could be said to indicate something more than what was to be the future positive history of philosophy; it is as if the excess of the *pharmakon* provided for the different unfoldings of the history of philosophy; as if it wrote the script for philosophy's failure to apply binary distinctions in an exhaustive and non-overlapping fashion, and the script for the constantly repeated frayings and reworkings of these distinctions to which Derrida's writings point. The 'root' provides 'reserves' from which new distinctions could be attempted, but which will, like their predecessors, be exceeded by that from which they derive.

This pattern is in action in the very rhythm and mode of Derrida's writing. Much of Derrida's work – his attention to what is pushed to the margins of our intellectual history, his policing of hesitancies in syntax and of non-sequiturs in argument – is a vigilance towards the gestures and indices which are indicative of that failure to partition once and for all the excess, indicative of the difficulty of resolving difference into opposition (a failure which is, of course, endemic to thought). But it has not always been recognized that this picking on symptoms of that failure is not merely critical, it is also enabling; it is a non-redundant measure of what we have; it is a treatment of the actual which, while it is non-positive, because non-endorsing, is also non-negative. It causes the actual to stand out against a 'possibly not'. Such a 'possibly not' is often given not just by Derrida's argument, but by the very texture of his writing, the sense of chronic doubt or suspicion which is injected by his changes of rhythm, his swerves in flying altitude, so to speak, in relation to what is discussed. The 'possibly not', whose interpretation is the crux of the disagreement with Searle, as we have seen in the preceding chapter, gives a negative underpinning to what actually is;[2] unlike Hegel's negations, it is not part of an oppositional system, it resists recuperation into a synthesis; but again, it is not endless dispersal either (unlike for instance Bataille's notion of 'dépense') and the very form of argument 'not . . . and not . . . ' I have used here in presenting it will need commentary in the next chapter.

Once more, it needs to be pointed out here that this is also an effect of the very way Derrida writes. The practice of quotation in his work goes beyond any defined insertion of clear-cut, penumbra-less phrases or words. What I have called lexemes do not appear to be very long-lived in Derrida's work (with the possible exception of *différance*), and the sense that they convey of being quotations, or special usages, while making them important in the texture of writing, imparts something transient, or at least insecure, to their use. So that when Derrida points out philosophically consecrated or sedimented nuggets of meaning in others (e.g. 'philosophemes', ALT, 76) or uses 'scare quotes', this is modified by the effect of his own writing and by the impression of epistemic modality and of constant attention to the way the commitment to the utterance may be qualified in the utterance itself.

The paragraph I have placed just above is an impressionistic even if accurate account of the relation between what is written and the way it is written. It is a broadly reflexive relating of theme of writing and effect of writing (pieces of Derrida's text, phrases or aspects, produce an effect in the reader in clear, almost mirrored relation to their theme). It is now necessary to take a step further towards describing the way in which phrases of Derrida's writing induce the formations which are the subject of this chapter.

Now, Derrida's writing often gives a different inflection to analyses of concept formation which are in fact traditional to a certain philosophy: to Nietzsche of course, but also to Locke. Take the already quoted '[le blanc supplémentaire] libère des effets de série, *fait prendre*, en se démarquant, des agglomérats – pour des substances' (D, 285) ('liberates the effect that a series exists; in marking itself out, it *makes us take* agglomerates for substances') (*D*, 254). The preceding chapter showed that in opposition to the thematic criticism of J. P. Richard, Derrida had argued that 'blanc' in Mallarmé could not be treated as merely a theme grouping white objects – snow, paper, swans' down, or whatever. On the contrary, these form 'series effects', liberated by the supplementary blanks on the page, in a looping between operation and theme. For 'blanc' is 'white', but also 'blank', and it has to be related to what is not there, the blanks between words on the page. What makes possible the actual words, allowing them to appear on the page, is also what stops them forming a tidy series (D, 285; *D*, 254). The blanks on the page are not complementary to the signifier 'blanc', as a ground might be to a figure; they are supplementary, in that they make the possible actual, by marking off the word against the ground, and the word 'blanc', which is the ground virtually, through the pun, thus points to the 'possibly not'. So the 'series effects' here are not mere illusions. They are 'freed' by gaps, by something which when verbalized is not really a noun, an entity, but a relation, a syncategoreme – the blanks are in fact 'between' ('entre'). (We saw that likewise at the level of a whole article, 'The double session' is not wall-to-wall conceptual carpeting, an aligning of terms or concepts, but on the contrary an operation, a bringing together of the hetero-geneous, a bringing together at an angle, a fold or 'pli'.[3] This halting or trammelled construction has been discussed in the previous chapter.)

Hence another feature of Derrida's mode of writing: the use in his own text of blanks, sometimes programmed (for instance, *The Post Card* with fifty-two spaces between sections or inside sections), sometimes not ('Parergon' where the spaces are irregular, but framed by a kind of enlarged bracket – the subject of the text being the Kantian imagination, which 'frames', that is, pulls into a synthesis). Such gaps change the status of what is written, quite apart from leaving it incomplete. They are like a negative version of Derrida's striking use of quotation discussed above, where in texts like *Glas* large portions of alien text are held in suspension, or where paragraphs are cut off from each other by blanks. The effect of this mode of writing is to make the violent lacunæ or the ferociously funny juxtaposition of words, spaces and quotes in *Glas* remind the reader that what they are reading is excerpted out of other things. What is being read may appear as a kind of phantasmatic production out of what is not there, or rather is somewhere else.

Phantasms and fetishes

This effect of the writing must now be related to what is thematized in certain texts, in passages concerned with ideology. It is in *Glas* that one type of complexity pertaining to such 'agglomerates' is made explicit and brought to the surface of the text (for the construction of *Glas*, see preceding chapter, p. 87). We shall see that the formations this chapter is concerned with have a relation to the roles played in *Glas* by the fetish and the phantasm, so that these appear like simpler oppositional versions of singularities, or what I have called 'strange attractors'.

Derrida, like other philosophers, pinpoints the linguistically compacted constructions with which we think but which are no longer enquired into as we think. His discussions of Freud, and of Marx on Feuerbach, examine the role of analogy in their 'unveiling' of ideological representation and the fetish, and suggest that their analysis relies on the unanalysed in an unanalysed way. For Marx, Feuerbach's criticism of religion is merely theoretical; it has located the 'secret' of the Holy Family in the human family, but the human family has been left unexamined, so that a mere representation, not the human institution, has been analysed. But Marx has then, the text of *Glas* implies, participated in the fetishizing he is laying at the door of Feuerbach. Founders of religion and destroyers of religion alike want to get beyond representation to the unsubsti-tutable (*Glas*, 230a, 204a), and this is fetishism.[4] 'Fetishism', or the particular fetish, has to have its own counter-quality, the particular 'truth', for which it has been substituted.[5] The very idea of the fetish, of the substitute, relies on the 'thing itself'. So Feuerbach found the secret of the Holy Family in the human family, and Marx in turn criticized Feuerbach for leaving intact the anthropo-logical concept of family (not to speak of religion). (It needs noting that in the choleric humour of *Glas* but also of 'Dissemination' and *Signéponge*, written round the work of the poet Francis Ponge, the 'thing itself' is as if represented by the theme of the column, and thus by the textual column, but also by the father of all columns, the phallus – both need monumentally to be got up, both need an erection. In these texts, symbols or orderings of the printed text interact in complex cross-cutting manner with the argument about the 'thing itself'.)

In the following parts of the Hegel column in *Glas*, Derrida's Freud is put into a difficult and funny three-part exchange with Hegel and Kant. Though he is made to employ different tactics, he uses the same structural opposition as Derrida's Marx – real thing/substitution, castration/fetish – to make the fetish decidable, to make it refer to what it is a fetish of. But, suggests Derrida, there is at the same time in Freud's account a much more paradoxical view, where the fetish points to a simultaneous denial of and assumption of castration, to an implicit assertion that the mother's penis is both present and absent, and this is why it needs a substitute, or at least its absence to be disguised. In this way a binary relation (real thing/substitute) is spliced with a non-binary relation (a substitute which at the same time might be merely a veiling of the absence of what it is a substitute for), causing the concept 'fetish' to work in an 'undecidable' fashion: (*Glas*, 234–5a, 209–10a) 'comme le battant d'une vérité qui cloche' ('like the clapper of a truth that rings awry') (*Glas*, 254b, 227b) (there is a complex reference here to Georges Bataille's not-so-sensible utterances on Genet, to *batail = battant = tongue of bell*, and to Bataille's use of his own name as a substitute for 'phallus'). Of this 'undecidable' relation of simultaneous denial and affirmation of female castration Derrida once again uses the term 'excess': 'puissance d'excès par rapport à l'opposition, vrai/faux, substitut/non-substitut, déni/afirmation etc.' (*Glas*, 236a) ('power of excess in relation to the opposition true/untrue, substitute/nonsubstitute, denial/affirmation') (*Glas*, 211a).[6] The use of the term 'decidable' here seems to me less happy than in *Origin of Geometry*.[7] Derrida, it seems, needed here a term which could apply to the simultaneous appeal to two contradictory operations; he also needed to suggest that there is, as a result of this, a limping, halting movement between the contradictories, which works against the 'either/or' of the contradiction. He is detecting in the Freud text the forcing of a relationship between an exclusive 'or' (in Latin *aut* – either fetish or truth, not both) which is the structure of Marx's concept of fetish, and a non-exclusive disjunction (in Latin *vel*, where either or both of the poles can be true). Though only affirmation or denial of castration seems to be possible, the fetishist seems both to affirm and deny it. This creates an unequally imbricated structure. Something like this pattern of argument seems to recur again and again in Derrida, and although one hesitates to force this particular example into a mould, it seems to be close to that already analysed in the preceding chapter à propos the phrase 'the dialectics of dialectics and non-dialectics'. Later in *Glas*, this work on the fetish is continued, in a passage where 'Kant' is made to quote Freud and to criticize the 'analogy' the latter sets up between the categorical imperative and taboos – both are negative fetishes according to Freud. (Derrida had in fact, as we have seen, preceded 'Kant' and questioned the status of analogy in Marx's critique of Feuerbach.)

Before advancing further in this account of the fetish, which takes us onto new ground in this book, one further point must be made. With the 'undecidable', we meet here a version of one of the problems encountered in Chapter 1: does the detection of invariant patterns ('noyau invariant'/'invariant kernel' of the fetish, *Glas*, 234a, 209a) become an invariant in Derrida's work? And would he not be subject to his own arguments which imply that such invariants are constructs which neglect or paste over the fragility of our distinctions? Now, as so often, the problem is one he himself flags. The 'undecidable' is not to be allowed to become a place of last resort, any more than any other term – in 'Entre crochets', a commentary on *Glas*, he suggests that to make the 'undecidable' a tool whose valency goes beyond the upsetting of binary oppositions is to make of it a 'safe investment', whose return is calculable – a second-order fetish precisely which will paralyse the halting rocking activity of the fetish, and will trump it ('Entre crochets', 110).[8] Invariant labelling of the activity of the fetish will itself be a fetish, a compact formation preventing further analysis. (A question is raised here which will be addressed in the final chapter: can the rocking movement created by the unequally imbricated structures be described without becoming a theme and thus running this risk of inappropriate critical emphasis? Is not this rather just the risk of using language?)

So at another level, then, that of conceptual self-commentary, a concept which acquires hegemony, which gets too big for its local context, becomes a fetish, and is used to 'cap' or put down what it is applied to. Yet as its conceptual peculiarities suggest, the fetish as such is a construction which is not simply debunkable – it exists because it allows contraries to be joined (*Glas*, 253b, 226b) and because one wants to join contraries. Now as the commentary proceeds (cautiously careful of context and of the scope of the thinkers quoted but also ambitious, bringing together a large number of works without dodging the huge intellectual problems[9]) it seems as if the concept 'phantasm' emerges via analogy (*Glas*, 248a, 221a) to succeed to the fetish. Both words 'trump', that is, present their concept as less than the truth, for both propose a truth or a reality behind the ideological set-up they are being used to pinpoint. Both allow a contradiction, or rather heterogeneity, to be profited from.

Out of the exchange between Marx and Feuerbach (since Derrida allows Feuerbach, through the device of extended quotation, a kind of implicit reply to Marx), which the reader gradually sees to be addressing, among other problems, that of how to escape from the coils of Hegelian dialectic, comes a development, slowly widening in its ambit, on the relation between Hegelian *Aufhebung* and Christianity (for the doctrines of transubstantiation and resurrection are reconciling and transcending syntheses); and out of the question of fetishism as a search for the truth behind the substitute, there is elaborated a commentary on the last two chapters of Hegel's *Phenomenology*, where the latter makes Absolute Knowledge succeed to revealed religion but drives between them a separation, which is that of representation, *Vorstellung*. Derrida pushes this word towards the psychoanalytic 'phantasm' to indicate the mastery of religion by dialectic (religion is *Vorstellung*, only a phantasm) and also to resist this mastery – on what grounds can the idea of phantasm dominate religion on behalf of the dialectic when it is itself determined by the idea of religion? Hegel trumps theology by philosophy in order to reinstall it in the guise of philosophy-as-the-dialectic. ('Phantasm', beyond its relation to Freudian analyses and Marxian accounts of ideology, allows Derrida reference to the doubles, the simulacra, discussed in the preceding chapter.) The religious consciousness for Hegel's *Phenomenology* stops just short of Absolute Knowledge – it still looks with desire to the future coming, and for it time is not collapsed into the timeless present of the Absolute. It remains with nostalgia and with representation, with retrospection and anticipation; it is not fully reconciled. But Derrida seems here to point to a phantasmatic basis of the dialectic: Hegel has derived from the sexual difference at the basis of Christianity (virgin mother, divine father)[10] a pair of mutually exclusive opposites which work into a structure of opposition in general. And then the phantasm is unavoidable, the phantasm of infinite control over the opposed pair. Hegel has been able to master religion in the dialectical process by stalling it as representation. But it is religion which provides the opposition and the very notion of phantasm (for Marx, it is the original ideology, the producer of ghosts: SM, 236; *SM*, 148). The knowledge of, that is, the truth behind, this phantasm is Absolute Knowledge. So it is the phantasm which has provided Absolute Knowledge. With Absolute Knowledge, the Hegelian reconciliation has occurred and we are in an infinite set of equivalences. To depart this loop of equivalences, we need to think, says Derrida, 'the remainder of *time*' (*Glas*, 252a, 225a). Derrida is commenting on the paragraph in which Hegel says that time is the Notion itself that *is there* and which presents itself to consciousness as an empty intuition: 'for this reason, Spirit necessarily appears in Time, and it appears in Time just so long as it has not *grasped* its pure Notion, i.e. has not annulled Time' (Hegel 1977: 487). Derrida's reader thus needs to think what it might be to think the remainder of time. Clearly, it involves not accepting a chain of equivalences, for a remainder is not equivalent, and cannot be substituted.

To speak of 'fetish' is to set up something as the 'real thing', subject to some kind of ban or taboo, for which the fetish is a substitute and some kind of equivalent. Likewise, the 'phantasm' in Derrida's analysis of the section of the *Phenomenology* on revealed religion is Hegel's representation, not philosophy. Now Derrida relates fetish and phantasm to each other through the taboo. (See also *Specters of Marx*, Chapter 5. In Derrida's recent work there is a growing connection of these terms with 'specter', and with analysis of the effect of the media.) There was implicit in Freud a more paradoxical concept of the 'fetish', one where the opposition of 'substitute'/'real thing' is complicated by an affirmation as well as a denial of castration. Likewise, in a text written in 1982, the 'phantasm' seems to be affirmed beyond the denial implicit in its very use as label. Derrida links Walter Benjamin's view of the text to be translated as untouchable with Heidegger's project of getting back to what the Greeks failed to think. Both are a desire 'of' an intact kernel; both desire that intact centre and also desire that it should be untouchable: 'Donc le désir ou le *phantasme* du noyau intact est irréductible mais *il n'y a pas* de noyau intact' (OA, 152–3) ('Thus the desire or the *phantasm* of the intact kernel is irreducible – despite the fact that *there is no* intact kernel') (*EO*, 115) (the term 'kernel' is that of psychoanalyst Nicholas Abraham). Derrida opposes to this desire the Greek necessity, *Ananke*, and points to the Lacanian real: 'A la place de Nécessité, certains pourraient dire "*réel*"'; 'In place of Necessity some might say "real"' (ALT, 92). Necessity is the otherness of this desire's aim, or rather the desire's limit in the other; the impossibility of fulfilment produces 'a phantasmal logic, a logic of desire that forgets necessity' (ALT, 93), a logic which, like desire, is continually reborn out of its very impossibility. Necessity reminds desire that its condition of possibility, its movement, is also its impossibility, its frustration. Once more the phrase occurs: 'its [desire's] condition of impossibility is also its condition of possibility' (ALT, 92). The phantasm, in this text, like the fetish, rests on simultaneous forgetting and forgetting that there is nothing to forget, a version in the negative of the Freudian fetishist's affirmation and denial: 'Ce n'est pas qu'il y a de l'oublié: on veut oublier qu'il n'y a rien à oublier, qu'il n'y a rien eu à oublier . . . qu'il n'y a jamais eu de noyau intact' (OA, 153) ('It's not that something has been forgotten; rather, one wants to forget that there is nothing to forget, that there has been nothing to forget . . . that there has never been an intact kernel') (*EO*, 116). (Heidegger's work is here radically traversed by Derrida, in that the 'forgetfulness of being', which for Heidegger is the 'impetus to metaphysical questioning', may appear to be another invariant object of desire.)[11]

So if Derrida's own discussion is not to align itself in the series it discusses as yet one more example of a trumping notion of truth, then care needs to be taken. (For truth trumps 'phantasm', which itself was designed to trump what is held to be only a representation; it trumps 'fetish', which trumps what is thought of as only a substitute.) *Glas* speaks of 'time's remainder' needing to be brought into play, that is, that 'one must give oneself' the rest of time. One must try to think a remainder of time which is not part of a mode of being or of presence (*Glas*, 252a, 226a). How may this be?

Time constructs

'Phantasm', then, is pulled into shape by desire and by the forgetting that the condition of possibility of desire, in the form of 'some other singular' (ALT, 92), is its running up against necessity as a limit, which is also a condition of desire's impossibility, its constant frustration. (Necessity here, Derrida admits, might be called the real if the real precisely did not threaten to become an immovable, a fetish, a backstop, instead of a tensor, a force which tenses desire.) 'Fetish' links two contraries in a double link (*Glas*, 253b, 226b), powerful because undecidable. (Whereas truth about the thing itself is decidable; moreover, Freud's discourse about castration decides: the fetish is, he says, 'a substitute for the penis'.) The 'phantasm' of self-sufficient contraries arises, on the other hand, from determining difference as opposition.[12] These intellectual entities are in the Freudian and Hegelian texts, and can be used by extension out of those texts, but Derrida also makes them refer to that very use: the 'fetish' may itself be a fetish, as was suggested in the previous section à propos 'undecidable'. This forces reflection on two levels, that of the constitution of a fetish or a phantasm, and that of the constitution of the concept 'fetish' or 'phantasm' as formations allowing the holding in focus of opposites, which are trained on each other, so to speak. It is neglect of these two levels, and of their interrelation, that has in my view led commentators (Fenves 1997) to worry that Derrida, in *Specters of Marx*, in fact equates the two formations and effaces the difference between the fetish and the phantasm, thereby eliminating also the 'effectivity' of the fetish. But it is precisely the distinction 'effective'/'unreal' that 'phantasm' or 'fetish' was set up to maintain within the Hegelian or Marxian argument, by 'trumping' in favour of the 'real', effective, or true against the substitute (religion/value of an object in the market). And the Derridean analysis is pointing to this pattern of maintaining the oppositions while favouring one pole.[13]

Now 'fetish' and 'phantasm' have long and fraught histories, and have seen service in past battles in philosophy. But one can wonder in what they differ from, say, *restance*[14] in *Limited Inc*. *Restance* is possibly relayed by 'reste' in the article '+r', in *The Truth in Painting*, which through its written similarity to the first two letters of *trace* may in turn relay that word, and certainly refers back to one of Genet's titles active in *Glas*, *Ce qui est resté d'un Rembrandt* . . . . It is presupposed, as has been indicated in the preceding chapter, by a minimal idealization (logical, mathematical, or just that idealization at work in ordinary speech): 'L'itérabilité suppose une restance minimale (comme une idéalisation minimale quoique limitée) pour que l'identité du même soit répétable et identifiable *dans, à travers* et même *en vue de* l'altération' (LI, 105) ('Iterability supposes a minimal remainder (as well as a minimum of idealization) in order that the identity of the *selfsame* be repeatable and identifiable *in, through*, and even *in view of* its alteration') (*LI*, 53). 'Reste' is a mathematical term and '+r' a mathematical formula for remainders – we might seem then to have got down to some vital minimum, some elementary particle, some 'intact kernel'; and thus something which could turn out like a phantasm or fetish. However, where Derrida's *restance* might seem to make possible a similar power to hold opposites in focus, it does not stall within the pair 'effective/unreal'. The neologism signals that the complicated situation, which I called 'trumping', at work in the structures Derrida analysed as 'phantasm' and 'fetish', has been catered for: as we have seen, he actually calls it 'une restance non présente' – 'C'est une structure différentielle échappant à la présence ou à l'opposition (simple ou dialectique) de la présence et de l'absence' (LI, 105) ('It is a differential structure escaping the logic of presence or the (simple or dialectical) opposition of presence and absence') (*LI*, 53). It is a paradoxical non-entity, the presupposition for *iterability* which 'makes possible that whose rigour or purity it makes impossible' (LI, 116; *LI*, 60). This remainder is a trace effect, but like a 'minimal point of adherence' (the term Derrida uses is from topology) it is being thought of as some kind of limit.[15] It has not stabilized, its strangeness is exhibited, for it appears to be a kind of *hapax legomenon*, a one-off coinage. In *restance*, the single occurrence and its repetition, in other words singularity and iterability, can 'fall together', that is, coincide, pulling into existence something that like certain sorts of mathematical limits, can be formulated, approached as closely as one likes, but not made present. 'Phantasm' and 'fetish', on the other hand, are structures which have not fulfilled the conceptual possibilities they might have had of allowing undecidable and decidable statements to be related (*Glas*, 235a, 210a). They have been made into stabilized units; they designate resultants of conditions of impossibility and possibility, which have been turned into elements and where the shadowy status is used to privilege the 'effectiveness' it is compared with. Whereas Derrida barely, as far as I know, returns to the word *restance*, and its spectrality thus can hardly be a form of mastery. As we shall see directly, it has as its matrix time.

In the article 'Ousia and grammé', in Derrida's *Margins*, time is discussed by Derrida à propos Heidegger's note on Aristotle on time, and Aristotle had Zeno in his sights: such overlaying discussion fits the overlayed view of time that emerges. If Derrida in some ways makes us insecure about concepts, and insecure about their difference (how we may divide them off one from another), Zeno has been interpreted as holding 'from Parmenides that there is only one thing in existence'[16] and thus aiming to show that our ways of dividing up the world, in particular temporally and spatially, and hence our concepts, were inconsistent. Aristotle in his *Physics* developed from Zeno the double view of the 'now', a present perpetually different yet perpetually same. There is 'on the one hand a succession of nows (219b 13–14, cf. 219a 25–9) yet on the other there is the one progressing now (219b 22–8)'.[17]

Before starting on Derrida's discussion, it is helpful to set out a rather different one, which also sees time as crossing over, as chiasmatic, but where the crux is the present, which is not, as we shall see, the case in Derrida. Dummett writing on McTaggart's problem of the nature of time suggests that we calibrate events in two different ways which seem incompatible: we count them as before, at the same time or after another event, but also as past, present or future. The first merely gives us order; only the latter allows change, but it seems inescapably linked to the position of an observer, in relation to whom things are past, present or future. Thus the expression of change is partial because it is token-reflexive, that is, expressed from a point of view, a deictic centre, and needing description by deictic expressions, in this case, tenses, which refer to the speaker–observer. These deictic references cannot be excised as they may be in the description of space, for one can describe a space one is not in, and need not refer in the description to the space one is in (the example Dummett gives is the visual field). These temporal expressions cause the sentence to have 'different truth-values according to the circumstances of its utterance' ('I am typing' may be true now but not at 9 a.m. tomorrow.)[18] The problem is that time seems both to be something that derives from things, in that they produce change; but it also seems to be a bath, a flux, within which change happens to things. It is change which causes our anxiety about units (can the 'now' exist if, when you try to pinpoint or fix it, it is always past or future?) and it is our insistence on the unit which makes Zeno's arrow seem not to fly.[19]

Now Derrida in this part of the article 'Ousia and grammé' (a long and probing discussion of Heidegger's attribution to Aristotle of the components of Hegel's view of time, the 'vulgar concept of time') suggests that already in Aristotle are wound together the two paradoxical threads: one, the question of the nature of the 'now' and whether it can be treated as an indivisible present point, with the consequence that it barely exists, because in the time you take to reflect on it, it is already past; two, the question of the relation between time and change, where the sense of time is the sensation of internal movement, without need of external sense content, which points forward to the Kantian time as a pure form of sensibility. In Heidegger's exposition in *Kant and the Problem of Metaphysics*, this pure form of sensibility is prior to a division between action and passion, where causing change and suffering change are the same.[20] (The linguistic concomitants of such a conception are the French reflexive verbs commented on in the preceding chapter.) Pure intuition for Heidegger means it is not actually time, that is 'nows', and 'now' as present, which are given, as they would be in empirical intuition, but time as a crossover of 'just now' (*soeben*) and 'very soon' (*sogleich*).[21] Pure intuition is not a field which contains what is already given, but is an act both passive and active,[22] and pure intuition is time, says Heidegger in his interpretation of Kant's first edition of *The Critique of Pure Reason*. But, argues Derrida, this time after Heidegger, a more powerful philosophical trend has privileged the 'now', and thus time as presence[23] and predication as a punctual point of synthesis between subject and object. The effect is to constitute intellectual entities in the sense of turning them into ob-jects, objectifying them, making of them already given objects of which something can be predicated, instead of working with our modes of apprehending them.[24] (Derrida develops this as a long and brilliant argument about the relation between philosophers' categories in general, and predication in particular, with the nature of language, and certain languages in particular, which will be discussed in the last chapter.)

In the complex account Derrida gives of Aristotle's aporia on time, and leaving aside his discussion of how time is represented, whether as line or point, there recur features of the constructs discussed earlier, 'phantasm' or 'fetish' on the one hand, and *restance* on the other. First: time as 'now', is a chiasmus, of past retrospected and future anticipated (we find here what is an occasional feature of Derrida's style, the future anterior). The 'now' as a present does not exist except as tension between these two: time tenses. *Glas'* 'phantasm' is called up within time by the 'already gone' or the 'not yet' of religion, from the perspective of what religion is not yet, that is extra-temporal and omni-temporal, Absolute Knowledge (*Glas*, 247a–8a, 220a–1a). Second: the 'now' cannot coexist with another 'now': yet for that to be impossible it must be the case that the other 'now', in everything the same except that it is different in time, is in fact coexistent in one sense, because appearing in a synthesis as non-coexistent at the point in time (M, 63; *M*, 55). *Restance*, like the 'now', is linked to the 'minimal possibility' for repetition of a sign, a paradoxical limit which is identifiable by not being what it is nonetheless being identified as (LI, 105; *LI*, 53, see above). It is as if *restance* avoids the attempted capping of arguments being operated by 'phantasm' and 'fetish'.

Now Dummett, in the previously mentioned article, summarizes McTaggart's argument for the unreality of time thus: 'McTaggart is saying that . . . a description of events as taking place *in time* is impossible unless temporally token-reflexive expressions enter into it, that is, unless the description is given by someone who is himself in that time' (Dummett 1978: 354). He shows that McTaggart's argument is that reality must be something of which there exists a complete description; none exists of time, because the describer is in time, therefore time must be unreal. But, says Dummett, if time is not an illusion, then the argument entails quite clearly important reservations about the possibility of objectivity, in that knowledge unrelated to its insertion in time is impossible. We shall see that Derrida's account of the insertion in time is different, but the consequence is the same.

Derrida develops Aristotle's argument on the non-being of time to suggest that it uses a precomprehension of time embedded in the tenses of verbs, and produces the following aporia: 'Il [le temps] est néant parce qu'il *est temps, c'est-à dire* maintenant passé ou futur' (M, 57) ('It is nothingness because *it is time, that is* a past or future now') (*M*, 50). Unlike Dummett, Derrida does not make of the inherent interlocking and overlapping in events' time a direct function of a relation to an observer's time (referring to the time of utterance of the statement, the then-present, and thus 'token-reflexive'). The *restance non présente* is cut from its point of production: we do not need to access its origin in an emitter to understand it – this is after all the point of Poe's Valdemar and the utterance 'I am dead', quoted by Derrida on several occasions. But Poe's statement should not be shorn of its paradox in relation to time:

> L'impossibilité (la coexistence de deux maintenants) n'apparaît que dans une synthèse (entendons ce mot de façon neutre, en n'y impliquant aucune position, aucune activité, aucun agent) disons une certaine complicité ou complication *maintenant* [the reconstruction of etymology is typical] ensemble plusieurs maintenants *actuels* dont *on dit* que l'un est passé et l'autre futur.
>
> (M, 63; the last two italicizations are mine)

The impossible – the coexistence of two nows – appears only in a synthesis; taking this word neutrally, implying no position, no activity, no agent – let us say in a certain complicity or complication *maintaining* together several *current* nows which *are said* to be the one past and the other future.

(*M*, 55)

There is then a synthesis; but Derrida has been careful not to anchor the synthesis in a point-like present, nor in a person (we have the impersonal 'on dit'), and he explicitly says that it implies no agent. Yet he has not excised the deictic temporal reference, though he has toned it down by use of the present participle, and the re-etymologizing pun on 'maintenant'; it has become a point of crossing. Derrida makes of 'present' a temporalization, a tensing of past and future, because all it is is a bringing together in one synthesis of determinations of time which are not contemporary, which appear to be contradictory and which 'are said' in a present tense which seems historic, unlocatable, and which is certainly not attached to a sayer.[25] As such, in a formulation which occurs as we have seen again and again in Derrida, 'present' is an 'impossible possibility'. Whereas Dummett's McTaggart carries presence into the past and into the future, in that the experiential present, whether it be past or future, underlies the deictic reference of the tense used.[26] But for both, for Dummett's McTaggart as for Derrida's Heidegger, time is the impossibility of escaping that synthesis whose index is the way tense operates in language.[27]

For Dummett as for Derrida, then, though in different ways, the description of an event brings together the time of what is spoken of and the time of the stating: uttering and utterance are inseparable, neither being eliminable. For Derrida, the present of the saying ('on dit') is not accessible directly, only as infinite overlaying in synthesis of past and present. Although 'token-reflexive' in its history is related to the logical paradoxes, this is not further explored by Dummett. Derrida, on the other hand, does so when he says: 'Le temps est un nom de cette impossible possibilité' (M, 63) ('Time is name for this impossible possibility') (*M*, 55). We have seen that *restance* and *phantasme*, one differential, the second a simplifying of difference into opposition, are also linked with conditions of possibility and impossibility, and thus with transcendentality and non-transcendentality. The yoking of possibility and impossibility within the same phrase, to lead to the aporia we have met before,[28] seems to suggest that underlying all these is time (which with language and the other was the object of intention without intuition; cf. Chapter 1). It is time which constructs such entities out of the infinite, infinitely embedded overlaying of projections and anticipations. The rest of this chapter will investigate such entities.

Singularities

The Derridean formations I am going to look at are relatively unstable; I claim that they may be examined together owing to the similarity of the circuits in which they evolve. Though repetition of such 'programmes' is a feature of Derrida's writings,[29] in the rest of this chapter I shall examine ones which are not always baptized with a name, and never with what I have called a 'lexeme'.

In other words, an argument which is not always explicitly signalled emerges from the text (hence my name for these, 'circuits of argument'). They are all connected with the problem of singularity.

The preceding sections contrasted 'fetish', 'phantasm' and *restance*. The first two were, Derrida had argued, designed to master the ideological formation they designated; the third, Derrida's nonce formation, in its paradoxical formulation as 'restance non-présente', expressed the definition of time as empty intuition. In the circuits of argument which will now be discussed, a similar process, each time localized, micrological, causes in each location, as it were, new formations, new resultants to appear. It is as if a set of floating conceptual currents 'seized' texts being commented on by Derrida and enabled them to be connected together by a process of projection from one current to another (one of the reasons why it is in fact inaccurate to say that Derrida comments 'on' a text, one of the pointers to the underlying problem of connection which will be treated in the last chapter). So that if Derrida is rightly held to throw suspicion on our mental furniture, on 'reality', on 'subject' (in the sense of 'autonomous subject'), on 'cause', it is also the case that by what one might almost call rewirings, strange collocations, such as might be reworkings of familiar conceptual *dramatis personae*, necessary to our thought, begin to swim into our ken. Each time different, the description of the process of their formation is similar, and to them I have attached the term 'strange attractors' (*singularités* in French) taken from theories of turbulence.[30] The formations are found embedded in some others' writing, Barthes or Levinas for instance; Derrida works on them by extending his own work into the work of the other he is referring to. He thus pays a kind of duty to that work, of care and respect, at the same time as causing it to spread out in ways that seem unpredictable. The second part of this chapter will examine the circuits of argument by which the singularities' functioning is described.

The negotiation of the singular reference

In 'The deaths of Roland Barthes', published in 1981, the plural of what can only happen once, of what is a singular event when it occurs to the bearer of a proper name, raises immediately the question of the singular and the question of the name. Moreover, the phrase, 'je suis mort', surfaces once again here. 'I do not exist' (see note 25) is in fact one of the canonic sentences when discussing whether using names implies presuppositions about the existence of the thing named. It gives a clue to what is going on in the article. Russell held that logically proper names are so to speak the cleanest proper names, clean of any modalizing implication about their sense, and in Kneale's interpretation of Russell on this point they provide a designation which can be guaranteed true. One such logically proper name is 'I', which cannot fail to designate – except of course in literature. So that – except in literature – 'I do not exist' (or in Derrida and Poe's example, 'je suis mort') is self-refuting. 'For here the denial of existence is incompatible not only with the existential proposition implied by the use of the subject term, but also with the fact that the remark has been made' (Kneale 1971: 599–600).[31] In such texts as Barthes', Derrida's and Poe's, even the logically cleanest proper name may fail to guarantee any sort of designation with true existential implication, any intact external kernel, to which the sense may be attached as to a reference.

The problem of the singular reference occurs crucially in the photograph (in a way it does not in painting): there must be an external originator which by its imprint on the film causes the photograph.[32] Barthes in his work on photography, *Camera Lucida*, had used a distinction *studium/punctum*, where *punctum* seems to lead back to the unique singular captured in the photograph, object of a regret which is *poignant* (a pun made via the word family and easily recognized in French). Apparently, then, there is a binary opposition leading to an end-station, the really existing, to which the photograph refers.

But Derrida gradually surrounds and orientates the duality, making of photography a process by which referring becomes possible, but without abutting on any intentionless 'real' 'out there', which might then become a point of arrest, an end-station. With patient rhythm, Derrida moves aside from the *punctum* as referent. He claims that the context 'reforms it' (Psy, 278; *RB*, 265). The reform involves movement in two opposed directions: the 'absolute singularity' of the other addresses itself to me, comes towards me. But the Referent is not simply a referent, it is a photographic image of a referent in which the sitter's presence eternally slips away, eludes me (Psy, 277; *RB*, 264). Nor, Derrida adds, is he merely suspending referentiality. Instead, Derrida takes the opposition *studium/punctum*, whose initials are made to suggest problems of predication ('S is P', in the usual formulation of philosophy textbooks in English) and causes it to exfoliate so that an object is not merely placed under a concept, nor a property predicated of a subject, but through the double movement described above an intensional relation is constructed. Reference can be aligned to that of an image in a photo, which can only refer to a sitter under a particular aspect, that of being unique: 'ce qui adhère dans la photographie c'est peut-être moins le référent lui-même, dans l'activité présente de sa réalité, que l'implication, dans la référence, de son avoir-été-unique' (Psy, 295) ('what adheres in the photograph is perhaps less the referent itself, in the effectiveness of its reality, than the implication in the reference of its having-been-unique') (*RB*, 285). It cannot perhaps do more than point, precisely. The intentional movement of reference (consciousness, like the camera, 'aims at' its object: 'Barthes recourt justement à la phénoménologie dans ce livre' (Psy, 292) ('Barthes does in fact appeal to phenomenology in this book') (*RB*, 281)) is this peculiar crossing movement, in double direction, aimed from the speaker outwards, but also described as working back from what is unobtainably out of reach. This movement is figured by the spectral nature of the photograph,[33] which cannot give access to the referent, and yet where the referent is not suspended.

Derrida's language suggests the two directions. First (so far we are in the photograph):

Un point de singularité troue la surface de la réproduction – et même de la production – des analogies, des ressemblances, des codes. Il perce, il vient m'atteindre d'un coup, me blesse ou me meurtrit et d'abord, semble-t-il, ne regarde que moi. . . . S'adresse à moi la singularité absolue de l'autre, le Référent.

(Psy, 277)

A point of singularity which punctures the surface of the reproduction – and even the production – of analogies, likeness and codes. It pierces, strikes me, wounds me, bruises me, and, first of all, seems to look only at me. . . . It addresses itself to me . . . the singularity of the other . . . the Referent.

(*RB*, 264)

This direction of address is called 'this range of the accusative or dative' (Psy, 278; *RB*, 264). (Cf. 'A l'instant du moins où le *punctum* déchire l'espace, la référence ou la mort ont partie liée dans la photographie' (Psy, 292) ('By the time the *punctum* rends space, the reference and death are hand in hand in the photograph') (*RB*, 281)) Second, in the other direction, there is '*punctum, le point de singularité*, la traversée du discours vers l'unique, le "référent" comme l'autre irremplaçable' (Psy, 295) ('*the point of singularity*, the traversal of discourse toward the unique, the 'referent' as the irreplaceable other') (*RB*, 284–5, my italics). To summarize: the 'point of singularity' then moves in opposed directions: on the one hand, out of the representation and towards me; on the other, through the discourse (or the crossing of discourse) towards the referent and the other (Psy, 278; *RB*, 265).

The other pole of Barthes' opposition, the *studium*, is that which the *punctum* traverses. It may be (though is not invariably) 'traversé, fouetté, zebré par un détail (*punctum*) qui m'attire ou me blesse' (Psy, 278–9) ('traversed, lashed, striped by a detail (*punctum*) which attracts or distresses me') (*RB*, 265). Medium, mediatory, it is always coded (Psy, 280; *RB*, 268) whereas the *punctum* is always out of the camera's field, out of the code. But *studium* and *punctum* are not mere complementary concepts; they do not in fact *oppose* each other at all: 'Séparés par une limite infranchissable, les deux concepts passent entre eux des compromis, ils composent l'un *avec* l'autre et nous y reconnaîtrons tout à l'heure une opération *métonymique*' (Psy, 279) ('Separated by an insuperable limit, the two concepts exchange compromises; they compose together, the one *with* the other, and we will later recognize in this a *metonymic* operation') (*RB*, 266–7). So one is an absolute other which 'composes' or, with a word which will recur in other texts, 'negotiates', does business with, its other through the strange chiasmatic movement discussed earlier (Psy, 295; *RB*, 285).[34] The *punctum* cannot be attained, it can only be described by this criss-cross movement, but because it composes with the *studium* it has substitutes, and can leave traces, engender substitutes (it thus comes within the pull of the Derridean *supplement*, a lexeme which has not been examined in this book). Such a force, such metonymy, is explicitly associated by Derrida with time:

> La valeur d'*intensité* dont je suis la piste . . . conduit à une nouvelle équation contrapunctique, à une nouvelle métonymie de la métonymie elle-même, de la vertu substitutive du *punctum*. C'est le Temps. N'est-ce pas la ressource ultime pour la substitution d'un instant absolu à un autre, pour le remplacement de l'irremplaçable, de ce référent unique par un autre qui est encore un autre instant, tout autre et encore le même.
>
> (Psy, 298)

> The value of *intensity* . . . which I am now in the process of tracking down, leads to a new contrapunctal equation, to a new metonymy of metonymy itself, to the substitutive virtue of the *punctum*. This is Time. For is not Time the ultimate resource for the substitution of one absolute instance by another, for the replacement of the irreplaceable, the replacement of this unique referent by another which is yet another instant, completely other and yet the same?
>
> (*RB*, 288)

To summarize: Barthes had said that the *punctum* was metonymic: a relation of substitution through juxtaposition. Derrida has interleaved this, so to speak, with his own concerns, he has made this metonymy reach out to other of his own writings. Like Aristotle's nows, an irreplaceable instant is replaced by one exactly like it (Psy, 298; *RB*, 288). Time is the metonymic form, Derrida says, which maintains reference by division of the referent. Less pointed to contradiction in its phrasing than the definitions of *restance*, the structural tension from which the spectral entity can arise is nevertheless the same, and once more its matrix is time.

In this way, we do not have 'some unsubtle theorems on the general suspension of the Referent' (Psy, 292, my translation). But neither, of course, do we have 'naive referentialism' (Psy, 299; *RB*, 290). Instead, there is gradually put in place a structure which, we gradually understand, may be the structure of reference. In this structure, the repeatability of writing, the 'iterability' of the 'mark', is cross-cut with the effect of this *punctum*, in which the effect constructs, or causes to emerge, the *punctum* which itself is 'offstage', 'out of focus' (*hors champ*), that is, the effect comes from the work of composition with, or negotiation of a relation to what is irredeemably other, what is extra-(photo)graphic. A relation of reference arises from the negotiation of the *studium* with the *punctum*.

This fragile and spectral pattern of strains and stresses, particular declensions which are allowed to inflect Barthes' work, recurs, as we shall see. It can be summarized thus: the circuit of argument, which Derrida puts in place by repetition of vocabulary, points to something which is off-limits and out of frame, and causes it to negotiate with or compose with, a process of infinite approximation. And my argument in this chapter will be that it is the strength of this buried argument which bears the complexity, the extreme and exfoliating density of Derrida's commentary on and his working within, his authors.

Cautiously, then, and with a kind of gently self-mocking homage to Barthes, as is right given the status of the text, Derrida's article probes the paradox of photography: a sense of singularity, of 'uniquely having been there' which is given by a technique enabling multiple reproduction. The questions of universals and particulars, of concepts and the actual object which 'falls' under the concept, of the law and the 'cases' to which it applies, all are evoked. In Barthes' 'science impossible de l'être unique', the chains of substitution, through images or words, only lead back to something which is a 'singular plural', a 'singulier pluriel' (*RB*, 272; Psy, 284). The unicity of Barthes' mother, of what we lose through death, is always out of focus: objects of desire are only phantomal, and their reality is not a cutting short of the chain, is not an end-stop, but the necessity with which their 'thereness' is unobtainable.[35] Like the secret names in Derrida's discussion with Lévi-Strauss fourteen years earlier, it is the inevitable lack of uniqueness of the linguistic sign, the lack of 'property' in a proper name, which makes language possible, but also painful in its intrinsic inability to reach the singular: it can only be signed by it (Psy, 284; *RB*, 272). This is what Derrida seems to imply in such a phrase as 'j'ai lu les deux livres *à la suite* comme si un idiome allait enfin paraître et développer sous mes yeux son négatif' (Psy, 276) ('I read these two books one *after the other*, as if the negative of a type of language were finally going to appear and develop before my eyes') (*RB*, 263) where in the pun on photographic 'developing' can be discerned the 'passage to the limit', that is, to the singular, the 'idiom', the *apeiron*, which is off-limits, which as we shall see can only emerge against the actual infinite. It is as if the circuit of argument from 'The deaths of Roland Barthes' discerned above points to an emergence of a singular from the negotiation of the actual infinite with a process of approximation.

Singulars and proper names

A similar circuit of argument in another of Derrida's works again seems to evoke another singular, this time not as the referent but as the name. There are of course different ways of referring to something. One can use a description in a way that implies one believes that there is one thing and one only satisfying the description, so that the description is successfully designating it ('definite descriptions'). A long tradition assimilates noun and name, referring and naming; to refer to an individual object is understood as using its name as its proper name as most people understand it, though it may not be unique, as 'Andrew Brown' is not unique, yet when used as a name has a unique referent, and refers to something that is singular. The non-uniqueness of this proper name can be sorted out and the actual references specified. 'Aristotle' to take the usual example, can refer to Plato's pupil, or to a shipping magnate recently dead, and which is the reference can usually be established even if it means labour in archives. The American philosopher Kripke[36] has suggested that such labour is precisely the verification of a chain back from the problem of whom the name refers to, or whether it refers to them, to the act of name-giving (or to the point when one of a set of given names was accepted). Such names Kripke calls 'rigid designators' because their designation would not change in any possible world (Kripke 1980: 48). For Kripke, a name refers by stipulation, which means that at some point the *act* of stipulation, of fixing the reference of the name and the archive leading back to that act, must be vouched for – what in Derridean terms might be termed the 'event'.

Frege 'was well aware that in ordinary language the use of a definite description . . . in a singular statement presupposed acceptance of a proposition not explicitly asserted' – that the object of the description existed, or that some people thought it did (Kneale 1971: 594). And, in Kripke's *Naming and Necessity* (1980) for instance, the proper name has acted, with the right guarantees, as a guarantor of a unique referent (since the fixing of the reference was exactly that). So in both types of theory, definite descriptions or rigid designators can both lead back to a referent. Now the poet Francis Ponge, Derrida points out, has been thought of by critics as returning to each singular thing, 'to the things themselves', as if under some Husserlian injunction (SéP, 23; SéP, 22). After all, the title of one of his collections is *Le Parti pris des choses*. Some other critics, Derrida also reminds us, have treated Ponge as returning to the question of language, that is, as a theoretician and practitioner of his own element, writing. Derrida moves against both these acounts of Ponge: the proper name does not supply an end-station 'out there'; it is written, he will show, all over Ponge's writings. A proper name becomes hard to distinguish from a common noun at the same time as it leads outside writing, because it involves signature, procedures for signing a proper name which then acts as authorization. And in the same way, for those things 'out there' on which Ponge appears to be meditating phenomenologically, they too are conveyed through language. Derrida in the series of works being considered in this chapter, will work on the 'idiom', the proper name, the individual style, the characteristic property of a specific, even in an example from the Greek dictionary, 'one's own death' *idios thanatos* – all examples of end-stations, and of apparent singularity. Derrida's title *Signéponge* with its pun already points to the way he will cause the opposition referent/sign to exfoliate by splicing it with problems connected with the proper name and with the signature. Once more, like the *studium* and *punctum* of the Barthes article, it points to the classical analysis of the form of the proposition 'S est P', whose elimination of modality and reliance on identity are suspect; in another version, 'Signe est ponge', it crosses use and mention, hinting at doubt about whether the distinction used to separate extensional from intensional functions is universally valid, that is, whether those functions which pick out the set of things to which the term can be applied (sign is (a) (s)ponge) and those which pick out the concept under which it is arranged (the sign 'sponge') can be cleanly distinguished (Kneale 1971: 607).

Derrida suggests that we need a 'science de l'aléa' (a science of hazard) and such *aléa* moves, in a very amusing way, against 'naming and necessity'. The *aleatory* nature of names as Derrida describes them (SéP, 119; SéP, 118) (which would correspond to *necessary* identity of the names through all possible worlds, a relation by *aléa*, by stipulation) can always be resemanticized and thus renecessitized (they then slide into descriptions, that are for Kripke non-necessary because they pick out properties which are not the same in all possible worlds).

The Kripkean question is thus asked of Ponge: with another name but being the same man, would he have been the same man, that is, written the same things – in Kripkean terms, not used by Derrida, would his designation have been rigid through different possible worlds?[37] Would he, in another possible world, have played around with his own name, in manner analogous to that of Francis Ponge with his name here? Does the rigid designator suddenly flop? Kripke would say no. 'Aristotle' is a name by stipulation, its bearer could have written none of his philosophical work, and in Kripke's definition he would still have been Aristotle. The relation between man and name is contingent in origin but necessary in function – a name is rigid through possible worlds; the proper name can be considered as assigned reference by stipulation. But in Ponge's case, in Ponge's poems, Derrida insinuates, by the mere fact of being linguistic, his name can acquire possibilities of sense, it can be remotivated, and thus rendered non-accidental.

Ponge

> déguise tous les noms propres en descriptions et toutes les descriptions en noms propres. . . . On ne sait jamais s'il nomme ou s'il décrit, ni si ce qu'il décrit-nomme, est la chose ou le nom, le commun ou le propre.
>
> (SéP, 119)

> disguises every proper name as a description and every description as a proper name. . . . You never know whether he names or describes, nor whether the thing he describes-names is the thing or the name, the common or proper name.
>
> (SéP, 118)

Derrida's reference to Russell's theory of descriptions is explicit. Russell (and Frege) held that the reference of a name was determined by a uniquely identifying description (Kripke 1980: 27) or a family of descriptions. That is a bit fast for Frege: but it is the case that he aligned every complete sign with the name: 'I call anything a proper name, if it is a sign for an object'[38] and that he 'undertook to supply a reference for every definite description in his system' (Kneale 1971: 594).

In a sense, what Derrida does, and what in *Signéponge* he says Ponge is doing, began already in *Of Grammatology* where, against Lévi-Strauss, he had denied that the 'proper name' constituted the final end of a naming chain. On the contrary, all naming is generalizing, no naming is absolutely singular. Thus Ponge sows his name in his work: Ponçage (polishing)-Ponce-Pilate (Pontius Pilate)-Eponge (sponge). The effect of Babel is that God has forced man to translate, to translate proper names by common nouns, and at the same time forbidden this (OA, 136–7; *EO*, 102–3). Derrida, who has done this with his own name – in *Glas* for instance – had also in *Glas* said that Genet's *Miracle de la rose* 'cultivates the grafts of the proper name', which like some occupying power begins to be found everywhere (*Glas*, 48b, 34b). This is a figure of rhetoric, 'antonomasia' (the use of a proper name as a common noun), and he links it by a pun in Greek with Genet's flowers and his own dissemination. So the proper name can be dissolved into the common noun, which in turn may fail to designate, to be a definite description. (Again, it is as if Derrida's current of thought seizes a bit of wood – Russell's definite descriptions – and makes it orientate itself momentarily in its stream.) *Glas* plays between remotivation and demotivation of phonemes and sememes (*Glas*, 169b, 149b).

Signéponge moves, then, on two opposed vectors as we shall see. On the one hand, Ponge's name is everywhere, it is monumentalized, turned into verbal monuments in astounding multiplicity, a multiple and atheological version of the *signatura rerum* (*signatura rerum* refers to an ancient theory explaining similarity in the appearance of things, especially of plants, to the particular body parts they are believed to treat). *Signéponge* (*Signsponge*), where Derrida makes Ponge's name creep out in a spreading network, is an onomastic version, a version through names of his own mode of construction, which takes place, however, not only through names, but, as we are seeing, through repetition of mini-circuits, cells of arguments, micrologies. On the other hand, the proper name is in fact a limit, a *locum tenens* of the 'offstage' singular, a version of the *apeiron*, that which cannot be reappropriated, that which generates necessity: 'Une limite marquée par l'autre comme autre, en tant qu'il est porteur de nom propre – qu'elle est porteuse de nom propre – en tant que concept' (ALT, 92) ('A limit marked by the other as other – in so far as he or she is a bearer of a proper name – in so far as it is concept') (my translation). Once again, as with the referent in 'The deaths of Roland Barthes', we have not come out into the daylight of a reality nor up to an end-stop. We have rather come upon the name as substituting for the referent, as the photograph did in that article.

Now the 'singularly identified', the singular, is arrived at when it has been completely determined, and is therefore a totality of determinations; as such it is positively infinite (according to what is usually picked out in the French analysis of mathematical limit). The paradox Derrida is addressing becomes clear when one notices that the French translation for Kripke's 'uniquely identifying' is 'singularisant'. The process of 'uniquely identifying' can never be completed, but has to be assumed for naming to take place. So that 'uniquely identifying' relies on a concept of a whole as condition of the parts, which is a version of the concept of the actual infinite, that infinite which is in some sense given already.

In a spreading net of commentary and puns, through the sponges, towels and soap of Ponge's poems, the sponge, as common noun and accretion round a proper name – *nom propre* is also the *non-propre*, the not-clear and undecidable – forcibly collocates proper and not proper, clean and dirty. Derrida, in a series of deliberately scandalous and inventive puns, spreads out the Ponge poems towards these names, he creates circuits which communicate with terms we have met before elsewhere in his work. 'Scandalous' because behind the 'proper' is Heideggerian *Eigentlichkeit* ('le propre' in French, usually translated as 'authenticity' in English). Derrida–Ponge's sponge might almost be a kind of subversive commentary on Heideggerian pathos round household objects. And against the *Ereignis* ('event'), the 'événement d'appropriation' as it is translated in French, the sponge is precisely that which has interminably to be dealt with, negotiated with, because it cannot be appropriated, rendered proper/clean.

The name marks then a paradoxical limit between proper and common; and Derrida's 'nom propre' (proper name) has then, like *restance,* a strange status – it is and it is not. It too makes possible, while being impossible in its purity (although the phrase is not used).[39] What is being explored is the nature of the idiomatic, if there is no defining set of unique characteristics which can be distributed to individuals (more recently, Derrida has pursued the question at a larger level, one of nation, or culture, see *Mal d'archive*). For clearly 'effects of idiom' do occur. *Signature* is a curious event whereby the unique signs itself doubly – you need to counter-sign at least once for a signature to be valid – and thus ends its uniqueness (the 'singulier pluriel' of 'Dissemination' and the Barthes article occurs here too: SéP, 81; SéP, 80). *Signature* is 'the absolute idiom of a contract' from the writer, but also for the written, in a phrase that reminds of *restance* without being identical, 'la forme de la signature, celle-ci restant *de l'autre*' (SéP, 51) ('the . . . form of the signature, this latter remaining *the other's*) (SéP, 50), as in the earlier theory of pharmacopy, it was the sign indicating some specific nature or quality (SéP, 49; SéP, 48). Here it is a trace then of something else, but that something is other, some extra-systemic force, something presumably beyond language.

Derrida sketches out three 'modalities of the signature':

1   as authentifying act;
2   as 'idiomatic' style;
3   as *mise en abyme* or reflexivity, where, by a kind of short-circuit cryptically expressed and to be looked at more closely, 'elle [mise en abyme] s'abîme et fait événement, c'est l'autre, la chose comme autre qui signe. . . . Ça ne se passe pas dans les livres, ça, seulement, mais aussi dans les révolutions' (SéP, 53–5) ('[it] is thereby decomposed and produces an event, it is the other, the thing as other, that signs. This does not just happen in books, not only, but also in revolutions') (SéP, 54) – as America's Declaration of Independence, Derrida will argue, will constitute the American people as a potential entity by referring to a nation which only exists in and after that very reference and the solemn signatures to the Declaration (see Chapter 4).

As with the proper name, so with the signature: it is inserted, through Ponge's dissemination/dissimulation of his name, into the body of the text; it is monumentalized – it is 'got up' like the column or colossos in *Glas*, but then it is reified, deadened, impersonal, 'une chose ou un nom commun. L'érection-tombe' (SéP, 57) ('a thing or a common noun. The erection-tomb falls') (SéP, 56). So the erection falls and becomes a standing tombstone and this is 'une dissipation sans retour', 'dissipation without return' (SéP, 51; SéP, 50). As such it is paradoxical: on one side, a Thing which loses singularity to become a common noun and a writing of the colossos; on the other, an assignation of pure idiom, which is impossible. Once again, the signature working by anagram or by juxtaposition, works like time, by metonymy: 'Condition de possibilité et d'impossibilité, le *double bind* d'un événement de signature' (SéP, 65) ('the condition of possibility and impossibility. The *double bind* of a signature event') (SéP, 64). The signature is written by following a contrary injunction (the 'double bind' of the Palo Alto school of psychiatry, crossed with a sexual metaphor: *double bande* from *bander* = to get an erection).

The thing and the event

In relation to Ponge, then, Derrida works with such end-stops as 'proper name' and 'signature'. These appear to lead back to a unique entity which, however, is out of our focus, which appears as the terminus of a not-yet-finished and possibly unfinishable process, as something whose unreachability imposes on us negotiation.

This process now needs further examination. Is its possible terminus a person, individual, characterizable? Is it an act, locatable in space–time? *La chose*, another apparent end-stop which cannot be one, is subversive as well as commonplace. As has already been suggested, the 'sponge', among other pieces of Ponge's household paraphernalia, appears as a very funny burlesque of Heidegger's everyday objects. (See, for instance, Heidegger's 'jug' in *Das Ding* [*The Thing*] and the relation there to the everyday object – in *Truth in Painting*, Derrida brings together the art historian and townsman Meyer Schapiro's account of Van Gogh's paintings of shoes with the commentary provoking it, the would-be woodsman Heidegger's.) Derrida picks up the 'exprimer' which is found in the poem 'orange' and applies it to the sponge: 'Il exprime son nom, c'est tout. A travers tout le corpus' (SéP, 71) ('He expresses his name, and that is all. Across the entire corpus') (SéP, 70). It doesn't merely rub the body, it expresses what the spreading network of names through Ponge's work suggests. As suggested above, the process is analogous to Derrida's circuits of argument, his in-spiration of related patterns into different texts.

'La chose' ('the thing'): *causa* in Latin, but bringing with it then references to and through Heidegger's *Ding*, to *bedingt* (conditioned) as the totally determined singular and thus to the infinite, as has been seen above, to Blanchot, and, who knows, to Lacan, is explicitly said to give way in the *mise en abyme*[40] to the event of the other, to be a place-holder for the other, which signs, leaves its mark: 'quand la mise en abyme réussit, donc quand elle s'abîme et fait événement, c'est l'autre, la chose comme autre qui signe' (SéP, 55) ('when the placement in abyss succeeds, and is thereby decomposed and produces an event, it is the other, the thing as other, that signs') (SéP, 54). The thing placed reflexively in a Ponge poem is a figure of the unrepresentable (and is therefore sublime?), but in a parodistic invocation, with echoes of religious language, it is also a bit of common bric-à-brac:

> Incroyable chose sans chose, nom de l'innommable qui peut s'affecter de tout, du propre et du non-propre, qui peut se souiller et se laver elle-même de ses souillures, se confondant ainsi avec' tout (la pierre et le savon par exemple) et donc s'excluant de tout, seule, unique à être tout ou rien.
>
> (SéP, 73)

> An incredible thing without thing, the name of the unnameable which can be affected by everything, by the proper and the non-proper, which can be soiled and can also wash itself of its stains, confusing itself in this way with everything (stone and soap, for example), and hence excluding itself from everything, unique in being all or nothing.
>
> (SéP, 74)

The thing is multiply double, so to speak: it is, for example, both example and particular – a particularity so great, a uniqueness so striking that it becomes an example, and thus potentially plural; or, like the Kripkean proper name, it is contingent (any old thing) but also necessary (SéP, 91–2; SéP, 90).[41]

Like the signature, it collects contradictory adjectives: Ponge's 'serviette éponge' (tissu éponge – 'towelling' – or texte éponge) is near and impossible, offered and refused, both another thing and the something different which makes it into a thing and, in a deliciously respectful parody of Heidegger, gives it 'la choséité, allons-y, de la chose' (SéP, 93) ('the thingness, shall we say, of the thing') (SéP, 92).[42] Like Barthes' *punctum*, it has double direction: it gives (an order), it addresses me; and yet 'I' go to it. In what is another circuit of argument, a new micrology, it makes the law:

> D'abord la chose est l'autre, le tout autre qui dicte ou qui écrit la loi, une loi qui n'est pas simplement naturelle (*lex naturae rerum*) mais une injonction infiniment, insatiablement impérieuse à laquelle je dois m'assujettir, quitte à tenter de m'acquitter ensuite.
>
> (SéP, 13–15)

> Beforehand, the thing is the other, the entirely other which dictates or which writes the law, a law which is not simply natural (*lex naturae rerum*),

but an infinitely, insatiably imperious injunction to which I have to subject
myself, even when this involves trying to acquit myself afterwards.

(SéP, 12–14, trans. mod.)

A law is applicable and available in general and to all. But the thing's law does
not pre-exist, and it prescribes absolute attention to singularity and to difference (SéP, 15; SéP, 14). For the law prescribed by the thing[43] is also no law, the
thing is singular, whereas a law is general and exemplary (SéP, 51; SéP, 50).
Like 'signature', it is a contradictory injunction, like 'signature', it provokes the
event.

Derrida splits apart the usual translation of the Heideggerian *Ereignis*, he
makes the dyad 'event of appropriation' separate.[44] Each event of writing is
unique, and must each time be reappropriated by a law, the law of the common
noun. Event for Heidegger is the moment, the unavailable moment, which yet
happens to human thought, and which momentarily tears open ontological
difference between Being and being.[45] Derrida will elsewhere relate 'event' to
'rencontre, décision, appel, nomination, initiale incision d'une marque [qui] –
ne peut advenir que depuis l'expérience de l'indécidable' ('meeting, decision,
appeal, nomination, initial incision of a mark [which] – cannot come about
except from the experience of the undecidable') (Par, 15, my translation).
(Event cannot then arise from what can be calculated – the undecidable is to
have no reason for choosing between two quite determinate and opposed
choices.) If 'appropriation' is perilous, rejected as 'mastery',[46] Ponge's own
constant reapplication suggests a struggle with an absolute, with something
absolved from relations, a struggle like Joseph's with the Angel, 'la lutte au
corps à corps avec l'impossible, avec quelque chose qui, dans le propre, dans la
structure même du propre, ne se produit, qu'à passer dans son autre' (SéP, 31)
('some hand-to-hand conflict with the impossible, with something which,
within the proper, within the very structure of the proper, is produced only by
shifting into its opposite') (SéP, 30). The appropriation of the thing is always
wiped out, or rather stopped short – one can only *want* to say 'my thing', and
Derrida uses the conditional (SéP, 49; SéP, 48).[47]

Before looking at this tension which Derrida injects into 'event of appropriation', what is the event, this strange entity? The title of his article on Austin's
work on illocutionary utterances: 'Signature event context' suggests a piece of
comparative philosophy. It suggests that the performatives, the illocutionary
acts that Austin is analysing are versions (to be then defined) of 'event' and
'signature'. The illocutionary force Austin spoke of might then be connected to
what is in Derridean terms the 'unappropriatable' in the event and the signature. As with the signature, so with the event: the unappropriatable both
structures and puts them out of reach. Now two modern philosophers, Saul
Kripke and Quentin Skinner, relate the using of names and writing. Kripke, as
has already been pointed out, when treating 'the logic of proper names' – the
title of the French version of *Naming and Necessity* – relates names back to an
act of baptism. (Cf. Derrida, on signing as self-baptism: 'En signant, je me

donne à moi-même chaque fois pour la première et la dernière fois, mon nom', SéP, 109; SéP, 108). Skinner suggests how history of ideas can be done without, on the one hand, making of reading the archives an activity sealed into a medium of words, there being nothing else, or, on the other hand, without considering that all writing is merely epiphenomenal, caused by other 'real' forces in society. He makes of writing an act (Skinner 1988). This baptism or stipulation, with Kripke, or production by writing with Skinner, are anchor points, chain ends in their work, chain ends which are attached to unanalysed or unfocused things. In both cases it is an act of enunciation to which the weight of analysis is anchored, an act which according to Husserl cannot be explored at the same time as the utterance itself. What Derrida may be doing in these explorations of ghostly shapes – thing, event, proper name – is showing what shape that unavoidable attachment to the necessarily out-of-focus takes.

The *chose* as 'entirely other', creates an injunction, yet at the same time it asks for nothing, for it has no relation to itself nor to another: in that sense it is death (SéP, 49; SéP, 48). Or again, later, as unique it is, like the sun is unique in its genre, inapt for metonymy, for substitution, and thus for language, 'référent sans substitution possible, sans réproduction et sans dissémination'; it is like the Platonic good – *epekeina tes ousias* (SéP, 141; SéP, 140), that is, the actual infinite. But the poet can revenge himself on Plato: by making a change of article, by language, the sun becomes 'a sun' and an example. Writing can tempt the sun; the thing's demand can only be acquitted by writing through which the thing can sign. And the writing of the idiom immediately cancels it as idiomatic by making metonymy necessary: the process has to be repeated. Subjacent here once more, but confirmed by repetition of word and circuit of argument, is a reference to time.[48] Time is the matrix of substitution in which unrepeatable and iterable meet, as time in 'The deaths of Roland Barthes' operated with metonymic force to suspend the referent while making that reference possible (Psy, 299; *RB*, 290). Derrida captures thus not just the elegiac mode of regret for Barthes' death, but also the particular mode of Barthes' writing in certain texts. So 'la chose' is both an unobtainable singular, and the possibility of common everyday things. The thing, like the signature and the event, is arising from the pulls and the tensions between what is beyond all approximation, and what is approached by infinite negotiation and interminable process.

Derrida is writing of writing: of an everyday thing constituting itself into a written through a process of writing.[49] But this process is being formed against a relation of non-relation with the other, the thing to which there is absolute obligation: there is an ethical thrust, a lesson even in Ponge's work (SéP, 53; SéP, 52).[50] So that a mediation is called for. Exactly as in 'The deaths of Roland Barthes', *studium* and *punctum* had to compose with each other, here:

Comme les deux tout-autres [producers of signature and of 'the thing'] (engagés-dégagés) sont hors contrat, inaccessibles et qu'on ne peut jamais que les laisser être (lui et la chose), ce qui intéresse, nous intéresse, nous engage à lire, c'est forcément ce qui se passe au milieu, *entre eux*, les

intermédiaires, (noms et choses) les témoins, les intercesseurs, les événe-
ments qui se passent *entre eux*, les intéressés.

(SéP, 53)

Since the two (engaged-disengaged) entirely others are outside of the
contract process, are inaccessible, and since we can never do anything other
than let them be (he and the thing), that which interests, or interests us,
and engages us in reading, is inevitably what happens in the middle,
between them: the intermediaries (names and things); the witnesses, the
intercessors, the events that go on *between them*, the interested ones.

(SéP, 52)

In writing, the thing as unobtainable other is inveigled into the thing written, I
'interest' the thing in signing (Derrida puns on 'intéresser' and squints towards
the Heideggerian *angehen*):

Reconnaissance de dette infinie à l'égard de la chose comme autre chose,
j'intéresse la chose qui me regarde, je l'intéresse à signer elle-même d'elle-
même, et à devenir, en restant ce qu'elle est, tout autre, aussi une partie
consignée de mon texte.

(SéP, 129)

an IOU made out for an infinite debt in regard to the thing as something
other, I interest the thing that regards me, I interest it in signing itself, by
itself, and in becoming, while remaining the thing it is, entirely other, also a
consigned part of my text.

(SéP, 128)

Like the double direction of 'le punctum . . . la traversée du discours vers
l'unique' – 'the traversal of discourse towards the unique' (Psy, 295; *RB*,
284–5), and 'le punctum déchire' – 'the punctum rends' (Psy, 292; *RB*, 281) in
'The deaths of Roland Barthes', such a double relation, here built round
intéresser,[51] makes possible the constitution of the thing in Ponge's poetic text.
In sum, patterns are emerging, cell-structures which recur, ghost-like, for they
are composed out of our fragile recognition of repeated circuits of argument,
and these seem to give rise to ghostly entities, 'chose' ('thing'), 'nom-propre'
('proper name'), 'événement' ('event'), 'référence' ('reference'). These are
doubles of what naively we might call 'real things' – 'real names', 'real events'.
They enable us to speak of 'thing', 'name', 'event', 'reference' without a naive
distinction between 'real world out there' and the world of the word, of
language and ideas, without abolishing necessary distinctions which enable
thinking. But they are in themselves doubles – 'signature' needs 'counter signature', 'chose' ('thing') points to 'autre chose' ('something different') for
instance. Moreover, such words in Derrida are not free-floating, for they have
an umbilical cord back to their context of nurture in Ponge or Blanchot. Like

strange attractors, 'singularités' in French, where prolongations of certain apparently chaotic series subside within the limits of a certain form, they have a double self-construction. They are produced both by what is beyond approximation and works through the double bind, short-circuit or violent interruption; but they are also produced by the negotiation which involves constant approximation.

Other

The question now becomes pressing: to what degree are the programmes discerned here the same? The vocabulary used of them is not uniform. Are the programmes then analogous rather than identical, the language used in them being mined by Derrida from the particular writer or philosopher in question in the particular writing, but the resemblance, on which the similarity they have to the reader is based, being one that is never fully secure?

Derrida, in his article of 1964 already discussed, 'Violence and metaphysics', showed how the nature of speech about the other is a point of difference between Levinas and Husserl. Both agree that 'the other' is not to be reduced, for two reasons: because perceptions are incomplete, and the phenomenological reduction is of necessity infinitely indefinite; and because the other is another person, whose experience is not 'proper' in the sense of not accessible to me as my own (propre) (ED, 183; WD, 124). But Husserl will yet speak of the other as an intentional object *for me*; whereas Levinas will refuse this, as a violation of the other; he will therefore, argues Derrida, speak of the other in fact, without any basis of justification, while making of the other something like the positive infinite. Derrida rejects this. He refuses to identify the actual or positive infinite with the 'infinitely Other': 'L'infini ne s'entend comme Autre que sous la forme de l'in-fini' (ED, 168) ('Infinity cannot be understood as Other except in the form of the in-finite') (*WD*, 114), that is indefinite, needing to be infinitely redetermined. So if this attitude is not denied in later work, then we should expect to need to find, what in fact we did in *Signsponge*, that the sun, the positive infinite, which is *epekeina tes ousias*, can yet be drawn into language, which is constant redetermination.

In another article on Levinas, 'At this very moment in this work here I am' (1980 – revised in small but significant ways for *Psyché*, 1987) – Derrida takes up the questions of language and the other, of the token reflexive and presence. For Levinas the relation to the other must be in terms of interruption.[52] Derrida, with three quotations from Levinas, shows how the apparently token reflexive written phrase 'At this very moment in this work here I am' ('en ce moment' or 'en ce moment même') is used in opposite ways (it was of course the token-reflexive nature of language which Dummett used to defend McTaggart on the unreality of time). It expresses language's systematizing power, since whatever the relation to the other, however open and unthematized, we nevertheless predicate, synchronize, organize, just by talking, in the very moment of talking. Yet the same phrase at a different point in Levinas' argument, says Derrida, expresses the way in which reference to the inter-locutor, openness to the other, tears or pierces ('déchirure', 'percée': the word 'déchire' was used of the *punctum* in 'The deaths of Roland Barthes') the text which discourse was making seamless and organized (Psy, 172). So that, Derrida points out, the distinction made by Levinas, between the saying, that is the act or moment of enunciation, and the said is not one that inserts presence into language through token-reflexivity. For Levinas, the reference to the inter-locution cuts in two nearly opposed ways: both to seam over by its very saying what is other, and to remind us of the interruption which has been congealed, sealed over by language. But in Levinas' writing the distinction between moment of enunciation and what is being said is *effaced* because it is being both mentioned and used (Psy, 173). What Levinas has thematized is in the one case thematization which obscures relation to the other, and in the other case what is non-thematizable in this relation; (we see the thematization of the thema-tizing and the non-thematizing, a variant of the 'dialectics between dialectics and non-dialectics' already discussed above in Chapter 2). He has done this using the same phrase 'en ce moment même', 'in this very moment'. Yet the distinction, Derrida says, between 'use' and 'mention' is unsteady, for Levinas by the temporal marker 'en ce moment' both enacts and talks, and enacts and talks about both the systematizing by language and the piercing, the tearing of language. This smudging of the distinction between 'uttering' and 'uttered' (which will be discussed again later) picks up the problem of the linguistic act, the 'anchor point' to which Kripke's naming and Skinner's history of ideas are attached.

We seem to return here to the analysis of time in the article on Aristotle, where the impossibility of the coexistence of different nows, in everything the same except that they were past and future, had to be stated by maintaining them together, a synthesis which was not anchored by any subjectivity in action. It is, says Derrida, the 'same' moment and yet it is different, for the 'same' follows the noun, and in fact in French means something more like 'very'. The occurrences of the *phrase* 'en ce moment même', 'in this very moment', in Derrida's article are altered at their quotation – Derrida by bending them towards each other prevents the phrase pointing to the present. He separates it from Hegel's 'this now' which represents the cross of time. (Hegel at the begin-ning of the *Phenomenology of Spirit* pointed out that when you say 'now', what you were referring to has already gone, and made thus of deixis and of token-reflexive expression, the start of reflexive consciousness in time.) On the contrary, says Derrida: 'Cela tient d'abord à autre chose; à la chose comme Autre. Ecoute' and he adds in the 1987 text, 'Ecoute c'est encore l'âme ou psyché'. As we shall see, the sameness and difference of the phrase is not merely because the 'now' is not the same 'now' as that which is past. In a parenthesis, it is as if Derrida suggests that language provides the subjective field within which the possible impossibility which was time becomes a responsibility towards what is outside the present window onto time (Psy, 173–4). A respon-sibility less toward than imposed by what is outside that window.

Now it is striking that many of the additions to the text for its re-publication are references to the title of the collection, to the 'psyché' (this is true too of other articles).[53] It has to be remembered (and Derrida reminds us in the preface to *Psyché*) that 'psyché' also means 'mirror'; that the relation between 'énoncé' and the saying can be considered reflexive, in that it is a mirroring of what cannot be incorporated into what is said ('énoncé'). Finally, 'In the last resort, all references to particular things or events in space and time consist in the location of them by relation to the act of speech'.[54] As was suggested earlier, token-reflexive expressions cannot be excised from language, as Russell seems to have wanted to do. Yet that point *punctum, stigmé*, the *moment* of attachment of language to its act is overlapped and interlocked in Derrida's view. It is not a simple insertion, not a moment of presence. It is not a positing by an agent. It arises from a negotiation, as from the relation between *punctum* and *studium*.

In shadowy fashion, besides 'la chose' ('the thing') which we have seen at work, there appears to arrive a new entity which might double the 'human subject' (without the limits of being defined as human, nor the limits imposed by being opposed to object and to predicate, nor any of the connections with a predatory, tool-using attitude to all that is not subject, as suggested by Heidegger in his analysis of *Gegenstand*). 'Psyché' may enable a comprehension of the presuppositions which float in our discourse and make the distinction between modal and non-modal language unsustainable;[55] were it structured like 'event' or 'thing' or *punctum*, it would be something which can yet be enticed into speech, into an unformalizable relation between what can and what cannot be formalized: 'at this very moment in this work here I am', 'en ce moment même me voici' as a tension, another counterpart to the other. The 'psyché' has constituted something like a place holder, a *locum tenens* for the 'subject' just as 'chose' had for the object, as has been seen above. But 'psyche', unlike the group 'event', 'thing', 'proper name', and unlike the Derridean lexemes 'supplement', 'différance', appears as if only lightly instilled into the texts in this collection, appears to have no future outside it. Instead, and more strongly, 'other' and 'gift' begin to emerge.

The second article on Levinas in fact opens slowly, with a hesitating step, moving round the questions of context, of writing 'on' someone when the article is also addressed to him; of the temporality of such a relationship (the future perfect, important in Derrida's own language use). It goes on to consider 'le don' – the gift.[56] 'Donner' (cf. 'The deaths of Roland Barthes' on the 'dative', the receiving of the *punctum*) is not an exchange of an object, nor is it an act. Derrida uses a Heideggerian reduplication (or rather here, triplication): 'Non, lui donner le donner même du donner' (Psy, 164) ('No, to give him the very giving of giving') ('At this very moment in this work here I am', 15), a form of expression which at the same time seems to purify and to infinitize. 'Donner' is once more, like the *pharmakon*, an excess ('étrange, non, cet excès qui déborde la langue à tout instant et cependant qui la requiert') which is more than language and yet necessitates language. As *punctum* 'holed' (*trouer*) the surface of our notions of resemblance and reproduction, so to give, 'donner', 'holes' the usual interpretation of the meaning of language, the usual 'extra-temporal' sense given to the infinitive, for it is usually held to refer not to a time, but to what is outside time ('Il faut donc que le "donner" troue ici le phénomène grammatical dominé par l'interprétation courante de la langue', Psy, 164; 'the "giving" therefore must perforate the grammatical phenomenon dominated by the current interpretation of language', 'At this very moment . . . ' 15) Derrida also repeats the word 'traverser' for this excessive movement through language: in 'The deaths of Roland Barthes' it was an ambiguous halting between objective and subjective genitive; between discourses' crossing towards the 'referent' or on the other hand the *punctum*, that is the 'point of singularity's crossing of discourse towards the "referent"'. In the Levinas article, the same excess which is more than language, also necessitates language, and sets it in motion at the very moment of 'traversing it'. And the same word, as has been said above, is used of these interrelations – negotiation.

Language as subjective field, always beyond what can be gathered into a site of present syntheses, is thus first the site of responsibility to the other. The excess beyond synthesis in language means that other meanings or the possibility of other meanings, future ones as well as past, have to be deferred to. But that responsibility may not be answered to – it is because it may *always possibly not* be answered to that there is an ethics. The new cannot be programmed for, and ethical response is not merely a result of calculation within any 'felicific calculus' or theory of 'social responsiveness' (we see here the link between the taking of risk and ethics which is evoked several times by Derrida).

Now for Levinas, this responsibility is not the reception of a given by a prepared receiver, primed for his or her reaction, nor an intentionality focusing outwards in a version of the traditional activity of the will. It is a kind of command which arrives from the other and lets the receiving subjectivity arise. There is a kind of force which words like 'should' indicate. The gift 'should' go to the unique, what the proper name has made unique. In this way, the binary structures of systems of exchange, of which language is one, and thus of the communication model for language, have been radically recast. Although there is an originator of the act, instead of a speaker exchanging words with a hearer, the two-dimensional grid of addresser and addressee has been effaced, as Derrida already pointed out in his early article à propos Austin, by the notion of force, 'illocutionary force' as Austin calls it. It is as if addresser has been etiolated, altered in the sense of 'othered', and the 'psyché' is no longer a focal source of an act. Once the primacy of 'S is P' is questioned, that is, the pattern of predication is queried, Derrida points out, there is an 'absolute dissymmetry', for 'I' is assigned from the place of the other (a version of the *punctum*'s accusative force) : 'une sorte d'agrammaticalité du don assignée depuis l'autre: *je* à l'accusatif' (Psy, 169) ('a sort of agrammaticality of the gift assigned from the other: *I* in the accusative, etc') ('At this very moment . . . ', 19). The conception of language as communication is being altered.

Such an assignation of a 'kind of agrammaticality' is through the 'gift': we do not have twinned entities of the same calibre, entities enterable in some binary grid; instead we have heterogeneous (even linguistically heterogeneous) and difficult concepts, the 'gift' being, one might almost say, at an angle to 'psyché' (see also Chapter 5).

> The gift, effacing all determination, sexual or otherwise, produces the destination. Supposing that a gift has been given, that supposes that, before it took place, the giver is not determined and the receiver is not determined. But the gift determines, it is the determination, it produces the identity of the given and the receiver. . . . That is why the gift is always a stroke of force, an irruption. . . . The one who responds, receives it, becomes the receiver. The performativity of the text produces its receiver, but in no way does it pre-exist it. It is the receiver who is the determining factor of the gift.
>
> (Beehive, 15)

The gift here alludes to the Heideggerian 'es gibt':[57] Heidegger's redefinition of it is part of his radical shifting of concepts of being and existence, and his recasting of the subject/object relation, his broadening, his fundamental altering of its relation with the problem of transcendence. Notions with long histories in philosophy, the 'datum', the problem of what 'actually exists', what 'is given', the problem of the relation between what we experience (things for us) and 'things as they are' – all are reworked through the 'ontological difference', that is, the distinction between Being and beings, and the exploration of transcendence (see above).[58] 'Es gibt' in ordinary German, the impersonal phrase for 'there is', has its literal meaning injected back into it by Heidegger (with it, it seems to me, come senses of 'charis', which allude to a kind of momentary grace from which all precise religious origin has been cut). Heidegger enlarges the idea of the given beyond the Kantian intuition through sensibility (KRV, A19, B33) into a co-implication with the transcendent, rendering impossible the partition of experience into subject and object. Beings are what they are, even if *Dasein* (being there, experience of the world) does not exist; however, 'Being (*Sein*) "is" not, but being is there [es gibt] in so far as Dasein exists. In the essence of existence there is transcendence, i.e. a given of the world prior to and for all being-toward-and among intra-worldly beings' (MFL, 153). Elsewhere, Heidegger will plot the development in western philosophy of the subject/object relation, and its relation to consciousness of the world as composed of discrete objects, available to a subject for use and mastery (*Gegenstände*; *Gegenständlichkeit* and its philosophical characterization, *Gegenständigkeit*).[59]

Such an analysis is crucial to Heidegger's critique of technology and science. Lest it sound merely nostalgic for a shadowy past of natural peasant respect for things and for the surrounding world, consider a possible filiation, which may sharpen realization of the extent to which Heidegger may be probing logical relations. Heidegger wrote a favourable review of Frege,[60] who precisely had taken *Gegenständlichkeit* – objectivity – as a necessary condition of objects. To be actual they must be individual objects.[61] From this kind of existence, Frege clearly distinguished the meaning of 'es gibt [ein]', which is not a statement about objects but about concepts.[62] It is as if Heidegger places this distinction between modes of existence in history and disengages an ontological signification to *es gibt* which serves to focus its relation to epistemologically contexted words like 'datum' and to theology, while at the same time setting in doubt such borders.

Derrida's 'gift' comes from the other, is suscitated by the other (this is only possible through an already opened anticipation, and this, which Derrida calls the 'yes, yes,' is in turn possible through the gift: neither precedes). Is it a counterpart, in both senses, that of replication and that of counter-move, to 'existence', stripped of notions of 'presence'? So that to the shadowy 'psyché', 'thing', 'proper name' which arose out of the double relation to the other, the relations of negotiation and of double bind, there might also arise a kind of ontological index? It is at this point in the article on Levinas, where the reader is speculating on the advisability of leaning on the philological relation 'es gibt' – 'don' – 'datum' – that Derrida enters into a consideration which had weighed explicitly in his first articles (in particular in 'Cogito . . . ') and in more shadowy fashion in the 'Supplement of copula' in *Margins*.[63] It is the question of the relation between thought and language, of the possibility of non-linguistic thought. Not, Derrida always hastens to add (with a pattern of argument that reminds of that used about transcendental reasoning), in the classical sense of thought as superior to its mere medium, language, not as a transgression of the limits of language, but as a relation to what has to be invented in and through language. 'Le passage au-delà de la langue requiert la langue ou plutôt le texte comme lieu des traces pour un pas qui n'est pas (présent) ailleurs' ('the passage beyond language requires language or rather a text, as a place for the trace of a step that is not (present) elsewhere') ('At this very moment. . .' 20) (Psy, 170). The tension, in this text drawn out by the 'other', like that which magnetized 'signature', 'proper name', 'event', into patterns like some strange attractor, seems to be that of representation, which is at the same time encouraged and forbidden.[64]

For the pattern of 'At this very moment in this work here I am', discussed earlier, shows in Levinas' writing both the necessity of relation to the Other and the necessity of interruption of that relation. The Other must be inaccessible, endlessly, or the Other will not be continually other, but will be a backstop, a place of last resort. But it must be accessible, it must make itself accessible in a paradoxical way, or else we are shut endlessly into the same, and there can be no Other. Between the two there must be negotiation, as Derrida picked out mediation and composition in the work of Barthes and Ponge. Language, Levinas' language, is already open to the quite other – but its possibilities have to be negotiated with in a way that leaves 'the non-negotiable intact'. The sense of language containing other possibilities – already expressed in *Marges*, 41, (*M*, 38) – is given by the analysis of the three passages with their 'en ce moment même' and the minimal readjustings that they mutually impose on each other, their 'contamination analogique' (Psy, 177), their 'analogical contamination'.

Moreover, in a debate on the work of Levinas, again expressing faith in negotiation ('je crois à'), Derrida distinguishes it from Hegelian mediation, which ingests the negative. It must be on the contrary a 'rapport sans rapport' (a possible translation is 'non-absolute absolute') which by a kind of reduplication in the negative allows the other to be the other (ALT, 82). The 'rapport sans rapport' can be glossed by an addition to the article for the 1987 book, where it is asked whether the name of the other must be invented (Psy, 163). If what is other is to be 'found' or 'created' (the two divergent senses in modern tongues of *invenio*) without being reduced to the same, then both the absolute unicity of the proper name *and* the possibility of indefinite substitution of names, must be safeguarded. The opening of lines out towards the new is made possible by the strange relation between the process of negotiation and the non-negotiable, which have structurally the shape of the negative or potential infinite and the positive or actual infinite.

As with the referent and the thing, there is a double relation to the Other: on the one hand a kind of double bind, impossible injunction based on a commandment from the Other, and a being pulled towards the other 'l'astriction au donner et l'extradition de la subjectivité à l'autre' (Psy, 169) ('the astriction to the giving and the extradiction of the subjectivity to the other') (trans. MRN) and, on the other, a negotiation, in the face of the wrong which is speech about someone, wrong because it is determination of that someone (Psy, 198). One might be tempted to make of Other the key to a series: as if 'referent' or *punctum*, 'thing', 'proper name', 'signature', perhaps even 'psyche', could by a double process of double bind and negotiation, of interruption and composition, be made to appear, be pulled into a process of substitution, but were also among themselves in a process of substitution for the Other, for the unrepresentable. But this will not do: though the Other is less local than these lexemes, it is comparable and co-appears in phantasmal form. It is not what is represented, but a pointer, of a slightly different status, to what cannot be represented.

This subjacent patterning in Derrida's work (of this period) is once more visible in the article 'No apocalyse, not now'. Here the strange attractor, the other, is aligned with what has not yet happened, the nuclear apocalyse (an unanticipatable 'entirely other') whose 'reality' then is, like the referent's in 'The deaths of Roland Barthes', out of reach. What we do have is the phantasmatic, the referent which can be signified but not intuited (Psy, 369; *NA*, 23). In the theory of nuclear war, the armaments are real enough, but they are manoeuvred by this phantasm. And Derrida edges his scalpel through the workings of nuclear strategy, its phantasmatic calculation, its estimations of what the Soviet strategists were thinking. But the unicity of nuclear war – we will only need one – enables us to think the essence of literature and its historicity. Once again, it is the 'possibly not' which reveals the actual (Psy, 377; *NA*, 27). For literature relies on its own archive – and if this were destroyed, it too would be destroyed. In so far as literature shows up the nature of other cultural practices, this would be true of them too. Derrida is neither here arguing that nuclear war would only destroy literature, nor that culture is equivalent to literature, but that the structure of most, perhaps all, cultural activity in the widest sense is one which implies the transmission, not of some core experience, but of the sedimentation, the superimposition of ways of doing things, and at a further but not distinguishable level, of accumulated modes of transmission.[65] All experience is stratified, held in quotation marks, modal, in that it is a set of modalized accretions. The 'thing', the 'referent', 'is there' as a tension, not as a nugget of the real. Which is why inventivity is possible, and why the new can be 'realized'. The new in this way is not the programmable outcome of a strategy for invention, but results from a tension between such a 'strange attractor's' power of interruption and the necessity of negotiation with it.

Nuclear war becomes in one sense the absolute referent which destroys such practice, and thus is the 'trace du tout autre' (Psy, 379) ('the trace of what is entirely other') (*NA*, 28). Though not there, it is the engenderer of strategies of negotiation, to put it off; of other ways of thinking 'pour différer la rencontre du tout autre avec laquelle pourtant ce rapport sans rapport, ce rapport d'incommensurablité ne peut être totalement suspendu, tout en étant la suspension épochale même' (Psy, 380) ('for putting off the encounter with the wholly other, an encounter with which, however, this relationless relation, this relation of incommensurability cannot be wholly suspended, even though it is precisely its epochal suspension') (*NA*, 28). It is just before this point that Derrida makes clear the relation between this kind of suspensive absolute, and themes he had treated previously: 'the end of history' and phenomenological *epoché*. The end of history in nuclear war would not be the achievement of absolute knowledge but its *epoché*, its suspension.[66] And allusively, in the references to Kant and to Hegel, and to the need to think the positive infinite in order to make the negative infinite work, Derrida makes a transition to the 'name'. Redoubling the name, 'le nom du nom', it can name what is beyond being (*epekeina tes ousias*) and which is a 'nothing' and for which other substitutes can act close to us, can engage us in compromise.

Singularity and the Law

What I have called the strange attractor acts as a kind of law; it puts the 'I' at the end of a process, either as recipient (dative, indirect object) or as accused (accusative, direct object) (see, for instance, 'The deaths of Roland Barthes'). The gift has words like 'demand' (exiger), 'is necessary' (falloir), 'oblige', used of it ('At this moment . . . '). A law generalizes the singular: yet in Kafka's *Vor dem Gesetz* (*Before the Law*) the force of law is singularizing: 'This door was only meant for you' says the door keeper to the protagonist at the end. In that, it is 'uniquely identifying' and thus acts like a proper name. Like the gift, it creates its destination, by a singular application. Derrida's work on Kafka's fable joins problems of 'antepredicative' judgements to questions about the nature of ethics. The title 'Fore judgements' points to the difficulties which have arisen when quantification is attempted in any logic which has not already set up distinct objects over which to quantify (epistemological and deontological or temporal areas, see notes 25, 55). This is a complex allusion both to the Kafka title and to its own opposition to the canonic predicative logical form 'S is P' (Pré, 93), where pre-existing subject and predicate are joined in a synthesis. For in Fregean terms, in a work of fiction the proposition's way of describing the objects of judgement specifies them. (Derrida begins in fact with a discussion of the singularity now considered – a view he holds at arm's length, but does not develop – to constitute a work of literature, a fiction where, precisely, names have senses but no reference.)[67]

Elsewhere, Derrida links such a law into a widening of the notion of 'ethics' and of responsibility, a refusal of it as a neatly presented philosophical realm. For the universality of the law has to face the 'singularité de la venue de l'autre' –

> je dirais que l'ouverture, ou l'attente, une certaine soumission, une certain fidélité à la venue, chaque fois, de l'autre singulier, a une dimension qui ne peut pas se laisser convenir dans ce qu'on appelle le domaine de l'éthique.
>
> (ALT, 71)

> The singularity of the coming of the other . . . I would say that the opening or expectation, a certain submission, a certain faithfulness to the coming, each time, of the singular other, has a dimension that can't be brought into what is called the domain of ethics.
>
> (my translation)

and Derrida suggests both how Kant tends to inscribe this singularity into what is generalizable, via a calculation (ALT, 72), and yet gives a strange status to the example, the singular used as generally valid (Pré, 108). The law specifies its destination: but what then is its right to judge? 'The law came, and I died', St Paul wrote. It is both forbidden and enjoined – 'terrifiant double bind' (Pré, 121); 'la loi procède d'un tout autre (la chose) qui ne demande rien . . . demandant tout et rien, la chose place le débiteur . . . en situation d'hétéronomie constante' ('the law proceeds from something quite different which asks for nothing . . . asking for everything and nothing, the thing places the debtor . . . in a situation of constant heteronomy') (my translation). A relation to it can be, in a phrase met with already, a 'rapport sans rapport' of interruption, a relation which whether interrupted or continued, is paradoxical, which involves guilt without fault.[68] What is being explored is the moral dilemma, is perhaps the paradox of guilt *tout court*, incurred by merely existing in the face of the Absolute, the unrepresentable, the absent God, 'La loi qui n'est pas loi' (Pré, 95) ('the law which is not law'). Derrida refers explicitly to the *anrufverstehen und Schuld* ('understanding the appeal, and guilt') of §58 of *Being and Time*, where Heidegger traces out a relation between the appeal, the incitation and guilt. The rigour with which Derrida follows through the pathos of such themes is coupled with a delight in probing the grotesque and the humorous in the theme of the nose in Kafka's text. In the Kafka story, the man from the country is placed in a double bind. But with this double bind come negotiation, composition and intercourse, with the relays of guardians, Kafka's Doorkeeper, encouraging his approaches (since there is a cursus to be gone through) and yet showing the hopelessness derived from the too-great-distance which separates the man from any goal, especially unknown. A version of difference which both forbids and incites. Even here, before Kafka's Law, we have both double bind and negotiation.

The Law was 'before the law' and there is infinite regress (familiar too in political theory of contract: a contract is needed on which to base the contract, and so on *ad infinitum*). Derrida seems to suggest that both in politics and in literature, a short-circuit can be created, an element can be bent forward to take two positions in a temporal or linguistic sequence, so that saying can be doing (see *infra*, on the *Declaration of Independence*, and on Ponge's *Fable*). The repetition of 'Before the law's' title in its first words, points to the story's enactment of the law of the singular as an enactment of its own application to us, both in law and in literature. Freud, Derrida points out, had related law and political foundation when he derived society and morality (the forbidding of murder and of incest) from horror and repentance at the primeval murder of the father. But here, too, there is a short-circuit, though one unacknowledged by Freud. If the murder inaugurates morality, how is the moral feeling for the repentance, which in Freud's account will drive men to self-repression, to be accounted for? Once again the Law is before the law (temporally before). Derrida relates it doubly to the phantasmatic: because the ghost father, the dead father in the imagination, is said by Freud to be much more powerful than the living father ever was – so much for the level of what is supposed to have occurred. But precisely the story which Freud uses to found morality is phantasmatic: a narration which is needed precisely to make that foundation. 'Evénement sans événement [. . . qui . . .] ressemble à une fiction, à un mythe ou à une fable' ('Event with no event [which] resembles a fiction, a myth, or a fable') (Pré, 117). The question of whether Freud thought this was historical or not is pointless. (One could add that 'It was and it was not' is the Arabic expression for 'Once upon a time' and in *The Arabian Nights* begins Schahrazad's different means of delaying execution.) 'C'est l'origine de la littérature en même temps que l'origine de la loi'. And this phantasmatic origin of Freud's Law explains why it is essentially inaccessible, producing double binds, and yet constantly promising itself, announcing itself, accessible to indefinite approximation. The whole antepredicative thrust of Derrida's work is to include relations of force which constitute psychoanalytic strata, not to exclude them by a process of abstraction.

In Kafka's *Before the Law* a double bind is formed from inaccessibility, and incitation to approach; a phantasm-fiction in Freud's derivation of morality makes of the Law something unattainable and promised. As in 'No apocalypse', the structure of referentiality is shown up but not the reference itself. Whereas, though Ponge's 'thing', Barthes' *punctum*, the signature, the name, Levinas' 'other', all seem to call for both responses, interruption and negotiation and to impose both, they act as strange attractors which form shadowy entities, enabling subjectivity and referentiality without presence. So that not merely is 'other' not any kind of common denominator for what is inaccessible in the entities discussed in this chapter, but each context in which the strange attractors operate allows a force to be active without it being easy to think of it as more than analogous to the others.

Now the very shape of the relation between negotiation and interruption, which enjoins and forbids, seems paradoxically folded back on itself, a relation between relation and non-relation, and thus dissymmetric and unstable. It is structurally the same as the 'dialectics of dialectics with non-dialectics' of the introduction to *Origin of Geometry*. Derrida contrasts elsewhere this dual mode of relation with Hegelian mediation, which as we shall see he holds to be 'recuperation' and 'appeasing' or 'purifying' of opposites, because 'raised up' without remainder into a higher level. Derrida insists that the relation of interruption is an opening of relation to the other:

> une autre expérience de la médiation, dans le rapport sans rapport: sous cette médiation je reconnaîtrais le mouvement du rapport à l'autre; c'est un rapport fou, un rapport sans rapport, qui comprend l'autre comme autre dans un certain rapport d'incompréhension.
>
> (ALT, 82)

> another experience of mediation, in the relation without relation; in the mediation I would recognize the movement of the relation to the other; it is a mad relation, a relation without relation, which comprehends the other in a certain relation of incomprehension.
>
> (ALT, 82, my translation)

Derrida proceeds in this passage to bring the two modes, interruption and negotiation, together as *différance*: 'Le mot dit ces deux choses à la fois et le rapport de ces choses, de ces deux logiques; une logique de l'économie et une logique de l'anéconomie, la médiation sans opposition et l'altérité radicale', for *différance* suspends opposition – 'on est dans l'économie', but by suspending opposition and dialectic, it is aneconomical and radical differance (ALT, 82); 'The word says these two things at the same time and the relation of these things, of these two logics; a logic of economy and a logic of aneconomy, mediation without opposition and radical alterity' (my translation).[69]

And in Derrida's recent work, *Force of Law*, justice itself seems to form what I have called a 'strange attractor'. It is not deconstructible (Force, 35; *Force*, 14); in the words of *Specters of Marx*, it is urgent, messianic, having the structure of a promise (SM, 266; *SM*, 167–8), undecidable and incalculable; it induces both 'irruption' (Force, 59; *Force*, 27) and negotiation from the basis of the inevitably necessary calculation of rights (Force, 62): a negotiation of the relation between the calculable and the incalculable.

This 'relation without relation' might seem to point to an aporia, like the 'impossible possibility' of time, or the condition of possibility which is also the condition of impossibility of desire or of the signature. But unlike that set of phrases, it is always used in texts with an implicit link to the work of Blanchot, and it may be substituted for by other phrases of which 'pas sans pas' ('step/not without the step/not') is the most common. The passages just quoted occur in response to an interlocutor's remarks about the negative which denies relation to negativity in the shape of loss, or in the shape of a dialecticizable opposite, to insist on affirmation (ALT, 81). It is with the question of Derrida's negatives that the next chapter will begin, to suggest precisely that they make possible a non-oppositional trellis of relations allowing a relation of non-relation with the radically new.

This chapter has shown that in Derrida's thought there may be put forward shaping forces or circuits of argument which are not baptized and which therefore do not attract attention. They arise from analogy between different passages in Derrida's text, and the resemblance between these becomes apparent without the patterns of argument being stably lexicalized. Indeed, it is the forces and the shape of the patterns which are similar rather than the component parts put into the patterns. It is to indicate this that the term 'strange attractor' was chosen. In fact, however, these patterns are textual, they are not presented as directly constitutive of knowledge, by Derrida or by this book. This question of the exceptional role of textuality in Derrida's work will be discussed in the final chapter.

4 Negatives and steps

'Pas sans pas'[1]

We saw that, in the Derrida writings discussed in the preceding chapter, singularities occupied a distinct role, one more diffuse in comparison with what I have called lexemes, but one possibly closer to the traditional frames of philosophy. The singularities are less securely lexicalized and appear to arise from repeated circuits of argument rather than by being flagged through characteristic vocabulary. They may act as what, in a term this book borrowed from dynamics, were called 'strange attractors'. They induce a pattern of negotiation, while imposing a relation of interruption – they attract but they are out of reach. For to attain the singular would be to specify it down to uniqueness and this implies having access to, as given, the totality of its possible determinations. In many cases in the last chapter, it seemed that such a given totality is implied by Derrida to be a kind of positive infinite.

Yet to determine is to limit. It is a cutting out from among the possibles: 'all determination is a negation'.[2] 'Différance', in that it refers to a differential process without sharp edges or limits, might seem, then, to refer only to a negotiation with the singular, not to an exhaustive determination. But at the end of the preceding chapter we saw Derrida claim that that lexeme also 'said' a relation to radical otherness: in that it is then structured like a strange attractor. The two forms of relation to singularities, negotiation and interruption, were not just picked out thematically by Derrida: the preceding chapter tried to show that they are connected with circuits of argument, micrologies, and that both of them are operating in the very way in which Derrida writes. The present chapter will begin by showing that there occur in Derrida's writing phrases which can be read as versions in the negative (not negations) of negotiation and interruption; such phrases are versions of both, as 'différance' was said to 'say' both. These negative versions of the micrologies are, like them, embedded in the text. But the exercising of these negatives through the argument forms a kind of process which is only partially conceptualized there; it is nevertheless at work in the text. This process is a kind of moving on. It makes possible an extension to a formulation of a position without the elaboration being pointed out to the reader.

This chapter will study this non-systematic, networked extension both in the writing and as it is written about, relating it to what was said in Chapter 2 about

replications, and to the question of the relation between history and the transcendental explored in Chapter 1. It leads to the questions of how what is new
in thought occurs, and how what is outside predictions and programmes can
happen. In that sense, a strong contrast with the Hegelian negative is made
from within Derrida's text. Hegel's negative is a kind of motor, it pushes the
development of the system on. The negative in the Derridean material this
chapter considers is, on the contrary, dissipatory. The system does not come to
a halt, but it seems to move on in aleatory fashion. It has a specific relation to
the negative. The end of the chapter will show that the havering movement
forward that Derrida's work is describing, or perhaps transcribing, allows a kind
of freedom to the other. In this, Derrida's writing is exploring, the final chapter
will show, a feature which he attributes to language: it is not a matter of technique and manipulation, because language does not rivet us to identity, and yet
the technique is there in language (CP, 207; *PC*, 192).

Negation and the infinite: two forms of relation

In reaction to the discovery that paradoxes could be developed in the Cantorian
or Fregean theory of sets (see Chapter 1), the Dutch mathematician Brouwer
undertook a radical overhaul of what could be admitted to mathematics. His
work, and the movement called 'intuitionism' he inaugurated, a movement
historically linked with phenomenology[3] in its attempt to rely in mathematics
only on 'the mind's clear apprehension of what it has itself constructed' (Kneale
1971: 678), picked out as source of the problems, not merely the actual infinite, but also negation and the principle of the excluded middle. Now, that the
infinite should be expressed as a negative had been remarked on since antiquity,
and held to show that what is not finite cannot be expressed positively, but only
by an infinite series of negative predicates. (This has been traditionally part of
'negative theology', and in *Psyché* Derrida discusses this description levelled
against him as an accusation: 'Comment ne pas parler: dénégations' – 'How to
avoid speaking; denials'.) This is the tradition in which Levinas can speak of
language as violence against the other, because it determines. So to doubt is to
un-determine, to unlimit.

It is in this way that we saw earlier that Derrida had discussed Descartes'
doubt. He had in 'The Cogito and the history of madness' (the second article
in *Writing and Difference*) interpreted against Foucault Descartes' meditations
as a carefully staggered increase in gravity of scepticism, proceeding through
doubt, madness, dreams and hyperbolic doubt, where it was supposed that an
'evil genius' had caused us to err even about intellectual objects. Such a movement, in a terraced augmentation, reached the *Cogito*: even if I am mad,
dreaming or tricked by an all-powerful Demon, I am still thinking (or more
properly, according to Russell, and more Derrideanly, there is still thinking
going on). The movement of doubt is a lifting of all possible determinations
and localizations of experience: a lifting of limits, beyond any determination and
thus beyond or prior to all contradiction (like the *pharmakon*). As such it is

invulnerable to particular, historically determined forms of classification, such as 'reason' or 'madness'; it is, says Derrida, an excess towards the positive infinite and as such, it is a thinking beyond the totality of determinate things to Nothing (ED, 87; *WD*, 56).[4] But the moment the point from which all limits can be lifted is talked of, it is in effect determined, and falls into history. Hence there is a movement between excess and fall into the determinate, a movement towards the ineffable, beyond time, and a fall into time. In this article, this movement is the very movement of the history of philosophy; it is also the price of being able to say anything at all. The very coming close to the silence of nothing creates the validity of speech: yet speech can only live by excluding Nothing, silence and madness.

(The rhythm of thinking set up here by Derrida is a version of a structure which has been called by J. P. Stern 'the dear purchase', and is related to theories of tragedy.[5] Value is created by an approach so near to catastrophe that failure and success are not clearly distinguishable, or even perhaps relevant criteria, and the value is lost at the moment of its achieving. Derrida has sketched a process which is interminable, not as with Foucault's exclusion of madness, once and for all: each stage of the process in Derrida's conception is historically local yet the whole process is not. He has got this by cross-cutting an experiential tragic rhythm with the more familiar fact/right distinction. Staten (1985) has explored this.)

That there is a complex intertext in this discussion (which I have simplified in order to show up the grain of the argument about the negative) has been suggested already in Chapter 1. Hyperbolic 'excess' ('hyperbolic' being a technical term used by Derrida in his early articles for Descartes' final stage of doubt – See Chapter 1) points to a series of writings by Heidegger dating from 1929. In one, Heidegger relays *Transcendenz* by a series of neologisms, including 'Überschwung' and 'Übersteig', to climb over (trans/cend) (GA, 9, 137; see above, Chapter 1) but related to 'übersteigen' – to exceed. The interconnection between 'excess' and 'transcendence' in Derrida's writing on Foucault and Levinas has been suggested above. The problem of the distinction between right and fact, reason and the processes of reason in history, is made to communicate not just with the history of the word *transcendence* as pertaining to conditions of possibility of experience in the Kantian tradition, but with Heidegger's highly original reworking of the Kantian distinction between things-in-themselves, and things for us, and with the sense of transcendence which Heidegger develops in the late 1920s. (His *Kant and the Problem of Metaphysics* was also published in 1929.) *Dasein* is itself the movement beyond, in the sense of the crossing over of beings, by which they become manifest, and become objects. This 'crossing over' is elaborated in *What is Metaphysics?* as an exceeding of beings[6] and as *Dasein*'s 'holding itself out into the nothing'. Quoting Hegel's 'Pure Being and Pure Nothing are therefore the same', Heidegger argues that this is not because both are unmediated and undetermined – nothing can be said of them[7] – but because beings are only manifested by the transcendence of Dasein. Such manifestation had earlier in this text been related to 'nichten' – 'to make into nothing' – whereby beings are manifest in their hidden strangeness as the merely other in the face of the Nothing, which is no mere counterpart to being but is what reveals it.[8] Heidegger later complained in a postscript added in 1943 that critics had turned the text into a document of nihilism; he claims on the contrary that *das Nichts* is not an empty negation of all beings, but that which by distinguishing itself from beings makes them determinate. *What is Metaphysics?*, like the lecture course *The Metaphysical Foundations of Logic*, is powered at least in part by an attack on the notions of representation and of objectivity in the contemporary logic and science, an attack made not from a position of total ignorance, even if one of total antipathy.[9]

It is the former text that Carnap famously chose to attack when he attacked metaphysics, and picked on the phrase 'Das Nichts selbst nichtet' – 'Nothing itself makes into nothing' – as an example of metaphysical language.[10] But both Heidegger and Carnap were claiming to move beyond metaphysics, and Carnap's article, for all its aggression, was not the cheap trading in misunderstanding it has sometimes been supposed to be. In particular, it has been suggested, the chief accusation against Heidegger, his 'ontologizing' of nothing, fails to take account of the history of philosophy he is disengaging and with which he is working: he is deliberately going back upstream beyond Parmenides, who first had turned Nothing into the negative particle,[11] and from whom the possibility of treating being as positive, and thus treating it scientifically, derives. The problem Heidegger is pointing to is that of justifying negation[12] – if in the Fregean way, by discerning two elements in negation, the affirmation and the negative particle, or rather the thought and the negating operator or connective which needs the thought in order to be complete, then the problem seems to be put back one stage into the nature of that negative affirmation; and if through extension, where a negation is said to mean 'corresponding to nothing in reality', then the definition seems to presuppose that the objects which do not fall under the concept are already there, and that reality consists of definite objects, or at least that we can cordon off some piece of reality which is so composed.

Not only does it seem that the basis of negation is assumed, that the negative connective is taken to be primitive in order to get logic going, but also that the connective is a one-place function, that is, that it corresponds to a distinction whereby non-membership of a class is identified with membership of the complementary class (principle of the excluded middle). But Aristotle points to a type of judgement (called 'infinite', it is said, as a result of a mistranslation by Boethius of the Greek 'aorist' = indeterminate)[13] as did Kant after him (KRV, A72–3, B97–8), where a different sort of negation appears. Kant gives the example, a telling one, since the judgement is 'infinite', of the difference between saying 'the soul is not mortal' and saying 'the soul is non-mortal'. The latter proposition is infinite in logical extension, for the judgement places the soul in an infinite set (of things which are non-mortal), but in terms of its content, it is merely 'limitative' because it doesn't further determine the soul (all we know is that the soul is non-mortal, not whether it is white, or individual or . . .).[14] An important modern treatment of the 'infinite' judgement has, referring to Aristotle and Kant, developed it in ways that focus on the nature of its negation. G. H. von Wright (1959) criticizes classical logic for its inability to differentiate between 'the denial of truth' and 'the truth of the denial'. He distinguishes two concepts of negation, one 'weak', to which the principle of the excluded middle applies (anything which can be coloured can be red or not red); the other 'strong negation', where it cannot be truthfully said that the subject either has the predicate or not (an idea can neither be said to be green nor not) – both the proposition and its negation are, says von Wright, 'removed from truth', but also are 'removed from falsehood'. This inability to say may occur, argues von Wright, because we do not know what sort of a thing the logical subject is, so that the negative proposition is 'open and unspecified'. Our lack of knowledge may derive from our needing to specify the subject (our judgment is indeterminate until we have done so); but von Wright also envisages the situation where the subject might be the sort of thing of which the predicate either is true or else is non-applicable: he calls these 'the ultimate genera', for they can never be invalidated (the predicate is either always true or never true).

It is striking that in Derrida's very syntax there appears to occur an enactment of these two forms of negation: phrases which can be read both as a 'weak' negation, which denies both sides of a pair of complementary opposites (and thus leads to paradox), and as a 'strong' negation, which denies opposites which are not exhaustive in a way which calls for further specification, or which suggests that the opposed predicates are inapplicable. There is a further point: such phrases appear to enact negatively the two modes of relation discussed in the preceding chapter. They are negative versions of the interruption, and of negotiation. The most striking such phrase (but there are others)[15] is:

(le *pharmakon* n'est ni le remède, ni le poison, ni le bien ni le mal, ni le dedans ni le dehors, ni la parole ni l'écriture; le *supplément* n'est ni un plus ni un moins, ni un dehors ni le complément d'un dedans, ni un accident ni une essence etc; l'*hymen* n'est ni la confusion ni la distinction, ni l'identité ni la différence, ni la consommation ni la virginité, ni le voile ni le dévoilement, ni le dedans ni le dehors, etc; le *gramme* n'est ni un signifiant ni un signifié, ni un signe ni une chose, ni une présence ni une absence, ni une position ni une négation etc.; l'*espacement*, ce n'est ni l'espace ni le temps; l'*entame*, ce n'est ni l'intégrité (entamée) d'un commencement ou d'une coupure simple ni la simple secondarité. Ni/ni, c'est *à la fois* ou bien *ou bien*; la *marque* est aussi la limite *marginale*, la *marche*, etc.)

(P, 58–9)

(the *pharmakon* is neither remedy nor poison, neither good nor evil, neither the inside nor the outside, neither speech nor writing; the *supplement* is neither a plus nor a minus, neither an outside nor the complement of an inside, neither accident nor essence, etc; the *hymen* is neither confusion nor distinction, neither identity nor difference, neither consummation nor virginity, neither the veil nor the unveiling, neither the inside nor the outside, etc; the *gram* is neither a signifier nor a signified, neither a sign nor a thing, neither a presence nor an absence, neither a position nor a negation, etc; *spacing* is neither space nor time; the *incision* is neither the incised integrity of a beginning, or of a simple cutting into, nor simple secondarity. Neither/nor, that is, *simultaneously* either *or*; the mark is also the *marginal* limit, the *march*, etc.)

$(P, 43)$[16]

In this extraordinary sentence, a lexically strange head term, one of Derrida's own 'quasi-transcendentals', is rapped out, to be followed by complementary opposites which the *definiendum* appears to reject. Each pair (no less than eighteen of them) appears to divide up the semantic space which has been opened, in an exclusive and exhaustive way, and yet they are followed by a pair which operates in a different and unexpected area, by no means related conceptually to its forerunners. In fact, the sentence can be read in two ways, which are incompatible, according to whether the negation is taken to exclude the middle or not.

In the first reading, the sentence is an argument by reduction to the absurd, where the antitheses are complete and the negative creates complementary sets. It is neither . . . nor, the opposites are complementary, and in each case, the result is that the lexeme is left hanging, an excluded middle, an impossible entity, intriguing by its oddity, its strange lexical status. Yet the jumps between the lexemes (they are linked by their status in Derrida's work, that is all) the jumps within each string between each pair of binary opposites impel the reader to move on to search for a solution, which is refused by the syntax and the sense. The 'lexeme', the strange term, retrospectively, is presented as a *tertium datur* but is also denied. This double gesture is that of the paradox in logical terms, of the double bind, in the terms of the Palo Alto school of psychiatry. We reverse it out of its negativity and demand that what is to be defined be one thing OR the other; yet it is a *tertium datur* which is both desired and rendered impossible by what is systematic abrupt interruption, powered by negative conjunction.

But if the disjoint effect created by the gaps between both the head terms and the relation of the couples within the strings is taken account of differently, the sentence can be read in a different manner. Then each pair constitutes a rejected, a negated area, but one which permits the adjoining of another area, in turn negated. The negation implies that it is not applicable, and the attempt to determine starts up again. Such an interpretation of the negation as infinite process (leaving an infinity of possibles to be run through in turn) seems to be a version of the 'negotiation' which must be endlessly continued in the work on Ponge, Levinas and Barthes.[17]

The analogy with von Wright's formalization of logics of negation probably cannot be drawn too far without abuse; it does nevertheless throw light on the curious structure of Derrida's mammoth sentence. Von Wright himself points out the relation between intuitionist theory of negation (with its rejection of the principle of the excluded middle) and his own theory of strong negation. His article illuminates the intellectual structure of the Derridean sentence, that of opposed pairs rejected after a head term, the 'pharmakon', it could be said, is neither remedy nor poison, it is a paradoxical entity, it must be one of two things (weak negation) and it is neither; or it 'is' neither speech nor writing, because not capable of being associated with these at all (strong negation).[18] In the very way it is constructed, Derrida's sentence seems to bring together both strong and weak negation, and to move between them. This has the further effect of increasing hesitancy, not just about the pairs, but about their relation to each other: are they additional or disjoint? And, finally, the whole clause's pattern is that of a set of syntactically identical circuits of argument each following and glossing its 'quasi-transcendental'. Now strong negation entails weak negation: there forms, as it were, a dissymmetric lattice pattern, with internal self-replication: head terms, followed by negated opposed pairs, stringing out the entailment. The pattern then echoes that diagnosed in other contexts in Derrida's work, that of *eidos* and writing for instance (cf. pp. 67–8):

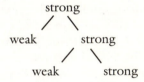

In this way, a non-oppositional pattern of negation is being constructed: it does not remain with the opposition of complementary sets (weak negation), that is, with the negation of a whole, totalized through sets of opposed pairs; it seems to put forward a pattern of dissymmetric but continuous extension through rejected pairs that would be negated, but from which there is constant movement on. And this pattern of extension is being carried by the writing, not made explicit. In other words, the shape of the argument is implicit and embedded in the writing.

Such a system is expressly anti-Hegelian. The long quotation given above occurs at a moment in *Positions* when Derrida is mobilizing against Hegel 'a work of simulacrum' ('un travail de simulacre'), a system of replication which makes the successful synthesis, the *Aufhebung*, impossible. For Hegel's dialectical process constructs itself out of terms which are disjoint and determinate;[19] it is because such terms are already negative that when negated they can produce something new (unlike classical negation, double negation in Hegel does not lead back to the original term). For this to be meaningful, 'the true is the whole. . . . It is to be said of the Absolute that it is essentially *result*, that only at the end is it that which it is in truth'.[20] But complete sets of possible determinations must be immanent in experience if double negation is to produce a synthesis which keeps the negative.[21] (From this derives what Michael Rosen, 1982, calls the 'post-festum paradox': only after having worked through the Hegelian system can one criticize it; there is no point external to it from which valid criticism can be made.) It is precisely this lack of independence in the negative which moves dialectical mediation and reappropriation, according to Derrida: 'ce dedans de la philosophie spéculative relève *son propre* dehors comme un moment de sa négativité' (D, 17) ('The inside of speculative philosophy sublates *its own* outside as a moment of its negativity') (D, 11).[22] Hegelian *sublation* is remainderless. Each stage of the dialectic has absorbed completely what has preceded it. But Derrida, it was shown in the previous chapter, suggests that to leave the system of equivalences one needs to think the remainder of time. We will shortly turn again to considering what that might mean.

Derrida has brought together in the mammoth sentence quoted above both strong and weak negation, so that the movement of negation is not recuperated as a 'work of the negative' by passing through immanent possibilities, nor is it stalled once and for all in paradox. What the sentence appears to enact are the negations of the two forms of relation discussed previously: interruption and negotiation, relations out of which emerge the 'singularities', the strange attractors. Analysis of Derrida's sentence is difficult: it also abuts on a major question, to be further considered in the last chapter: what is the status of Derrida's use of the the term 'logic', what is his attitude to logic, what of the suggestion he makes that 'trace' cannot be filtered into a logic of identity? What relation do these claims bear to those of Derrida's actual writing which, it was suggested in the previous and present chapters, are put forward through repeated 'micrologies', circuits of arguments that are not thematized nor conducted explicitly at every point? For, in the example above, the syntax itself suggests a movement between negation through sets of opposed pairs and fragile suggestions of something beyond, to which those opposed pairs are inapplicable. The syntax itself edges beyond a trammelling of the argument, by suggesting a cautious extension through replication.

It seems then as if, in this sentence and elsewhere, a development of Derrida's argument is indicated by the very way the writing operates. That the argument is not spelled out, but allowed to develop, underlines in paradoxical fashion the sense: what is not there – not present – is able to make itself felt.

Différance and Hegelian negation

In the difficult article on Levinas, 'Violence and metaphysics', Derrida, as has been seen, explores the radical way in which Levinas has sought to guarantee the otherness of the other, in which preserving the integrity of the negative is given a kind of ethical function: the other is kept whole, so to speak, by the inadmissibility of speaking of it (ED, 224; *WD*, 151). So that it is as if, at least in this stage of Derrida's work, Levinas becomes the contrary of Hegel; but, as Derrida points out, this also leaves the problem of how this moving beyond speech can in turn be spoken of. Whereas, on the contrary, the whole force of the Hegelian speculative process is to bring together without residue, if not speaking and what is spoken of, then the consciousness and content created by the consciousness, 'source and product in the self-particularizing movement of Thought's development'.[23]

Derridean *différance* develops what might be called, then, varieties of negation; ones which seem to work against Hegelian *sublation*. Deconstruction shifts classical philosophical oppositions. But by showing that there is a neglected partner of the opposition, it destabilizes and delimits the opposition itself. *Différance*, where the vowel change brings together differentiation and deferral, logical and temporal distinction, uses change in the form of an infinite chain of extension. *Différance* and *dissémination*, one could argue, operate like von Wright's 'strong negation', where proposition and its negation are 'removed from truth' and 'removed from falsehood': 'ce qui n[e] se laisse pas plus intégrer qu'il [ne] forme la *simple* extériorité sous l'espèce de l'échec ou de l'impossible' (P, 120) ('that which can no more be integrated . . . than it can form the . . . *simple* exterior under the heading of its failure or its . . . impossibility') (*P*, 85–6).

Glas brings the critique of Hegel into violent enactment: the columns set Hegel against Genet, state-upholding professor against petty thief, homosexual, writer. If the very disposition of the pages of *Glas* suggests opposition, this is made more complicated by the non-linear reading they impose. The eye is constantly drawn from one column to the other, they answer each other in counterpoint. This is not just two complementary expositions of themes (though it is that); the effect of opposition is fragmented, literally, by the printing. In each column, windows of white open between what may be sections; each has at least two typefaces, one for the commentary close to the text, one for the commentary which may be on other writers (Freud, Beckett), but which is thus marked as being at a different angle to Genet or Hegel; and each column may have inserted hanging paragraphs of text. The monolithic oppositional nature of each column is frittered, etiolated, altered by localized interferences (Heidegger in the seminar round his lecture 'Time and Being' related Hegelian negativity not so much to Absolute Consciousness, but rather to 'Fragmentedness' – *Zerrissenheit* – SD, 52).

In the first article on Levinas, absolute otherness, it seemed to be said, keeled over into empiricism, that is the speaking without any suggestion of how one might justify one's speech (see above); in Hegel, the speculative process was held ultimately to resolve the negative, the other, without remainder. The very printed form of *Glas* makes opposition less secure, while keeping Hegel and Genet prised apart in separate columns. But with *Glas* there is complex criticism of the Hegelian system, often saturnine or cruelly funny, eccentric, not merely because interrupted, because flowing from the commentary, but because of the very angle from which it is done: an angle, as has been suggested, altered by the accompanying Genet column – by the typeface. Derrida violently acronymizes the controlling point towards which the Hegelian system is orientated: 'Absolute Knowledge', 'savoir absolu', using the initials 'SA'. But this recalls, it has often been pointed out, one pole of the structuralist binary opposition SA/SE, *signifiant/signifié*, signifier/signified – the absolute point and the signifier are thus projected one onto the other, two very different systems brought into contact and made less secure. At this point in the Genet column, Freud's work on the fetish is being discussed and, via Derrida's quotation of Beckett, Fonagy's on the drives as the (phantasmal) bases of phonation. This reinforces the insinuation in the Hegel column that SA is, at least for structuralism, a fetish, and the suggestion that the phantasm is a way of stalling the process of *différance*. The 'Absolute Knowledge' is the master of Hegelian time, the pulling into a circle in whose end is its beginning (*Glas*, 252, 225) (which thus links with Derrida's work on the relation between Aristotle and Hegel's view of time in 'Ousia and grammé' in *Margins*). Against this Hegelian movement Derrida, playing on the Genet title 'Ce qui est resté d'un Rembrandt mis en morceaux et jeté aux chiottes' ('What's left over of a Rembrandt torn up and thrown into the bog'), suggests a remaindering time, one not dialectically reappropriatable, one which is suspended between the regularity of the movement of finding the remainder and the irregularity of the remainders. A movement, then, which is halting, suspensive, and much of whose power of suspension comes from the inscription in columns, the cross-cutting of their senses, the elaborate self-context Derrida has constructed for his own text.

A suspension, once again, quite unlike the effect of Hegelian dialectic. Again, Derrida makes the initials IC (immaculate conception, Iesus Christus, categorical imperative, Immanuel (C)ant) bring together in a violent synapse what are highly differentiated concepts and references. But within Hegel's *Phenomenology*, Derrida argues that the opposition makes possible the phantasm, as has been seen in the previous chapter. Rodolphe Gasché, in the course of an illuminating article on *Glas*, shows how Derrida explores the power of the Hegelian system, the vice-like grip of the 'post-festum' paradox; the passages on Marx and Freud, for instance, show that these writers fail 'to dislodge the speculative bond', but also, taking account, as does Derrida, of Hegel's critique of Kant (see Chapter 1) that Hegel 'formulates a limit of the bonds of thinking that is no longer simply its limit'.[24] Now the passage in *Glas* on the religion of light in Hegel's *Phenomenology* suggests a moment possible before the bending into Hegelian exchange and relief of the opposition into new synthesis. It is as if there is a moment in the development of the Hegelian system where its self-swallowing nature is not yet activated.

Part of what is at stake here is the assimilation of philosophy to religion by Marx, as by Freud. The previous chapter showed how Marx used Feuerbach's critique of Hegel, but to argue that it stays representational, theoretical (though Marx's account of the way in which Feuerbach stops short in criticizing Hegel is in fact already contained, Derrida's commentary suggests, in Feuerbach's account of the Protestants' relation to the dogma of the virgin birth which

Derrida supplies for the reader – *Glas*, 230a, 204b). It seems that it is Marx, like Freud, who stops short his critique by relying on the trumping idea of 'fetish', and on unexamined analogies. But, as we also saw, Hegel makes of religion only representation; he blocks difference and thus ensures that Absolute Knowledge can trump the 'phantasm':

> Dès qu'on détermine la différence en opposition, on ne peut plus éviter le phantasme (mot à déterminer) de l'IC: à savoir un phantasme de maîtrise infinie des deux côtés du rapport d'opposition. . . . Toutes les oppositions qui s'enchaînent autour de celle-là (actif/passif, raison/coeur, au delà/ici bas) ont pour cause et pour effet le maintien immaculé de chacun des termes, leur indépendance et par conséquent leur maîtrise absolue.
>
> (*Glas*, 250a)

> As soon as the difference is determined as opposition, no longer can the phantasm (a word to be determined) of the IC be avoided: to wit, a phantasm of infinite mastery of the two sides of the oppositional relation. . . . All the oppositions that link themselves around the difference as opposition (active/passive, reason/heart, beyond/here-below, and so on) have as cause and effect the immaculate maintenance of each of the terms, their independence, and consequently their absolute mastery.
>
> (*Glas*, 223a)

The putting in place of oppositions, maintaining them there, is an act of power, which creates the phantasm of mastery for Hegel, since it prevents religion being assimilated to speculative philosophy, and creates, within the oppositions, intact poles: virgin mother/spiritual father. By its very use of discontinuity, the dialectic becomes a serpentine structure which has no external limit, and from which it seems impossible to escape (*Glas*, 252a, 225a).

But at this point two things happen. First, the order of the sections from the *Phenomenology of Spirit* is changed as if to pick up hints from the Feuerbach passage. The 'nature of light' as religion is discussed by Derrida *after* Hegel's sections on revealed religion and absolute knowledge. Marx, upstream of himself, so to speak, with Feuerbach, had suggested that by the latter the negation of the negation is conceived of as insecurity, not resolution, as 'affectée de son contraire, doutant d'elle même' (*Glas*, 226–227a) ('burdened with its contrary . . . doubtful of itself') (*Glas*, 202a). Derrida's reader cannot but relate this insecurity to that instilled by certain of Derrida's texts. Likewise, Hegel's 'Lichtwesen' ('God as Light') allows for a stage of religion as 'a game without essence, pure accessory of substance which rises without ever setting, without becoming subject and without stabilizing its differences through itself' (*Glas*, 266a, 239a; PG, 506; PS, 419). In both these sections, it is as if Derrida suggests there is a preliminary phase to the process, one which is Derridean, but which settles into something different, into Hegelian or Marxian dialectic.

Second, a Derridean relay of terms, playing on the structure, begins to double it, thus forming the structure of its own which Derrida seems to suggest is under and before this process: a shadowing of Hegelian dialectic which has, so to speak, got there before the setting up of the dialectic. The tone of such a shadowing may well be ironic (see Chapter 5). This moment of the religion based on light leaves no trace of its passage (*Glas*, 265a, 238a; PG, 506; PS, 419) and there seems to be no remainder to continue the dialectic (*Glas*, 267a, 240a). But 'the implacable force of sense [direction] of mediation, of the hard-working negative' (*Glas*, 267a, 240a), the twists and turns of the circuit of recuperation cause the fire 'to retain itself'. In its appearing as what it is at the moment of its disappearance, it has a 'for itself', a consciousness, and it 'offers itself up as a sacrifice' [*Opfer*] to being-for-self (PG, 507, 420). The dialectic process may then be able to start up. This holocaust (Derrida's translation, he points out, of *Opfer*) opens history in the Hegelian sense. It cannot but do so. But before this, with the 'gift', the 'sacrifice', there 'is, was, will have been' the 'irruption of the event' of donation. These are more than ontology, but can only bring ontology and dialectics into being, set them on their circular courses (*Glas*, 269, 242) (a reference here to the circle as the prime lieutenant for the Infinite, cf. 'White metaphor' in *Margins* and 'Plato's pharmacy' in *Dissemination*, but also to Heidgger's *Ring*). The gift and the sacrifice are prior to being, they *are* not, although 'es gibt' ('there are', literally 'it gives'); but as in the religion of light, pure light sacrifices itself, so the fire, says Derrida, burns itself as sacrifice, is pulled into reciprocity to itself, 'and begins to be' (*Glas*, 270a, 242a).

Derrida makes at this point of *Glas* a link between reciprocity and 'for the self': the appearance of the gift, its 'for the self' creates this link. In this way there is debt from the moment debt is determined; it appears, it becomes appearance, it is pulled into a circle of giving and obligation, it becomes a contract between giver and receiver. 'Le mouvement annulaire re-streint l'économie générale (compte tenu, c'est à dire non tenu, de la perte) en économie circulante' (*Glas*, 271a) ('The annular movement re-stricts the general economy (account taken and kept, that is, not taken or kept, of the loss) into a circulating economy') (*Glas*, 244a); the reference is to the work of Bataille and to Derrida's own article 'From restricted to general economy: a Hegelianism without reserve', in *Writing and Difference*. What is created by this constraining into a cycle of exchange is return and reappropriation, that is, what is created are the opposites of dissemination (Derrida retraces this movement etymologically as well, through *cadeau* derived from *catena*, chain). It is the reflexivity that starts 'history, the dialectic of sense, ontology, the speculative' (*Glas*, 270a, 242a). 'Le sacrifice se sacrifie' ('The sacrifice sacrifices itself', 271a, 244a). Giving without hope of return turns the gift into sacrifice; what Derrida calls the 'axiom of speculative reason'. And as sacrifice, the gift works to use its remainders, it calculates (270a, 241a).

The necessity for what is more than a structure of exchange to become one, to become dialectical, is called by Derrida 'striction' (*Glas*, 270a, 242a). It is as

if the predialectical 'striction' which produces the dialectic also forms a structure which is even preontological:

> La striction ne se laisse plus cerner comme catégorie ontologique, ni même,
> tout simplement, comme catégorie, fût-ce une trans-catégorie, un transcen-
> dental. La striction – ce qui sert à penser l'ontologique, ou le
> transcendental – est donc *aussi* en position de trans-catégorialité transcen-
> dentale, transcendental de transcendental.
>
> (*Glas*, 272a)

> The (con)striction no longer lets itself be circumscribed as an ontological
> category, or even, very simply, as a category, even were it a trans-category, a
> transcendental. The (con)striction – what is useful for thinking the ontolog-
> ical or the transcendental – is then *also* in the position of transcendental
> trans-category, the transcendental transcendental.
>
> (*Glas*, 244a)

In post-Kantian philosophy, as we have seen, the transcendental is the set of
conditions of experience and thus of conditions of possibility, of discourse.
'Striction', then, in this passage appears not just to show how the 'gift' can
become exchange and dialectic, which imply some kind of regulated reciprocity,
but how this can be thought. 'Striction' encapsulates the structural context of
the ontological, or the transcendental in a thinker's thought, not as a field or
background, but as a force. This is a move typical of Derrida's way, which goes
to another more general level, or changes mode, so to speak. Striction is the
force, we are told, by which what is excluded from such conditions in fact structures them. It is a tension whereby what had been excluded is put into a
structuring position, and moves to a meta-level: it becomes 'transcendental du
transcendental' – but, as Derrida immediately adds, it is 'false transcendental'
('simili-transcendental') or, in a pun already met with, 'contre-bande transcendentale' – transcendental smuggled goods, and yet also an 'erection against'.
(*Glas*, as has already been said, is about getting many things up, and the
vocabulary of 'potency', 'annulus' and 'counterband' can bear very funny,
mildly obscene, second meanings.) Now, how does this structuring by what is
not there (because excluded) differ from a Hegelian work of the negative?
Through temporal differentiation, for 'contrebande' is 'not yet' dialectical
contradiction:

> [elle] reste autre chose que ce que nécessairement elle est à devenir. Telle
> serait la loi (non-dialectique) de la stricture (dialectique), du lien, de la liga-
> ture, du garrot, du *desmos* en général quand il vient serrer pour faire être.
>
> (*Glas*, 272a)

> [it] *remains* something other than what, necessarily, it is to become. Such
> would be the (nondialectical) law of the (dialectical) stricture, of the bond,

of the ligature, of the garotte, of the *desmos* in general when it comes to clench tightly in order to make be.

(*Glas*, 244a)

Note the relay of terms; the member *stricture* which has a future in Derrida's work is like *différance*, a variant by one letter on a philosophical buzzword. It forces a short-circuit between paths that the dialectic would like to organize into remainderless synthesis. It is as if this *stricture* – double bind in the sense of being, forces pulling in opposite directions by chiasmatic tension, by strangulation, as the constricting of the throat produces the first phoneme of *Glas* – is a parodistic double of *sublation*, but subverts it, and is itself doubled by other terms.

The term 'striction' had appeared earlier in *Glas*, at one point in relation to Hegel's early texts, and Hegel's own relation to Schelling, in an earlier 'approach' to the way the Hegelian dialectic works, to its annular throttling effect.[25] And through the term *Potenz*, which anticipates the 'moment' of the dialectic, can be shown the organization of Hegel's text, which has the same structure. His text 'repeats and anticipates, yet marks a bound, a jump, a rupture in the repetition, while making sure of the continuity of the passage and the homogeneity of a development' (*Glas*, 121a, 105a). It mirrors the patterns of change being presented in the Hegelian text (*Über die wissenschaftlichen Behandlungsarten des Naturrechts . . . – On the Scientific Methods of Treating Natural Law*), that is, discrete reversals through absolute opposites:

> Cette structure – bond discontinu, effraction et séjour appaisé dans une forme ouverte à sa propre négativité – n'a aucune limite externe. Grâce à sa limite interne, à ce renversement ou à cet étranglement qu'elle se donne, elle évite de se perdre dans l'indétermination abstraite (ici, par exemple, le cosmopolitisme 'sans forme' ou la république mondiale etc). Mais sa généralité ne rencontre pas d'obstacle au-dehors. Elle règle le rapport entre l'esprit absolu et toutes ses 'puissances' ou figures déterminées.
>
> (*Glas*, 123a)

> This structure – discontinuous jump, breaking-in and allayed stay in a form open to its own proper negativity – has no outer limit. Thanks to its own inner limit, to this contradiction, or this strangulation it gives *itself*, this structure avoids losing itself in abstract indetermination (here, for example, cosmopolitanism 'without form' or the world republic, and so on). But its generality meets no obstacle outside. This structure regulates the relation between absolute spirit and all its 'powers' or determinate figures.
>
> (*Glas*, 107a)

Hence the difficulty of exiting from the system: the only way is to displace the kind of reading that the Hegelian text imposes, and thus escape the dialectical law (*Glas*, 123a, 107a). The very form of *Glas* indeed arranges such a displacement. Moreover, *Glas* overtly discusses what it is to read Hegel badly at least three times: at 254a, 227a; 258, 231; and in the story told by Kierkegaard, that the dying Hegel said he had never been understood except by a man who had not understood. So that it is as if the form of *Glas* provides for Hegel a contradiction (with the Genet column) but also a displacement (within the Hegel column). There has been not a negation, which would then have stayed within the dialectical ambit, but differentiation and spacing.

We have seen that the Hegelian pattern diagnosed by Derrida is one of 'striction', relayed by 'stricture . . . when it comes to clench tightly in order to make be' (*Glas*, 272a, 244a). This pattern is that whereby the 'gift' 'begins to be' after the reflexivity of fire burning itself. The dialectic is the spark which jumps between the poles of the circuit. But the movement is more than that: there is suspension, countermovement within the poles 'sans la striction suspensive et inhibitrice, l'absolu ne se manifesterait pas' (122a) ('without the suspensive and inhibiting constriction, the absolute would not manifest itself') (106a). This suspension and inhibition relates it to the double bind. But the 'striction' and, still more, 'stricture' connect through tension. What exactly, then, connects them, or rather what connects? It is here that Derrida's tracing of Hegelian argument from the unstabilizable pattern of differences in the section 'Lichtwesen' ('God as Light') to the 'gift', the 'striction' and the dialectic, reaches through the relayed term 'stricture' to other philosophers and other circuits of argument. Derrida has differentiated both type of negative and its function in this section of *Glas*. We shall see that *stricture* has a future in his work.

The double bind and *stricture*

The double bind was one of the movements of tension in *Signéponge*: 'sans relâche ni relève ni annulation' – neither relaxation nor sublation nor annulation (references here to the circle-ring through the pun on 'annulation' as well as to Hegelian *sublation* through *relève*) which moved constantly and chiasmatically between recto and verso (like a Moebius strip: 'renversement . . . au renversement de renversement' (SéP, 85) ('reversal [or] the reversal of reversal') (SéP, 84). A '*double bind* of an event of signature' which was 'the condition of possibility and impossibility' of signature (SéP, 65; SéP, 64). As such, like the Law in 'Préjugés', it is enjoined and forbidden (Pré, 122); it is a violent version of the 'noose' in 'En ce moment' ('Le lacet de l'obligation, sa stricture incomparable' (Psy, 182) ('The lace of obligation. . . . Its incomparable stricture') ('At this very moment . . . ', 30) or in 'The deaths of Roland Barthes' where, as has been shown, there is both movement towards ('traversée') and a movement of irruption into ('trouer') the *punctum* or the other. It seems to work like a dynamization of repression (Pré, 111) – the analogy being made possible for Derrida's reader not by thematization, but by the proximity of the discussions in Derrida's text. This analogy through proximity will itself have to be further discussed. For *double bind*, *noose*, *stricture* are a set of terms alike and different (as was the case with *différance*, *trace*, *spacing*); not a series, for they are not developed by a law: they are apposed in Derrida's lists, through contiguity and through separation by punctuation; they are comparable through the crossing tensions they seem to bear.

In another text, *The Truth in Painting*, *stricture* is set off first from what I take to be *striction* and then from *double bind*:

> La logique du détachement comme coupure conduit à l'opposition, c'est une logique, voire une dialectique de l'opposition. J'ai montré ailleurs qu'elle avait pour effet de relever la différance. Donc de suturer. La logique du détachement comme stricture est *tout autre*. Différante, elle ne suture jamais. Elle permet ici de tenir compte de ce fait: ces souliers ne sont ni attachés ni détachés, ni pleins ni vides. Un *double bind* y est comme suspendu et tendu à la fois, que je n'essaierai pas ici de rattacher strictement à un autre discours sur le *double bind*. . . . Toute stricture est *à la fois* stricturation et destricturation.
>
> (VEP, 389)

> The logic of detachment as cut leads to opposition, it is a logic or even a dialectic of opposition. I have shown elsewhere that it has the effect of sublating difference. And thus of suturing. The logic of detachment as stricture is *entirely other*. Deferring; it never sutures. Here it permits us to take account of this fact; that these shoes are neither attached nor detached, neither full nor empty. A double bind is here as though suspended and imposed simultaneously, a double bind which I shall not here attempt to attach strictly to another discourse on the double bind. . . . Any stricture is *simultaneously* stricturation and destricturation.
>
> (*Truth*, 340)

'Striction', in *Glas*, a dictionary word, has disappeared, though its work is described, in favour of *stricture*, non-existing in French, punning towards 'structure' but also towards the English word meaning 'blame'; and *stricture* is then doubled, positively and negatively, into 'stricturation' and 'destricturation'. As the process of 'striction' undercuts Hegelian use of negativity, which is presented as stalling in the 'phantasm', 'stricture' occurs here as the counterpoint and counterpart to the process of the fetish. In his commenting on the art historian Schapiro's and Heidegger's opposing commentaries on one of Van Gogh's paintings of shoes (it is not quite certain which painting, though both write as if it were), Derrida remarks just before the quoted passage that neither art critic nor philosopher has entertained the possibility that they could be two shoes of the same foot, that, in other words, the possibility of fetishism has been effaced.

In *Glas*, it was suggested that Freud had elided the process of fetishism, seeing the fetish and its contradictions as a counterweight between the double bind of desire and counter-desire (*Glas*, 235a, 209a). The simultaneous tension of denial and affirmation concerned with the fetish tended to be reduced to a substitution for a truth, a one-place function. Here then, the loosened shoes painted by Van Gogh (they are half-unlaced) are invested by Heidegger with values of detachment, modesty and finally attachment to the earth, an investment in fact, Derrida gently suggests, which involves an unadmitted tightening of other bands, subjective ones, linking to choices and penchants, which are not thematized by Heidegger and which give rise to symptomatic contradiction (VEP, 387; *Truth*, 339). For the fact that Heidegger is being worked by such a tightening and loosening of intellectual and political constraints explains the surface contradiction between his insistence on the lack of determination of the shoes (he says they are 'just a pair of shoes') and his attribution of this lack to a peasant and to a woman. The shoes are used to show lack of usefulness; from the inadvertent investment in this comes the possibility that they are fetishized, a possibility repeated by Heidegger, when the painting (a painting serves no use) of old shoes (ditto) serves to show the workings of truth: again a hint that the fetish is a precipitate from contradictory forces of argument, or contradictory forces in the subjectivity (VEP, 395; *Truth*, 346).

Derrida implies that Heidegger and Schapiro are in agreement to try for a reattachment of these shoes to their owner: to look for a true subject and support for this bereft painted twosome (VEP, 322; *Truth*, 282), and they agree there must be a pair so that the complex reversed symmetry of the whole human body in its spatial orientation is preserved. 'Detachment is intolerable' (VEP, 324; *Truth*, 283). There must be connection for both Heidegger and Schapiro; and their connections, Derrida shows in amused and yet respectful fashion, reveal them: the former, Heidegger, is an admirer of grounded peasant life, and the latter is a townsman, even an uprooted cosmopolitan.

But this double bind – expressed as a 'neither–nor' disjunction, the shoes being neither done up nor undone, nor full nor empty, we are told – moves away from the oppositional negation to the negotiating negation. Gradually through the Derridean dialogue is sketched out a '(metaphorical?) doubling' (VEP, 331; *Truth*, 290) by Heidegger for Van Gogh, and by Derrida for Heidegger: the Heideggerian distinctions which Schapiro has homogenized, made to operate equally, are on the contrary not distinctions so much as connections. And in a long parenthesis the looping curves of connection, in the passage Derrida refers to from Heidegger's *Origin of the Work of Art*, between the thing, the product and the work of art, are developed by Derrida as the lacing on the boots, so that 'each mode of being' of the thing passes like a lace inside and then outside the other (to be untied partially by analysis – VEP, 298; *Truth*, 261). The movement (also called fort/da, which, we shall see, is also then a movement out to another of Derrida's texts) makes the 'thing sure of its gathering . . . by a law of stricture'.

So that with the 'stricture', we find moves between opposites without stalling into oppositions; it is a movement by which Heidegger's speech doubles after what it speaks of; which does bring together, does 'gather' up something by its connection. This question of gathering or connection will have to be investigated further. But it also points to what is not explicit, what is 'unthought' in the sense of unworked out, unworked on, as if 'stricture' worked under opposites, pulling them into a tension different from that which they are given explicitly whether by Heidegger, Hegel, Freud or Marx. It is as if 'stricture' works by producing a fetish of the idea of the fetish, a phantasm of the phantasm, but also by sending these away, undoing them, so that things may move on, so that lines develop out of their texts which are not wholly contained in them. The developments are more than what could be programmed out of the texts Derrida is discussing; in each case precise account is being given by Derrida of how more goes on in the texts than is thematized and explicitly acknowledged. But the parallel with the preceding chapter suggests that if the flow of Heidegger's text causes a 'structure' whereby objects are 'gathered', that is, precipitated out of tensions, only to be then absorbed back in, exactly the same might be said of Derrida's own text and about such 'objects' as 'double bind', or 'stricture'. There is a particularly complex interweaving in Derrida's work between text and commentary, of mutual but not reciprocal moulding.

To advance further, one needs to look once more at the relation with the negative. If the double bind can be related to exclusive or weak negation, what of the inclusive or strong negation, which it was argued above had a relation to negotiation? In the long phrase quoted above the exclusive negation was as if overprinted with the inexclusive negation, with the disjunctive 'ou bien', a negation that could be indefinitely specified by further determinations. In 'To speculate – on "Freud"' (in *The Post Card*) 'stricture' is a negotiation between opposites, is a differential, a 'moderating stricture'. In its deferral, its commitment to a future, to further specification, it allows extension without that extension being aligned on prediction, on the future being laid down from a situation in the present.

Stricture: connecting and constituting

But in other work, Derrida develops what have to be called other types of negatives – for instance, in his 'To speculate – on "Freud"' on Freud's text, *Beyond the Pleasure Principle* (1921), where Freud considers how his pleasure principle might be rendered compatible with his patients' repetition of traumatic events. What pleasure can there be in repeating events which have damaged the psyche? Freud entertains the possibility of wholly other principles being at work, the death principle or the reality principle. In his work *The Uncanny*, dating from the same period, which likewise deals with the compulsion to repeat, Freud wonders à propos of death whether it should be considered extraneous to life or on the contrary a necessary part of it: 'Our biology', he says, is undecided whether death is the necessary fate of each living being, or only a regular but avoidable accident within life. In this Freudian pair of alternatives, there is once again the exclusive and the non-exclusive negation: death as interruption, or death as an approximation, a 'composition' or agreement. 'To speculate – on "Freud"' can be thought of as giving meaning to 'our biology's failure to decide which should apply; as negotiating in non-exclusive fashion between the exclusive and the non-exclusive negations.

But first, Derrida, in a way to be examined more closely later, points out that the manner in which Freud writes in *Beyond the Pleasure Principle* is hardly distinguishable from what he writes about. Freud is dealing with neurotic repetition and its compatibility with the pleasure principle; he writes about these in a way which, though controlled, nevertheless repeats and constantly returns to the pleasure principle. Freud 'entertains' various hypotheses, he tries them out and then returns to base. He 'speculates' as he himself says, using a word in which other senses lurk: intellectual speculation, but also the sending out for gain, and the reflecting of the self in the *speculum* (mirror). More, the famous game of his grandchild, which Freud is describing, where he sends out a bobbin on a string from his cot and retrieves it, announcing 'Fort/da' ('away/there'), has also the same pattern: and, moreover, in Freud's recounting of it, there clearly appear lineaments of his relationship to his progeny both physical and intellectual: a 'scène d'héritage' is going on, Derrida points out, Freud is working out his relation with an institution, which is likewise being spun out into existence, and which will bear his own name.

The problem for Freud, then, is that pleasure must operate between two poles which are equally distributed: too much pleasure, and too little pleasure both mean interruption, the death of pleasure. Derrida argues that in Freud's developing conception, the reality principle (or death principle) which might seem to be opposed to the pleasure principle, is in fact a version of it: the two poles between which pleasure operates make of all pleasure a detour between them. The apparently opposed principles are differentiations one of the other (CP, 302; PC, 283). The pleasure principle is in fact only deferring to its own principle when it allows for reality: there is no oppositional clash, but pleasure for its own purposes moderates itself, it gains by losing, makes possible continuance by some forbearance. There is self-moderation, of one principle, which involves the incorporation of the other, a self-differentiation which makes death internal to life (CP, 305; PC, 285). Derrida refers to these problems both with the phrase 'life/death' and by the 'arrêt de mort' (death sentence or suspension of death) through which he points to Blanchot's novel of the same name, tracks it, so to speak, traces his own work on it, picking out the title's slippage between subjective and objective genitive (for it can mean both 'sentence of death' and the 'stopping of death'). Bringing together exclusive and non-exclusive negation, interruption and negotiation, in this way makes possible a halting connection. As we will see, it becomes possible to think a development of self, of psyche, which is neither subjective nor objective, where ideas of self-regulation and purpose can be rethought in a way that is new and illuminating.

This is set in motion also at a level of commentary – Derrida allows various Freudian terms to communicate with his own. Freud had worked on these processes in terms of *Bindung* – binding – where a primary process is replaced by a secondary process, and the drive towards satisfaction relayed by a complex group of 'partial drives'. Derrida relays the word *Bindung* through *Band* to 'bander' and to 'contrebande', terms whose trail leads to *Glas*: 'le principe même du plaisir se manifesterait comme une sorte de contre-plaisir, bande contre bande qui vient limiter le plaisir pour le rendre possible' (CP, 426) ('the very principle of pleasure would manifest itself as a kind of counterpleasure, band contra band which comes to limit pleasure in order to make it possible') (*PC*, 399). But the 'contrebande' or the 'stricture', as it is called on the next page, is local and plural, not the 'deconstructive gesture' of Iaveh, of the double bind which demands and forbids (CP, 179; *PC*, 165), but 'des différences de bandage' – 'differences of banding' (CP, 426; *PC*, 399). *Striction* in *Glas* 'comes to clench tightly in order to make be'. In 'To speculate – on "Freud"', *stricture*, more diffuse though more particular, nevertheless liaises, bends together poles, makes them communicate, makes connections.

This occurs through Derrida's reworking of Freud's account of his grand-child's game. 'Fort/da' are poles, but Freud's account of the child brings them together, and then starts again. In doing so, Freud causes the child to create a track for himself – Freud's grandchild keeps the self going through the repetition of throwing the cotton reel out to an extreme and hauling it back. This is not a game in which mastery is acquired through some kind of intermediate object; the child strings the self out (Derrida puns on *fils*, 'son' and *fil*, 'thread') and pulls it back; it is the track through differential relations to the self which gives power over the self, by having constituted it. Trajectory, not entity, seems to make the self.

The directions in which Derrida will tease out Freud's account are multiple. In a complex pun, the child is said to talk to himself on the telephone.[26] The game enables him, in a phrase to be further investigated, to 'call himself back' – for he is on the line to himself. Telephone lines appear a good deal in Derrida's writing round about 1980 – but they refer back, we shall see, to his first publication on Husserl's *Origin of Geometry*, to Husserl's 'return question', *Rückfrage*. (Sam Weber has suggested that there is also a punning reference to Heidegger's *Anruf* – 'appeal', for example in *Being and Time*, but also 'telephone call'.[27]) Such hints are serious jokes, for the 'collect call' builds in complex temporality to the child's tracing out of the self: what comes later can affect what is earlier, in a paradox no longer so paradoxical since quantum mechanics, in a way that permits, as we shall see, relations to the future which are not simply ones of intention or purpose or projection from the present. There is perhaps also here a sideways glance at a passage in the analysis of *Dasein*'s temporality in *Being and Time* §69, where it holds itself out beyond, and in coming back (*da*) comes upon being: 'the world is transcendent. It must already have been ecstatically disclosed . . . in temporalizing itself [temporality] comes back to those entities which are encountered in the "there"' (SZ, 366; *BT*, 417).

The child's trajectory, Derrida sugggests, is yet more involved: the child's repetition of *fort/da* is not repetition of the same cycle; once it is repeated it is repeated as a unit, like a knitting loop which becomes a stitch in a jumper, or a computer loop as an element of a programme:

> Il s'agit du *re* en général, du revenu ou du revenant, du revenir en général. Il s'agit de la répétition du couple disparition/réapparition, non seulement de la réapparition comme moment du couple, mais de la réapparition du couple qui doit revenir. Il faut faire revenir la répétition de ce qui revient, à partir de son revenir.
>
> (CP, 339)

> In question is the *re* in general, the returned or the returning – to return in general. In question is the repetition of the couple disappearance/reappearance, not only reappearance as a moment of the couple, but the reappearance of the couple which must return. One must make return the repetition of that which returns, and must do so on the basis of its returning.
>
> (*PC*, 318)

This pattern is of repeated two-stroke cycles which are not end-to-end leaps between opposed poles (+–+–+) but which compose a rhythm of obligation 'which must return', a rhythm of expectancy – 'one must make return the repetition'. 'Autos' as relation to the self develops through these journeys between opposed states, and then journeys round a circuit which is now composed of the expectation and of repetition of the couple: 'Tout être-ensemble même . . . commence par *se lier*, par un se lier dans un rapport différentiel à soi. Il s'envoie et se poste ainsi. Il se destine. Ce qui ne veut pas dire: il arrive' (CP, 429) ('Every being-together . . . begins by *binding-itself*, by a binding-itself in a differential relation to itself. It thereby sends and posts itself. Destines itself. Which does not mean: it arrives') (*PC*, 402) (the last phrase being a reference to the famous remark of Lacan, that every letter arrives at its destination). Derrida throughout this text plays on 'post' – after – and 'post' as a sending forward in time: a contradiction in one syllable which pinpoints the tension of 'stricture'. (It should be noted that *spannen*, German for 'to put under tension', and *sponte*, Latin for 'of one's own accord', are etymologically related.)

The child constitutes itself, not as object but as process; the psychoanalytical movement is constituted as an institution, the text of *Beyond the Pleasure Principle* is constituted by this process of havering and halting, of detour, of speculation, sending out and back an idea, of accumulation through repetition, as the text of 'To speculate – on "Freud"' itself accretes.[28] This account is not just psychoanalytical nor ontological, it requires a logic (Derrida uses the word). Unlike mathematical logic, it will not use ready-constituted objects and relations: it will use as negative, not a binary operation of opposition, but one whose multiple values are on a kind of sliding scale, which can go all the way to 'radical alterity': 'Une logique de la différence – qui peut être altérité radicale – et non plus de l'opposition ou de la contradiction' (CP, 436) ('a logic of difference – which can be radical alterity – and no longer in a logic of opposition or contradiction') (*PC*, 408).

But in these pages, Derrida makes the weave between Freud's matter and his manner tighter. The 'power drive' (*Bemächtigungstrieb*) makes its appearance; it is called by Derrida 'tautological' (one cannot but wonder whether there is here a cross-cutting with the English word 'taut' towards the sense of 'stricture'; such wordplay, as we shall see in the final chapter, seems to allow language to gather in meanings rather than to operate with intentions which must be expressed). Now the self is applied to the same in self-differentiation, not in a structure created by the criticism of the reality principle as against the pleasure principle, but a self-settling into localized points of compactness and diffusion, differentiation and tension caused by a looping back of the same principle, at work on itself as on another (compare what was said about the 'gift' above). This same structure is the drive (it is another 'être ensemble'):

> La pulsion d'emprise doit être aussi le *rapport à soi* de la pulsion . . . D'où la tautologie transcendantale de la pulsion d'emprise: c'est la pulsion comme pulsion, la pulsion de pulsion, la pulsionnalité de la pulsion. Il s'agit encore d'un rapport à soi comme rapport à l'autre, l'auto-affection d'un *fort:da*, qui se donne, se prend, s'envoie et se destine, s'éloigne et se rapproche de son propre pas, de l'autre.
>
> (CP, 430)

> The drive to dominate must also be the drive's *relation to itself.* . . . Whence the transcendental tautology of the drive to dominate: it is the drive as drive, the drive of the drive, the driveness of the drive. Again, it is a question of a relation to oneself as a relation to the other, the auto-affection of a *fort:da* which gives, takes, sends and destines itself, distances and approaches itself by its own step, the other's.
>
> (PC, 403)

This is more than a Pynchonesque logic (through the use of well established structures, those of a *rapport à soi*, 'self-relation'), more than a binding together into some nomad tent of language from different areas, logical, Freudian, Heideggerian. Active, passive, auto-regulation, are being thought in a way that is new. The 'transcendental'[29] of the instinct for mastery, the *Bemächtigungstrieb*, is that it is a fundamental relation between and over the drives, and the plotting of this relation will permit Freud to decide whether the pleasure principle or the reality principle is dominant. But the domination is not of one drive over another: in phrases like 'la pulsionnalité de la pulsion', which reminds both of Heidegger and of other texts by Derrida ('l'événementialité de l'événement', 'la choséité, allons-y, de la chose' – 'the thingness, shall we say, of the thing') (SéP, 93; SéP, 92), the recursion 'X of X' makes feedback possible. What seems to point to possession and passiveness through an objective genitive (the drivenness belonging to the drive) also points to action and clarification with the sense of essence (the drivenness performed by the drive) as a subjective genitive. In the case in point, the pleasure principle and the drive to power are no different: they are differential forms of the same, what Derrida calls the postal principle.

The postal principle and the 'pas sans pas'

'To speculate – on "Freud"' develops a complex of analogies (a term which will itself be held up for inspection in the next, final, chapter) for the constitution of Freud's text, and for the little boy Ernst's constitution of his own self. All establish connection: travel system, railways, the postal services, the radio-linked computer network. All are transit systems.

> Un groupe de pulsions se précipite en avant pour atteindre le but final de la vie le plus tôt possible. Mais, division du travail, un autre groupe revient prendre place en arrière du même chemin (*dieses Weges zurück*) pour refaire le trajet et 'allonger ainsi la durée du voyage' (*so die Dauere des Weges zu verlängern*). Entre les deux groupes, sur la même carte, un réseau ordonne, plus ou moins bien, plus ou moins régulièrement, les communications, les transports, les 'petites' et 'grandes vitesses', les aiguillages, les relais et les correspondances. On peut décrire ce grand ordinateur dans le code du réseau ferroviaire ou du réseau postal. Mais l'unité de la carte est toujours problématique, et même l'unité du code à l'intérieur de l'ordinateur.
>
> (CP, 384)

> One group of drives rushes forward in order to reach the final aim of life as quickly as possible. But, division of labor, another group comes back to the start of the same path (*dieses Weges zurück*) in order to go over the route and 'so prolong the journey' (*so die Dauers des Weges zu verlängern*). Between the two groups, on the same map, a network coordinates, more or less well, more or less regularly, communications, transports, 'locals' and 'expresses', switch points, relays, and correspondences. This great computer can be described in the code of the railway or the postal network. But the unity of the map is always problematic, as is even the unity of the code within the computer.
>
> (*PC*, 361–2)

Derrida, punning on 'pas' as both 'step' and 'not', relates to the negative the havering, halting, self-differential movement built out of infinitesimal frequency alterations – 'se rapproche de son propre pas' (CP, 430) ('approaches itself by its own step' in the passage just quoted, *PC*, 403). Picking up his own work on Maurice Blanchot in 'Pas', reprinted in *Parages*, the phrase 'pas sans pas' (untranslatable, this: the phrase commutes disjunctively 'not' and 'step'; it is varied in such phrases as 'lieu sans lieu', 'place without place'; 'mort sans mort', 'death without death', etc.) might seem to be a version of the non-exclusive negative discussed above. For Blanchot's title *Le Pas au-delà* may be a forbidding of further movement, or, on the contrary, a step beyond, according to whether 'pas' is read as the negative or as 'step'. The 'identity of the double in the name' ('l'identité du double dans le nom') troubles the law of identity all the more as a noun and a particle are being spliced (cf. 'entre' and 'antre' in Chapter 2). But the Hegelian dialectical negative is also excluded (for Hegelian logic, 'not not-A' is not equivalent to 'A'). 'La structure du pas exclut que le double effet du pas (annulation/conservation de l'audelà) soit une négation de la négation revenant à inclure, intérioriser, idéaliser pour soi le pas' (Par, 45) ('the structure of the step [not] excludes the double effect of the step (annulation–conservation of the beyond) being a negation of a negation, coming down to being an inclusion, an interiorization, and idealization of the step for itself') (my translation). If we neglect such an effect of '*sans* sans *sans*' '*without* without *without*' (CP, 428; PC, 401) or of 'pas sans pas', of the negative burrowing under identity, of negation working on itself, then says Derrida (in what is itself a negative formulation) we forbid, we stop ourselves paying any attention to the 'venir de l'événement', to the coming of the event which is not parousia but 'éloignement du proche' ('distancing of the near') – both estrangement and approach.[30]

So the 'pas sans pas' is not just a tramelling negative, but a speculating, halting gait between different hypotheses, an establishment of an intellectual heritage (in a wild cross-lingual pun of Derrida's 'legs de Freud' [legs/heritage]). 'Il faut que le pas le plus normal comporte le déséquilibre' – 'The most normal step has to bear disequilibrium' (CP, 433; PC, 406). The text limps (as the devil, incarnation of negativity, is supposed to), but so too does the living organism which at each set of points, changes very slightly in direction. It is *via*, way, detour from the nothing before birth to the nothingness that is death, but the way, with its filamentary structure, its walks between nodal points, is created out of a deferring of death, a 'living on', to quote one of Derrida's titles. The identity of an organism is not homogeneity, but one of trajectory, where there is not a distinction between transiting object and route traced, but instead a destabilizing self-replication, which, by repeating the self, relays the self: 'L'organisme (ou toute organisation vivante, tout "corpus" tout "mouvement") se conserve, s'épargne, se garde à travers toutes sortes de relais différenciés, de destinations intermédiaires, de correspondances, à court ou long terme, de court ou long courrier' (CP, 378) ('The organism (or every living organization, every "corpus", every "movement") conserves itself, spares itself, maintains itself via every kind of differentiated relay, intermediary destination, correspondences of short or long term, short or long letters') (PC, 356).[31] Such a relay system, at the same time furrow and plough, path and pathfinder, works through constriction, through binding free energies, rendering them bound, postulated or posted in the military sense, and thus limited either in their tendency towards pleasure or displeasure. It is the measure which is the condition of possibility of pleasure, but measure is the measuring out of pleasure: 'the postal principle': 'Poste' refers to the temporality of the 'fort/da', already discussed, and to positing in an intellectual sense; but is also translated in crabwise fashion, via lateral dictionary definitions perhaps, or perhaps out to English and back as 's'envoyer' which brings together a vulgarism 'to get oneself' and a reference to Heideggerian *Geschick*, destiny, which is an 'ecstasis' out, coming back from which there is *Dasein* and world (see *supra*, p. 166) and which in Heidegger's (correct) etymology, is related to *schicken* and *Geschichte*.[32] But the 's'envoyer' also refers to Freud's forerunners of death, the *Trabanten des Todes*, sent out as scouts to come back.

As is suggested by the word 'corpus' (in the quotation *supra*, p. 170) such an account doesn't merely refer to the psyche, and to the pleasure principle, it refers to Freud's text, and by extension to Derrida's text too. All are constructed via repetition, by a posting out, used like networks. Ernst constructed himself ('gave himself'; in the mathematical sense, this means to take as example: 'on se donne un triangle') not by linear repetition, with no stages in procedure at all, nor by an embedded repetition, like Russian dolls, where the stages are separate, but by a movement which can loop between stages, which 'boots' in the computer sense. It is a tangled hierarchy.[33] Likewise, Derrida's commentaries loop between text and metacommentary: they cannot be prised off what they comment on, and this is true in detail too: if one pattern of thinking, of grouping of texts, of drives, seems to have hegemony, it is soon turned like a glove, re-sited, becoming part of what it seemed to control. All meaning is transit, movement through relays, adders and gates, so that the postal serves as a metaphor for all transport, as: 'La possibilité même de l'histoire, de tous les concepts, aussi, de l'histoire, de la tradition, de la transmission ou des interruptions, détournements etc' (CP, 74) ('The very possibility of history, of all the concepts, too, of history, of tradition, of the transmission or interruptions, goings astray, etc.') (*PC*, 66). But immediately the transcendental postal service is cancelled, or rather relocated as part of what it is trying through its metaphors to control and express (a gesture of Derrida's argument which will be examined in the next chapter). 'Un minuscule envoi dans le réseau qu'elle prétendrait analyser (pas de métapostale) seulement une carte perdue dans un sac, et qu'une grève, et même un accident de tri, peut toujours retarder infiniment, perdre sans retour' (CP, 74) ('A minuscule *envoi* in the network that it allegedly would analyse (there is no metapostal), only a card lost in a bag, that a strike, or even a sorting accident, can always delay indefinitely, lose without return') (*PC*, 66–7). The controlling metaphor is looped back and becomes part of what it was trying to array in its network.[34]

This is not a topologist's version of the structuralist tool, the *mise en abyme*. The mirror image is not complete, we shall see; the speculation is a sending out of what will not arrive back completely. When Derrida recounts Freud's movement between death as dissolution, lack of cathexis, lack of pleasure, and death as over-intensity, too strong a cathexis, he seems to repeat the movement discerned before, the dialectic between dialectic and non-dialectic, the havering connection between interruption and connection. 'L'irrésolution appartient à cette logique impossible. Elle est la structure spéculative entre la solution (non-liaison, déchaînement, desserrement *absolu*: l'absolution même [absolute as

dissolved] et la non-solution (*reserre*ment *absolu*, bandage, paralysant etc.)'
(CP, 428) ('Irresolution belongs to this impossible logic. It is the speculative
stricture between the solution (non-binding, unleashing, *absolute* untight-
ening: absolution itself) and the non-solution (absolute tightening, paralysing,
banding etc.)' (*PC*, 401). Once again, this is a structure where the operation
relating the two sides of an opposition has the form of one of the sides; for
although it is unloosening and bringing together which are joined, that
joining is part of the bringing together. We are referred once more to effects
which are 'predialectic', in that they bring forward dialectic effects without
being based on opposition. Thence comes the substitutability which makes
movement forward possible.

The movement is like the negotiation of the second article on Levinas
already discussed, *supra*, where negotiation negotiates what is non-negotiable
with negotiation:

> Cette négociation n'est pas une négociation comme une autre. Elle négocie
> le non-négociable et non pas avec tel ou tel partenaire ou adversaire mais
> avec la négociation elle-même, avec le pouvoir négociateur qui croit pouvoir
> tout négocier.
>
> (Psy, 171)

> For that negotiation is not merely a negotiation like any other. It negoti-
> actes the non-negotiable and not with just any partner or adversary, but
> with the negotiation itself, with the negotiating power that believes itself
> able to negotiate everything.
>
> ('At this very moment', 20)

A vectorized power (negotiation as 'pouvoir négociateur') is contrasted with a
substantivized adjective, but the contrast, the operation which brings them
together is itself one of negotiation.

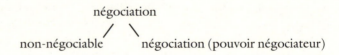

Derrida's structure in *The Post Card*, which he calls 'one-two-three terms' which
gives the 'structure d'altération sans opposition' (CP, 305) ('a structure of alteration without opposition') (*PC*, 285) is a structure like one we have already
met, a structure of which one leg repeats the structure itself, putting itself out
into a trellis on one side. The replication is not a mirrored embedding, but an
extension.

Sending

Derrida's 'To speculate – on "Freud"' precedes in *The Post Card* an article on Lacan's seminar on Poe's story *The Purloined Letter*. Both Lacan's article and Derrida's are work from their respective seminars 'on' Freud's *Beyond the Pleasure Principle*. Comparing them exhibits the difference between the idea of relation to the self in Derrida and in Lacan. Whereas Lacan uses a relation of containing to build the self's relation to itself, for Derrida the relation is constituted out of extension and trajectory.

In a famous article,[35] Barbara Johnson argued that though Derrida had demonstrated that Lacan tailors Poe for his own demonstration, he too had omitted part of Lacan's account, a difficult part in which the latter deals with symbolic determination and random series. Yet more: Derrida himself has shown the impossibility of fixing a frame for a text. So that in one and the same gesture, Derrida is both guilty of that whereof he accuses the other, Lacan, and inconsistent. And Johnson both alters and aggravates the charge: such apparent incoherence is no local accident, no slip-up. It is endemic in natural language itself, for language and meta-language cannot be held separate. Thus any act of reading in the strong sense operates within a double bind. Johnson says: 'the total inclusion [of the frame of interpretation] is both mandatory and impossible' (Johnson 1977: 481).

This double bind 'mandatory and impossible' is in fact a pair of bounds, within which anyone, but especially Derrida in this context, must move, according to Barbara Johnson. Derrida's work has been reprojected on to itself, and this has the effect of containing himself within part of himself, of enclosing him. This is, relevantly, an example of Lacan's definition of intersubjective communication: 'Selon la formule même . . . de la communication intersubjective où l'émetteur . . . reçoit du récepteur son propre message sous une forme inversée' (Lacan 1966: 41) ('According to the very formula of intersubjective communication where the emitter receives in inverse form from the receiver his very message') (my translation). The sender's message is mirrored back to them, the relation between sender and receiver is specular and thus bounded. For if the sender's message is reversed and sent back by the receiver – the analogy with the mirror image is patent and indeed is developed with great learning and invention throughout Lacan's work – then it is moving by ricochet between limits (the mirror and the eye, the sender and the receiver). Likewise the turning back of Derrida is only possible within a system of limits.[36] The complex relation to meta-language in Derrida, the tangled hierarchies have here been collapsed into a simple conjunction of opposites, 'mandatory and impossible', which exhaust possibilities not by enumeration, but by creating limits (a barrier through a norm, in the case of 'mandatory', a practical barrier for 'impossible').

The nature of those barriers, and why they do not fit Derrida's text, becomes clearer further on in Johnson's article. Derrida is said to have found in Lacan an uncovering of an original meaning, a backstop, and thus himself has brought to a halt an interpretative process which in Lacan's text is ambiguous. The original meaning Lacan gives to the purloined letter is lack of meaning, but in assigning this to Lacan's 'Seminaire sur la lettre volée', Derrida too, Barbara Johnson says, has supplied an original meaning. Yet on examination, '"Lack of meaning" is the meaning Lacan gives' is not a backstop, as Johnson alleges, not an end to an algorithm; it is an infinite nested series, for the phrase 'lack of meaning' can be indefinitely embedded in the meaning it replaces. Not a stop, but once more, a movement within bounds. This embedding process can be indefinitely prolonged, but it is always working within opposing limits ('lack of meaning' and 'meaning'). It is close, as Derrida points out, to Lacan's acount of truth, which is a version of the Heideggerian hiding/revealing:

> Aussi bien, quand nous nous ouvrons à entendre la façon dont Martin Heidegger nous découvre dans le mot *alethis* le jeu de la vérité, ne faisons-nous que retrouver un secret où celle-ci a toujours incité ses amants, et d'où ils tiennent que c'est lors qu'elle se cache qu'elle s'offre à eux *le plus vraiment*.
>
> (Lacan 1966: 51)

> As well, when we are open to hearing the way in which Martin Heidegger discloses to us in the word *alethia* [*sic.*] the play of truth, we discover a secret to which truth has always initiated her lovers and through which they learn that it is in hiding that she offers herself to them most truly.
>
> (Lacan 1977: 51)

The movement of truth is always within bounds (and must be related to Lacan's account of the unconscious, which, he says, can only be satisfied by 'finding the object fundamentally lost' – 1966: 45). Derrida's reading of Lacan then is not one which inappropriately eliminates Lacan's ambiguity. On the contrary, it is based on Lacan's often reiterated account of truth, which is an oscillation between bounds, although that oscillation can be infinite.

The importance to Lacan of these nested oscillations is confirmed by the way he develops the account in Poe of a schoolboy's remarkable ability to guess whether his opponent had an odd or even number of marbles in his hand (the very passage Johnson accused Derrida of omitting in his article and a crucial passage, because it brings together the random and prediction). Lacan's elaboration of the passage in Poe even takes place, as he points out, in a series of embedded parentheses. He is relating automatic repetition, one of the themes of *Beyond the Pleasure Principle*, to Freud's conception of memory implied by his conception of the unconscious. It is from a chance alternation of presence and absence that Lacan presents symbolic determination as developing. But this symbolic determination occurs between poles: 'L'homme littéralement dévoue son temps à déployer l'alternative structurale où la présence et l'absence prennent l'une et l'autre leur appel' ('Man literally devotes his time to unfolding the structural alternative in which presence and absence take their appeal') (Lacan

1966: 46; my translation).[37] The kind of pattern present for Lacan's mirror effect is not random – the process which can achieve a transition of the form *abba* is structurally dependent and the history of the process affects each move (in terms of the mathematization of the problem that he uses, the history of the choice path must be taken into account in estimating the next move). The history of the set of choices determines the choice to be made in accordance with a law that structures the whole sequence. Lacan seems to wish to combine chance and structural determinants: out of the permutation, in groups of three, of absence and presence, he elaborates a hierarchy which he relates to his own concepts of the 'real', the 'imaginary' and the 'symbolic' and then to the mirror relation which is his model of intersubjective communication. (That Lacan may not have been satisfied with the relation established in the article between, first, a random series; second, a notation which contains a kind of memory function; and, third, the mirror relation, is suggested by the addition in 1966 of the section 'Parenthèse des parenthèses'.)

Lacan sees the hierarchy he constructs as one which contains earlier levels: 'Dans la nouvelle série constituée par ces notations [il apparaît] des possibilités et des impossibilités de succession que le réseau suivant *résume* en même temps qu'il manifeste la *symmétrie concentrique* dont *est grosse* la triade' (Lacan 1966: 47; my emphases) ('In the new series constituted by these notations there appear possibilities and impossibilities of succession which the next network *sums up* at the same time as it shows forth the concentric symmetry which the triad *is pregnant with*') (my translation). The specular effect is here thought of as contained in the random series. In general, the specular structure is crucial in every way to Lacan: the fact that a specular effect is of necessity a movement, however indefinite, *within bounds*; the relation of subject and meaning set out by Lacan is always 'over against' – 'positions over against the subject' (*ibid.*: 231); his repartition of his groups of four to obtain chiasmatic reversal is seen by him as the simplest formalization of exchange (*ibid.*: 49). It is this that constitutes the locus of difference with Derrida. Derrida's occasional references to the *tain* of the mirror, that is, to the other side, the mercurized side of the glass, pinpoint this difference; his work does not remain within opposed bounds, heads/tails, mirror/spectator, receiver/giver. 'Speculation' moves outwards from the movement of 'fort/da' from the other side of the mirror, from other meanings of 'speculation'. The 'Séminaire' is part of Lacan's work on *Beyond the Pleasure Principle*; and as neurotic injuries take a chance event and invest it with compulsive necessity, so he suggests how a series of chance binary outcomes, heads or tails, can be taken up and made complex, forming different necessary sequences. This absorption into a non-overlapping hierarchy is quite different from the Derridean work on the same Freudian text. And it has struc-tures: mirror, rhythmic oscillation, exchange, which are not those Derrida is privileging. As suggested already, Derrida is attentive to the different frequency at which forces operate. But we have seen that their relation to each other in Derrida is not one of subsumption; nor do they operate within bounds, but 'speculate' in the economic sense, send out for gain: they move on.

Lacan's famous seminar in its first version, without addenda, ends with the words: 'A letter always arrives at its destination'. In *The Post Card*, 'To speculate – on "Freud"', together with his article on Lacan, 'Le facteur de la vérité' ('The factor/postman of truth') are prefaced by what is a kind of letter novel. *Envois*, not unlike *Glas*, binds together disparate material in a humorous way. There is even a comparable use of blanks: the periodic insertion of fifty-two blank spaces. In the novel, themes of sending, of destination, of destiny seem to dislocate the complementarity of sender and receiver. It does this both by edging into the Heideggerian terms *Geschichte-Geschick-schicken* (history, fate, sending) and by going upstream from them. For Heidegger, the submerged puns are gnomic indications of paths of being. While not belying the intensity of Heidegger's tone, Derrida reflates the puns in a very funny way: by bringing together 'notre histoire', a kind of love story, a sense of destiny, constant travelling of people and missives, and the postal services which pass on postcards, transmit telephone calls and love letters (in fact, the keeping in play of very different tones is one of the novel's qualities).

Now the idea of this packet of 'missives' needs discussion. At two points in *Envois* Derrida seems to point to an idea of network which would not be a pathway joining pre-existing point of origin and point of arrival, but one where the actual pathway (rather like lightning) would determine such points (cf. the 'gift' in Chapter 3). In both passages, Derrida considers whether a 'postal' version of Heideggerian *Geschick* is one that is dependent on a particular historical location, on an 'epokhé', a particular historical configuration and particular localization, sufficiently determining a singular, an identity. Derrida suggests that it is 'post' or 'posting' which, far from being implicated in a metaphysical technological determination of Being, is in fact the rhythm of Heidegger's *Geschick des Seins*. So that when Heidegger makes *tekhné* and technology derivative, some kind of falling off from the 'sending of being', he forgets that the very closing into a linked epoch of his history is postal. Whereas, Derrida counter-argues ('against "Martin"'), from the moment that 'there is', 'il y a', 'es gibt', there is destination, and the post is 'la possibilité "propre" de toute rhétorique possible' (CP, 73) ('the 'proper' possibility of every possible rhetoric') (*PC*, 65).

Heidegger had suggested many times that the subject/object distinction is a recent refinement of a much more diffuse, less technological–utilitarian relation between *Dasein* and the *Seiende*. In Tugendhat's words, that 'horizons of praxis and intersubjective history are more original than objects' (Tugendhat 1965: 255, my translation). It is as if Derrida widens this so that the very notional end-points themselves are 'post' the missive, the sending; individuation is not prior to but coeval with the individuating. It is not a question of exchange, not an atom-letter or missive on a circuit between terminals.

The differences with Lacan are therefore profound. There is not a structure of sending and receiving between stations which are clearly opposite each other; Derrida's structure does not, he tells us 'noyer toutes les différences, mutations, scansions, structures des régimes postaux dans une seule et une grande poste centrale' (CP, 74) ('submerg[e] all the differences, mutations, scansions, structures of postal regimes into one and the same great central post office') (*PC*, 65). The history of the postal *tekhné* is the tendency to assume transit between pre-existing sender and pre-existing receiver; identity and destination are treated as the same. But the nature of any kind of mark, and so anything that can be sent, is to *divide* both itself and its destination, because it is coded, and takes on several values in one (CP, 207; *PC*, 192). The possibility of error and loss is always there. Contrary to Lacan's famous assertion, that a letter always arrives at its destination, Derrida implies that any trace (merely because it is 'material') is divisible, and can be lost.

Tangled hierarchies

What for a moment will be called the postal 'analogy', we have seen, cannot provide a key:

> une telle 'histoire des postes' ne serait qu'un minuscule envoi dans le réseau qu'elle prétendrait analyser (pas de métapostale), seulement une carte perdue dans un sac, et qu'une grève, et même un accident de tri, peut toujours retarder indéfiniment, perdre sans retour.
>
> (CP, 74)

> such a 'history of the posts' would be but a minuscule *envoi* in the network that it allegedly would analyse (there is no metapostal), only a card lost in a bag, that a strike, or even a sorting accident, can always delay indefinitely, lose without return.
>
> (*PC*, 66–7)

The history of the postal services turns inside out on itself and becomes part of what it is analysing. A concept that might have seemed to dominate has been looped back, history is a tangled hierarchy. Are we merely 'in' a set of utterly unrelatable, utterly local pockets of events, knowing the location because we are there, so to speak?

What the 'postal services' give is the possibility of thinking differences, of not assimilating them, even of facing radical discontinuities:

> On peut tenir compte de ce qui se passe d'essentiel et de décisif, partout et jusque dans la langue, la pensée, la science et tout ce qui les conditionne, quand les structures postales font un saut, *Satz,* si tu veux, et se pose ou se poste autrement.
>
> (CP, 74)

> one can account for what essentially and decisively occurs, everywhere, and including language, thought, science, and everything that conditions them,

when the postal structure shifts, *Satz* if you will, and posits or posts itself
otherwise.

(*PC*, 66)

Derrida here puns on the German word for 'jump' and for 'phrase', and also for
intellectual postion ('Ansatz'). Derrida suggests that it is the postal analogy, the
postal principle, which allows a way of thinking liaison through time. He speaks
of, not this time 'condition of possibility', then, but a more tentative and
remote 'concerned with the very possibility' of history. (But if the postal service
is not a metaphor, not an analogy – and it is suggested that it is not – then what
is it? Not historically localizable, as part of the history of being, nor a-temporal,
neither metaphorical nor literal, it might seem to be a reworking of 'trace' with
the paradoxes of time, of anterior future and future-in-the-past, built in. The
question of this non-metaphor will be taken up in the final chapter.)

I am going to take the postal principle for the moment as pointing to something in the way thinking goes on, capturing the 'step/not' of thought's
movement. It might seem that to write history, some kind of transcendence in
consciousness is necessary, of even a momentary nature. You have to stand sideways to the process, a position which can be provided by an origin, placed
outside and supporting the historian's web, or else provided by *telos*, by an end
towards which the whole historical process is moving. Neither of these is available in the 'postal principle'. It seems as if, then, from these pages of a
philosophical novel, a view of history emerges which is a web of differences:
each point is heterogeneous, each point is local. Yet at the same time, the points
emerge, they do not pre-exist. And that emergence is a 'destiny', *Geschick*, as
well as a sending, a destination which is not available until the event has
occurred. In ways again to be analysed in the next chapter, it makes possible a
thinking of missives without purpose, without connection to each other
through the preplanned end-point of their cursus, but only after the event.
Where possible-past-histories were unconnected at each turn to possible-future-
histories, the movement can yet be described: in Markovian terms, as a 'random
walk'; in Derridean terms as 'concerned with the possibility of history', as posting
or sending ('poster', 'schicken'). This sense of destiny is concerned, not with
knowledge about where the history is going, but with a sense of extreme vulnera-
blity to those slight shifts in conditions which are the waverings of the random.

Derrida says of Freud's speculation that it is not a meta-discourse: the
description is also part of what it designates or can become so. Thus devices of
hierarchy or of logical type, developed to defeat paradox,[38] are left unavailing,
perhaps because paradox is always reconstitutable. Saying and saying 'that' are
in communication: the transcendence of conscious speculation is always looping
back to what it appears to fly over. Derrida himself brings together commentary
and meta-commentary:

Je fais comme si cela même qu'il [Freud] paraît analyser, par exemple le
rapport entre les deux principes [principe de mort, principe de plaisir],

c'était déjà un élément de la structure spéculaire en général . . . au sens enfin de ce qui déborde la présence (donnée) du présent, le donné du don. Je fais tout cela et je prétends qu'il faut le faire pour accéder à ce qui se joue ici au delà du 'donné', au refusé, retenu, repris, au delà du principe de ce que Freud *dit* présentement, si quelque chose de tel était possible, *au sujet de la spéculation*.

(CP, 303–4)

I am acting as if the very thing he appears to analyze, for example, the relation between the two principles, were already an element of speculative structure in general . . . in the sense of that which overflows the (given) presence of the present, the given of the gift. I am doing all this, and I am alleging that this must be done in order to gain access to that which is played out here beyond the 'given', to that which is rejected, withheld, taken back, beyond the principle of what Freud presently *says*, if such a thing were possible, *about speculation*.

(*PC*, 283–4)

This is a complex sentence: Derrida 'behaves as if' Freud's 'using' of speculation were also a 'mentioning' of it. But to 'behave as if' in its present statement of hypothesis involves separation of Derrida's own use and analysis (treating Freud as speculating, analysing Freud's speculation) which are or have been the same act. Simulation and action, use and mention, are not joined and not separated. This is not a performative 'doing things with words';[39] it is a tangled hierarchy where action and acted on (CP, 304; *PC*, 284) are not truly separable, or not for long, where no set of concepts is proof against all others:[40] 'Celui-ci [le discours théorique] se trouve ainsi inclus, partie prenante et prise dans l'objet même qu'il prétend analyser' (LI, 136) ('This discourse thus finds itself an integral part – part and parcel, but also *partial* – of the object it claims to be analyzing') (*LI*, 71). Freud's analysis follows the rhythm of Ernst's game with the bobbin, as Heidegger's analysis of Van Gogh, discussed above, follows the lacing of the half-unlaced bootlaces: in all these, there is a halting back-and-forth movement forward.

Derrida, in the passage just quoted, implied that such intrication is necessary to get to the 'refused, held back, taken back', to what is beyond what Freud is actually saying at that present moment (with the implication that when one uses such a phrase, it is shorthand for the complex tangle of said and half-or-not-said). More, then, is going on in texts, or they are going in directions other than those they admit to.[41] Notions of intention are opened out and revised to a kind of headless direction 'sans origine, sans émission, et sans destinataire' (CP, 363) ('without origin, without emission, and without addressee') (*PC*, 341) with a reference to Kant's *Critique of Judgement* and its 'purposiveness without purpose': 'Télé – sans telos. Finalité sans fin. La beauté du diable' – 'Tele without telos. Finality without end, the beauty of the devil'. Intention, meta-language, both are inadequate as structuring principles, which might allow valid connection or give direction. This points to his account of his own way of working: 'Stratégie finalement sans finalité, on pourrait appeler cela tactique aveugle, errance empirique', but Derrida immediately brings up the question of responsibility, and thus of answering to: 'si la valeur d'empirisme ne prenait d'elle-même tout son sens de son opposition à la responsibilité philosophique' (M, 7) ('Finally, a strategy without finality, what might be called blind tactics, or empirical wandering if the value of empiricism did not itself acquire its entire meaning in its opposition to philosophical responsibility') (*M*, 7). Philosophical responsibility does not bring with it *telos*: the responsibility to the unknown, we shall see, is not one that can be preplanned. There is no pre-given structure – and Derrida has coined the term 'destinerrance' for such a movement. Yet he has also said, of his own work: 'If I saw clearly ahead of time where I was going, I really don't believe that I should take another step to get there'; but this does not mean 'I never know where I'm going'.[42] So that there may be a kind of 'stepping out' which is neither towards a goal nor aimless, which is an uneasy tension relating movement to the random and to the transcendent infinity of the *alea*, in a way illuminated by a remark of Blanchot: 'the experience of chance is, as André Breton saw it, the experience *within* immanence of a kind of transcendence of unknown essence' (EI, 147, trans. MRN).

This 'purposiveness without purpose' might be found in the aerated, disconnected architecture of the Maison des Sciences in Paris, with its pavilions along connecting walkways – as if random walks; its architects certainly refer to Derrida's work. Such a network of circuitry can be modelled by the Markov chain (the arrival of calls along a network into a telephone exchange is so modelled): when Derrida uses the telephone exchange, that 'interminable réseau de branchements d'écoute *en allo* qui oblige à compter avec la pièce rapportée' (*Glas*, 136b) ('interminable network of listening lines *en allo*, in hello, that compels reckoning with the insert, the patch') (*Glas*, 118b); the reply ('hello') is placed in the same phonemes as Aristotle's 'in another' (*Physics*, iv, 218a; M, 65; *M*, 57), responsiveness and allogeneity are placed then in never-ending, branching networks of calls.

Return calls and histories

The structure of the telephone exchange, and the possibility of constant havering extensions out from where the call is received, is precisely the net of routes of possible return calls, of possible answers to the other. The structure of return here is not symmetric to the call, or not certainly so.

The child Ernst's 'calling himself back', Freud's 'posting' himself, writing back to himself from a position not yet existing, have a strange temporality; they have time's chiasmatic structure. They are versions of 'return calls'. But just as the history of the postal service was concerned with the very possibility of history (see above) so the return call, *Rückfrage*, is a Husserlian term, which appears in Derrida's earliest published text and which describes 'the pure form of any historical experience' (OG, 36; *OG*, 50). To it Derrida restores its

> résonnance postale et épistolaire d'une communication à distance. Comme la *'Rückfrage'* la question d'un retour se pose à partir d'un premier envoi. A partir du *document* reçu et *déjà* lisible, la possibilité m'est offerte d'inter-roger à nouveau et *en retour* sur l'intention originaire et finale de ce qui m'a été livré par la tradition. Celle-ci, qui n'est que la médiateté elle-même et l'ouverture à une télécommunication en général, peut alors, comme le dit Husserl, *'se laisser questionner'*.
>
> (OG, 36)

> postal and epistolary reference or resonance of a communication from a distance. Like the *Rückfrage*, a return inquiry is asked on the basis of a first posting. From a received and *already* readable *document*, the possibility is offered me of asking again, and *in return*, about the primordial and final intention of what has been given me by tradition. The latter, which is only mediacy itself and openness to a telecommunication in general, is then, as Husserl says, 'open . . . to continued inquiry'.
>
> (*OG*, 50)

Any history, it might seem, of the child, of the Freudian institution, or in general, is not a collection of acquired experiences so much as the openness to receiving and placing calls, to taking up and sending on.

Husserl, in his work on the origin of geometry, made of the present whole of culture a continuity of parts which entail each other, each constituting a present for us of past culture, a present which is a sediment of originary sense, but which the act of understanding reactivates and makes living. Yet the events of geometry's history were once projects, that is, acts creating sense. This sense turns into sedimented mathematical objects; but these are in turn justified by the present's power not to treat them as dead, but to give them meaning, to bring them alive in understanding, to reactivate their meaning. This is how the network of phone calls can model geometric tradition, and it is underpinned by the phenomenological basis given to time by Husserl: for him, the activity of consciousness, says Derrida, is the criss-cross of protentions and retentions in dialectical relation with the Living Present (dialectic of dialectic and non-dialectic, the structure of relation to relation and non-relation discussed many times already – OG, 158; *OG*, 143). Time is not phenomenologically succes-sive: it is unified by this net of protentions and retentions, of castings back and projectings forward, and the unity of this movement appears to consciousness as indefinite.

In *Origin of Geometry*, this rethinking of the implications of the Husserlian Living Present, of the Present as weaving together futures in the past, and past in the future, occurs at a moment when the problem raised by Jean Cavaillès[43] à propos Husserl has been differentiated sufficiently to be absorbable into the text's argument. The question of how there can be *developed* through mathematical praxis or geometric norms, which then are treated as transcendental; and that question's generalization, the question of what is the relation between constituting act and constituted meaning, which was the centre of Cavaillès' meditations, are enlarged. They are elaborated into the question of how past sense is reactivated, and into the question of the temporal synapse of activity and passivity within consciousness – whether receipt of stimuli or of ideas precedes activity. For if geometry has sense and can progress as a tradition by a co-implication of sedimentation and reactivation, then there is a receptivity to that sedimented meaning at the heart of the subjectivity, which makes of it a new project in meaning (OG, 158; *OG*, 143). (The relation between praxis and the tradition in philosophy and logic will be raised again in the final chapter, as it is deeply imbricated with the question of language: that is, in effect, in the Husserlian context, with the presence of historical facticity at the heart of the development of geometry. For the emergence of the mathematical object is the emergence of objectivity and the conditions of its logical availability are the conditions of its historical constitution. The logical 'if' is, then, also the historical condition, the *a priori* in the chronological sense. And the availability is *linguistic*: the mathematical object is embodiment, not expression. Language and facticity, as conditions of ideality, are one and the same. The question of history, even the history of mathematics, leads to the question of language, not as a formal syntax for any statement, but as necessary localization.[44])

The 'return call', the return inquiry of *Origin of Geometry*, then, prefigures the child's game, Freud's speculation, indeed, the generality of telecommunication in the later texts. In Derrida's development, they are tradition, they make possible a continuation of tradition which is one of extension neither programmed nor aimless, which is 'open to continued inquiry'; and a consciousness which, in its structuring by the criss-cross nature of time, is neither active nor passive simply, but where the receptiveness styles the creativity which works out of it.

The unknown and the neuter

Husserl's history of geometry had to explain how new theorems can be 'found': are they inscribed in the laws of logic, always existing in some sense, so that they can be cranked out? Or are they in some sense constructed, out of a particular moment of geometrical knowledge? (OG, 193; *OG*, 172–3) With formal calculations which are 'blind' (Leibniz) or perhaps unreactivatable (Husserl in OG, 196) in spite of the fact that they originated our knowledge? The 'collect call', the questioning back is not just historical, but is the exploring of logical implication: epistemology and history are not separable and this movement forward of any axiomatics is a projection back through such implication. It allows the new which is connected to but not programmed by tradition. The 'openness to continued enquiry' of the Husserlian *Rückfrage* is for Derrida the openness of responsiveness to the other, like an on-line modem, or like the phatic signalling of a cellular telephone. But what is the nature of that connection, if there is no overarching medium or logic for us all, and not even the directional rationality of Husserlian *telos* is available? Does the community of knowledge develop in other ways than by this halting pair of negatives we saw earlier? And what might it be? Can the non-known be drawn into the sphere of the known, and yet not be embedded in its grid? How do we allow for the not-known? Is it found or does it just appear?

Blanchot (in *L'Entretien infini*, in three articles originally published from 1963 and 1964, as in *Le Pas au-delà*, 1973) repeatedly brings together the unknown and the neuter: 'The unknown is verbally a neuter' (EI, 440). French has no neuter, and the recourse to the masculine to express Greek or Latin neuter expresses its lack of gender, rather than its assignation to one. Not hesitant between gender, nor between objective and subjective disposition, it has, says Blanchot, been effaced by philosophers. (By Sartre, when he speaks of the 'pratico-inert' which can make any dialectic collapse, that is, suspend any binary opposition; by Freud when he makes the Id out of drives and instincts which are not neuter, by Heidegger, with the dispensation whereby understanding and being correspond and do not diverge.) These rectifications of possible differential mismatch, says Blanchot (EI, 441, my translation). Blanchot insists, in what appears to be a version of the two infinites, negative and positive, that the relation to the unknown that he is proposing is neither that to an unknown object nor to what is an exceeding into the 'absolutely unknowable' which refuses all expression. The unknown must be approached by a relation which protects it without infinitizing it or incorporating it into the known. Its form is a 'passive action' ('Le pas au-delà'). It is a 'nec uter', 'not-either of two', not a mere word for the negative – there is no work of the neuter, as there can be talk of Hegelian work of the negative. It juxtaposes an affirmation and an indefinite series of negations (Blanchot 1973: 105) spawning into a plurality with each attempt to approach it.[45]

These passages from Blanchot working in what might be described as an intertext between Derrida and Heidegger are themselves, as it were, distressed (in the sense that material may be 'distressed') and spun out by Derrida in a series of writings on Heidegger and sexuality. First, he has shown how in Heidegger's writing on *Dasein* and sexual division, neutralization is both the result of negativity induced by sexual division, and the effacement of such a negativity, moving towards a neutralization which is neuter in the sense of non-binary, not bigamous (Psy, 402).[46] As such, it is associated with chance and the random, for it is a movement (a gift) between determinations which are not pre-given, but which exist after the trajectory (Beehive, 4; Blanchot 1973: 103). In the strange temporality of telepathy or psychoanalysis, or, one might add, sufficiently complex analyses of cause (Taylor 1964), the causes may appear to post-date the caused.

If the neuter, the 'negative without the negative', is a pattern for the unknown, but without assigning to it causal force, which would make of it a pre-existing future object, how *does* it work, or come about, without 'the negative's work' (Par, 15)? In Derrida's work, there seems to be constant reference to two ways which cross-cut. One, the destabilizing limping, the 'pas' as 'step'. Two, the paradoxical, self-programming of a short-circuit where, by 'booting up' out of contradictory conventions or the double bind, the 'now' is created.

In respect of this second way, through the double bind, Derrida has spoken several times – in 'Women in the Beehive', *Otobiographies* and *Psyché* – of the American Declaration of Independence. There is always a 'necessary undecidability' (Oto, 20): 'Without this experience, would there ever be the chance of a step being made?' In the case of the Declaration of Independence, the dependent colonists sign themselves free: their representatives declare themselves what they will only be after the Declaration – free; their act is undecidable between a constation of their freedom, and a making of it by the act of signature. For fact can never make right, and the legitimacy of a situation is not guaranteed by its factual existence, yet the search for the naturally right is then reduced to infinite regress. In the political *de jure/de facto* dilemma of legitimation, Derrida shows that it is precisely the undecidability, the necessary clash, which produces 'the desired effect' (Oto, 21).[47]

'La signature invente le signataire' – 'The signature invents the signer' (Oto, 22; *Oto,* 10). It is through signature or through quotation that this effect is obtained. Self-signing and self-quotation link founding subjectivities and effects – a people or, in another case, the poem, to emerge. He has discussed several times the beginning of Ponge's poem *Fable* in this respect:

> Par le mot *par* commence donc ce texte
> Dont la première ligne dit la vérité

> By the word *by* begins thus this text
> Of which the first line says the truth

Here there is not merely self-reference (that would exist in 'Ce texte commence par le mot "ce"') but performance: it appears to be describing (something which might then pre-exist), but is actually materializing as the description occurs (clear if the difference with '"Par" commence ce texte' is considered). Derrida argues that the distinction between 'use' (first 'par') and 'mention' (second 'par') is insufficient to describe the effect (Psy, 23; 'Inventions', 33). The strange effect of the altered word order is that the first 'par' is in fact already a part of a designation of the whole phrase, as the text talks about itself and not merely an expression of the sense, which would only then be designation by the second 'par'. 'L'événement inventif, c'est la citation *et* le récit' (Psy, 23) ('The inventive event is the quotation and the narrative') ('Inventions', 33). This short-circuit, where constative and performative, use and mention, are cross-cut, can inaugurate a text, as it inaugurated the American people, for out of the repetition, the iterability which seems to confirm what is, there can come the new which destabilizes it: 'Le mouvement même de cette fabuleuse répétition peut, selon un croisement de chance et de nécessité, produire le nouveau d'un événement' (Psy, 58) ('The very movement of this fabulous repetition can, through a merging of chance and necessity, produce the new of an event') ('Inventions', 59). In this text, the short-circuit between poles takes the form of 'infinitely rapid oscillation' (Psy, 25; 'Inventions', 34), and that constitutes the event.

The undecidable is undecidable in respect of two determinate alternatives. A movement takes place within Derrida's article at this point, for the question of invention, of what cannot be allowed for, anticipated, the question of the incalculable, emerges. The term 'incalculable' relays perhaps the 'undecidable', but must differ too: there is not a binary, impossible choice. With the incalculable come notions which cut across the distinction between the necessary and the random, between the aleatory and the willed. The incalculable is a letting come of the other, a respecting of its difference. But the reader cannot in this context lean on a binary distinction of 'event' and 'aleatory advert' (Psy, 59 note; 'Inventions', 65 note 23); the text will not warrant it. In reading this text, written shortly after the death of de Man and in his memory, a problem we have encountered previously appears: one is not sure whether the 'singular event' (Psy, 25; 'Inventions', 34) can be related to the singularity, the strange attractor of the previous chapter. There is a sense of working with circuits which appear to be projectable out to other Derridean texts (the 'oppositional logic' here is deconstructed by the event of this poem by Ponge and by its 'fabulous economy'; in *The Post Card*, the small series of painful rhythmic impulses in Freud's pleasure principle makes impossible a logic of opposition (CP, 436; *PC*, 408). Yet it is not clear that in the different context they can be truly connected, much less identified. The irruption of the other, the 'invention de l'autre' in the article's title, seems to be comparable to those singularities, and thus to the positive infinite:

> la venue aléatoire du tout autre, au-delà de l'incalculable comme calcul encore possible, au-delà de l'ordre même du calcul, voilà la 'vraie' invention, ce qui n'est plus invention même de la vérité et ne peut advenir que pour un être fini: la *chance* même de la finitude. Elle n'invente et ne s'apparaît que depuis ce qui *échoit* ainsi.
>
> (Psy, 59 note)

> the aleatory advent of the entirely other, beyond the incalculable as a still possible calculus – beyond the very order of calculation, – there is 'true' invention, which is no longer [even] invention of truth, and can only come about for a finite being: the very *opportunity* (*chance*) of finitude. It invents and appears to itself only on the basis of what *happens* thus.
>
> ('Inventions', 65 note 23, trans. mod.)

Here, then, we have invention from a position of finitude, invention that is only possible from there, but which has been exceeded by invention *of* finitude from the excess implied by the 'beyond', the 'au-delà'. We seem once again to have the two movements of the strange attractors, on the one hand their imposition of a position of relation incorporating finitude, or on the contrary of a movement towards finite receptivity from the absolute. The circuits of argument move out to a 'completely other', which once again links possible and impossible in a paradox (Psy, 59; 'Inventions', 65). Like Pascal's account of grace, the coming of the other can be prepared for, but not made to happen: it is an incalculable of a different order from the calculable,[48] and in question and answer we are told that it is impossible, and thus the only possible invention (the title of the section is 'Invention de Dieu (politique de la recherche, politique de la culture)' (Psy, 55) ('Invention of God (politics of research, politics of culture)') ('Inventions', 60). We thus come right up against questions – of circuits, of their similarity and difference – which will be discussed in the next chapter. But it needs to be noted here that what the reader is dealing with is precisely the subject of the Derridean article: how from within the change, within repetition of the same, an invention may spring. As in Ponge's fable, in exhibiting the rules of its own working, an opening is waiting. Within the echoes and resonance of what seem similar programmes of phrases, micrologies, a further way-station emerges in the network of Derridean themes.

Derrida, then, trusts to the play within the French word 'pas' – opposition ('not') and extension ('step'). His negatives, which it is possible to oppose to the Hegelian work of the negative as to the Lacanian reversed reciprocity, work between irruption and negotiation, as do what this book calls the 'strange attractors'. Indeed, in his commentary on Hegel and on Marx, in *Glas*, it is as if Derrida enjoyed catching a system before it has crystallized, to show us what is its working in an earlier, pre-oppositional mode. He is not however studying these systems in themselves, in terms of their own development.

We will see that some of the features of the very way Derrida writes allow opposition and extension to work with each other. The next chapter will consider connection further, which might be thought to be the converse problem of negation. However, in some of Derrida's writing, it is as if we begin to adumbrate the development of the new from under, so to speak, what may be its opposite.

5   Contacts

Nous devons pour des raison essentielles, traiter ici les choses par contiguïté (we must for basic reasons deal here with things that follow on from each other).
(UG, 115; *UG*, 56)

This final chapter will consider the question of connection in Derrida's work, both as an idea and as a practice in his writing. Discussion of Derrida's work in the first years of its reception tended to concentrate on the way some of the most frequent frames of connection in philosophical ideas – causality, intention, ground and common origin, purpose – seemed to have been repudiated in his thought, or at least to have been made to seem insecure. It has been pointed out in preceding chapters that there are ideas developed in Derrida's writings which act instead of or take the place of these frames – as the title of one recent collection, *Psyché*, might warn us, there are in his writing important reworkings of concepts which have functions that are familiar. But even so, it is not the case that Derrida has in wholesale manner refashioned our intellectual furniture into entities with similar if revamped functions. And it is the case of this book that connections are built between the arguments of Derrida's work, his books and articles, in ways that make new versions of consistency possible.

This case may seem to work against the tendency of some of his recent writings which suggest that the new and our access to the new must be protected, the latter a paradoxical enterprise (see for instance 'Inventions of the other', in *Psyché*). The incalculable is in such work the descendent of the earlier 'unheard of' ('inoui') (given value in such an article as 'Structure, sign and play', in *Writing and Difference*). In *Psyché*, the new should not be forseeable, and its lack of predictability must be maintained. In that way, its link with the present is likely to be tenuous, otherwise it will be the probable rather than the new. Yet in terms of the coherence built up in Derrida's arguments, this chapter will argue that there are forms of writing in these texts which allow consistency of an unusual sort. This building up of coherence is precisely not explicitly linked by Derrida with questions of consistency, nor is it even tagged by commentary to any degree; but it nevertheless engenders the sense the reader has both of exploration and of coherent suite in the development of an idea. This particular role of the style of exposition creates an effect which cannot be summarized merely by the explicit statements in Derrida's work. As the terms used of it in the previous chapters suggest (syntax, lexemes, circuits of argument), it is derived from the patterns of the use of language, and goes beyond the ideas which are explicitly expressed. Discursive content here is part of something more than the sum of the phrases. In that sense, this chapter is arguing that a distinction like that between 'force' and 'meaning', which often seems to repeat the traditional distinction between style and content at a different level of unit, is not one which can address part of the effect of work such as Derrida's (nor that of other philosophers either, Wittgenstein, for instance). Indeed, a striking effect, as we shall see in this chapter, is the bringing together of disparate or even contradictory meanings within the same phrase. The phrase engenders an oscillation between these, and the reader is thus obliged to take into account a meaning beneath the meaning whose force may be very different. When this happens, the reader allows effects of writing to influence their understanding in ways that may not be exposable from within the ambit of the surface meaning.

The end of the last chapter saw the bringing together of event in a text and historical event (America's Declaration of Independence). Through that text, the origin of the American people, a political event which is also a textual one becomes possible. It is a result, Derrida argued, of an interference between performative and constative uses of language.[1] Likewise, in Derrida's first essay in memory of Paul de Man, in the section on *Fable* by Francis Ponge, repetition and report, quotation in performance and constation, led to the new. More clearly here than in the text on the Declaration of Independence, the Derridean commentary also begins, at one point at least, not just to narrate, but to allow a meaning to emerge which overwrites the sense of its own phrases. As Derrida recounts it, the Ponge poem seems, in strange fashion, to make the new emerge from the already-there-as-possible. With repetition, something begins which is not what is reported:

> Le mouvement même de cette fabuleuse répétition peut, selon un croisement de chance et de nécessité, produire le nouveau d'un événement. Non seulement par l'invention singulière d'un performatif, car tout performatif suppose des conventions et des règles institutionnelles; mais en tournant ces règles dans le respect de ces règles mêmes afin de laisser l'autre venir ou s'annoncer dans l'ouverture de cette déhiscence.
>
> (Psy, 58–9, already partially quoted)

> The very movement of this fabulous repetition can, through a merging of chance and necessity, produce the new of an event. Not only with the singular invention of a performative, since every performative presupposes conventions and institutional rules – but by bending the rules with respect for the rules themselves in order to allow the other to come or to announce its coming in the opening of this dehiscence.
>
> ('Inventions', 59–60)

It is as if the repetition just *is* respect of the rules and conventions for the performative. But the phrase Derrida uses of the rules is ambivalent and can bear nearly contradictory meanings: 'en tournant ces règles dans le respect de ces règles mêmes' – 'inflecting the rules in respect of these same rules' or, 'getting round the rules in respect of these same rules'. The near-negative lying under the phrase, as it were, causes an interruption, an interference. This chapter will discuss other examples of such two-way phrases which appear, by a kind of linguistic short-circuit in the present case, to build out the complication which, we have been told, allows the event. In the example before us, that very respect of the rules both acknowledges and exhibits the precariousness of the distinctions with which the rules do their work, preventing structures of thought from hardening so as only to be able to produce a combination of the already there. Perhaps, Derrida says, that is what is called 'deconstruction'.

The consequence would be that texts do not simply 'bottom out' in some non-textual reality, which can then be thematized harmlessly back up into commentary. Nor are they simply conjoined to historical (or poetic) event, as witnesses or tools for interpretation of something beyond themselves (though of course they are that also). The American Declaration of Independence was clearly an act as well as a text, but that is true of all acts, which enact or obtain comprehensions and misreadings, and of all texts which are interventions in situations. It is here that the Derridean formation I have called the 'strange attractor' shows its power: it allows for more than, or other than, what we can say, or write. But at the same time, we cannot access it, only receive its irruptive force, and we have to repeat the process by different, further writing, further negotiation. So that a writing might develop, and a written notion of that writing, which allows some way for this delaying to be registered. This seems to me to be the source of one of the striking aspects of Derrida's mode of writing: the layered effect of the extension through the negotiation.

The end of the last chapter in fact shows the way in which all that has been summarized in the four paragraphs above raises questions about Derrida's own writing. Derrida's working of the question of connection, through the problem of invention, had led to the incalculable, which cannot be programmed for. Now in this present chapter, this question of connection in his own writing will be examined. How might it be possible to link what I have called circuits of argument from one context to another? Are apparently similar micrologies each time different? Is their reappearance identical or merely similar? The nature of the continuity or discontinuity needs investigation (this is of course to ask the question of difference). The problem of this chapter is to begin to understand what is going on in the language of this work, to understand the 'or' in Derrida's phrase 'the discursive or textual event' (DP, 286).

So this chapter will consider the question of language in Derrida, and also Derrida's language. In particular, the peculiar play of contact and interruption of contact both thematically and in the texture of the writing will be looked at in relation to consistency, that is, a standing together occurring through language. This will not involve giving a full thematic account of what Derrida says about language (though that is of itself of great interest, and will be evoked), but looking at the way the actual Derridean writing induces consistency – with the effect of what I have called syntax, lexemes and circuits of argument. Now, Derrida's work in part can be seen as a constant drawing of attention to the fragility of the distinctions, to the insecurity, for instance, of the separation of inside from outside which the great tradition of logic relies on, to the paradoxes generated by these distinctions (in which he is working in totally different mode, but in the same direction as some of the great recent logicians). His work can be seen as pointing, in other words, to the question of consistency.

My use of the term consistency, though intended to draw attention to the technical problem of consistency in logic, is philological in an everyday sense. I want to suggest that besides the power of Derrida's arguments, his writing has a textual coherence. But does my suggestion that there may be a consistency induced by writing imply a contradiction in Derrida's work between what is said and the saying? (It would thus be a linguistic version of the usual argument against scepticism; and a mode of consistency would be evolved in the writing which went against the theme of the fragility of distinctions.) Now, reduction of meaning to controllable semantic kernels is imperfect, and any thematization partial and provisional. A certain sort of consistency is associated with thematization and the possibility it provides of clear and concise conclusions; it will seem directly threatened by such insistence on the importance of what many would hope would be the fringes of meaning, the etiolated outer edges of a focus. But there may be modes of consistency which are not part of thematics, nor using methods usual in discursive writing, but operating beside them, or sometimes in lieu of them. Such modes are textual, and, it will be argued, provide for a networked extension of a position not by explicitation, or not always by explicitation, but by repetition, tacitly and occasionally, an extension to somewhere which then has to be consolidated thematically *post hoc*. The connection is built out after the position has been adopted, or at least, it becomes visible afterwards. In this way recognition of the connection yields something new going beyond the pattern of meaning made available by the repeated elements in themselves.

So this chapter will show how Derrida induces a consistency which may allow discontinuity. In this way, it allows that language and thought are not seamlessly joined, nor separable either. The new for Derrida may come about from this sense of proximity and discontinuity. This sense is certainly the source of one of the striking effects of Derrida's writing – that something important and difficult is just coming into our comprehension.

The random and connection

The incalculably new is a random coming (Psy, 58; 'Inventions', 59). Even in the domain of the scientific, with the planned use of the random there arises the question of the unconscious: random numbers have to be mechanically generated, and used by a mechanical procedure. Otherwise the mind's links to the event are not broken – projections, expectations, memories will spin a web between the past and the experimental future. What this may mean in terms of Derrida's own text, and the scope it takes pains to allow to an unconscious, will be discussed at the end of this chapter. At this present point, the relation Derrida sketches out between language and the random will be discussed, or if what I am trying to pinpoint should only be called the random with many precautions, then at least it may be compared, for like the random, it consists of tiny sequences of events not subsumable into deterministic laws.

In an article on incident, on chance, and the 'falling' that is commemorated in those words, for both are derived from the Latin verb 'to fall'; on Freud, Sterne and the use of the trivial detail as indicative, Derrida has suggested that a willingness to allow for the fragility of distinctions, for their essential mobility, is in appearance (only) very like the forms that superstition can take, in that it relates the apparently disconnected (MC, 34; *MC*, 26).[2] Two apparently severed sequences of events may, under certain conditions, be brought within each other's frequencies, as it were, and the connection be made, that is, transference out of random collocation begin. (The importance of the analogy of 'wire less' telegraphy, of electromagnetic interchange riding along branching networks, will be again apparent in this chapter as it was in the previous.) In these processes, causality and communication cannot be separated, as event and narrative cannot: the diminutive size and fleeting nature of what is thought of as in process make the separation impossible.

Increase or even stability in information exchange involves energy consumption (and thus energy intake). It involves entropy, one could say, 'dissemination'. As autoregulation increases, so does the disorder. In the thought experiment of the English scientist James Clark Maxwell, a demon sorts white and black balls that are moving randomly in a closed container, by allowing them preferentially to move into separate compartments according to colour. He thereby increases the order at one level. But the demon must be regarded as being a thermodynamic part of the system, so that if the system is closed and the process of sorting were to continue, the disorderly Brownian motion of the demon would itself increase. This is because the creating of order for the balls requires the importation of further energy from outside the system to keep it stable. If the further energy is not forthcoming from the demon, it is removed from farther down the whole system, at the molecular level. Such an effect is true of any system of records, of 'traces', argues Derrida. The recording cannot be separated from the recorded, and the lack of closure, the impossibility of Maxwell's demon, means that the system is not one of regulated exchange. No real homeostasis is possible, there are always minute seepages, small leaks of energy, small *restes* which may cause the instability to accumulate at one point, and the system to fissure and collapse. So that the divisibility of the letter which Derrida insists on so many times implies the impossibility of balanced exchange: any stabilization or homogenization into stages (into 'phase space') is an abstraction which neglects the minute flickering interchanges of energy always at work. The thin line between inner and outer is an unstable area of differential exchange.

Even more, the retroactivity typical of living systems, where future goals, not yet existing except in a programme or intention, affect what will become their own past, cannot be the result of exchange, but only of filters, channels and differences. Language serves here, as it does frequently for Derrida, as an example of this, a kind of boom box for the effects of the random: like other systems of 'writing' it simultaneously increases the random variation and inde-terminacy, and the effects of coding, that is of self-regulation (MC, 5; *MC*, 2).

In this kind of connectedness, then, there is no whole and no overarching form: but neither is there rhapsodic improvisation (D, 62); like Kant's 'purpos-iveness without purpose' attributed in the *Critique of Judgement* to beauty, it is a 'stratégie finalement sans finalité' (M, 7) ('a strategy finally without finality') (*M*, 7), a 'télé – sans telos' (CP, 363) ('tele – without telos') (*PC*, 341). Unlike for Lacan, for Derrida not merely can the letter always fail to arrive at its desti-nation (thus breaking the circle of exchange as a basis for communication, since it may always possibly not occur, not close), but it does not exist before its itinerary:

> Il n'y a rien qui précède le mouvement, le trajet ou le transfert, rien qui ait la forme de ce qu'on appellerait couramment une lettre, voire un objet, rien dont on puisse dire: c'est posé là, devant, existant quelque part avant l'envoi.
>
> (Aff, 79)

> Nothing precedes movement, journey or transfer, nothing that may have the shape of what would commonly be called a letter, or an object, nothing about which one can say: it is lying there, before us, existing somewhere before the sending.
>
> (Aff, 79, trans. MRN)

In a related conversation with anglophones, the word 'random' is used of what seems the same process, but in relation to gift and receipt of gift (Beehive, 14).[3] It seems as if connection in this kind of case is *ex post facto*; it is one of way, of trail and of its having been beaten (a process which itself implicates a near-miss relation to the self, to one's own position, which is created by a series of move-ments out with the stick or hatchet to cut the path). The linear temporality of the usual concepts of causality is thus perturbed: defining a movement where the effect can influence the cause, Derrida says of his 'kind of novel' *Envois* (in *The Post Card*) 'une lettre n'y précède jamais son trajet' ('in it a letter never precedes its journey') (Aff, 81) in the sense that it is determined by the reply; with the linguistic consequence that pure deixis, pointing without right of reply, so to speak, and so often the explanation given of the origin and direction of speech, does not exist (Aff, 81). Even to point at something is in effect to bend to an answer. The causality and temporality of the process Derrida is describing cannot, then, be linear. The consequence seems to be that a system of lateral connection is functioning: everything can always be joined up with everything else, can always be arranged in a complicated trajectory. So that such a procedure allows what might be called an ergodic consistency in argument. As in probabilistic systems, where the trajectory of the particle can get arbitrarily close to every point in the phase space in the long-enough term, so over the long-enough term, textual connections can always be made.

How these can be made remains to be seen. This can and should be applied to certain examples of Derridean writing (not to all – and not uniformly – Derrida also writes in more plain-sailing fashion). Rigour may be created by the replications – or reapplications; as in the child Ernst's engendering of the self, there is a gradual filling out of the argument through similar forms and semi-repetitions, through circuits of argument which confirm the extensions of the argument as they occur. This sheer written density of patches of the text and its tissue will be examined through certain examples below. Coherence and rigour are an effect of the writing, they are constructed as things go along, through a placing of what I have called lexemes; or through a repetition of the micrologies, where there is a maximization of the points of contact between the closely similar but not exactly similar circuits. The anxiously havering, Brownian motion-like movement of the argument Derrida is mounting puts out filaments, stems and extensions, which gradually and over time put out discursive space through semi-repetition and occupy it. Take, for instance, a passage from the Genet column in *Glas*: 'Les sciences, toutes, doivent ici enregistrer le coup de dé. Et la force d'aléa, en clinamen. . . . Tout s'entraîne à faire cas de la chance. Elle ne peut jamais bien tomber' (263b–4b) ('The sciences, all of them, must record here the throw of the d(ie). And the force of chance, as *clinamen*. . . . Everything is moved to attach importance to the case of chance. It can never fall well') (*Glas*, 236b). Almost every word constitutes a node in a filament of Derrida's reflection, and could be glossed, for example, by moving back to 'The double session' (the second article of *Dissemination*) and forward to 'My chances' (1984). The words develop consistency out of their very mutual insistence ('entraîner', 'cas', 'chance', 'tomber') and point to future or past extensions round each of them. It is as if Derrida throws back ropes to his own work, while allowing the future to come to us not as a set of calculated compossibles, but as a force proceeding back to us from strands that have been projected out. For such a mode of composition, the phrase is like a point of accumulation in its context, it acquires weight and effect in a way which is not in simple posteriority to the situation it is in.

This is, I repeat, only one among many kinds of arguments mounted by Derrida – there is, for example, in 'The double session' a marvellously accurate résumé of the structure of seventeenth- and eighteenth-century theories of mimesis, which for all its brilliance and illuminating power is of a much more familiar kind (see above, Chapter 2). But to be aware of the filamentary construction of some of the writing helps the realization of why it is so very hard to summarize or paraphrase some Derridean arguments. This difficulty which crops up (but once again, not everywhere, not all of the time) is in fact akin to the problem faced by certain kinds of computer program. It may not be known whether a complete program is an algorithm and will come out to an answer, or whether two program of sufficient complexity could intersect at one point (an actual problem for those constructing program for flight paths).[4] The sequences of programs cannot be compressed or subsumed into terminating programs (Chaitin 1971), the information embodied in the digital series cannot be summarized to any useful extent. A summary which can be raised to the level of theme, of next-level program, is simply not possible. Such types of binary series suggest that the much more variegated strings of signifiers in natural language may likewise not be summarized without loss, by imposition of law-like program or summary equation one to another of different scales of detail and signification – what can be called generally 'thematization'. The elements of the series can only be taken at the level of singulars.

For Derrida, a philosophic or fictional text is neither a code which is inter-preted, nor a programme which is 'run'. (This stance takes the form of occasionally explicit resistance to a commentator in *Jacques Derrida* and is one of the sources of humour there.) Paraphrase and summary seem to fail to make purchase at least some of the time. And if this failure of summary is upsetting (what else occurs in the present book, for instance?), there are features of some Derridean texts which seem to exacerbate and exploit it. They have points of accumulation, as suggested à propos the example above, where filaments reach out to arguments in other of his texts; a connection with another text may derive from a dense patch of difficulty; or again they can, within their own surface, put out fragments of meta-language, as we shall see, which do reflect on and thus consolidate them, but do so only partially and momentarily. So there is a modular construction by circuits of argument, lexemes, and larger-scale patterns, which enable different types of connection through language to lock into each other, as it were. And with these connections, there come also different types of discontinuities: apparent counter-movements of meaning, parody and what I shall argue later in the chapter is a form of irony, prevent meaning being entirely at one with the words on the page.

At one point where Derrida speaks of such connection, he shows that it works not with continuity, but with construction between discontinuities. Derrida's second article on Levinas develops round a certain type of such construction, and in its investigation of connection, might be thought to develop certain problems of the first article on Levinas, round the question of coherence and rationality (ED, 224; *WD*, 151). For language cuts loose what is said, it departicularizes, it separates from origin, from speaker – it can never be purely anchored in the deictic centre of origin, it is shared with others. Yet, surely, it *is* also located, it has deictic connection – somebody said it, some-where, once, from the centre of where things looked like that. This difficulty forms the basis of the second article, in which in a punning complex way, an account is offered to Levinas of his work which can in fact be applied to Derrida's own, and to his own vocabulary (Psy, 165; 'At this very moment',

16). The argument proceeds via the question of the difference between different repetitions of the same 'micrology', the question raised at the beginning of this chapter. 'En ce moment même' (in this very moment) a phrase repeated several times in Levinas' *Differently From Being or Beyond Essence* (*Autrement qu'être ou au-delà de l'essence*) is *not* quotation, says Derrida; its instances may be the same phrase, in different contexts, and thus departicularized, but they are also singular. For the first use of the phrase in Levinas points to an act by which language, even in indicating singularity, unique location, undoes the singularity and the uniqueness by reappropriating words and placing them within different webs of meaning; the second use points to an interruption in the circulation of meaning, constituted by the pull of the interlocutor, an interruption without which meaning is not possible. Between these two, we have seen, there is a negotiation, which once more takes the form of the dissymmetric embedding picked out in the present book so often: 'une nécessité: celle qui, pour n'être pas formalisable, reproduit régulièrement la relation du formalisable au non-formalisable' (Psy, 178) ('a necessity: one which, although unformalizable, regularly reproduces the relation of the formalizable to the nonformalizable') ('At this very moment', 26). The 'en ce moment même', then, both interrupts ineffably and garrulously interweaves.

The pattern of negotiation discerned by Derrida is given greater range when it is related to Levinas' title, *Autrement qu'être ou au-delà de l'essence*, whose 'beyond essence' points to the Platonic *epekeina tes ousias*, the dwelling of the good, which the first article on Levinas, 'Violence and metaphysics', had related to the actual (positive) infinite. So that the negotiation in the second article on Levinas by Derrida may take on the value of relation, not just between interruption of relation and relation, but between the Positive Infinite, that which infinitely transcends, and the Negative Infinite, that which itself negotiates, which is an infinite travail/travel of interminable approximation. The Derridean article can be read, then, with these two infinites at work in this strange dissymmetric embedding structure, a structure which seems to undercut both the empiricism which gives up attempts at transcendental rigour of language in the face of the unattainability of such an Absolute (ED, 224; *WD*, 151) and those formalisms which efface difference and rely on the general. Empirical and transcendental determinations would, then, be neither contradictory nor complementary (see Chapter 1, for a broader-scale arguing of this point).

Here a preliminary conclusion can be made. In the 'syntax' suggested in Chapter 1, it is the complexity and strength of the relations being cast between the empirical and the transcendental which formed a kind of undercurrent to Derrida's relation to philosophy. But shadowed by the relation between the positive and negative infinites, the syntax enables Derrida's own writing to wander without being 'empirical' in his sense; like a palaeontologist clearing some fossil from the stratum in which it is embedded, he disengages the outlines of the tensions and cross-cutting of the empirical and the transcendental, the genealogical and the structural in the writers he writes on, in Husserl, Foucault, Lévi-Strauss, Levinas. The structure of what I have called 'strange attractors', in particular the urging of microstructures and micrologies in others' work into this particular embedded dissymmetry, enables Derrida to relate others' work to his own concerns without simplified general repetition of a general form.

But there is more. In Derrida's article on Levinas, this 'relation without relation' is given consistency via, so to speak, the Levinas text (and thus respects and repeats the tensions in it). The latter had linked together thematizing, and coherence:[5] the holding up of an idea as object-theme, its 'objectivation', makes possible consistency and system but does violence to the absolute and to otherness (to the absolute of the context, then). And yet the reference to the other inherent in all discourse tears apart this web of linguistic coherence. Such discourse is compared by Levinas to a 'fil renoué' ('fil' = reknotted thread, but also a near-homophone of 'fils' = 'son') and is thematized as a trace which itself records interruption, like a knot. But one knot (homophone of 'not' in French as in English: 'il faut des noeuds pour faire un pas' ['you need knots to make a step', as Derrida has punned on the negative 'ne . . . pas']) does not suffice to withstand reappropriation. It is, says Derrida, a series which structures through gaps:

> J'ai choisi pour nommer cette structure le mot de *série* pour y nouer à mon tour *series* (file, suite rangée conséquente, enchaînement ordonné d'une multiplicité regulière, entrelacement, lignée, descendance) et *seira* (corde, chaîne, lasso, lacet etc). On acceptera la chance de trouver dans le filet de la même lignée l'un au moins des quatres sens du *sero* latin (entrelacer, tresser, enchaîner, rattacher) et l'*eiro* grec qui dit (ou nomme) l'entrelacement du lacet et du dire, la symploké du discours et du lien. . . . Le risque est . . . inscrit dans la *nécessité* . . . de la stricture.
>
> (Psy, 180)

> I have chosen to name this structure by the word *series* so as to tie together, in my turn, *series* (file sequence, range, consequence, ordered enchainment of a regular multiplicity, interlacing, line descendance) and *seira* (cord, chain, lasso, lace, etc.). We will accept the chance of finding in the net of the same lineage at least one of four Latin *seros* (to interlace, plait, enchain, reattach) and the Greek *eiro* which says (or ties) together the interlacing of lace and saying, the *symploké* of discourse and binding. . . . And the risk is . . . inscribed in the *necessity* . . . of stricture.
>
> ('At this very moment', 28)

These series of terms reach out to other Derridean texts, especially to *Glas* (*Glas*, 272a, 244a) and to its list of links, to *desmos*, *stricture*, to the necessity of the double bind explored in that text. In doing so, the series confirms, but also collects, the filaments which had started elsewhere. The *series* is then both the collection and the element; the series of a series (though one should beware of the word series, which implies a law regulating the relation between the items in the series).[6]

But this series, says Derrida, is multiple in its complication: the knots which are retied and reknotted insert interruptions and prevent even continuity in the interruption. And Derrida continues his sentences in this work on Levinas in a style which brings together contradictories, but which makes their discontinuity unabsolute.[7] He may use a flowing rhythm, a syntax which sweeps subordinating phrases into coordination, thus giving a sense of addition; the near-contradiction emphasized by repetition, where each time the phrase with a 'but' seems to move aside to avoid in the nick of time the contradiction; with the puns ('ab-solu', 'noeud', 'sans fil', 'wireless', the old name for radio, but which could also be heard as its opposite, 's'enfilent', 'thread on after'), all these suggest both the interweaving and the interruption, the very process by adjunction of near negatives which is being described. The minimal coherence which 'series' was allowed to describe is one of patterns of interruption, for which language has to turn to geographical reference:

Les noeuds de la série contaminent [une fatalité qu'il faut assumer] sans contact, comme si, à distance, les deux bords rétablissent la continuité par le simple vis-à-vis de leurs lignes. Encore ne s'agit-il plus de bords, puis qu'il n'y a plus de ligne, seulement des pointes effilées, absolument disjointes d'une rive à l'autre de l'interruption.

(Psy, 182)

The knots in the series contaminate without contact, as if the two edges established continuity at a distance by the simple vis-à-vis of their lines. Still, it is no longer a matter of edges since there is no longer any line, only filed points absolutely disjoint from one shore to the other of the interruption.

('At this very moment', 30)[8]

Derrida is bringing together the ideas of linking and of interruption into a paradoxical relation, but takes this relation further: the account of intellectual relation by what is a kind of geometrical/geographical description (line, river-bank) is a taking seriously of the instability of any unit. It suggests a construction out of intersected spaces (as a material object, seen close enough up, is an agglomeration of atoms in large spaces) and a kind of intellectual force field into which shifting gaps inject structures.[9] There is connection across spaces as it were – connection as contamination through alignment. (As we have seen, some of his own texts – *The Post Card*, 'Parergon' – use blanks on the page as grouping devices.)

Derrida's writing in this article reflects on what is being drawn out of Levinas, drawing it in to a different movement. His article, like his first article 'Violence and metaphysics', does seem to construct a possible support for discourse which goes beyond thematizing or logical speech, but also turns beyond the Levinasian reference to the interlocutor which had made possible a speech which might be more than 'discourse'. Levinas puts in question 'relation' as a narration of discourse which homogenizes the singular and speaks the ineffable; he presents relation as an act of mastery through language, which imposes coherence and unity. But this Levinasian questioning, for indeed what is suggested is beyond language, is pulled round by Derrida, so that the nature of that coherence can be worked on, can actually be salvaged so to speak. Normative constraints in language are presented as tending to wipe away any givenness to the other in speaking; Levinas' phrase (the title of Derrida's article) on the contrary forces language to contract with or negotiate with that which is not discursive, is not the 'dit', the 'said'. For in the phrase, Levinas comments on what he is actually doing, as he does it. But Derrida, by picking up the repetition, makes the appeal to his reader given by Levinas one that does not represent the appeal of the speaker, but a composition with the interruption of the discourse that is the appeal. Indeed, it makes possible the saying of what is not discursive, not 'said' in language, but which is neither reduced to silence. There can then be saying which is not thematic. Moreover, construction can occur out of interruption, it is suggested. It is related almost immediately to other concerns connected with 'tying', 're-ligio' and 'obligation', in a complex suggestion of new forms of subjectivity and responsibility (the addition [Psy, 173], points to this: 'Ecoute, c'est encore l'âme, ou *psyché*' – 'Listen, it is once again the soul or the psyche' – since it is added to the book version, enacting precisely the kind of linking which is the object of the present discussion).

Levinas' phrase, 'en ce moment même' appears to be distributed between what he himself calls 'dit', that is, the 'said' temporally located, homologized, coherent language, and the same phrase as 'discourse', that is, the pull of the interlocutor whereby what is coherent is complete in that it is seen as totalized (Levinas says 'en totalisant l'Etre', Psy, 172 – 'In totalizing being', 'At this very moment', 22). The latter 'discourse' is made possible by something beyond, 'by the excessive relation', to which phrase Derrida adds in his book 'of the psyche' (Psy, 174), as if excessive relation which totalized (cf. Chapter 1) were the counterpart of absolute interruption. And yet the Levinasian phrases are the same, and the effect of the text, says Derrida, comes about from their being in a series. There has to be a relation between them, 'une sorte de contamination analogique entre les deux' (Psy, 177) ('a sort of analogical contamination between the two') ('At this very moment', 26); (they are after all literally the same phrase) which is not folded back immediately into the domain of the 'said', that is, relation cast as thematization and narrated. Analogy which is contamination, like the contamination of the odd grouping of 'pointes effilées absolument disjointes' (Psy, 182) ('filed points absolutely disjoint') ('At this very moment', 30) (where the *pointe* gives a geographical, fractalic, shape to what might have been a notional point) brings together what is one more suggestion about the nature of relation.

Here, a connection is made between assembling and resembling. Levinas' writing, in its knotty discontinuity, resembles the discontinuities of official discourse, 'the logical discourse of the state, of philosophy, of medicine'. For example, after a long quotation from Levinas, we pass to Levinas' writing:

> L'interruption laisse ses marques, mais autrement. Des noeuds s'y forment, rattrapant les déchirures, mais autrement. Ils laissent apparaître le discontinu dans sa trace, mais comme la trace ne doit pas se *rassembler* dans son paraître, elle peut toujours *ressembler* [my italics] à la trace que le discontinu laisse dans le discours logique. . . . La trace doit donc s'y 'présenter', sans se présenter, *autrement.*
>
> (Psy, 179)

> The interruption leaves its marks, but otherwise. Knotted threads are formed in it, recapturing the tears, but otherwise. They allow the discontinuous to appear in its trace, but since the trace is not to be reassembled into its appearance, it can always resemble the trace which discontinuity leaves within the logical discourse. . . . The trace should therefore 'present' itself there . . . otherwise.
>
> ('At this very moment', 27–8)

The process brings about what seems to be a presentation without presentation. In the passage between the repeating of 'moment', argues Derrida, another connection forms, which knots together not continuous threads, but interrupted ones, and like the ply in any thread, internal to the interrupted threads are further interruptions. The Levinas 'knots', in the long quotation from his text *Autrement . . .*, are urged towards a process where the trace cannot be turned into a phenomenon, that is, into that which can appear.

By the play on *ressembler* and *rassembler* (resemble and assemble, words which are cognate) a type of connection is suggested which tacitly refers to, but also undoes, an important Heideggerian theme about relation as assembling or gathering. In Heidegger's analysis/history in *Introduction to Metaphysics*, appearing was first a 'bringing itself to stand in togetherness', creating space for itself; and logos was 'decision concerning the truth', where utterance (logos) was gathering, assembling and unconcealment. In a series of 'departures', 'fallings off', the standing became (mere) appearance and the logos became a statement which is correct or incorrect (IM, 180–6). The 'standing in togetherness', the consistency, is developed in, for instance, Heidegger's 'The age of the world picture', into a 'sending' of being. And in 'Envoi', published in *Psyché*, Derrida shows that sending relies on an assembling, or using a term which also occurs à propos Freud's grandson Ernst, in 'To speculate – on "Freud"', on a 'being together' which though it does not have the unity of a totality or a system, is still part of the same sending, and can thus be spoken of. 'C'est en faisant fonds sur cette indivisibilité rassemblée de l'envoi que la lecture heideggerienne peut détacher des époques' (Psy, 135) ('It is basing itself on this grouped indivisibility of the *envoi* that Heidegger's reading can single out epochs') ('Sending', 322).

Though the reference to Heideggerian sending is only through the word 'rassembler', it is as if Derrida is suggesting ways in which the Levinasian text can connect, without effacing gaps and imposing the discursive unity that Levinas himself rejects (what he called the 'discours de l'Etat'). The 'knots' of the Levinas article reveal the discontinuous trace which cannot appear, for it cannot gather itself to appear; nevertheless, as we have seen, it can always resemble the other discontinuity (Psy, 179; 'At this very moment', 28), found in a different sort of discourse (the 'discours de l'Etat'), which is made of the knotting of continuous threads. Instead, the discontinuous trace knots together interrupted threads, which themselves are made of knots. There is, we have seen, presentation without presentation, 'autrement' in a reference to Levinas' title. The structure of the 'knot' in Levinas, the difference, we are led to expect, between the two instances of the same phrase, enable us to read the trace as trace of something not appearing as a phenomenon. In Derrida's discussion, the Levinasian text is respected; but it is also urged towards a supplementary process, towards one where interruption becomes interruptions. They are absolute but plural and not thus stable units, but refer out to other knots, other interruptions. The coming-to-presentation is without being-over-against (object) and without assembling. The consequence is that the interruption is non-phenomenalized, is gone beyond by a repetition between the 'moments' (of the repeated phrase), by a resemblance. Resemblance, and, it may be added, replication, which ensures 'non-present remainder' (Psy, 180) (the term 'restance' from *Limited Inc.* is used). There is thus connection where there are no clearly limited units, only infinitely dissolvable traces; such a connection from disconnection is fragile, at best analogical.[10] With the resembling knots in Levinas' work, Derrida suggests then a relation of negotiation with rupture, where the tacking steps of the negative infinite cross-cut the positive infinite.

Elsewhere, resembling and reassembling are connected by Derrida. In the previously quoted article 'Envoi' ('Sending: on representation'), the unity from gathering – the 'logos' according to Heidegger – is further queried and linked to representation. Here we come up against the very nature of connection. The history of being has less than the unity of a centred system, but it still has a sort of postal unity of 'envoi' ('sending'), 'une sorte d'indivisibilité du destinal' (Psy, 135) ('a sort of indivisibility of what is destined') ('Sending', 322), which makes up the unity of the eras in the Heideggerian history of being. For the earliest Greeks, according to Heidegger, phenomena appeared not as appearance of something, but as a conquering of space against which the appearing detached itself (IM, 183) and as a result the appearance was not copied but produced space. Yet almost inevitably, the appearance was gradually seen in a kind of frame. Vision and the inherent 'opposite' of the visual field made of that appearing an 'already furnished visual space' and thus an appearance, and a virtual copy. In Heidegger's history, then, what was not a copy becomes one. Such a history as 'falling-off' is challenged by Derrida. There has, however tenuously, to be something that falls off, something that continues throughout time, and is in the process of degrading. But in Heidegger's history, says Derrida, this process of falling-off, and the Heideggerian work of separating out the process of suspensive eras in which it occurs, are the same: the very *rassemblement* which is the being together of presentation is also the *rassemblement* which causes the eras to gather themselves and to appear as distinct. As Derrida expounds Heidegger, the era of representation detaches itself from that of presence (*Anwesenheit*) but it thus represents *Anwesenheit*, it stands in, substitutes, for it; and thus, paradoxically, continues it. Against this Derrida places a difficult conception: because representation is primary, and being is always plural, there is not one main river of being from which tributaries flow, not one core element which is carried forward through a history. There is only process: a process of substitution and dissemination.

The problem of connection is, then, acute: connection can be neither archaeological nor teleological, controlled neither by beginning nor end. Further, the connecting 'renvois', we are told, have a structure which is not that of representation, nor is it symbolic nor metaphoric (Psy, 142). They are an urging to 'penser tout autrement' (Psy, 143), 'to think quite differently'; and this involves thinking how references may function without representation.

It might seem that, as already suggested, the connection in such 'renvois' can only be retrospective and performed linguistically; that when Derrida said famously 'there is nothing outside the text' (strictly, 'there is no outside-text'), even if 'text' is interpreted widely, to include or even to privilege non-linguistic traces, there nevertheless has to be a looping back into language from the not-quite or already-not-linguistic. Though that utterance was revised in the second publication of *Limited Inc.* to imply 'there is nothing outside the context', we are still within the linguistic web. This account I believe to be broadly accurate,[11] but it fails to take account of at least three essential qualifications to that picture. First, the mediated nature of that web's relation to the non-linguistic (for 'traces' are not necessarily or even primarily linguistic). Second, the role of what I have called the 'strange attractors' in Derrida's writing. This allows for entities which are out of the web of traces, which are unintuitable and unpresentable, but to which we can have some sort of access, paradoxically and imperfectly, by a process of negotiation and contamination. But there is a further point. Such an account also fails to account for the 'dissociation of thought and language' which Derrida mentions at various points. Before turning to this, however, the 'assembling' which language provided must be further examined.

'Assembling' in language or in a particular language

If language is held to 'group' or assemble, we have then to consider whether what is meant is language in general, or whether the particular language is considered. Now, for Levinas silence protects the other from the violence of language; such a view, Derrida has already pointed out, makes of violence 'L'origine du sens et du discours dans le règne de la finitude' (ED, 189) ('The origin of meaning and of discourse in the reign of finitude') (*WD*, 129), as we have seen. Assembling and classification are inherent in language, and are a restriction in that they assign connection (without that restriction, thinking and logic are not possible at all – see Chapter 1). Classifying traditionally operates with a tree-like hierarchical form, and at least since the *Logic* of Port-Royal, the particular thing is arrayed under the term which applies to it (extension); or attributes are associated by definition with an idea (comprehension or intension) and thought of as contained in it. These orderings can be generalized as forms of the relation of containing.

Now Derrida speaks in many different contexts of this relation, but often suggests that it cannot perform for our thought in the way it is meant to. What is part and contained turns out to be as great or greater than the whole and thus containing; the separation between member of the set and set itself, token and type, particular and general, singular and universal, turns out, he argues, not to be reliably stable. For language has generalizing force: words tend to turn what is one-off, 'descriptive intuition' or description of a piece of empirical data, into something which, because it is both particular and general, is capable of bringing with it both the intended and also unwanted senses.[12] *Glas*, we have seen, undercuts Fonagy's notion that, at the phonological level, sounds uttered are specified by drives, and are thus determined in their material form by extra-linguistic referents. But this undercutting points to the way the grouping at work in language is uncontrollable: the co-functioning of generalization and classification is not foreseeable. Derrida plays with the phoneme *gl*: *glas* is contaminated to *cl* by its derivation from *classus* and thus pulled towards the sense of class; the name, which seems to individualize, may rather activate a dilution of particularization.

Nor can the sound itself be specified by the name: onomatopoeic words can often be shown to have developed towards effects of mimicry or more generally onomatopoeia, but may not have started that way; or they may start that way, and lose the relation with sound (as the derivation of 'pigeon' from 'pipio' has done in French). 'Pas d'idiome absolu': no proper name is entirely proper, conversely the general example may turn out to be oddly personal:

> Par exemple, (l'unicité de l'exemple se détruit d'elle-même, élabore aussi la puissance d'un organe généralisateur) au moment même où nous prétendrions y ressaisir, dans un texte déterminé, le travail d'un idiome, relié à une chaîne de noms propres et de configurations empirico-signifiantes et singulières, *glas* nomme aussi la *classification*, c'est-à-dire l'inscription dans des réseaux de généralités entrelacées à l'infini, dans des généalogies d'une stricture telle que les croisements, les accouplements, les aiguillages, les détours, les embranchements ne relèvent jamais simplement d'une loi sémantique ou d'une loi formelle. Pas d'idiome absolu, pas de signature.
>
> (*Glas*, 169b)

> For example (the uniqueness of the example is destroyed by itself, immediately elaborates the power of a generalizing organ), the very moment we would claim to recapture there, in a determined text, the work of an idiom,

bound to a chain of proper names and singular empirico-signifying configurations, *glas* also names *classification*, that is, inscription in networks of
generalities interlaced to infinity, in genealogies of a structure such that the
crossings, couplings, switchings, detours, and branchings never simply
come under a semantic or formal law. No absolute idiom, no signature.

(Glas, 149b)

Language interchanges general and particular, it assembles and disassembles.
And likewise, in these few lines, there is a double-decker effect, where *glas* refers
both to the word and to the book we are reading, and thus points to a particular
effect in Derrida's writing: the use of a lexeme, a strange word, particular in both
senses of that term, in a general way, but a use which by a kind of performative
baptism ('nomme') marks the passage. There is also the effect of accumulated
plurals of semantically related though distinct words ('croisements' (crossings),
'aiguillages' (switchings), etc.), all suggesting that words are the crossroads of
constantly latticing senses. Language is not to be divided into on the one hand
the arbitrary and on the other the motivated; classification is concomitant with
language and is always ineffective, yet the conceptualization inherent in language
cannot be done without, and concepts enable connection, what Derrida calls
'sewing'; they are what makes ideas linkable (VEP, 107; *Truth*, 94).[13]

But here we touch on a problem that will be returned to. The language is
always in effect – in its examples, for instance – a particular language and is
always operating in a historically bound way. Concepts are developed in particular words or phrases in a particular language and at a particular moment.
Understood in this light, philology becomes then a philosophical tool and
cross-linguistic comparison enables one to get a purchase on change.[14] But the
difficulty of such comparison, in particular the problem of where to stand,
linguistically so to speak (the linguistic version of the historical problem
encountered in Chapter 1), is intricately revealed by Derrida's example of
Heidegger's example in the *The Origin of the Work of Art*. De-sedimenting
accretions and channellings of sense round 'subject' and 'substance' in the
history of philosophy, Heidegger does not notice that he has transferred the
very 'discours d'attribution . . . déclarations de propriété' (VEP, 331)
('discourses of attribution, declarations of property') (*Truth*, 288) which he
declares typical of the discourse on the subject in 'western thought' to the shoes
painted by Van Gogh he is discussing. Heidegger fetishizes the shoes, accretes
round the representation of everyday material objects the very kind of mass he
is trying to liquefy, and in particular passes from a showing up of the conceptualization of a thing, of the determinations of it as a substance, a support, as
under, to a valuation of what is under, or supposed to be under, the peasant's
shoes. Ground, rootedness, strength – and all that such values entail in the
Germany of the 1930s (VEP, 331; *Truth*, 290) is shown negatively by
Heidegger to be lacking or to have been lost in 'western thought' and its
'groundlessness'. But further, in this metaphor of ground bringing up the
undisclosed link in Heidegger's treatment of the word 'substance' and the

fetishizing of the things, the shoes, lies a more general problem, which goes beyond questions of particular language: how does one speak of ground without standing somewhere – whether the 'groundlessness' of 'fallen' western thought may not be the 'groundlessness' of thought *tout court* (VEP, 332; *Truth*, 291), that within history, which is the only place we can stand, there is simply no place from which there can be a stable distinction between metaphor and ground: the ground is another metaphor.

The question of metaphor is then not the ultimate question that can be asked. In a sense, admitted in the passage quoted above at note 14, some of what Derrida does is most readily understood as a history of ideas. To say such a thing appears surprising, since, as we see, he questions the principle of assembly for such a history. Take for instance the principle of assembly of a 'tendency to act in a specific way':

> When we say as part of our evidence for someone holding the seventeenth-century conception of 'idea' that they believe that words and thoughts can be separated, we ought to understand this as analogous to the claim that it is evidence for someone having the concept 'brown' that they systematically pick out brown things. It is a belief then, not in the sense of a mental state, but as a propensity to organize discourse in a certain way.
>
> (M. Rosen 1982)

Derrida's own work has often shown up such an organization in others; or, in a negative mode, how a particular organization or concept may be avoided by a philosopher (Heidegger and *Geist* for instance). But the Rylean 'propensity' in the quotation locates a statistical pattern firmly inside a personal disposition 'to organize'. Derrida's sense of intellectual system is quite different. Such a propensity, a regularity in pieces of behaviour, is not tracked further. The statistical model, and its implications, are allowed their head, so to speak, but from them are explored and set out tentative configurations of words, patterns of ideas and links which can be active in a tradition; they are not brought back to the habitual doings of an individual, his or her 'propensities'. Moreover, though such patternings and connections work through language, and through tradition in language, they are inflected by the particularities of the particular language, as Derrida, via quotations and brackets, reminds us.

So that metaphor is not merely a question of style. It is never merely expressive, and never avoidable. It limits as it locates. Now Derrida, in his work on Husserl, on Levinas, on Foucault, discussed in the first chapter, has – in each case respecting the context – worked on language and the limits of language. But the implications of Derrida's work seem to fold together two opposite views of language: on the one hand, 'language' as some kind of more-than-linguistic set of conditions for all languages and, on the other hand, the implication that different languages, like different jargons or different terms within the same language, induce different ways of grasping things. We speak and write in specific languages, and then in subsets of a specific language, subsets constructed by processes of imitation or borrowing, through admirative choice or unaware contamination. There is no other way. (This is true of formalizations too, even if to a lesser degree – a mathematician has to learn to read eighteenth-century formulae.) Our particular language is both our horizon within which we focus as if it were not there, in ways that neglect it, and a labyrinth in which we try to move around. Derrida, by paying attention to this, is examining tradition rather than history, the tradition at work in the choice of example, of reference and of language. In tradition, there is neither a disjoint set of epistemes – disjoint epistemological phases – 'une coupure sous chaque pas' (VEP), as Derrida comments satirically, with a side glance at Foucault; yet neither is there linguistic and cultural continuum, but points of accumulation, jumps, scatterings of density apparent according to the point from which the tradition is approached. Nor are there ideas to be studied like individual atoms, incorruptible, interacting without changing; for indeed constellations of other words may suggest notions where earlier one word did the work; or, conversely, the same word may take on subtly or radically different significations even within similar contexts. To this is added something further. Any discussion of ideas alters those ideas *in situ* – Heidegger's discussion of Aristotle's ideas is in a sense programmed by Aristotle, but changes them for others who read Aristotle ('Ousia and grammé', in *Margins*). As we have seen, a model for such connection over distance, with possible interference in the line, is the telephone or telegraph.

There are no 'perennial problems' handed down the ages intact and unsited in a tradition. But what then are the constraints within which we may consider tradition? The historian of ideas Quentin Skinner (1988) has argued powerfully that elucidation must move out of the 'texts themselves' (Skinner 1988: 52) by looking at possible writing strategies of the time. Writing is investigated as deliberate intervention in a debate, and he takes as the constraining values for this view of understanding those expressed by the adverbial phrases 'voluntarily', or 'with conscious intention'. Skinner has shown that the 'texts themselves' school he is attacking has usually equated text and subject in an unsustainable way. If, however, an exclusion zone is not thrown around texts by treating them as individual objects, individual projects of one mind, but if in addition they are allowed to be part of a larger circulation of meaning (if, in other words, language's disseminating power is accepted), then the view Skinner is attacking does crumble, but the values of 'conscious' or 'deliberate', which are there, we are told, to guarantee minimal scholarly standards, are not left unscathed either. This does not mean that any interpretation is relevant, all connections equally valid. But it would mean that the connections the critic establishes would be borne by language and textual conventions; they would be philological and linguistic. Skinner accepts that introspection is an unreliable and frequently impossible guide to intention, but still insists that an author's intentions must be established, though by reference to other texts, which form a context. Yet in writing, as in any kind of action, a 'plea for excuses' must be made. A text can go somewhere not explicitly intended in the complex way we accept in agreements of custom; and intentions, relevant intentions, may be more complex than conscious ones.

Against this, Skinner refines the conception of intention: 'The relevant logical consideration is that no agent can eventually be said to have meant or done something which he could never be brought to accept as a correct description of what he had meant or done' (Skinner 1988: 48). This does not exclude the possibility of a fuller account being given than might have been available to the agent, but it does exclude

> the possibility that an acceptable account of an agent's behaviour could even survive the demonstration that it was itself dependent on the use of criteria not available to the agent himself. For if a given statement or other action has been performed by an agent at will, and has a meaning for him, it follows that any plausible account of what the agent meant must necessarily fall under and make use of the range of descriptions which the agent himself could at least in principle have applied to describe and clarify what he was doing.
>
> (Skinner 1988: 48)

Now the problem pointed to is in fact the problem of interpretation in the strict sense, the one speakers of several languages deal with when moving between them. For the 'range of descriptions' will be in the language of the agent; or will be connectable to that language by the commentary and interpretation used in difficult questions of translation.

Skinner (1988: 66) takes slavery as his example, and sharply demonstrates that Plato cannot be dragooned into discussing participation in democracy in a context that would be a useful model to moderns, for slaves are excluded. But such an argument will apply equally on a micrological scale to the description of intention we might try to supply for him. Any linguistic expansion of meaning, as required by Skinner in the quotation above, will certainly involve relating it to another epoch's conceptions, and indeed, more important, to other languages and their concepts. This necessity will certainly leave a 'non-present residue': meaning that cannot be mapped, cannot be accounted for, might not even be seen, though it might be designated at a different time and in a different language. (This is itself one of the reasons, in the narrow terms of the present discussion, why it is possible to make progress in the comprehension of intentions at all.) The alienness Skinner accepts in past configurations of meaning is internal to language; the respect for the historical other that he recommends has also to be extended to the languages worked in. While the respect for the context, and for the other's understanding of that context built in to the Skinnerian position are indispensable, the limit of conscious intention, or intention which can with explication be made conscious, may not be absolute. Nor plausible: as individuals, we do mean things we do not consciously intend; and our language, especially when used by masters, may be freighted with its own future development which their very selecting and filtering activity will end by bringing about. The process Skinner imagines, 'the bringing to accept', for the agent is after all often dead, is in fact a careful accommodation and extension through glosses and explanations of past linguistic configuration to our point in time and in the shared tradition. Of course, the process is one the past also persuades us to accept about its ideas and culture; but such an accommodation, in either direction, is not straightforward, not without what Derrida has called violence.

Take, for instance, the work of Vernant and Vidal-Nacquet on Greek tragedy. It has involved comparing classifications of concepts of willing for Greeks and showing their great difference with those of the twentieth century. It is not certain that Aeschylus would have found the work relevant or acceptable – nor whether to say that even makes sense; for insofar as Vernant and Vidal-Nacquet work on the horizons of Greek tragic vision, it might well be that they point to what could not have been focused on at the time without fundamental shifts in conception and perception of the world, shifts which, though adumbrated in that perception, would have already destroyed it had they occurred. Modality, of will or of knowing, is complex in language, in all languages, and the very patterns of modality differ between languages, substantially for instance between Greek and English. It is as if the problems of language and meaning have as a major component problems of translation, translation momentarily into a version of our native tongue from which we are already travelling away into some kind of awareness of its particularity.

Before turning to this problem, and to whether the problem of language being addressed here can be subsumed under the question of translation, the question of the nature of linguistic classification must be reverted to.

Nominalization and metaphor

Though words with the same reference may assemble senses differently in different languages,[15] or indeed in the same one, all languages seem to share the word as their unit. Now Derrida has often expressed suspicion of the word as unit, both as part of the opposition word/grammar and as the linguistic version of the individual, whole and self-standing without need of relation ('The double session'; 'Ja, ou le faux-bond'): 'On ne peut nominaliser que ce qui prétend – ou qui dès lors prétend – à une signification complète et indépendante, ce qui est intelligible par soi-même, hors de toute relation syntaxique' (M, 278) ('Only that which claims – or henceforth claims-to have a complete and independent signification, that which is intelligible by itself, outside any syntactic relation, can be nominalized') (M, 233). (The question of the unit will be further developed in the next section.) Derrida shows, in his article entitled 'White mythology' (1971) how closely connected in the history of rhetoric have been the notion of noun and the notion of metaphor as transfer of signification from one noun to another (M, 279; M, 234), a notion neglecting the function of syncategoremes in language. Nouns are categoremes, units, and may be treated as intelligible outside any syntactical relation (the subversive point of the

Derridean puns *entre/antre*, *pas/pas* is once again apparent, where a syncate-goreme is placed in punning relation with a categoreme). But, Derrida suggests, the word itself may not be unifiable, it may have no 'supporting sense' guiding usage as a stake guides a plant. A propos of 'don' and 'donner' (gift), Derrida argues that there is no semantic focus which might unify all contexts in which the word or expressions containing it appear. One might as a result only consider actual instances of usage in context: 'les usages, les jeux, les fonction-nements contextuels des idiomes, si même on pouvait encore parler d'idiomes en ce sens' (DT, 68) ('usage, play, and the contextual functionings of idioms, if indeed it were still possible to speak of idioms in this sense') (*GT*, 48). Dictionaries might eschew definitions, and give only lists of occurrences. There is however a twist to this argument: it is mounted not generally, but in regard to 'don', and it is suggested that for the notion of the 'core sense' of gift might be substituted the notion of 'dissemination'. But if dissemination is allowed for, as against core or underlying invariant meaning, then that is sufficiently like the 'gift' whose dissemination is being discussed (the potlatch of Native Americans) for the separation of example and argument, or word and meanings, to become insecure. It is as if the sense of 'gift' is being allowed to be reflected in a language about the gift (the gift of the gift, perhaps) so that it in strange fashion both unmakes and remakes some kind of unity. Meta-language and language are distinguished and yet are as if overprinted on each other in this example.

I have just connected 'gift' and 'dissemination' in Derrida's text by the phrase 'sufficiently like'. It would be possible to excavate from his writing what would amount to a critique of analogy. At the same time, at other points, analogy is turned to (cf. D, 248; *D*, 219). That it does in some instances induce extensions in argument, in particular allowing for the bridging of opposites, Derrida shows by Freud's account of the categorical imperative (and, in a text I have not discussed, by Condillac's negotiation of the relation between 'germ' and 'development' – in itself not unlike the opposition between structure and genesis of Chapter 1, see especially *Glas*, 242a, 216a; but also AF, 26). Can it be that it is resemblance which allows (momentarily, it is true) reassembly, that it is the comparable proportion which is analogy, which can allow extension of argument and connection between micrologies?

The basis of metaphor is traditionally held to be the comparison in point of resemblance between signifier and signified, but even more, between signs, one designating the other, leading to transport of sense (M, 255–7; *M*, 215–17). Metaphor in the history of rhetoric (and the history of rhetoric has to be under-stood as a continuous transformation as well as epistemic rupture) allows a transference which is controllable, Derrida argues, because the transference takes place between units. It has a direct relation to what can be nominalized (M, 278; *M*, 233). The result is that, traditionally, connections are made by metaphors between units, but not syntactically (Derrida shows how Bachelard, for instance, interprets what is syntactic coordination as thematic or semantic bundles). They are made on the basis of similarity, which ultimately is directed by a teleology of writing (*rassemblement*) of future sense.[16] Philosophy, Derrida argues, has always held metaphor to be provisional loss of sense, a loss to be made good by the resemblance in the metaphor, which brings us back to proper meaning, and hence to the death of metaphor. But there is a deconstructionist double of that argument which makes metaphor die, not by return to proper meaning, but by proliferation – metaphor is irreducibly plural, it thus must be at work syntactically and not just semantically, for it takes any text beyond its sense and its thesis; and this very possibility means that it can only 'construct its own destruction'.

If metaphor is everywhere, then there is no clear demarcation of metaphorical language; if the whole opposition between metaphorical and proper use is thus undermined, if there is no centralizing force which holds metaphor and proper apart gravitationally, if the opposition between semantics and syntax is set in doubt (words as bearers of certain sorts of meaning/reference, and syntax as rules governing their combination into well formed sentences), what connections in thought *are* valid? If not guided by the resemblance which brings metaphor back to base, relations will be nothing but a relation, one that is *post hoc*, visible from after, based on the word seen as a bearer of historical sediment, which is not to be neglected, yet which does not gravitate in any continuation of thought, but on the contrary which engages at different historical points in work within quite different systems.[17] Though we try to tie it as figure to a proper sense, to nomination, metaphor seems, then, to be a disseminative entropy and a continuing generation of sense, constantly moving on.

But in the later 'The *retrait* of metaphor' ('Le retrait de la métaphore') (1978, republished in *Psyché*) this is pushed further in a way already indicated by the title. For it has opposing directions, both 'retreat' and 'redrawing', that is, retracing. This two-way movement is continued by such phrases as 'plus de métalangage, plus de métalinguistique, donc plus de méta-rhétorique, plus de métaphysique. Toujours une métaphore de plus au moment où la métaphore se retire en évasant ses limites' (Psy, 85) ('[no] more meta-language, [no] more meta-linguistics, so [no] more meta-rhetoric, [no] more metaphysics. Always one more metaphor at the moment when the metaphor retires in widening itself at its limits') (my translation) where the 'plus de' can mean 'more' or 'none', as is spelled out in the English version quoted. The negative meaning runs under the positive one. Such a sentence then becomes an exploration of what it means to efface the distinction between the figurative and the proper, on which rhetorics have based the use of metaphor, since we are simultaneously to have more metaphor and no metaphor. For Heidegger, we have seen, metaphors run throughout 'western' intellectual history because 'a suspensive drawing back of being' creates a unit of historical time, within which metaphors supplement for the withdrawal of being, but where the determinations of being for which metaphors are made (modes, etc.) are themselves metaphors. The uniting thus revealed by assembly or resemblance just is the language of metaphysics, part of which is metaphor. But in turn Being has retreated and can only be named quasi-metaphorically; there is no literal sense available. Metaphysics is a retreat of Being and cannot be departed from except by retreating from that concept, that is, by retreating from metaphor (itself given room by the suspensive retreat of being) that is by retreating from the retreat of Being. Being cannot be spoken of except by continuous displacement of quasi-metaphor which is already inside metaphysics: 'répétant en la déplaçant la métaphore intra-métaphysique' (Psy, 80). Underlying this is a containing–contained relation between metaphysical discourse and metaphor: the first contains the second, but is itself quasi-metaphorical and thus contained by the second. Neither the notion of metaphor nor that of proper meaning can act as base for language. But can we do without Being?

Gradually the article edges to where there arises in its slipstream, so to speak, a question from *Of Grammatology*, but returned to in other texts – the ontological status of what is designated by the verb 'to be'. The 'retrait' as Heideggerian *Entziehung* (removal) and the 'trait' as *Riss* (stroke or tear, the two words brought together for the first time, Derrida suggests, in *The Origin of the Work of Art*, 1935–6) appear as a grammatological version of the programme associated with Heideggerian Being, hiding and revealing, and as a relay of 'trace' or 'différance':

> N'étant rien, il [trait] n'apparaît pas lui-même, il n'a aucune phénoménalité propre et indépendante, et ne se montrant pas, il se retire, il est structurellement en retrait, comme écart, ouverture, différentialité, trace, bordure, traction, effraction etc. . . . Son inscription, comme j'ai tenté de l'articuler de la trace ou de la différance, *n'arrive qu'à s'effacer*.
>
> (Psy, 88–9)

> Being nothing, the line does not appear itself, it has no phenomenality for itself and independently, and not showing itself, it withdraws, it stands structurally slightly back, as a gap, opening, differentiality, trace, hem, traction, effraction etc. . . . Its inscription, as I have tried to articulate about the trace or about difference, only comes about in effacing itself.
>
> (Psy, 88–9, my translation)

'Retrait' is neither subject nor product, neither active nor passive, neither single nor multiple, but the source of possibility. Yet it is not a root, not a node, in a trellis of concepts which can thus dominate and contain; for it changes level, by reduplication, and if it seems to 'bottom out' in a linguistic locality, it will have removed itself from there:

> Il ne se confond pas plus avec les mots qu'il rend possibles, en leur délimitation ou découpe (y compris les mots français ou allemands, qui se sont ici croisés ou greffés) qu'il n'est étranger aux mots comme une chose ou un référent.
>
> (Psy, 92)[18]

It does not become confused with the words it makes possible, any more than in cutting them out or delimiting them (including the French or German words, which have crossed themselves or grafted themselves here) it is foreign to words, like a thing or a referent.

(Psy, 92, my translation)

Then by a movement, perhaps the movement of withdrawal from under the words so to speak, something beyond words appears to make itself felt.[19] This kind of remark allows for meaning which is not fully thematized, but which cannot be just pinned into the effect of rhetoric. Such a possibility appears to allow for dissociation between thought and language; it appears to allow for meaning to be engendered which is not discursive, or thematic, which is beyond the discrete effects of item-like words arrayed in a sentence.

'A non-classical dissociation of thought and language'

Derrida in an early article speaks of the common root of reason, as of language and historicity, not as a positive origin, but as one derived from a wordless and non-historical negativity, 'le fonds non-historique de l'histoire', 'the non-historical capital [basis] of history', where finally a non-classical dissociation of word and thought is made: 'Il s'agirait alors d'une négativité si négative qu'elle ne pourrait même plus se nommer ainsi' (ED, 55 note) ('It would be then a question of a negativity so negative that it could not even be called such any longer') (*WD*, 308). The 'classical dissociation between thought and language' Derrida speaks of at several points is one where thoughts are matterless and have then to be clothed in language. (The idea is clearly connected in many earlier writers with the idea of the language of the angels.) Nietzsche in order to attack metaphysics had, Derrida argued in a kind of *tu quoque*, used what were metaphysical schemata: the arbitrary nature of the sign, the divorce between thought and language (M, 213; *M*, 179). (This was not, as we have seen in Chapter 1, an accidental or empirical incoherence on Nietzsche's part, but an essential one.) Now, Derrida himself has several times spoken of a divorce between thought and language, albeit cautiously, as if aware of the problematic nature of the suggestion. He speaks of 'une dissociation de type non-classique entre la pensée et le langage' (ED, 55 note) ('a non-classical type of dissociation between thought and language') (*WD*, 33 note 4, cf. 1986a: 26; 1987b: 170) one to which concessions have to be made but of which 'perhaps' can only be said, and thus effaced, in philosophy.[20] For language in general is the structure of rational thought. There cannot then be a simple passage beyond language; the text – texts like Blanchot's – may as it were contain in them traces of the passage 'beyond' language, but do not secondarize the *logos*. Now in the earlier article on Foucault, as in that on Levinas, a double-edged argument had been mounted: that language can never be fair to negativity, must always make it secondary, pull it into its area of influence, or never fail to set it to work, in dialectics for instance. In the long note in *Writing and Difference*, already discussed in the first chapter, this is immediately related to how we talk – even to talk of nothing is in this perspective to recuperate it, for the paradox which arises is that the schism between thought and philosophy as discourse can only be said in philosophy, which thus effaces the schism as it is spoken of (ED, 55 note; *WD*, 33 note 4). But language is also that which allows relation to the other, and thus protects silence which may be the other's unforced response. The first article on Levinas has thus a double attitude to logic and language which is developed, in very different tone, in the second one. Such a movement towards a nothing which cannot be said and which must be pulled back into language is at the same time an opening towards a truth, which was necessarily an effraction within the domain of language. So writing like Blanchot's can hint at the beyond of the limits of language without neglecting these constraints.

The gaps Derrida leaves in some of his writings then appear as a textual reminder of what is not said, cannot be said, or has been effaced. And Derrida admires Blanchot's writing for making negativity perceptible, and for venturing most, because removing something from the order of language while accommodating itself to it ('Voilà une écriture, la plus risquée qui soit, soustrayant quelque chose à l'ordre du langage qu'elle y plie en retour avec une rigueur très dense et inflexible' – 'Here is writing, the most adventurous there is, subtracting something from the order of language which it folds there as a return with a very dense and inflexible rigour', my translation). Derrida reflects on what has been subtracted, and asks whether it is the element of thought – a scandalous thought for a 'certain modernity' (Par, 26). It is a risk which has to be run, the price to pay in order to think differently the 'outside language' of thought (one sense Derrida gives to Blanchot's title *Le pas au-delà*). Hence also we have seen the pun on 'pas' announcing a 'pas au-delà de la langue' (Par, 51) which suggests at the same time that there is no going outside language, and that there is. (For the 'step' reverts through its meaning of 'not' to 'stuff' which is prediscursive – 'Un pas au delà de la langue qui revient à du phonème et du graphème prédiscursifs', Par, 50–1.)

The divorce between language and thought in Levinas does not secondarize language, says Derrida (Psy, 170; at this very moment, 20), for it is possible for the other of language to be within language. (This is how we may not be being quite silent about the things we cannot speak of, and are not speaking of.) There may be differences internal to language which abut onto the unsaid. Under 'the old name' in writing such as Blanchot's work, there may be something else which 'comes to go over its limit in remarking the generality of the process' (Par, 73, my translation). The word given as example in this passage, 'oubli' (forgetfulness), has a charged history, which as in the case of 'don' (gift), discussed earlier, affects what is said about the 'old name', 'this X' as Derrida calls it. In Heidegger's *Zur Seinsfrage*, the overcoming of the 'forgetfulness of Being' ('Seinsvergessenheit') (ZSF, 36) is the over-coming of metaphysics, the possibility, however fraught, of a return to something we have lost. Within Derrida's paragraph, then, 'oubli' may link to Heideggerian forgetfulness, but also goes out of that limit but not as a transgression of it. There may be nowhere else to go from metaphor and from language; no original Being, no proper meaning, no languageless thought may be accessible. But that does not mean that there is no room for moving. One further example of the same pattern: in an article on the question of philosophy's relation to a specific language (Descartes and French is the example), translation is not a simple bijection from one language to another (the example Derrida [DP, 308] gives is the Latin translation of the *Discourse on Method* which actually leaves out the commentary on its language because presumably it starts by referring to French); translation is already at work within the French, it is intralinguistic as well as interlinguistic. In Borges' story, Pierre Menard (Menard is a fictional character but both Pierre and Jean Mesnard, whose surname is indistinguishable in pronunciation from Menard, were real French critics) attempts to produce *Don Quixote* as if *ab initio*. Yet, says Derrida, the Spanish of Borges is marked by a Frenchness which is lost in a translation into French, so that the Borges text makes insecure the very concept of a particular language as a system, and thus of the possibility of clean translation from one linguistic system to another (OA, 134; *EO*, 100). Moreover, translation operates between two poles, either of which wipes out its necessity: if the other is seen as so exquisitely and irremediably different that there is no contact, then there can be no translation – not by definition as might appear, but because the appreciation of difference means that understanding has already started.[21] Yet if, as Pierre Menard's experience suggests, the very same words (and not just words, but complex chains of sentences putting forward plot and character in a cumulative belt of chapters) may not signify the very same thing when written at a different point in time in different circumstances, then *a fortiori* – it has become a commonplace to admit it, but the consequences are often dodged – interlinguistic translations will never be innocent matches of words or phrases, but will mean grafting into a different linguistic and intellectual tradition, with the implications of incision, heterogeneity, and dovetailing of filaments that this entails.

Derrida's own writing insists that words convey an open set of senses: it is not possible to tone this down by claiming that there is a 'basic' or 'central' or 'main' one which can be summarized without defect or expressed in other words.[22] But this also means that particularly careful study, philological and contextual, is needed, which respects the filiation both of the words studied and their systematic relation (M, 302; *M*, 253), as well as of the concepts used in their study. Sense then is linked, Derrida implies, both to the word – however problematic this nominalization is – and to a specific language.[23] He expresses this as a refused concession in a phrase in *Of Grammatology*, whose importance for the present book is hard to over-emphasize. In discussing Heidegger's statement that the word 'being' is an 'originary' word, which allows the possibility of words in general and is pre-comprehended in every language, Derrida admits that the sense of being is not the same as the word 'being' nor the concept of being, but continues: 'Mais comme ce sens n'est rien hors du langage et du langage de mots, il est lié, sinon à tel ou tel mot, à tel ou tel système de langues (concesso non dato), du moins à la possibilité du mot en général' (G, 34) ('But as that sense is nothing outside of language and the language of words, it is tied, if not to a particular word or to a particular system of language (concesso non dato), at least to the possibility of the word in general') (*G*, 21).

It is to the refusal of this concession that we must turn. In it is raised the question of the connection of philosophy to the language in which it is conducted. Heidegger, as has often been pointed out, praised the German and the Greek languages as the most powerful of all languages in regard to the possibilities of thought (IM, 57). From the other end on, so to speak, one might recall in the Britain of the 1960s criticism of the ordinary language philosophy associated with J. L. Austin and the questioning of the worth of his investigation of the implications of our English turns of phrase: the questioning of their philosophical relevance, and their lack of translatability. Now, the refusal of the concession might seem to lead to a position which is related to the work of Benjamin Whorf: philosophy is tied to a language, and thus must be affected by the nature of the language, even if it does not produce a 'world view' tied to that language.[24] The second part of this position was Benveniste's and has been attacked by Derrida in particular in the article 'The supplement of copula', republished in the collection *Margins*. Benveniste had argued that Aristotle's categories are an unconscious extrapolation from Greek grammar, an ontologizing of grammatical categories specific to Greek. Benveniste had argued that this could be shown by comparing the notion of 'to be' in different languages. In its functions of copula or identification it is by no means lexicalized, turned into a word, in every language, and thus is not the same as a designation of existence. Derrida shows that the fact that Benveniste ignores the historical localization of his own argument, is historically a restricting of the scope of Aristotle's. Benveniste treats philosophy as if it were a self-service shop, from which he deploys arguments with little inquiry into the reasons for their presence on the shelves.

But it is precisely this kind of tissue of connection which Derrida is interested in, without bending it to the purpose of historical reconstruction. Derrida warns:

> On aurait tort de croire à la lisibilité immédiate et anhistorique d'un argument philosophique, comme on aurait tort de croire qu'on peut, sans une élaboration préalable et très complexe, soumettre un texte métaphysique à telle grille de déchiffrement scientifique, qu'elle soit linguistique, psychanalytique ou autre. Une des premières précautions concernera l'origine et l'appartenance métaphysique des concepts qui constituent souvent cette grille 'scientifique'.
>
> (M, 225)

It is a mistake to believe in the immediate and ahistorical legibility of a philosophical argument, just as it is a mistake to believe that without a prerequisite and highly complex elaboration one may submit a metaphysical text to any grid of scientific deciphering, be it linguistic, psychoanalytic, or other. One of the first precautions must concern the way the concepts that often constitute this 'scientific' grid belong to metaphysics.

(*M*, 188)

The very notion of category, and perhaps of language, is held in a tradition deriving from Aristotle: treating philosophy as if it could be as a limited whole, distinct from, and even contained by, linguistics or rhetoric, is using a defining notion, a *definiens* which has been produced by what is to be defined, by the *definiendum* (M, 274; *M*, 230). And a parallel argument is possible in rhetoric, and is indeed mounted in the article 'White mythology'. It is not just that philosophy and linguistics are related by tradition, by language: philosophy has *preceded* linguistics, it was there before, it is not a separate region but an older one, upstream. Benveniste has treated a philosophical problem, that of category, as existing separately from its location in a specific language, tradition and thinker (M, 220), and has moreover used to define it terms which are anachronisms, being in fact Kantian (M, 221), while at the same time arguing that Aristotle's treatment of it is determined by the Greek language.

Derrida does not take the 'Whorfian' position, i.e. that of a world view being imposed on its speakers by a language and its determination of conceptions through grammar and lexis; but the implication both of the refused concession and of the very way he writes, with constant reference to the other languages which his texts may be written in, are that some such moulding is inherent in intellectual as in linguistic tradition, without being dominant or even simple to pick out. Whorf's ideas have suffered an eclipse since his death; yet not to be saying exactly the same thing in another language which one speaks well is a matter of daily experience for the large numbers of the world's population who speak more than one language. It may well be that the extreme view of the relation between understanding of the world and language is untenable because in a sense circular (our evidence for a world view is likely to be largely linguistic); nevertheless, the reworking of an experience of time, for instance, which is implicit in moving between languages which have different tense systems, precisely does allow this sense of gap between language and thought which Derrida appears to be exploring.

How does this sense of gap function in the area of philosophy? The wrap-round relation between philosophy and linguistics, where the tools that linguistics seems to provide in order to exhibit the limits of philosophy, are in fact part of what they seem to limit, is a macroversion of the translation problem. Ewe, a Ghanaian language, Benveniste shows, does not lexicalize the functions of the verb 'to be', but distributes them across several verbs. However, since some Indo-European languages do the same, and there is no determinate semantic content to 'to be' which, it could be claimed, is absent in such languages, the limits between word and concept must be seen as fuzzy and unclear. With such a verb as 'to be' and such a notion as 'existence', the relation between empirical grounding (embodiment in a particular language, a particular philosophical tradition) and transcendental category (condition of possibility of thought) becomes especially fraught and tangled.

Aristotle treats the question of how being says itself/is said (*legetai*) (*Metaphysics*, E 2 1026 a 33).[25]

> La catégorie est une des manières pour l'"être' de se dire ou de se signifier, c'est-à-dire d'ouvrir la langue à son dehors, à ce qui est en tant qu'il est ou tel qu'il est, à la vérité. 'Etre' se donne justement dans le langage comme ce qui l'ouvre au non-langage, au-delà de ce qui ne serait que le dedans ('subjectif', 'empirique' au sens anachronique [pour Aristote] de ces mots) d'une langue.
>
> (M, 218)

> The category is one of the ways for 'Being' to say itself or to signify itself, that is, to open language to its exterior, to what is in that it is or such as it is, to truth. 'Being' is given in language, precisely, as that which opens language to nonlanguage, beyond what would be only the ('subjective', 'empirical', in the anachronistic sense of these words) interior of a language.
>
> *M*, 183)

Words are in specific languages, yet against Benveniste, or rather pushing his arguments about the relation between the 'notion of being' and philosophy further, Derrida points out 'la relation absolument unique entre le transcendental et la langue' (M, 234) ('the absolutely unique relationship between the transcendental and language') (*M*, 195).[26] It is 'being' as a transcategorial notion which makes possible the passing between categories of thought and categories of language (M, 236; *M*, 197), which limits the incommensurability of the different languages with each other, which enables comparison, which makes translation possible at all.

If use by philosophers of a particular language, Greek, seems to have set the notions of category, predicate and their relation to being on a particular cultural and philosophical journey, that journey has involved treating them as more fundamental than any particularities of a specific language, rather, indeed, as particularities of language and thought in general. But Derrida shows, in relation to Benveniste, that we are not able to step outside these: this is the way things look to us, for they have been built into the way things look to us; we cannot just sum up Aristotle by deriving his notion of category from the particularities of Greek.

Yet at the end of the article 'The supplement of copula', before an extended quotation from Heidegger, we are warned that if 'being' is not identified with what can be linguistically individuated, neither is it a determination of meaning separable from actual existents. So thought and language are not identified, but on the other hand, neither are they cleanly and clearly dissociated. Heidegger had, in works other than the *Introduction to Metaphysics*, insisted on a precomprehension of being as a condition for language at all. Derrida reminds us of this in *Glas*, but does not tarry with 'pre-comprehension', although it points to his discussion later of 'pre-judgments' in 'Devant la loi', and will be discussed very briefly in the next section. In both texts under discussion (*Grammatology*; 'The supplement of copula') Derrida turns immediately to the problem of the lexical unit (the turn is especially clear in 'The supplement of copula' – it occurs at the end, and has been little prepared). Heidegger, we have seen, had argued that 'being' was an *Urwort*, glossed by Derrida as 'Le mot transcendental assurant la possibilité de l'être-mot à tous les autres mots' (G, 34) ('The transcendental word assuring the possibility of being-word to all other words') (*G*, 20) and Derrida immediately queries in the earlier text the pre-eminence of the word, in the later text the distinction lexis/syntax. This turn is important. For Heidegger had presented the predominance of the third person of the present indicative of the verb 'to be' as a copula which gradually took over the direction of the interpretation of being; yet many languages lack the form, and express through, for instance, reiteration, what in many but not all European languages is done by the copula. The question of language as transcendental, of the forms of language as the conditions of possibility of our thought, which is clearly present in much twentieth-century thinking, from Wittgenstein to Chomsky, and which helps explain the explosion of philosophy into a nebula of disciplines – linguistics, anthropology, psychology – is immediately turned away by Derrida from channels one might have expected, from considerations of language 'in general', of 'base structure' or of 'language games', towards the problem of its elementary particles, of whether such things be, and to whether such things be words. It is important to note that the transcendental here and at this point is not some kind of frame, but the question of whether there need be such units at all, such units being, each time, of a particular language.[27]

Are we locked into one particular language, does translation from one language to another provide the only tightrope from which we can at a height both slight and dangerous survey the abyss of our thought and its relation to language; or are there structures, whether overt or 'deep', common to every language?[28] These problems in Derrida's work probably develop from the experience of translating Husserl and lead out of Husserl's concern with eidetic form in history, his concern for logic as the fundamental structure of language (M, 191) and yet awareness in his very late writings of the crucial role of language in making intersubjectivity possible. The development of the transcendental as a condition of possibility was in Derrida's argument on the history of philosophy in *Of Grammatology* the condition for a passing beyond various formalisms without falling into empiricism (G, 89; *G*, 61).

A brilliant interpretation of the late work of Wittgenstein by Bernard Williams points in the same direction. In charting a movement from 'I' to 'we', and thus from a position which might look like solipsism to a concern with human activity, Williams suggests that while 'the "we" of Wittgenstein's remarks often looks like the "we" of our group as contrasted with other groups, this is basically misleading' (Williams 1981: 160). Wittgenstein is not speaking, in Whorfian fashion, of the way in which our particular language might inform and condition our particular view of the world. Yet he, and Dummett after him, have put into relation conditions of assertion and truth conditions: to know what justifies an assertion is to know the conditions for its truth. This, undoubtedly, Williams points out, refers to a human practice, with the consequence that what has been a subject of practical decision – decisions about geometry for instance, during the formulation of the science – becomes something of a kind which it is nonsense to say has been determined by decision, precisely a (non-empirical) mathematical truth (*ibid.*: 163). This can be sharpened to an aporia: our statement appears to be if true, then false: if something has been determined by decision to be a mathematical truth, then it is the kind of thing which cannot be made true by decision.[29] In this sense our language would show us how things are in relation to our concerns and practices, though it would be as it is without being an empirical explanation of those concerns and practices, and these would not determine the language.

This shows something, argues Williams, of the later Wittgenstein, of what it is for things to make sense for us, what he baptizes 'the transcendental facts' (namely for Wittgenstein), that is, the shape of our language outside which it is impossible to climb. This kind of thinking of language could not be explained by looking at how our (particular) language conditions our view of the world as against the Hopi Indians (the Whorfian example), for that is still internal to language. Nor could it be explained in, for example, Marxist terms, as conditioned by other factors, for there are no ideas outside of it to condition it.

> However, while we could not explain it in any of those ways, we could in a way make it clearer to ourselves by reflecting on it, as it were self-consciously exercising it; not indeed by considering alternatives – for what I am presently considering can have no comprehensible alternatives to it – but by moving around reflectively inside our view of things and sensing when we begin to be near the edge by the increasing incomprehensibility of things regarded from whatever way-out point of view one had moved into. What one would become conscious of, in so reflecting, is something like *how we go on*. And *how we go on* is a matter of how we think and speak and intentionally and socially conduct ourselves, that is matters of our experience.
>
> (Williams 1981: 153)

So that the collective enterprise 'we' undertake is both transcendental and piecemeal.

This account is strangely near to and yet far from that explicit in Derrida's writing. In the refused concession with which my discussion started, Derrida is more willing than Williams to allow the specificities of a particular language to be part of the conditions of thought, to be inseparable from, or at least of no categorically different status to the other aspects of assertion conditions. They are built in to what makes sense. But at the same time, and perhaps because

Derrida is willing to sharpen the aporia above, we do not have the empirical (particular language) being identified with what makes sense. We have returned to a linguistic version of the problem raised in the first chapter à propos Lévi-Strauss and Foucault. Derrida is not making an empirical event of a transcendental condition. But the transcendental condition is not separable from the language in which it is enunciated. We can indeed think of language in general, but we will always trip over specifics, in the particular language we are working in. Conversely, we may be able to 'think in another fashion', 'penser autrement' under the specifics, that is, produce a kind of tremor by the hampered gesture that is not being able to think differently (M, 41; *M*, 38).

'A subjectless transcendental field'?

Merleau-Ponty said that Lévi-Strauss' structuralism was 'Kantianism without a transcendental subject' (Schmidt 1985; Frank 1983: 37, attributes the remark to Ricoeur); Derrida quotes Hyppolite's interpretation of the result of the Husserlian 'epoché' where writing is a 'subjectless transcendental field' independent of any actual empirical subject (OG, 84; *OG*, 88). And the epigraph to the first chapter of the present book shows a not dissimilar viewpoint in Blanchot about Foucault's structuralism. Derrida suggests that it is writing that for the later Husserl makes possible transcendental historicity, since it liberates a piece of language from the actual intentionality of a subject, and even from a particular community of speakers. Writing (as traces carrying records) is the enabling condition of Husserl's pure subjectless transcendental field which is the final goal of his reductions: it makes absolute objectivity possible, because it frees meaning from the circumstances of its production. Yet for Husserl, Derrida points out, this liberation of objectivity can only take place by a strange interleaving of the transcendental and the empirical. The transcendental field of writing can function without a subject (indeed it may post-compose the subject); however, the whole structure of intentional meaning postulates a virtual subject as a condition of its possibility. But, Derrida affirms, the subjectlessness of the field is empirical each time and the beautiful last phrases of a paragraph in his introduction to *Origin of Geometry* [30] enumerate icons of loss of meaning and point to the transcendental sense of the facticity of death.[31] The value (or 'effect') of transcendentality is created, says Derrida, by the structure of writing and the virtual absence of any receiver of the writing (M, 375; *M*, 315). The importance of the 'possibly not' implied by the possibility of empirical loss, the angle at which transcendence and fact are set in a language, makes of language both a structure which 'is the limits of our world', and a particular language, with particular empirical features. If language for Husserl seems to be a transcendental field, intelligible for a subject only through its intentionality and its direction to a subject in general, in writing that absence, that subjectlessness is factical (since the possibility of the subject's presence is a constraining condition on meaning, it has to be *meaning for*). So that transcendental condition and empirical fact are both part of writing's structure.[32]

Derrida reminds us in the introduction to *Origin of Geometry* that it is language which disrupts that regression to conditions of possibility; he quotes Herder against Kant (as Fink against Husserl) to suggest that language is always rooted in cultural and rhetorical circumstance, which will nullify the *a priori* of synthetic judgement and cannot be (not just is not) fully thematized. And this view of the particularity of language is itself rooted in historical circumstance: here, then, is a return, with Herder, as with Heidegger, to a facticity which is not an abandoning of the transcendental, but a recognition of a further structure of transcendence ('un retour à la facticité comme droit du droit' (OG, 61 note) ('a return to facticity as the de jure character of the de jure itself') (*OG*, 70 note, trans. mod.). Whereas Levinas makes of this dynamic a transcendental fact, Derrida points to a 'zone' where language has irreducible proximity to original thought, which, however, cannot be phenomenalized or thematized. He uses notions associated with the undecidable (the note in question has all the signs of being a marker put down for further exploration). Unlike Levinas, he allows an imbalance between language and thought,[33] between language as discourse of reason and particular language, to continue indefinitely.

Derrida's admission of a 'non-classical' dissociation between language and thought is one where the field of language is as if transcendental to the individual's thought. Yet in such a conception, nevertheless, language is not the spectacles through which thought views the world; thought is of a different order, which is how it may be the dissociated negative of language.

Prelogic

The problem of the relation between the structure of logical activity and logic as a norm had been the crux of Cavaillès' last work, as has been seen in the previous chapter (note 43). Historically, logicians had defined logic as 'the art of reasoning', the art of giving rules to thought, yet it was from the thought of the mind that that art was supposed to come. For this to work, formal structures had to be refined of any material content, and in that way could be said by Kant, for one, to resemble universal grammar in that refinement (Cavaillès 1947: 5–6). But not merely was the divorce between form and matter difficult to sustain (and words are not the matter of formal syntax; both words and syntax have invariant and variant elements, Cavaillès points out). In addition, the idea of the individual mind and its operations seemed hard to bypass. In Cavaillès' account of the development of ideas of logic, it was from the intellectual faculties that logical structure was held to proceed, seeming thus to involve infinite regress: the structure is needed to regulate the faculties, but itself derives from them. The moment there is reference to acts of thinking, these seem only to have sense ultimately in relation to an actual consciousness. In Husserlian terms, there seemed to be an infinite regress between constituting acts of consciousness, and constituted structures. The later work of Husserl, in trying to understand the origins of geometry as historical and not merely as genesis within a single mind, had pointed to a state of consciousness which could be called 'pre-objective', in which there was not a constituted subject opposite a correlated object, nature. In the words of Merleau-Ponty (1968: 116), whom I am following here, 'une couche naturelle à l'esprit est comme enfouie dans le fonctionnement concordant des corps au milieu de l'être brut' – 'a layer natural to spirit is as if buried in the coinciding functioning of bodies in the middle of gross Being' (trans. MRN).[34]

There is discernible through Derrida's work a concern with this 'pre-objective' mode of being (and thus with the permeability of the distinctions between mental and physical, non-logical and logical). Where he insists that *différance* is not a condition of the possibility of thought (and thus not transcendental), he takes care to insist on 'des possibilités prélogiques de la logique' ('prelogical possibilities of logic') (LI, 173; *LI*, 93) which cannot be ruled by constituted logic, a development of Cavaillès' argument. But these 'prelogical possibilities' are not primary, nor a condition of possibility for logic. It might seem, then, that they cannot be called 'logical' at all. And in what might be seen as a further raid, so to speak, on 'constituted logic', Derrida relates these possibilities to a 'quasi-transcendental' activity of concepts like 'trace' and 'différance': they both belong and do not belong to the conceptual space they are organizing. (I take 'quasi-transcendental' to have a different status in Derrida's text from 'simili-transcendental' whose dynamics were discussed in Chapter 4 à propos 'striction'.)[35]

The first point to make is that this further exemplifies how much the relations of containing and being contained, belonging and not belonging, act as a filament in the Derridean text. These are involved in the paradoxes of infinite sets and self-reference, which, it has been recalled (see above), caused such tremors at the beginning of the century, and which provoked the discoveries made by Gödel and, ultimately, Paul Cohen. For precisely the fragility of such distinctions at vulnerable points of our universe of discourse suggests, if not that the latter is not monolithic and that there is a plurality of logics at work, then at least that it is a highly striated and variously compacted structure, with local discontinuities and inevitable aporia.[36] In the course of a lecture remarkable for being one of the very few discussions of Derrida's work from a point of view at once resolutely open-minded and that of an analytical philosopher, Tom Baldwin has jibbed at the suggestion that 'supplementarity' or even grammatology 'can somehow evade classical logic'. A similar stance has been taken by Proust's 'postface' (Proust 1991), helpful in its wish to bring out differences rather than score points. Baldwin insists that the contexts in which 'we have to countenance the acceptability of contradictions' are restricted, and that these are 'at best unwanted by-products of the classical categories, requiring strict policing'. To discuss this in detail one would need not just to examine carefully each of the examples Baldwin gives, but to separate out, for instance, the three classical principles of negation: the law of non-contradiction, the law of excluded middle, and the law of double negation. This is not the place for this.

I have tried to suggest in earlier chapters that through the phenomenological tradition, Derrida shares in some of the concerns of intuitionist logic – that unqualified assertion of the principle of the excluded middle may imply that all problems are resolvable, for instance. Here, however, a quite general point must be made: it certainly is the case that Derrida resists the overarching claims of classical logic. And given the way his thought works with the implications of the infinite, this is hardly surprising. But he is not, at one extreme, jettisoning the entire function of contradiction (indeed, the textual process of deconstruction makes extended use of it, but in a sometimes unfamiliar context, as Chapter 4 of this book has suggested); nor is he at the other extreme, doing, in however unfamiliar mode, some 'logic of the infinite'. I have suggested throughout this book that the remarkable daring of what he is doing is to work with a highly detailed and nuanced account of language, one that can take acount of the most complex sites of its activity: poetry, effects of style; the modalization inherent in most of natural language.[37] His writing actually builds into itself precisely those effects of the development of logic which some have tried to make incommunicable as 'unwanted by-products'.[38] And I have tried to show that when Derrida takes the paradoxes of the infinite radically, so to speak, this does not lead to a stalling into repetition of aporia nor to an abandoning of rigour. It has the result of building in awareness of language in ways that are uncommon: the question of linguistic particularity, the inherently modal nature of most language, the difficulty of the separation between content and comment on that content.

But what prevents Derrida's pattern of argument, and his use of the word 'logic', from being a kind of 'trumping', where classical logic – which, however short it comes in accounting for the way we use language to reason, has at least the merit of working clearly and distinctly on the set of problems it approaches – is put down in favour of what amounts to a sheer statement of diversity, and permeability of distinctions? Several things. First, Derrida's work exhibits, amply and persuasively, the heterogeneity at work in our thinking, the shifting value of the distinctions we are obliged to work with. But we have dynamic demonstration, not mere description. Second, that demonstration is not designed to inhibit thinking and logic, but to build into their shape recognition of the paradoxes. When Derrida says: 'Tout concept qui prétend à quelque rigueur implique l'alternative du "tout ou rien"'(LI, 211) ('Every concept that lays claim to any rigor whatsoever implies the alternative of 'all or nothing') (*LI*, 116) this is not an attack. Derrida actually says that it is illegitame as well as impossible to make a philosophical concept outside that logic of all or nothing. It is a reminder that we have to aim at a rigour which is at its limit impossible. To be aware of this, though, does not mean that one abandons rigour. Third, it may make the kind of rigour and consistency aimed at of a particular or new sort.

These 'pre-logical possibilities' then, seem to be what is more than (strictly) philosophical in language ('son assise philosophique', 'its philosophical jurisdiction', LI, 173; *LI*, 93). It has been argued, particularly in Chapter 3, that there is a sense in which Derrida's work begins, in a barely thematized way, after a process both patient and complexifying, to make possible the use of reconstituted items of linguistic furniture. Take 'subjectivity'. In *Psyché*, especially in the changes made in the already published articles it is composed of (see above), there are pointers which involve a working on a pre-subjective subjectivity, if I can call it that, a 'psyche' which hardly disengages from the text, which is inseparable from it, but which at knots in the argument appears as a kind of underlining, a kind of building out of corrections in the text (only clearly thematized in the title and the *avant-propos*). Like Merleau-Ponty's 'pre-reflexive' root-ends or strands of form in perception, there begins to be suggested an embryonic intentionality: 'Force pré-performative, qui sous la forme du "je" par exemple, marque que *je* s'addresse à de l'autre . . . marque, avant de vouloir-dire ou de signifier: "je-là"' (UG, 126) ('pre-performative force which, for example, in the form of "I" (*je*) marks that "I" as addressing itself to the Other . . . marks, before meaning or signifiying, *I-here*') (*UG*, 62–3). Derrida develops the call, the telephone call, what he calls the 'yes', the openness of response, and suggests that this 'minimal and indeterminate' address gets translated into 'I' and thus into a positing when it is put into language (UG, 127; *UG*, 63). This 'yes' is logically and historically prior to the I and to any performative act (for which, as Cavaillès has shown, a subject is needed). In a phrase whose structure must now be familiar:

> L'autoposition dans le *oui* ou *Ay* n'est pourtant ni tautologique ni narcissique, elle n'est pas davantage égologique même si elle amorce le mouvement de réappropriation circulaire, l'odyssée qui peut donner lieu à toutes ces modalités déterminées. Elle garde ouvert le cercle qu'elle entame. De même, elle n'est pas encore performative, pas encore transcendentale, bien qu'elle reste supposée par toute performativité, *a priori* par tout théoricité constative, par tout savoir et toute transcendentalité. Pour la même raison, elle est préontologique.
>
> (UG, 132)

> The self-positioning in the *yes* or the *Ay* is, however, neither tautological nor narcissistic; it is not egological even if it commences (*amorce*) the movement of circular reappropriation, the odyssey that can give rise to all these determined modalities. It holds open the circle that commences it (*entame*). In the same way, it is not yet performative, not yet transcendental, although it remains presupposed in any performativity, *a priori* in any constative theoricity, in any knowledge, in any transcendentality. For the same reason, it is preontological.
>
> (*UG*, 66)

Once again, though differently, the relation of transcendental to empirical is being redrafted; a preliminary fragile drafting of the 'pre-ceding' answering which is a kind of bearer-field out of which action as performative utterance and

positing, a placing within defined fields, can occur. And this is done in a tenta-
tively complex way, so that terms, themes and even syntax reach out in such a
passage to other Derridean texts and contexts, for extension, substantiation,
further qualification. The mode of construction gives a sense of openness, for
extensions are always possible, either into Derrida's own work, or into that of
other writers. Derrida's work on Joyce, for instance, fills out and modifies
remarks on him made right at the beginning of his own writing, in *Origin of
Geometry*. The connections are made by this moving back and forth, this sense
of careful movement between points in a trellis of references.

Writing and consistency

> The performativity of the text produces its receiver but in no way does it
> pre-exist it. It is the receiver who is the determining factor of the gift, not a
> message structure, for a message presupposes that 'x' sends 'y' for 'z' and
> in the situation of the gift there is no message. It is only the other, at the
> moment when it receives it, who decides the destination and who says 'it is
> me who answers' or 'it is me'.

> (Beehive, 15)

Derrida's writings are, by and large, texts round or on texts; his writing often
seems to perform this reception of the gift, making sense by a 'question back'
from the reception of the text, by a becoming-aware of repetition and extension. An example of this is the way, in the reprint in the book *Parages* of the
article 'Pas', there are several times added references to the title of the volume,
to 'parages'. But these do not straightforwardly reinforce links, for one at least
is made within the context of absence of links: 'On se trouve ici, sans y aborder,
en des parages de la pensée, où le voisinage conceptual est même impossible, et
l' "air de famille" (*family resemblance*)' (Par, 66, also 67, 71, 95) ('We find
ourselves here, without landing, on the strands of thinking, where conceptual
neighbourhood is even impossible, and family resemblance') (my translation;
Derrida gives 'family resemblance' in English). Here then there is a reinforcing
of textual connection (for the reader 'finds themself' and the words used echo
the title of the volume) at the same time as the connection is said to be
impossible.

But a reverse textual movement may be engineered in changing the text. For
instance, two separate words, of dissonant sense, are replaced by the same.[39] So,
by a kind of backstitching, further links are made in and between the articles in
this collection, by reinforcing a connection between what is declared dissimilar
or which actually has dissimilar meaning. In these examples from *Parages*, as in
the texts collected in *Psyché*, we have seen that there are additions which have
the effect of bringing together senses which are distinct, even as the distinction
may be pointed to. In *Psyché* it is not one word, but a series of phrases referring
to the other, or to 'psyché', or to the soul, so that they knot together and make

up filaments, lines of communication. These begin to form a network which was much less evident in the original articles.

Now, that this can happen is at least in part because of the cultivated density and complexity of what Derrida writes: he does not usually conduct a theme through a set of predefined stages to a conclusion. There is in his mode of writing something private and even privately eccentric (Derrida has called this mode of his 'athèse'). Tightly packed, often difficult sentences develop round what are already often deliberately odd phrases in the host writer, or in a phrase that has, so to speak, caught his ear: 'Feu la cendre' – 'The late ash', or 'Fire the ash', a title, for instance, or 'il y va d'un certain pas' – 'moving with a certain pace' (*Apories*). Or they will echo with, signal out to, other phrases in other texts. For instance, in a close discussion of Freud on the fetish, he picks out the word 'monument' to say: 'Le fétiche s'érige ici comme un "monument", un "*stigma indélébile*", un "signe de triomphe". Cette érection monumentale d'une colonne supplémentaire est une solution de compromis' (*Glas*, 235a) ('The fetish erects itself here as a "monument", a "*stigma indélébile*", a "sign of triumph". This monumental erection of a supplementary column is a compromise solution') (*Glas*, 210a). Here the 'column' is a sign of triumph and also a compromise solution. It refers to the columns of the text, but also beyond that to the 'column' of another work of his, 'Dissemination', where it is likewise facing in two ways. For here the phallus and fetishes of unmodalized utterances are identified as being of authority. Yet the column in the same text, once decapitated and captured, makes possible something beyond self-identity and authority: 'le passage innombrable de la dissémination et le déplacement joué des marges. Elle n'est jamais elle-même, seulement l'écriture qui la substitue sans fin à elle-même, la dédoublant dès sa première surrection' (D, 381) ('the innumerable passage of dissemination and the playful displacement of the margins. It is never itself, only a writing that endlessly substitutes it for itself, doubling it as of its very first surrection') (D, 342). Only the clash between such statements makes it possible to 'identify' (D, 405; D, 364–5) the column with the fetish of identification. But then the column, through suggesting the operation of identification, operates a movement of expansion through the identification. However, this spreading of the column is less than a theme: the whole procedure, in its sketching of links, is necessarily tentative, and indeed it is the clash, or at least the friction, between such statements which makes it possible to 'identify' the column with the fetish of identification, and thus cast doubt on the whole 'assembling' round the column, even as it is occurring. We have here one more example of an argument which undoes itself even as it is put forward.

The filamentary structure of the texts can thus provide for extension into other texts. But Derrida's syntax may often provide for a set of extensions within one phrase:

> Quelle que soit entre eux la différence [between Joyce and the commentary] et jusqu' à l'incommensurable, le texte 'second', celui qui fatalement

fait reférence à l'autre, le cite, l'exploite, le parasite, le déchiffre, c'est-sans doute la minuscule parcelle *détachée* de l'autre, le rejeton, le nain métonymique, le bouffon du grand texte antérieur qui lui aurait déclaré la guerre en langues.

(UG, 25)

Whatever the difference between them [between Joyce and the commentary] even if, as in the present case, it is immense and even incommensurable, the 'second' text, the one which, fatally, refers to the other, quotes it, exploits it, parasites it and deciphers it, is no doubt the minute parcel *detached* from the other, the metonymic dwarf, the jester of the great anterior text which would have declared war on it in languages.

(*TWFJ*, 148)

This sentence moves forward by a process which starts with a concessive clause, admitting disjunction and then moving to nullify it, 'c'est sans doute'; it then apposes by throwing forward what is a 'texte second', and the series of accumulated verbs – exploiting, parasiting, decoding. Then the plural identifications of the second text – metonymic dwarf, fool – extend its capacities only to have them swallowed up by an anterior text and made tentative by a conditional in the past. (Incidentally, we have once more the relation of contained and containing, and an amusing picture of the Joycean leviathan swallowing up the minute parcel of commentary which has tried to stay detached from it.) In other words, stratifications, pushes and pulls in intellectual relationships, are syntactically embodied.

But, of course, they are also lexically expressed. Typically of Derrida's written style, an accumulation of lexically related words in the plural will suggest rigorous and proliferating distinctions, as much as connection: 'Une citation au sens strict implique toutes sortes de conventions, de précautions et de protocoles contextuels dans le mode de réitération, de signes codés comme les guillemets ou d'autre artifices typographiques' (Par, 254) ('In the strict sense, a quotation implies all sorts of conventions, precautions and contextual protocols in the mode of reiteration, of coded signs like quotation marks or other typographical artifices') (my translation). The sense of a struggle of ideas is often given by use of the French reflexive, which can be interpreted either as passive or as active:

Or la rive se partage en son trait même, et il y a des effets d'ancrage, des effondrements de bord, des stratégies d'abordage et de débordement, des strictures de rattachement ou d'amarrage, des lieux de réversion, d'étranglement ou de *double bind*. Ils sont constitutifs du procès même de l'athèse.

(CP, 279)

Now the shore is divided in its very outline, and there are effects of anchoring, collapses of the coastline, strategies of approach and overflow, strictures of attachment or of mooring, places of reversion, strangulation, or *double bind*. These are constitutive of the very process of the athesis.

(*PC*, 261)

The ghostly half-metaphors of seafaring develop out of 'rive' ('riverbank' or 'seashore') which is both linked to writing and to water; but the whole derives from a commenting on his own vocabulary, on *dérive* – 'J'ai abusé de ce mot' – where we move, as so often, from the commenting of what is going on in Freud's text to the act of commenting set against it, to this account of the way a piece of writing does something different from what it explicitly proposes. So that there is not writer-subject and text-object, but a putting out of tentacles of connection between writer, reader and text commented-on. At the same time, Derrida's text does do what it proposes: it evokes in its own syntax the 'athesis'.

Here there is some kind of replication.[40] In the examples just discussed, the replication through syntax is shadowed by negatives and by a style which is as if nagging at doubts in the semantic or rhetorical development of the phrase. But the contrary may occur: Derrida may use lexemes or phrases which allow their opposite house room. He takes from Blanchot 'pas', 'step' and 'not'; from Plato 'pharmakon', 'poison' and 'medicine', as we have seen, and sets them in the foreground of an argument so that the lack of identity in the senses of the word is allowed to function – in different ways, in the two cases. The Platonic instance is conceptually unsettling: Plato uses both senses in the *Phaedrus* with the effect of a kind of contradictory reiteration. Whereas 'pas' and even more the pun on 'entre' and 'antre' in 'The double session', again bringing together a syncategoreme and a noun (in the case of 'cave', a noun which is a philosophical *locus classicus*), cause a syntactic instability to be set up in some of the sentences they appear in. In, for instance, the phrase 'l'allusion perpétuelle au fond de l'entre qui n'a pas de fond' (*D*, 248) ('this perpetual allusion being performed in the background of the entre that has no ground') (*D*, 219). Derrida here speaks of a peculiar swinging effect produced – the suspension between the senses is operated by the way the words are placed, by the syntactic ambiguity provoked (*D*, 254; *D*, 225). These words, we are told, 'appartiennent en quelque sorte à la fois à la conscience et à l'inconscient, dont Freud nous dit qu'il est tolérant ou insensible à la contradiction' (*D*, 250) ('they belong in a sense both to consciousness and to the unconscious, which Freud tells us can tolerate or remain insensitive to contradiction') (*D*, 221).

In a another disquieting phrase, Derrida speaks of 'faire l'économie du saut', which means both 'to go through the hoop of the jump' and 'to economize on the jump'. This, used of Kantian methods of preventing the contaminating effect of analogy, suggests that by embedding contradiction in a circuit, Kant ultimately does without it (*Glas*, 242a, 216a). A further example of such a turn of phrase which contains its own opposite, as it were, was discussed at the beginning of this chapter. These strange words or phrases with their two-way stretch make opposition and relation fluid and uncertain;[41] far from focusing a double meaning within the ambit of a pun or a phrase, they disperse it, cause it to have a ripple effect. The puns stop functioning as foci, centres, and begin functioning as junction points. The phrases are poised on the page, swinging in relation to the sentences adjacent to them, hijacking other grammatical functions, leaving the reader aghast and amused.

In such a text as 'Plato's pharmacy' or 'The double session', the Derridean coinages 'pharmakon' or 'hymen' contradict themselves unstably in a kind of internal fission: remedy or poison, separating membrane or fusion in marriage. These are load-bearing terms, and are very visible. But they point to micro-movements in Derrida's texts, which wordplay engenders. For example, he at different points establishes a relation with the Platonic cave when he says of Mallarmé that he 's'y connaissait aussi en grottes' ('he was a connoisseur of grottoes') but uses a word which at different points is rephoneticized to 'glottes' (e.g. D, 239). The wordplay picks up, of course, a trait in the poet himself, just as the reference to Plato picks up Mallarmé's 'idealism'. But the punning is not just a movement away from one word to another, not just a parody of Mallarmé's puns, but on the contrary an effect where the parody and what is parodied slip into each other. Derrida in fact makes the effect of such terms insecure, by the very way he writes.

In such phrases I believe there is at work a radically original form of irony. Original, for irony has, in some at least of its history, been applied to a kind of meta-linguistic effect, hovering above the text, implying through its tone a transcendence of what is said. Such is the irony of Voltaire, for instance. The reader of such irony reads under what is said to implications which are radically different. There is no such transcendence implied by such Derridean phrases and terms; they are local, partial, provisional. Where they occur, the text becomes at that point a resonance between different actualizations of sense. For instance, analysing Mallarmé's three rewritings of one sentence of *Mimique*, Derrida shows how a changing of the place of a noun can make it syntactically ambiguous, either subject or object of a relative clause. But the ambiguity is not ambivalence – possible readings are not equally weighted, and this is why the effect is one of such instability: 'un effet de flottaison indéfinie entre deux possibles' (D, 254) ('an effect of indefinite fluctuation between between two possibilities') (D, 225). Such a floating of meaning certainly has ironic effect. It is, however, one that is not related to a human or more-than-human mind with an ironic overview. On the contrary, it comes off, so to speak, syntactic units which join together in unstable ways, it acts like a perturbing force field round certain words or phrases. (Kierkegaard [1830: 48] in his account of Socratic irony spoke of 'telegraphic communication'.) The syntactic irony available at certain points in Derrida's text is not that of signals to a reader sent out by a transcending consciousness; it is much more like a sudden change of frequency in emission, which can momentarily be received in a different way and at a different place.[42] In that way, what I have called irony develops the 'polylogues' in Derrida's texts, the fact that quite a few of them are multivoiced dialogues, in which different voices are active without there being speakers who are personalized to any degree, in which arguments can be set out in more diffuse ways, which allow a non-linear progression ('Restitutions of the truth in painting' – the last article in *The Truth in Painting* – and *Mémoires d'aveugle*, for instance). These 'polylogues' cannot be reduced to dialogism. But irony, in its relation with the negative, given the fact the phrases and lexemes are allowed to give their own opposites house room, produces a much less gentle, less genteel, effect at the points at which it operates. For these phrases and lexemes take a feature of Derrida's own writing, and sharpen it.

This feature is that Derrida's arguments in the main advance by fractions, by small segments of discursive prose – in which there are at work what have been called in this book 'circuits of argument' or 'micrologies'. These circuits, repeated or almost repeated, analogous lexically (as pointed out in Chapter 3) or even of similar rhythmic pattern, form different connections in the different segments in which they are embedded. Their repetition, or semi-repetition, it has been argued, allow for consistent extension through very different contexts and through different texts of what at this late point in my argument will have to be called Derridean positions: on deconstruction, on the question of beginnings, on identity, for instance. The two-way phrases just discussed, however, point to where this account stops short. They indicate a hiatus in the flow of argument, they pivot, they both open up and close down connections. They force attention to the segmental nature of the mode of construction of argument; they induce by their negative counterpoint to their own positive sense a momentary shifting, an ironic underscoring. But that ironic underscoring is local, and it is sited quite clearly in the language of a segment of prose, not in the effect of some broader consciousness. Might this effect be called 'quasi-transcendental', as Derrida calls the tonality of laughter in *Ulysses* (UG, 121; *UG*, 61)? Here, in his work on Joyce, there is a double valuation, not this time of a phrase, but of a whole, or at least of *Ulysses*, and of its tone and its affect. The laughter here represents the totalizing mastery, the 'hypernesic' net that is the novel, catching in a burst of affirmation, so we are told, everything there has ever been of tales, knowledge, culture, aiming to contain everything in one sardonic act, aiming at encyclopedic reappropriation – it is compared to Hegelian absolute knowledge assembling itself to itself (UG, 120; *UG*, 60). But at the same time, and in a way that is said to be 'quasi-transcendental and supplementary', the laughter is quite different – it moves to its near opposite 'quasiment amnésique' (UG, 120; *UG*, 60), a gift which is not part of exchange, an affirmation which allows room to the other, something which has no proper name. Here Derrida refers to the place left for Elijah at his feast, not as the chief programmer of all references, but as the other. And yet here the other has a kind of shadowy reference, to Derrida himself.[43]

This lack of identity within the unit at the level of lexeme, phrase, or even description of tone, as in the last example, enacts in its very writing the questioning going on throughout Derrida's work of the distinctions which enable us to mark off units, or to neglect the differentiated nature of the tools we employ to think. In this is an exacerbation, a bringing up violently of the problem discussed above: can circuits of argument be connected from one context to another without reduction or paraphrase? Are apparently similar micrologies each time different? Chapters 3, 4 and 5 of this book have made connections between Derridean phrases which allow patterns of the unpresentable – the strange attractors – to be discerned, and which suggest ways in which negatives may be allowed to run under what is on the surface of the phrase. They have also shown that through the relation to the negative, through the 'yes and no' of some of his phrases, a way of writing is developed where there is as if an internal dissociation of language and thought played out without thematization. It is as if more is there than in the actual work performed by the words of the phrase.

Consistency and repetition

Poststructuralist 'strategies' have been said to be 'oriented toward the dismantling of stable conceptions of meaning, subjectivity, and identity', and Derrida has been incorporated into the developers of such strategies (Dews 1987: xi). I hope that this book has suggested in detailed fashion that there are in Derrida's work reworkings of conceptions of subjectivity, meaning and identity, among many others. Such ideas are not broken up, but rather revised. They are powerfully renewed. Yet historically the concepts mentioned have not been stable, as a reading of the Oxford English Dictionary entry under 'identity' will convince. The question then might become whether there is in Derrida's work an *orientation* towards a *dismantling* of stable conceptions as they are held in the late twentieth century. There can be no doubt that Derrida shows that much of what we think is haunted by the search for ground or origin. But whether the exhibiting of such a search is irresponsible, as is frequently implied against Derrida, may be doubted.

The ground of the investigation has to alter. I have tried to show that both in lexemes and in phrases, Derrida constructs effects of language which frequently allow something which acts as a negative to work under what is said. Yet the effect is not straight contradiction, but rather of the slight offbeat sense, which is not said but not left in silence either. It is as if there were a 'yes-no' which allows for the new, not as formulated but making space for future formulation. Neither 'force' nor 'meaning', the usual terms, can adequately cover what is pointing to that formulation. What Derrida develops from the circuits and syntax in his argument is not something which can be fully expressed in themes; the order and repetition it is presented in are part of its significance. So is what I have called its 'havering' quality. What one has is a pattern of thought whose recognition yields a new idea which is not yet thematized – an opening of lines, as the subtitle of this book suggests.

Lexemes, recurring in different texts, or whose function at any rate recurs ('chose', 'loi', 'différance', 'supplement'); micrologies or circuits of argument which are repeated or nearly, in different texts, serve to make Derrida's writings stand together: these supply a consistency which becomes a consistency of approach, or gait. On a larger scale, there is also what I have called the syntax of argument: the repeated concern with the imbrication of the transcendental and the empirical, and with the structure of paradox (or rather, of certain paradoxes, those of the infinite). Here, at the broadest scale, the importance of repetition is likewise striking. With all three functions, syntax, lexemes and circuits of argument, it is through recurrence that they come to the reader's attention.

Some of the examples I have discussed allow very similar phrases to be attached to lexemes or leading terms which are quite different. Take, for instance, a couple of phrases which are indicating a movement outside opposition: 'La trace ne serait pas le mixte, le passage entre la forme et l'a-morphe, la présence et l'absence, etc, mais ce qui, se dérobant à cette opposition, la rend possible depuis l'irréductible de son excès' (M, 206, note) ('The trace would not be the mixture, the transition between form and the amorphous, presence and absence, etc., but that which, by eluding this opposition, makes it possible in the irreducibility of its excess') (*M*, 172); or, 'la mobilité indécidable du fétiche, sa puissance d'excès par rapport à l'opposition (vrai/nonvrai, substitut/non-substitut, déni/affirmation etc)' (*Glas*, 236a) ('the undecidable mobility of the fetish, its power of excess in relation to the opposition (true/nontrue, substitute/nonsubstitute, denial/affirmation and so on)') (*Glas*, 211a). The context of these phrases, indeed their very vocabulary, is different; yet there is a circuit of argument recognizable, in the one case with regard to trace, in the other with regard to the undecidability of the fetish, connected with an 'excess' which, though not thematized by being picked out as what I have called a lexeme, is a crucial element in the way the instability of intellectual distinctions is studied (cf. Chapter 1).

Or take:

> Qu'est-ce que cette écriture nous apprend de l'essence du rire quand il rit parfois de l'essence, aux limites du calculable et de l'incalculable? Quand la totalité du calculable est déjouée par une écriture dont on ne sait plus décider si elle calcule encore, et mieux et plus, ou si elle transcende l'ordre même et l'économie d'un calcul, voire d'un indécidable qui serait encore homogène au monde du calcul?
>
> (UG, 51)

> And what does this writing teach us of the essence of laughter if it recalls that laughter to the limits of the calculable and the incalculable, when the whole of the calculable is outplayed by a writing about which it is no longer possible to decide if it still calculates, calculates better and more, or if it transcends the very order of calculable economy, or even of an incalculable of an undecidable which would still be homogeneous with the world of calculation?
>
> (*TWFJ*, 157–8)

which is close, without being repeated, to the phrase:

la plus géniale inventivité qui soit pour se préparer à l'accueillir [le venir de l'autre]: pour se préparer à affirmer l'aléa d'une rencontre qui non seulement ne soit plus calculable mais ne soit même pas un incalculable encore homogène au calculable, un indécidable encore en travail de décision.

(Psy, 60)

the most genial inventiveness is needed to prepare to welcome it; to affirm the chance of an encounter that not only is no longer calculable but is not even an incalculable factor still homogeneous with the calculable, not even an undecidable still caught up in the process of decision making.

('Inventions', 60)

The first is a question about the Joycean text and the nature of the laughter it evokes; the second an exploration of the aporia that the only possible invention (in the strong sense that the whole text, 'Inventions de l'autre', is striving to define) would be the invention of the impossible. But nevertheless both point to something heterogeneous to calculation, which in *Force of Law* is also called undecidable.

The incalculable is never subject to the ambiguity of a 'yes–no'. Yet this effect runs through much of Derrida's writing, which, the last two chapters of this book have suggested, sometimes yokes negative to positive in a trellis pattern of argument, or allows a contradiction to run under the surface of a phrase. Justice, Derrida says, is undeconstructible. It has the form of what I have called a 'strange attractor' in that it is not presentable, and it certainly cannot be calculated. But like the strange attractor, it has to provoke negotiation (Force, 62; *Force*, 28), a negotiation between the calculable and justice's incalculable. So the shape of Derrida's 'deconstruction' is ultimately not partitionary or negative, it is not operating an 'either/or'.

This book has been interested in a type of effect of repetition in Derrida's writing which allows a refrain which does not quite repeat, precisely refrains from doing so. It can be related to what above was called 'irony'. Such repetition becomes a 'metalangage sans surplomb' (Psy, 24) ('its metalanguage has nothing to set it off', or rather 'its metalanguage has nothing to enable it to gaze down') ('Inventions', 34, in a context dealing precisely with Paul de Man's account of irony). The closely similar circuits bring themselves to notice as such, as just that, similar, as well as innocent bearers of the argument. They act crucially in the way that Derrida gradually urges the text he is reading into the eddies of his own concerns, connecting in a flexible and powerful fashion its terms with his own, its micrologies with his: take for instance 'To speculate – on "Freud"', where we pass from an account of the psychic apparatus in *The Interpretation of Dreams* to Chapter 5 of *Beyond the Pleasure Principle*, where there is implied but not explicited a negotiation between the primary and the secondary processes in their purity:

Une zone médiane, *différante ou indifférente* (et elle ne peut être différante qu'en étant indifférente à la différence oppositionnelle ou distinctive des deux bords)...une *zone*, autrement dit une *ceinture*...ni serrée ni desserrée *absolument*, toute en différance de stricture.

(CP, 373)

A median, differing or indifferent zone (and it is differing only by being indifferent to the oppositional or distinctiive difference of the two borders)...a zone, in other words a belt...neither tightened nor loosened *absolutely*, everything *en différance de stricture*.

(*PC*, 351)

Derrida here leans on the 'stricture' of *Glas*, and *Truth in Painting*, and urges Freud towards it, since a reading of Freud's account of the fetish and its excluded middle has lead into the emergence of 'stricture' in *Glas*. As Derrida says in an amusing analogy, the cyst, the blister of meta-language, forms with any systematization. But it is soon burst again (*Glas*, 186b, 165b). Derrida resists the mastery of commentary, the commenting on a text from a great height. His outworking and outweaving allow filaments to form from his own texts to others: his work is neither citation nor apparently innocuous objectivity: if the deconstructionist trawls for unmeant senses, his own work is trailing possibilities for connection which allow future commentaries to proceed out of the projections. The work is consistent owing to effects of writing as well as to effects of argument. And the effects of writing, by working out patterns which are common to a series of thoughts, allow the reader a perception which is not what has already been recognized, but which is sensed as moving out into ideas which cannot be thematized immediately but which are entering our cognizance.

In the allowance for effects of writing, there is room allowed for the unconscious. The originality of what has here been called irony, the reshaping of meta-language, is precisely that a relation to the unconscious in language is made room for.

Peur parce que sans cesse le cheval que j'enfourche, le texte, la force textuelle sur laquelle je monte doit être plus forte que moi, ne pas se laisser dominer, dompter, maîtriser par le mors qu'elle a que je lui mets ou que je lui prends dans la bouche.

(JA, 12)

Fear because incessantly the horse I am astride, the text, the textual force on which I am mounted must be stronger than I am in order not to let itself be dominated, tamed, mastered by the bit that it has, that I put on it, or that I take from him in the mouth.

(JA, 12, my translation)

'Reconduire l'effet de loi à une instance qu'un sujet ne saurait maîtriser' ('Entre crochets', 107) ('Bring back the effect of the law to a factor which a subject would not know how to master') (my translation). This is allowing language to have its head as it were. Elsewhere, à propos Nietzsche, he gradually suggests that the apparent persiflage of the Nietzschean pronouncements on women is not 'infinite mastery', not transcendental irony, in the terms of the present book. On the contrary, the parody 'suppose toujours quelque part une naïveté, adossée à un inconscient, et le vertige d'une non-maîtrise, une perte de connaissance' (Epérons, 78) ('No, somewhere parody always supposes a naivety withdrawing into an unconscious, a vertiginous non-mastery. Parody supposes a loss of consciousness') (*Spurs*, 79). Language is the incalculable, in this perspective, and parody allows some kind of access to it.

Coda

Derrida's circuits, the programmes attached to lexemes, are local but also extensible: what they are not is universally valid forms, systems of relations outside any linguistic or historical situation, and the deliberate alteration of vocabulary, its occasionally highly invested nature, forces this recognition. These circuits cannot form themselves into a meta-language, or at least not for any length of time. Indeed, the very lexical recklessness of some ('double invagination chiasmatique', for instance) was no doubt intended to warn of this. But that does not mean that there cannot be rigour in the undertaking. Derrida's extreme attention to the complexities and confines of language, his careful working with the strange structures the infinite appears to induce in our thought (the 'strange attractors'), provide rigour; the tacit acknowledgement of the complexities, the urging of them into forms of consistency, occur through the way he writes.

Writing, Derrida tells us Hyppolite had suggested, might act as a subjectless transcendental field (subjectless because the emitter like a reader could always be absent, OG, 84; *OG*, 88.) Such an absence, however, Derrida points out, is for Husserl factical; writing is haunted by the ghost of a virtual intentionality who could read it, but a particular subject does not have to be there. However, I have tried to show in the final chapter of this book that Derrida's writing uses methods to make this distinction not impossible, but less secure. The methods are, some of them, related to surrealist techniques. Their interest in his work is that they cannot be put down to the account of 'literature'. They do have a 'philosophic' effect. We have seen that some of Derrida's phrases allow their sense to move between positive and negative, capable of both. They develop their sense as if within themselves, and the reader does experience a disarray from what is contradiction even if it is also allowing the sense of a new thought. For instance, in examining the phrase 'la *tekhné* n'arrive pas à la langue ou au poème' (CP, 207) ('tekhne does not happen to language or to the poem') (*PC*, 192) he points out that the phrase might mean 'doesn't get there', which would make the exception of the language and literature, or that it doesn't just happen, it is always already there.[44] Derrida is concerned to protect the new, to allow for the incomplete.

This allowing room for the new means, then, that sense in and for Derrida cannot be only thematic sense (the translatable is a mark of thematic sense, as is the possibility of summary). In his work repetition, order, development within a sense which is different – all give the possibility of meaning which is not ready to go, which has to be worked on and worked out. The picking out of patterns like those which in this book have been called 'circuits of argument' enables a meaning which goes beyond the thematic sense of the circuit. Such a meaning is new but perhaps not yet thematizable.

In this, Derrida's writing is exploring something that is not a matter of technique and manipulation, because language does not rivet us to identity, and yet the technique, which is there in language, tends to do so (CP, 207; *PC*, 192). We have thus to allow for what makes for part of meaning but which is not yet verbalized. We can, by thinking over what is said, get abreast with it, so to speak, but even so are conscious of what is not fully associated with the words.[45]

> Man has the impulse to run up against the limits of language. . . . This running-up-against Kierkegaard also recognized and even designated it in a quite similar way (as running-up against Paradox). This running up against the limits of language is *Ethics*.
>
> (Wittgenstein 1989: 80, a remark about Heidegger)

Notes

Introduction

1 There is, or was, a UK record company called Deconstruction.
2 The first to point out the quality of Derrida's writing is, to my knowledge, Jean Genet, in a letter published in *Lettres françaises* (Genet 1972). I owe this reference to Ian Magedera.

Chapter 1

1 Translations where the entry in the bibliography mentions none are my own, or by Marianne Ronflé-Nadaud (marked MRN); modifications are my own in every case.

   In the passage quoted as epigraph to the chapter, Blanchot is alluding to structuralism. The transcendental is here presented as a grid of relations. The grid is differential (it does not unify) and is determining (the elements in the grid are determined from out of their differences). Blanchot argues in this article that humankind, far from having been expelled from the new, structuralist, human sciences – Lévi-Straussian anthropology, Foucauldian history – as was the then current accusation, has been implicitly integrated into them, as a formalized set of operations which shape the objects studied. (Blanchot's article is in fact a kind of recommendation of a 'sort' (EI, 392) of humanism, one pared down into cry or protestation.) The final chapter of this book will look, in relation to Derrida, at a similar possibility, that of a 'subjectless transcendental field' conceived not as a set of determining operations, but as writing.

2 The text Derrida translated appears as 'Annexe III', in *Husserliana VI* (1954), The Hague: Martinus Nijhoff, 365–86. According to note 1 in this text, the title seems to have been given to Husserl's work by E. Fink.
3 Stanley Rosen (1969), discussing *différence* in relation to linguistic philosophy, makes of it an operation combining both affirmation and negation (52). Deleuze develops a shadowy logic round difference, by making it a kind of negation, and repetition a kind of logical identity (Deleuze 1968: 1).
4 'Being is different than beings, and only this difference in general, this possibility of distinction, ensures an understanding-of-being. . . . We thus term this distinction that first enables something like an understanding-of-being the *ontological difference*' (Heidegger, MFL, 151–2) (lecture given in Marburg, summer 1928).
5 Heidegger has a series of careful and important distinctions round the 'fact'. 'Factical' (not 'factual' nor 'actual') can often be translated as 'as a matter of fact'.
6 Merleau-Ponty (1968), in his *Collège de France* lectures of 1952–60, had spoken of a certain 'gap' ('écart') necessary for meaning (1968: 12), a term Derrida will use, in harness with *différance* and *trace*. More generally, he had spoken of an 'attempt to

take into account the finitude of consciousness' (*ibid.*: 11). In particular, the lecture notes in a section on Descartes point to thought's necessarily 'coming after' being (*ibid.*: 98), which might be related to what Derrida will call the 'originary delay of thought over being' ('le retard originaire de la pensée sur l'être').

7 Kristeva's *intertextuality* is the necessary correlative of the 'death of the author'. The group of writers associated with the review *Tel Quel* (Kristeva, Sollers and Goux) were instrumental in forging this moment. Barthes and Derrida could be said to be with but not of the group. Their materialism, their canon of writers – Bataille, Blanchot, Artaud, Roussel – marked it. They were interested in China, and their information about the Chinese discussion of the probable effects of a switch of writing systems from the traditional ideograms to the PingYing romanization is mentioned obliquely in *Of Grammatology.*

8 The influence of linguistics seeped beyond language study through Jakobson, his work on literature and his mediation of the work of the Russian formalists. He had a profound effect on the anthropologist Lévi-Strauss, and on the work of Roland Barthes, who did not merely develop methods for textual analysis based on structuralist linguistics, but in a seminal way brought together the study of ideology with the study of signs, and claimed that all of cultural life could be treated as a general sign system (see Moriarty 1991).

9 See for example G, 128–9 (*G*, 86–7) and its note 35 where the end of the epoch of linear writing and of the book is proclaimed, not in the sense of 'end' as 'finish', but in the sense analysed by Simon Critchley (1992) as 'closure'.

10 The problem I have here is that the powerful diagnostic tool, hierarchized opposition, is not liftable out of the circumstances in which Derrida developed it (because that goes against his work's extreme attention to context); at the same time, if it is not taken out, the homology between the various pairs becomes frail.

11 Pattee refers to the work of the great mathematician Emil Post. With both Pattee in regard to Derrida, and Post in relation to concerns developed later in this book (he worked in particular on the problems of undecidability and unsolvability in logical systems), the time frame is relevant.

12 There is a submerged suggestion, it seems to me, in these passages of Dummett's work, that we in practice use realist notions of truth (presumably by some kind of passage to the limit which has been built into language [FPL, 468]) though we cannot in practice justify them.

13 Rodolphe Gasché (1986) has discussed the relation between Husserl's *Abbau*, Heidegger's *Destruktion* and Derrida's *déconstruction* (111–14). Compare Kant's 'architectonic' – 'the art of *constructing* systems' (KRV, A832, B860, my italics). 'Deconstruction' has become – without acknowledgement – a standard translation of Heidegger's *Destruktion* and *kritischer Abbau*, see MFL, translator's note, 27. One could argue that something of what Derrida's philosophical writing is concerned with is the danger and consequences of this kind of translation (cf. Derrida, CP, 285; PC, 267).

14 It is striking that only a little later than these works of Heidegger, Rudolf Carnap's logical positivism proclaimed the 'overcoming of metaphysics' and famously used examples from Heidegger's *Was ist Metaphysik?* (1929) to show that they could not be turned into logical–syntactically well formed sentences (Carnap 1932). It is conceivable that Carnap chose Heidegger, because he had known of Heidegger's reversal of Bertrand Russell's thesis that Leibniz' ontology was in some sense at least derived from his logic (see Kneale 1971: 323; and Heidegger, MFL, 28 note 3). Carnap seems to have known Heidegger's work more than superficially: he chooses it, he says, because of its strong influence (see Chapter 4 note 9). The probable link between them is the logician Oskar Becker. Carnap is tolerant of Nietzsche because what he wrote was 'literature'.

15 Perhaps in Kristeva's tone there is the triumph of having reached it, and in Derrida's a Moses-like never-entering it.

16 Though as discerning a reader as Sam Weber thinks it necessary as a kind of Archimedean point, where the lever may rest to move the world.

17 I gesture here to realist theories of truth and meaning which ultimately need the language of the angels, and God's knowledge, as ways of thinking of wordless language. (See Dummett 1993: 10–11, quoting Frege, *Posthumous Writings*. Dummett's account in FPL seems to suggest that this 'trap' is unavoidable, see note 12 above.)

18 Derrida has said '*Il faut* la vérité' ('*we must have* truth') (P, 80 note; *P*, 58 note 32); but this truth, which is probably not multivalued in his thinking, is certainly not used as some unique absolute.

19 The 'tu quoque' turns a thinker or speaker's arguments against him or herself. Its forensic context, together with its modern form of the logical paradox and the double bind, can, like the Aristotelian *antikategorein*, be both logical and rhetorical, a question of proper predication and a question of turning of arguments against their origin.

20 Cf. Tugendhat, who argues, à propos the same philosophers, that Heidegger in examining the presuppositions built in to the *Lebenswelt* (the lived world) has to move beyond the transcendental perspective of Husserl, a movement which is not, however, a falling back into a pre-transcendental position (Tugendhat 1965: 255).

21 My translation of Husserl, *L'Origine de la géométrie*, trans. Derrida, 1962, 203.

22 The relation to the work of the great historian of medicine, Georges Canguilhem, is clear though largely implicit in this consideration of the role of the pathological.

23 Expressed for example by the fact that any possibility between '1' for certainty and '0' for impossibility in some formalizations of probability theory is written as a fraction.

24 Derrida is deliberately coupling together in some of this list what much of philosophy has considered polar opposites.

25 See 'Can an effect precede its cause?' in Michael Dummett (1978), where it is argued (329) that 'an event can be counted as a sufficient condition of a previous event only in cases where the later event can be called "the means of finding out whether the earlier event had occurred"'. Here, as in Freud, the point of departure for tracing cause is in effect the cause, since through it past event is discerned.

26 See Taylor's powerful analysis of the relation between behaviourism and linear punctual time; causes must be separately identifiable from effects (hence the insistence on punctual time, ensuring separability) so that 'for the sake of' is not a valid connection between one behaviour pattern and another (Taylor 1964). The typical behaviourist criticism of explanation of behaviour through intention is that the effect becomes part of the cause. The similarities and differences in Taylor's and Derrida's relation of cause and effect are probably linked to Merleau-Ponty's teaching and influence and the different relations to phenomenology implied in his earlier and later work.

27 For problems with this account, see Hobson 1982.

28 The inflection on Derrida's texts during their reception in the US is here particularly visible. This was the first text by Derrida translated into English, and the one by which his work first came to American attention. For the history of the translation of 'jeu' in this passage as 'free' play, which relates it to the spontaneity of the Kantian free play of the judgement rather than to the play in a machine, see Hobson 1986.

29 Saussure's work on general linguistics is principally known through lecture notes taken by his pupils (the *Cours de linguistique générale*). This has to be complemented by his own notes, published by René Godel, and by the edition of Tullio di Mauro, as well as by the previously unpublished material appearing in the *Cahiers Ferdinand de Saussure*.

30 This is another of the micrologies, the circuits of discourse, which function in the construction of his argument (see Chapters 3 and 5).

31 Rodolphe Gasché calls such terms 'infrastructures'. This word is not particularly Derridean and has a hierarchical sense which detracts from its pertinence. 'Transcendental' has to take its meaning within the specific philosophical terms of reference set by each thinker

32 This has become clearer still with the publication of his thesis for the then *diplôme d'études supérieures, le problème de la genèse dans la philosophie de husserl* (1990b).

33 Cf. Alféri 1989: 15–28.

34 'When I speak, I am always exercising a power relation, I belong, whether I know it or not, to a network of powers which I use, fighting against the power which is being affirmed against me. Any speech is violence, violence all the more awesome that it is secret, and the counter-secret of violence, violence which can be exercised already on what the word names and what it cannot name except by removing its presence – a sign, as we have seen, that death speaks (this death which is power) when I speak. At the same time, we know that when we are arguing, we are not fighting. Language is the enterprise through which violence accepts to be not open, but secret' (Blanchot, EI, 60, article dating from 1959, my translation).

35 This is a traditional materialist argument about the nature, and indeed often the invention, of writing. Lévi-Strauss' view of the power of intellectuals here is a version of the eighteenth-century materialist d'Holbach's account of priestly power.

36 In an aparté, Foucault is said to be treating 'folie', which is a term, like any other, subject to extreme historical variation and 'borrowed from an unverifiable reserve' (ED, 66; WD, 41, trans. mod.) as if it were stable and invariant (ED, 65; WD, 40–1); in fact, as covering all that could be described as negativity.

37 Foucault's reply (1972) takes up the argument over the exacerbation of doubt and assumes feedback, so that the doubting subject does not undo the work of the medi-tating subject. He insists on a mutual action in the process of meditation between the different versions of the enunciating subject: it is when 'doubting subject' and 'medi-tating subject' can be simultaneously active that the Cogito works, and I can be, even if I doubt, because I think that I doubt; but this excludes madness because it would not be possible 'to remain qualified as a subject conducting rationally his meditation through doubt to an eventual truth' (Foucault 1972: 21). In other words, the whole process of methodic doubt is impossible. It must always assume what it seeks to prove: 'that which characterizes the actuality of the meditating subject' is in fact what convinces me of the rational character of my understanding. The meditating subject can become doubting subject only through the example of dreaming, because there actuality can be doubted and simultaneously the self can validly continue a medita-tion. (Foucault seems to assume what he wants to prove: the subject at work on itself – his definition of meditation – has to be a continuous underlay to the meditation; therefore madness is rejected. But this assumes that sanity and meditation are co-terminous, whereas the whole point of hyperbolic doubt is to suggest that they are not, no more than not-dreaming, or not being victim of a trick played by an evil genius.)

38 Here Derrida implicitly links his defence of Descartes with his work on Artaud, Bataille and the *poètes-fous*.

39 This 'réduction à l'intra-mondanité' ('reduction to intraworldliness') (ED, 88; WD, 57) is being related to phenomenology (cf. ED, 93; WD, 60). Husserl is said to relate more and more the theme of normality to that of the transcendental reduction; in other words, Husserl more and more thinks of the reduction as a movement towards certitude via normalization of the fuzziness of the empirical, though of course the phenomenological reduction is the reduction of and not to mundanity.

40 'L'Etre étant histoire [pour Heidegger], il *n'est pas* hors de la différence et se produit donc originairement comme violence (non éthique), comme dissimulation de soi dans son propre dévoilement' (ED, 220) ('Since Being is history [for Heidegger] it is *not* outside difference, and thus, it originally occurs as (nonethical) violence, as dissimulation of itself in its own unveiling') (*WD*, 148).

41 As a result, as Tugendhat (1970: 198) points out, empirical and transcendental are not, as they are with Kant, totally opposed.

42 *Dasein* is the term Heidegger uses to avoid the anthropological implications of 'man' and the psychological one of 'subject'.

43 Heidegger uses a neologism *Überschwung*, a hybrid word between *überschwenglich* (rapturous) and *sich schwingen* (to leap, vault over), to express this transcendence which leaps above and withdraws at the same time: 'Die *Transzendenz ist entsprechend den beiden Weisen des Grundens überschwingend-entziehend zumal*' (GA, 9, 167, original italics) ('transcendence is corresponding to the double nature of the foundation vaulting over and drawing back at the same time') (my translation).

44 This is not a criticism of a very fine article. Williams refers to Dummett on Wittgenstein, and the substitution of assertion conditions for truth conditions, the point of which is to accommodate a non-realist view of truth, where precisely a determinate utterance is only possible within a finite set of meanings which can determine it.

45 Compare a possible nontemporal version of this: 'Tout concept qui prétend à quelque rigueur implique l'alternative du "tout ou rien"' (LI, 211) ('Every concept that lays claim to any rigor whatsoever implies the alternative "all or nothing"') (*LI*, 116).

46 Descartes, *Meditatio tertia* (1647) I, 201. For the history of the two notions, see Moore 1990, to whom I am much indebted in what follows.

47 Smith (1923), when tracing the different chronological layers in Kant's text, argues that the section giving the nature of the solution to the trancendental problems of reason – that it can never be found in experience and that the Ideas of Reason (Kantian Ideas) exhaust their inherent meaning in their empirical reference – is earlier than the constructive uses of the Ideas of Reason (1923: 500).

48 Gadamer (1977) relates Kantian ideas to neo-Kantianism rather than to Kant himself.

49 As in the commentary on Foucault, Derrida shows how this Idea is both condition and example for Husserl; it is at once general and 'European' (OG, 120; *OG*, 114).

50 Kisiel shows that with facticity, Heidegger adapts a neo-Kantian term, giving it a radically different sense. Cf. note 45 (Kisiel 1993: 116).

51 I have adopted the translation by Boyce Gibson of the Husserl passage, not that of *Origin of Geometry*.

52 Derrida points out the role the infinite plays for Husserl in clearing a difficulty (Genèse, 100, note).

53 It should perhaps be emphasized that for Derrida, Husserl is the most rigorous thinker of objectivity.

54 Jakobson 1971: 132.

55 Derrida in a sense works with and develops the setting up of the problem by Cavaillès (1947, written during the war), and his criticism of Kant. Kant had used already-constituted transcendental subject, and already-constituted objects (OG, 25; *OG*, 42); Husserl's work is moving beyond this.

56 I cannot agree with Geoff Bennington (1988) that *différance* 'just is the postponement to infinity of the Kantian Idea' (105). There is a further complication, in that the postponement is stepwise, a series of looping failed advances. For infinity (totality of determinations) is inaccessible because unintuitable, and yet it is this that would guarantee the consistency of experience; infinity is approachable through form, each

step being finite, but the extensions of these steps to infinity is paradoxical, part of a regulated possibility which cannot justify itself and which neglects its own finitude.

57 Poincaré 1905, quoted by Kneale (1971: 656): 'Il n'y a point d'infini actuel. Les Cantoriens l'ont oublié et ils sont tombés dans la contradiction' ('There is no actual infinite. The Cantorians forgot this and fell into contradiction'). Cf. a letter from the great nineteenth-century mathematician Gauss: 'In mathematics infinite magnitude may never be used as something final; infinity is only a *façon de parler*' (Fraenkel 1966: 1).

58 In set theory as now usually practised, or at least taught, a universe of discourse is set up, within which the theory is to apply, and an axiom of choice instituted, which allows the selection of one object from each of the mutually disjoint subsets of the set under consideration; in other words, the context is carefully defined, and it is accepted that the act which starts the manipulation has to be justified by a separate axiom (see Fraenkel 1966: 34–5).

59 This can be shown in many different ways; for instance, by reference to the work of Oskar Becker on 'mathematical existence', which was published in the same volume of the *Jahrbuch für Philosophie* as *Sein und Zeit* and which is quoted by Heidegger in different places. They (had) both belonged to the circle round Husserl (Hobson 1993).

60 'All the truisms of general logic are accessible to us, but there is no procedure by which for any given formula we can make sure of deciding within a finite number of steps, whether or not it is a truism. That is to say, however long the time we have spent in systematic but unsuccessful search, a proof may yet be found' (Kneale 1971: 737).

61 This is especially clear in *Genèse*, 169 note 89:

> Au lieu de dévoiler la conscience absolue d'une finitude essentielle, il donne par idéalisme un contenu concret à un indéfini. C'est ici que se fait le partage entre l'idéalisme Husserlien et une philosophie de l'existence. Celle-ci partant à la fois de la possibilité ou de la nécessité existentielle de la mort et de l'idée d'une possibilité indéfinie du temps, nous conduit à conjuguer l'impossibilité du possible et la possibilité de l'impossibilité.

> Instead of unveiling the absolute consciousness of an essential finitude, idealism makes him [Husserl] give a concrete content to an indefinite. This is the dividing point between Husserlian idealism and a philosophy of existence. The latter, starting out both from the possibility or the existential necessity of death and from the idea of an indefinite possibility of time, leads us to link the impossibility of the possible and the possibility of the impossibility.

> (my translation)

62 Impossibility, not mere absence; the Heideggerian relation between what will act as subject and what as object is built into the use of the idea of possible.

63 The naming of death, the resoluteness in its face, appears then as an elision of death, whose function in this aporia repeats its function in other aporias. The relation of this aporia to the work of Oskar Becker on reiterated modalities is striking.

64 Derrida returns, as has been indicated, briefly to this at different points in his works: cf. for instance *Aporias* on Heideggerian mortality; see also Göbel 1984; Peddle 1980; Wolff 1981; and for a French account of the relation between the Hegelian dialectic and Kant, Guéroult 1977.

Chapter 2

1 Cf. Bennington and Derrida 1991: 248 *et seq.*

2 Kant, *Metaphysische Anfangsgründe der Naturwissenschaft*, quoted Heidegger, BP, 324. Kant, in refining what he means by *a priori*, gives as an example of a lax use of the term a judgement which brings in the conditional perfect, that is, the tense expressing the unreal, what is merely there in possibility: 'Thus we would say of a man who undermined the foundations of his house, that he might have known a priori that it would fall, that is, that he need not have waited for the experience of its actual falling' (KRV, introduction §1). It is lax because we would still have had to know from experience that unsupported heavy bodies fall.

3 Cf. Heidegger, BP, §22, 324–6.

4 Again, Derrida applies the term 'racine graphématique' ('graphematic root') to the difficulty Austin says he has in separating out performative and constative use of language (M, 388 note 10; *M* 325 note 14) .

5 In later work Derrida will relate this to the chora of Plato's *Timaeus* (Derrida 1993a). That the *a priori* is endowed with some kind of privilege by this, even if that privilege is not logical priority, seems clear. Cf. Lloyd 1990.

6 Cf. Freud 1923, 'Une nérvose démoniaque au XVIIe siècle', quoted Kofman 1974: 174.

7 Derrida relates it linguistically to the Heideggerian *Gleichheit* (likeness), which is not identity: 'Cette double participation . . . ne mélange pas deux éléments préablement séparés, elle renvoie au même qui n'est pas identique . . . au medium de toute dissociation possible' (D, 145) ('This double participation . . . does not mix together two previously separated elements; it refers back to a *same* that is not the identical, to the common element or medium of any possible dissociation') (*D*, 127). Cf. Heidegger, ID, 10, translating the Eleatic stranger of the *Sophist*, 251d: 'Nun ist doch von ihnen jeder der beiden ein anderes, selber jedoch ihm selbst dasselbe' ('now is then each of the two something different, nevertheless himself the very same thing to himself') (my translation). Derrida denies that the *pharmakon* is a Cusean *coincidentia oppositorum*, but cf. Nicholas of Cusa, in Hübener 1971: 123.

8 As suggested at the end of the preceding chapter, empirical events would then be held to be transcendental; the inauguration of logic as transcendental was an historical act.

9 'Le lien vraiment divin, qui unit entre elles les parties de la vertu' (D, 144) ('This most godlike bond [that] unite[s] the elements of virtue') (*D*, 126) quoting Plato, *Politics*, 310a.

10 Le mouvement de la différance, en tant qu'il produit les différents, en tant qu'il différencie, est donc la racine commune de toutes les oppositions de concepts qui scandent notre langage . . . sensible/intelligible, intuition/signification. . . . En tant que racine commune, la différance est aussi l'élément du *même* (qu'on distingue de l'identique) dans lequel ces oppositions s'annoncent.

(P, 17)

The movement of *différance*, as that which produces different things, that which differentiates, is the common root of all the oppositional concepts that mark our language . . . sensible/intelligible, intuition/signification. . . . As a common root, *différance* is also the element of the *same* (to be distinguished from the identical) in which these oppositions are announced.

(*P*, 9)

'La trace ne serait pas le mixte, le passage entre la forme et l'a-morphe . . . mais ce qui, se dérobant à cette oposition, la rend possible depuis l'irréductible de son excès'

(M, 206 note 14) ('The trace would not be the mixture, the transition between form and the amorphous . . . but that which, by eluding this opposition, makes it possible in the irreducibility of its excess') (*M*, 172 note 16).

11 'L'eidos, la vérité, la loi ou l'*épistémé*, la dialectique, la philosophie, tels sont les autres noms du *pharmakon* qu'il faut opposer au *pharmakon* des sophistes et à la crainte envoûtante de la mort' (D, 142) ('The *eidos*, truth, law, the *episteme*, dialectics, philosophy – all these are other names for that *pharmakon* that must be opposed to the *pharmakon* of the Sophists and to the bewitching fear of death') (*D*, 124).

12 Cf. Kojève 1947: 486 note:

> It seems then necessary to distinguish at the heart of the dialectical ontology of revealed being or of mind dominated by the totality a non-dialectical ontology of Nature (dominated by identity) which was inspired by the Greeks and by tradition, and a dialectical ontology (inspired by Hegel, but modfied consequently) of Man or of History (dominated by negativity) . . . since Kant, Heidegger seems the first to have posed the problem of a double ontology.
>
> (my translation)

13 Cf. *Genèse*, 8:

> L'existence de toute genèse semble avoir pour sens cette tension entre une transcendance et une immanence. Elle se donne d'abord comme indéfini ontologique ou temporel et commmencement absolu, continuité et discontinuité, identité et altérité. Cette dialectique . . . est à la fois la possibilité d'une continuité de la continuité et de la discontinuité, d'une identité de l'identité et de l'altérité.

> The existence of all genesis seems to have as a meaning this tension between a transcendence and an immanence. It first gives itself as an ontological or temporal indefinite and absolute beginning, continuity and discontinuity, identity and otherness. This dialectic . . . is at the same time the possibility of a continuity of continuity and of discontinuity, of an identity of identity and otherness.
>
> (trans. MRN)

14 'Il s'agit de re-marquer . . . une nervure, un pli, un angle qui interrompent la totalisation: en un certain lieu, lieu d'une forme bien déterminée, aucune série de valences sémantiques ne peut plus se fermer ou se rassembler' (P, 62–3) ('It is a question of re-marking a nerve, a fold, an angle that interrupts totalization: in a certain place, a place of well-determined form, no series of semantic valences can any longer be closed or reassembled') (*P*, 46).

15 The phrase, and its rewritten version, are:
'Ce rôle, moins qu'un millier de lignes, qui le lit comprendra les règles ainsi que placé devant un tréteau, leur dépositaire humble' (1891). 'Moins qu'un millier de lignes, le rôle, *qui le lit*, tout de suite comprend les règles comme placé devant un tréteau, leur dépositaire humble' (1897) (D, 255).

'This role, less than a thousand lines, whoever reads it will comprehend the rules as if placed before the stageboards, their humble depository' (1891). 'Less than a thousand lines, the role, the one that reads, will instantly comprehend the rules as if placed before the stageboards, their humble depository' (1897) (*D*, 225).

Mallarmé, in the later version, by altering the word order, has made it possible to interpret the role as reading the mime, as well as the mime, or any other reader, as reading the role.

16 Cf. Dällenbach 1977.

17 It would, in fact, enable a thinking through of a standard critical problem (the relation between texts) though it has never been developed by those who claim to use deconstructionist methods, perhaps because it entails extremely minute attention to tiny variations of texts within a filiation.

18 *Blanc* has an ancestor in *Of Grammatology: espacement. Espacement* picks up Heidegger's work on space and time in *Kant and the Problem of Metaphysics*, on the very root of the distinction between passive reception of experience and active synthesis:

> Le rapport entre la passivité et la différence ne se distingue pas du rapport entre *l'inconscience* fondamentale du langage (comme enracinement dans la langue) et *l'espacement* (pause, blanc, ponctuation, intervalle en général, etc) qui constitue l'origine de la signification.
>
> (G, 99)

> The relationship between passivity and difference cannot be distinguished from the relationship between the fundamental *unconsciouness* of language (as rootedness within the language) and the *spacing* (pause, blank, punctuation, interval in general, etc.) which constitutes the origin of signification.
>
> (G, 68)

Just as 'trace' brings with it the 'devenir immotivé du signe' so *espacement* is the 'devenir inconscient du signe': they both refer to what *cannot* be made completely present.

19 Selon la structure de supplémentarité, ce qui s'ajoute serait donc toujours un blanc ou un pli: l'addition le cède à une sorte de division ou de soustraction multipliée qui s'enrichit de zéros en s'essoufflant vers l'infini, le plus et le moins n'étant séparés/unis que par l'infime inconsistance, le presque rien de l'hymen.

> (D, 294)

> According to the structure of supplementarity, what is added is thus always a blank or a fold: the fact of addition gives way to a kind of multiple division or substraction that enriches itself with zeros as it races breathlessly toward the infinite. 'More' and 'less' are only separated/united by the infinitesimal inconsistency, the next-to-nothing of the hymen.
>
> (D, 262)

20 'The dice throw will never abolish chance because it contains chance in its practical essence; yet however the player performs an act, he throws the dice in a certain way, he reacts in one way or another to the numbers that come up and tries, in the following moment to use his good or bad luck' (Sartre 1971–2,. I: 60, referring to Mallarmé; see also Sartre 1977 [1952]: preface).

21 My discussion of this owes much to Frank 1983. Howells (1993) has discussed the attitude to the subject but not in relation to language.

22 The relation between the practice of perspective and Cartesian epistemology was explored by Panofsky (1975), in his work on perspective as a symbolic form. It is likely that there is a link between Panofsky and Heidegger's work round the subject of the subject (Hobson 1992).

23 'Transcendental illusion . . . does not cease even after it has been detected and its invalidity clearly revealed by transcendental criticism. . . . We therefore take the subjective necessity of a connection of our concepts, which is to the advantage of the understanding, for an objective necessity in the determination of things in themselves' (KRV, A297, B353); and, important in the line of the developing argument of

this book, Kant relates this to the tension between absolute infinity and potential infinity, between the assumption that the infinite totality of conditions is given and the thinking of a series in the process of becoming, rather than presupposed in its completion.

24 Pointed out by Manfred Frank (1983).

25 The phrase deliberately and parodistically echoes Pascal: 'Par l'espace, l'univers me comprend et m'engloutit comme un point: par la pensée je le comprends' (Pascal 1962: 67).

26 Dissemination in Heidegger's *Sein und Zeit* was applied to Dasein's facticity (SZ, 56; BT, 82), for Dasein always already had been split up into determinate ways of Being in the world.

27 See Rorty 1991 for discussions of this question and Derrida, in Mouffe 1996.

28 'There lives in [some ancient and modern poems] a real transcendental buffoonery. In the inside, the mood which looks out over everything and lifts itself up endlessly over everything which is limited, even over its own art, virtue or genius; on the outside, in the execution, the mimic manner of the averagely good Italian clown' (F. Schlegel, in Schmitt 1975: 102, my translation). Cf. Kierkegaard 1830: 19, where though the ironic totality is 'infinitely bottomless' (a paradoxical phrase), it is indivisible.

29 Frank (1972) and now Bowie (1996). Szondi's work on irony and utopia (1964) might be related to the idea expressed by Derrida in Mouffe 1996 that there is a messianic structure that belongs to all language.

30 I would suggest, but cannot develop here, that this form of irony could be related for instance to writing techniques in Kafka and perhaps Babel.

31 'Je crois qu'un texte comme *Glas* n'est ni un texte philosophique, ni un texte poétique, il circule entre ces deux genres . . . ou, si on veut à tout prix définir des genres, on pourrait historiquement renvoyer à la satire ménipée, à l'"anatomie" (telle *l'Anatomy of Melancoly*), à un genre comme parodie philosophique, où tous les genres sont convoqués à la fois, la poésie, la philosophie, le théâtre' (OA, 186) ('Think that a text like *Glas* is neither philosphic nor poetic. It circulates between these two genres . . . [or] if one insists on defining genres at all costs, one could refer historically to Menippean satire, to "anatomy" (as in *The Anatomy of Melancholy*), or to something like philosophic parody where all the genres – poetry, philosophy, theatre, etc – are summoned up at once') (*EO*, 141).

32 'In short blind chance brought about the strangest connections and frequently coupled persons and things the most heterogeneous; things so opposite in their nature and qualitites that no man alive would ever have thought of joining them together' (*New Foundling Hospital for Wit II*, new edn, 1784, London: J. Debrett, 237–8).

33 I owe these references to Rose (1979) who is very perceptive on parody. See also Riha 1971.

34 The function of the distinction is to reconquer for semantics what Leibniz' rule of the substitutability of different names for the same entity *salva veritate* had lost (Angelelli 1967: 51). In a letter to Husserl of 24 May 1891, Frege argues that in poetic use of language, expressions do not need reference, but they must have sense. Angelelli interestingly uses one possible translation of *Bedeutung* (reference) as 'importance' to suggest what lies behind Frege's distinction. Frege himself says 'For the poetic use it is enough that everything has a sense, for the scientific [use] references must not be lacking' (Frege 1976: 35, letter to Husserl, May 24, 1891, my translation). Gareth Evans (1992) suggests that Frege introduced the distinction to accommodate literature.

35 Cf. 'Although it can also be identified in other ways, a thought or a sense generally, is something that can be used to identify itself, precisely because it can be expressed;

and it can be expressed because it is already a means of identification, although, in the first instance, a means of identifying, not itself but its referent' (FOP, 311).

36 It has been argued that Dummett's reduction of the hierarchy of indirect speech occurs one level too early.

37 Cf. what is said about Levinas: 'Nous nous prenons sans fin dans le réseau des guillemets. . . . Nous ne savons même plus comment citer son "oeuvre" dès lors qu'elle cite déjà, entre guillemets, toute la langue, la française, l'occidentale, et même au delà'. (Psy, 186) ('We endlessly get caught up in the network of quotation marks. . . . We no longer even know how to quote his "work" any longer, since it already quotes, under quotation marks, the whole language – French, Western, and even beyond') ('At this very moment', 33–4).

38 'Ce dont nous avons besoin, c'est de déterminer *autrement* selon un système différentiel, les *effets* d'idéalité de signification, de sens et de référence' (P, 90) ('What we need is to determine *otherwise*, according to a differential system, the *effects* of ideality, of signification, of meaning, and of reference') (*P*, 66). Derrida is here pointing out that the word 'effect' gets its thrust from hovering between effect, as something caused, and effect, as non-essential, part of appearance. Elsewhere in the same text Derrida says 'truth is needed'.

39 If sense is the way we conceive of the reference, then it will naturally vary according to context; if sense is not really determined by context, but rather has meaning determined by convention, then the context helps decide which sense is relevant where the sense of the word is ambiguous and it is sense which is stable and with context determines reference.

40 IFP, 53, cf. Angelelli 1967: 44–6, 53, 80 note 23.

41 Frank has failed to take account of the fact that *différance* is not an entity for Derrida but is entirely process; the process of meaning. Frank's 'individual' acquires the same kind of status as Leibniz' monad: it is not a human being, but it does seem to be an entity. For Frank the Individual becomes the transcendental condition of sense and understanding (Frank 1983: 460); it founds meaning whose exchange makes communication and intersubjectivity possible.

42 Ryan (1982) makes of *différance* his own 'History'.

43 Even where Derrida speaks of 'une certaine identité répétable' that is also said to be divided and contaminated at the same time as repeated (LI, 119–20).

44 Austin 1962. Derrida, who by his attention to the compacted shorthand in the way we think is in this very like Austin, refers to Austin's denunciation of the 'fetish of the opposition *value/fact*' (M, 385; *M*, 323–4). Cf. Fish 1981–2: 717.

45 This is another version of the reiterated modalities studied by Becker (see Chapter 1 note 59).

46 Staten, in a book (1985) which has not to my mind had the attention it deserves, has examined this in excellent fashion. If Searle is both crude in argument and rude in tone, Derrida certainly gets his own back, though with a much more closely argued matter, and milder style. Searle does in fact contradict himself, as those who rely on tone in argument sometimes do, when arguing that Derrida has illegitimately brought together two forms of iterability: permanence and that of which quotation is an example. For Searle then allows the physical realization of signs to be on both sides, quotation and permanence. In the latter case it is because the text has a permanence that it can survive the disappearance of the author (Proust 1991: 11). In the former, following it would seem a Carnapian view of quotation, and thus obviating the Fregean problem of locating the reference of a phrase in reported speech, Searle states that the quotation can always be divorced from its meaning by thinking of it as a series of sounds or of written marks, that is of phonic or written symbols. But Searle in a note admits the 'abnormality' of such a view of quotation. In most quotation the sense of the linguistic symbols *is* at work. Yet Searle makes of it a speech act,

programmed by conventions, which simply *is* the speech act of quotation, whereby we make the quotation a topic of discourse, but does not account for how the sense of the quotation can be at work in the act. (Searle 1969: 76). For Derrida, the *event* of enunciation is not a piece of individual action, any more than it is with Searle, but it is not governed remorselessly by conventions either. Typically, as we will see in Chapter 4, it has a random component built in. It can go not according to plan, do something else, or not work. It is always at risk. Enunciation is always a venture.

47 Frege in *Der Gedanke* speaks of a third realm, whose objects, like representations (of the mental realm), cannot be perceived by the senses, but which like things (of the physical realm) do not need a bearer in whose consciousness they need to be implanted (Frege 1971a: 184). Frege is a Platonist, so that such objects are eternal and immutable. But they are only to be grasped as the sense of a linguistic expression (Dummett, IPF, 51) since 'we think in some language' (IPF, 80), as a sense of a particular linguistic expression. It is this tension between embodiment in an actual language, an embodiment thus contingent and particular, and ideal meaning which means that the idea of a Husserlian transcendental historicity is doomed. It is this tension which Derrida captures in the notion of 'writing'.

48 Precisely Derrida's point, in tune with current history of sciences, is that maths never is quite that ideal objectivity, as the development through time of mathematical symbols seems to prove.

49 The *Logical Investigations* is critical of psychologism, and scepticism, warning against confusing the ideal unities of judgement and content with the individual real act of judgement (Husserl 1970: I, 142). Truth and falsehood are ideal functions of the content of judgement, outside and independent of causal factors. 'Essence of meaning is . . . not in meaning conferring experience but in its 'content' the single self identifies intentional unity set over against the dispersed multiplicity of actual and possible experience as speaker and listener' (*ibid.*: I, 327).

50 This is stated very strongly:

> Analysis into necessary and sufficient conditions [is] likely to involve (in varying degrees) idealization of the concept analyzed. In the present case, our analysis will be directed at the center of the concept of promising. I am ignoring marginal, fringe and partially defective promises.
>
> (Searle 1969: 55)

51 Cf. Frank 1983: 517. Frank points out that Searle has made speech acts into timeless transactions, independent of context.

52 Cf. Davidson 1984: 81. Proust (1991) is right to emphasize how unusual the exchange between Searle and Derrida is, in that many philosophers ignore work in other traditions; but she stays tranquilly with the distinction 'use/mention', using it as a unquestioned tool, whereas Davidson and Kneale, for instance, both of whom are working in Searle's tradition, have been interested in cases where it does not function unequivocally. However, she puts her finger on a fundamental aspect of Derrida's work to be discussed in the final chapter: that he uses words like 'truth' in oppositional fashion, that is within traditional academic discourse, but that he also uses them in trumping fashion, in that they are reinscribed in different contexts. I would argue that this is a powerful and conscious version of the procedures of intellectual innovation in general – the token or instance altering the rules.

53 Further back in Derrida's production, the 'originary synthesis' in Husserl and its relation to time, its bringing together of the 'constituting' and 'already constituted', that is, of active and passive, is explored in *Genèse*, 122–4.

54 Petrosino (1983: 158) has rightly pointed to the importance of the possible in Derrida's writing. Rosen (1969) relates Heidegger's 'preference for possibility' to the

concept of time. Possibility is prior to actuality (1969: 97) higher than actuality (1969: 94). 'The Being process or pure differentiation, is higher (more powerful) than any of the elements of that process of differentiation (1969: 99). Cf. 'Higher than actuality stands *possibility*. We can understand phenomenology only by seizing upon it as a possibility' (SZ, 38; *BT*, 63).

55 Frank (1983, 515–6) argues that this is no way for events to happen, since Derrida will not accept individual acts which actualize; on the other hand, Searle's 'power of conventions' assumes what needs examining. But Frank points out that there is a minimal consensus between them, in that both cut out the individual subjectivity as an active force in changing meaning.

56 The double procedure of deconstruction comes about in the following way. Searle has chosen *successful* performatives, fulfilled intentions, which is only half the story. Derrida on the contrary takes the 'failed actions'. These two are not contraries: Derrida argues that there is a 'fold' and that what opens the possibility has been taken as the inferior partner of the binary double.

57 Searle (1969: 15) does indeed evoke the possibility that this could in some way be contested: 'A serious demand that I justify my intuitions that "bachelor" means unmarried man, if consistent, would also involve the demand that I justify my intuition that a given occurrence of "bachelor" means the same as other occurences of bachelor'. It is the way that this is being contested by Derrida that needs to be defined.

58 Cf. Skinner 1988: 54, though in the more circumscribed context of histories of 'an idea': 'My concern here . . . is not empirical but conceptual, not to insist that such histories can sometimes go wrong but that they can never go right'.

59 In other words, the second Becker reduction principle is refused. The reiterated modality is a logical structure which was investigated by Husserl's assistant Oskar Becker (see Chapter 1 note 59). (There is a historical connection through Husserl to Derrida, with interpretations of the intuitionist propositional calculus.) The equivalent of this principle in relation to epistemic modality – 'if a proposition is not known to be false then it is known that the proposition is not known to be false' (Kneale 1971: 556) – makes it clear why Derrida would not accept it, as von Wright does not: an argument cannot be mounted about second-level knowledge from a position of ignorance. In other words the closing off of the reiterated modalities is arbitrary, even if we cannot do anything with them.

60 The phrase was developed in 'Spéculer – sur *Freud*' (Derrida 1980).

61 Baldwin 1992.

Chapter 3

1 Heidegger, VA, 129, my translation.

2 'C'est parce que le sens auquel nous avons accès n'est pas l'être de l'événement, parce qu'il peut toujours ne pas s'incarner, s'éteindre ou ne pas naître, que le *pourquoi* tient sa gravité d'une certitude phénoménologique' (OG, 168) ('It is because the sense to which we have access is not an event's being; because this sense can always not be incarnated, it can die out or not be born, that the 'why' owes its seriousness to a phenomenological certainty') (*OG*, 151, trans. mod.).

3 As suggested by Derrida's phrase 'mots anglés' which puns on Mallarmé's title, 'Les mots anglais'.

4 This section of *Glas* is very complex: it considers how to get out of the Hegelian dialectic, the nature of representation and the role of the negative. The set-to with Marx is largely implicit, done with juxtaposed quotation, though it has become clearer since *Specters of Marx*'s final chapter.

5 Cf. J. L. Austin on 'trouser concepts', pairs of concepts where 'one wears the trousers'.

6 'La mesure de solidité ou de consistance serait donc le ligament entre des contraires, ce double lien (*doppelt*, *geknüpft*) et la mobilité indécidable du fétiche, sa puissance d'excès par rapport à l'opposition (vrai/non/vrai, susbtitut/non-substitut, déni/affirmation)' (*Glas*, 236a) ('The measure of solidity or stability would be the ligament between the contraries, this double bond (doppelt geknüpft) and the undecidable mobility of the fetish, its power of excess in relation to the opposition (true/non-true, substitute/non-substitute, denial/affirmation)') (*Glas*, 211a). The passage is a pointer forward to the ligature, lien or desmos which appears later in *Glas* and in *The Post Card*, which will be discussed later. Beside this account in the Genet column is a long quotation from Genet about Stilitano and his 'postiche' of haberdashery grapes worn over his penis, which is less a fetish than a false wound (a case of a double negation not making a position, which account of negation is also discussed in *Glas*) and Derrida makes the word group Stilitano/style/stilites (column) interact.

7 Cf. Chapter 1. A Gödelian 'formally undecidable' formula is 'one that cannot be proved with the resources of the system [in which it has arisen or been constructed] although it must be true unless the system is self-contradictory' (Kneale 1971: 714).

8 See Agamben 1988: 66, and the relation of the word 'fetish' to *Factizität* – not mere factuality, but made, non-original. Derrida points to Hegel's use of the word (*Glas*, 234a, 210a).

9 Any work on *Glas* owes a great debt to *Glassary* (1986), constructed by J. P. Leavey, which gives the sources of the quotations Derrida places in his text.

10 Derrida uses the acronym 'IC' – categorical imperative, immaculate conception – to force together the 'negative fetishes'.

11 'It becomes clear to anyone who follows our thinking that being *as such* is precisely hidden from metaphysics, and remains forgotten – and so radically that the forgetfulness of being, which itself falls into forgetfulness, is the unknown but enduring impetus to metaphysical questioning' (Heidegger, IM, 19). Derrida has shown in lectures that the 'as such' may itself function in this strange phantasmal way in Heidegger.

12 It is in origin the same word as 'phantom' (Derrida has appeared in a film called *Ghost Dance*) – in Greek it could mean 'vision' and yet in the plural 'phenomena' (Diogenes Laertius, 749–51, quoted Long and Sedley 1987: vol. I, 236: 'An impression [phantasis] is different from a figment [phantasma]. A figment is the kind of fanciful thought which occurs in dreams, whereas an impression is a printing in the soul'). Derrida points out the relation with 'phenomena' at the end of the section in *Glas* bearing on the last two chapters of the *Phenomenology*. From the standpoint of Absolute Knowledge, once it has been arrived at, the showing of the phenomena available to each stage of consciousness has been the showing of phantasmata.

13 In the final chapter of *Specters of Marx*, Derrida shows in Marx's text (*Capital*, Book 1, ch. 4) how the fetish has a ghostly character and also how religion is the model for the construction of the concept of ideology. 'Le caractère mystique du fétiche, tel qu'il marque l'expérience du religieux, c'est d'abord un caractère fantomal' (SM, 236) ('The mystical character of the fetish, in the mark it leaves on the experience of the religious, is first of all a ghostly character') (*SM*, 148).

14 The function of the non-standard formation is discussed in LI, 104; *LI*, 52.

15 But *reste* and *restance* elsewhere function more simply as what may never have existed, like Rousseau's state of nature, but which nevertheless structures what is going on: 'Le reste qui travaille en silence la scène de cette coopération est sans doute illisible (maintenant ou à jamais, telle est une restance au sens où je l'entends)' (CP, 324) ('The remainder which in silence works upon the scene of this cooperation

is doubtless illegible (now or forever, such is a *restance* in the sense in which I take it)') (*PC*, 304).

16 Owen 1986: 45, 'Zeno and the mathematicians'. Cf.

> If you want to say that there are a number of things in existence, you have to specify *what sort of thing counts as a unit in the plural*. If there can be no such individuals as you claim, there can be no such plurality either. And if your individuals have to be marked off by spatial and temporal distinction, *you have to be sure that your way of making such distinctions is not logically absurd*.
>
> (Owen 1986: 46, my italics)

Cf. also 'His [Zeno's] arguments seem designed to close not some but all avenues of escape to anyone holding the unremarkable belief that there is more than one thing in existence' (*ibid.*: 55). Owen goes on to show what consequences 'Aristotle's surrender to Zeno' (*ibid.*: 61) had for the history of dynamics. But cf. Caveing for another interpretation. In terms of Derrida, and his account of Hegel's relation to Kant discussed in Chapter 1, it is interesting that Caveing argues that the difference between a 'real' solution of Zeno's paradoxes and Aristotle's solution is that the latter only introduces a potential infinite into them, whereas what was needed was the actual infinite (Caveing, 1982).

17 Owen 1986: 306 ('Aristotle on time').

18 Dummett 1978: 353.

19 Zeno argued that whatever occupies its own space throughout a period of time is at rest throughout that period. So that at any instant an arrow (say) must be at rest. But this is tantamount to saying that the arrow cannot move, which is absurd (Moore 1990: 25).

20 'Time is only pure intuition to the extent that it prepares the look of succession from out of itself, and it *clutches* this as such *to itself* as the formative taking-in-stride [*activité réceptrice et formatrice* in the French translation]'. And after an account of the chiasmatic nature of time as pure intuition 'in general':

> As pure self-affection time is not an acting affection that strikes a self which is at hand. Instead, as pure it forms the essence of something like self-activating. However, if it belongs to the essence of the finite subject to be able to be activated as a self, then time as pure self-affection forms the essential structure of subjectivity.
>
> (KPM, 129)

21 'The taking-in-stride [*acte réceptif*, French trans. 229] of pure intuition must in itself give the look of the now, so that indeed it looks ahead to its coming-at-any-minute [*Sogleich*] and looks back on its having-just-arrived [*Soeben*]'(KPM, 119). The German of Heidegger makes the distinction between active and passive much less clear-cut than does the French translation.

22 'Pure intuition is "original receptivity", i.e. a taking-in-stride of what it, as taking-in-stride, lets come forth from out of itself. Its "offering" is one which "produces"' (KPM, 123). The extent to which Heidegger's work profoundly modalizes the whole domain of traditional philosophy is apparent here. Indeed, KPM points out that Kant removes pure reason from conditions of immersion in time in order to conserve the principle of the excluded middle (that is, a weaker form of binary opposition – the excluded middle will admit that the p of p v – p might not apply to the object). Kant modifies profoundly in 1787 the sections of KRV dealing with the transcendental deduction of the pure concepts of understanding, and thus, Heidegger suggests, the relation between synthesis and time (KPM, 128, 166). Heidegger's interpretation

(*Deutung*) of Kant really applies to the first edition of KRV, as he came to admit (Sherover 1971). Kant already in the second edition of KRV builds in external perception much more explicitly; reacting to 'German idealism', he argues that 'without the intuition of space and without objects in space, we would have no actual internal sense, and thus no temporal determination of our existence' (Kant 1988, notes conserved in the Leningrad library, ed. Brandt, 49, my translation).

23 In a sense, what Derrida (and Heidegger) are doing is to skein out the historico-philosophical threads to be found in an analysis of Aristotle on time, such as G. E. L. Owen's:

> Aristotle does not discuss the nature of moment in abstraction from the idea of the present. . . . The word for 'now' brings together what seems to us two distinct concepts, that of the moment and that of the present. When he speaks of the lapses of time as marked by different nows in order of earlier and later we think of moment. When he speaks of the now as progressing through time in a way comparable to that of a body, progressing through a moment collecting different descriptions according to the stage it has reached, we think of the present as something continuously overtaking such successive moments. When he claims to show how the now is perpetually different yet perpetually the same – since it can be thought of as a succession of nows and as one progressing now – we cannot think of him as distinguishing the two concepts but rather as conflating them.
>
> (Owen 1986: 306)

24 Derrida in long notes in *Marges*, 203–5, on the historical complicity of form, that is, *eidos*, and the copula 'is', shows how Husserl's concern to ensure the logicality of pre-expressive thought leads him to privilege statements of meaning in 'doxic' form, substituting them for the modalized ones, e.g. 'being valuable' instead of 'valuable' (Husserl 1913: 331–2).

25 Prior (1957) rejects for his system *Ut* the formula 'if it is possible that something fs, then there is something that possibly fs' (the 'Barcan formula'; 'f' being a formula holding a place for a verb) – the question being whether there can be already facts about objects which do not yet exist. It is interesting that he starts the rejection with a discussion of 'I do not exist', contradictory when said by 'I', and interpreted as 'there are no facts about me'. He shows (of himself, Prior – but the examples would need detailed commentary) that 'it was not the case 100 years ago that I existed' is true, but not 'it was the case 100 years ago that I did not exist' – there were no facts about me, even the fact that 'I' did not exist, 'though it is *now* the case that there were no facts about me then' (Prior 1957: 34).

26 Cf. Lyons 1977: vol. II, 821, on the 'Augustinian view of time'.

27 Lowe's attempt (1987) to defuse McTaggart's paradox seems to me to fail, and the reason for the failure to be hinted at by his choice of the term 'indexical' in lieu of Dummett's 'token-reflexive' – we more readily accept paradox of the 'token-reflexive'. Lowe reimports the problem at the level of the pragmatic context: an event cannot be spoken of without reference, through tense of verb, to the act of enunciation about it (clearly, I am not accepting, in saying this, that there can be such thing as a 'tenseless' use of the present tense). The term 'indexical', through its relation to its meaning of 'expressive', allows us to forget the cross-cutting of time of event and time of utterance, which occurs in the tense we assign to the utterance, and which brings them together. As a result, Lowe is obliged to assert that 'the statement that I now express by saying, for instance, "*e* will happen tomorrow" is the same as will be expressed tomorrow by saying "*e* is happening today"', which, if it is not patently false, then seems to turn a statement made at a time into a statement

made about a time (cf. Prior 1957: 25). For 'token-reflexive' and 'indexical' see Lyons 1977: vol. I, 15.

28 Some further examples of the same phrase: 'La signature *rebus* . . . condition de possibilité et d'impossibilité' (SéP, 65) ('The rebus signature . . . the condition of possibility and impossibility') (SéP, 64); 'Parce que cette impossibilité même est la condition de la possibilité de la demande' (SéP, 15) ('Because this very impossibility is the condition of the possibility of demand') (SéP, 14); 'Le code étant ici la possibilité et l'impossibilité de l'écriture' (M, 377) ('The code being here both the possibility and impossibility of writing') (*M*, 317).

29 For a striking example: '[Fétiche] puissance d'excès par rapport à l'opposition vrai/nonvrai' (*Glas*, 236a) ('power of excess in relation to the opposition (true/nontrue)') (*Glas*, 211a); *trace*: 'La trace ne serait pas le mixte, le passage entre la forme et l'a-morphe, la présence et l'absence, etc mais ce qui, se dérobant à cette opposition, la rend possible depuis l'irréductible de son excès' (M, 206).

30 Strange attractor is the name given to a process pattern into which a type of turbulence appears to be tending (at infinity) to settle.

31 Cf. for instance

Le 'Je suis donc mort . . . ' n'est pas une proposition parmi d'autres. Partout où elle se répète, se monnaie, se détaille, elle donne un coup d'écriture (où de *déjà*) à toutes les forces qui s'aggrippent au présent, à la vérité comme présence.

(*Glas*, 26b)

The 'I am therefore dead . . . ' is not just one proposition among others. Everywhere that it is repeated, cashed, retailed, detailed, divided, it imparts a writing (or *already*) stroke to all the forces that cling to the present, to truth as presence.

(*Glas*, 19b).

32 Whereas in painting theory, the related and extremely interesting problem of if and how we know a portrait is a portrait, an idealized portrait, or an 'ideal head' has barely been discussed since the eighteenth century.

33 In a brilliant aside, Derrida links Barthes' *punctum* to the 'detail' – derivationally 'cut' – and Walter Benjamin's account of mechanical reproduction and its relation to the work of art, once the very emblem of uniqueness; but also to psychoanalysis' seizure and enlargement of details.

34 [Barthes] a d'abord mis en valeur irréductibilité absolue du *punctum*, disons l'unicité du *référentiel* . . . L'hétérogénéité du *punctum* est rigoureuse, son originalité ne souffre aucune contamination. . . . Et pourtant, ailleurs, à d'autres moments, Barthes . . . fait droit au rythme requis de la composition. . . . Il lui faut en effet reconnaître, et ce n'est pas une concession, que le *punctum* n'est pas ce qu'il est. Cet autre absolu compose avec lui-même, avec son autre absolu qui n'est donc pas son opposé, avec le lieu du même et du studium.

(Psy, 295–6)

[Barthes] first highlighted the absolute irreducibility of the *punctum*, the unicity of the referential as we say. . . . The heterogeneity of the *punctum* is rigorous, its originality suffers [no] contamination. . . . And yet, in other places, at other times, Barthes . . . accedes to the requisite rhythm of the composition. . . . It is indeed necessary for him to recognize, and this is not a concession, that the *punctum* is not what it is. This absolute other composes with the same, with its absolute other which is thus not its opposite, with the locus of the same and of the *studium*.

(*RB*, 285)

35 'The singular plural' pushes further the unacknowledged contention with Sartre in 'Dissemination' where such a concept is impossible because the totalizing it implies is impossible, and can never be performed. The extent to which such works as 'Les morts de Roland Barthes' have moved on from 'Dissemination' is clear from such a comparison. The paradoxical 'singulier pluriel' enables the singular as *punctum*, the unique individual, to be part of a structure of reference without being posited as elementary particle, or irreducible end-station.

36 Kripke (1980) argues against Russell and Frege that fixing a reference is not to give a description, it is to use contingent marks of the object to specify what we are talking about. Kripke's is quite unlike what were the recent philosophical theories of designation, which held that the reference of a name can be determined by a set of unique identifying marks, some unique properties which only the bearer of the name can lay claim to. But these definitional definitions of the proper name seem to get caught in a circle, in that the unique properties are defined by and define the proper name.

37 Kripke (1980: 49) argues 'intuitively' that proper names are rigid designators, for although the man (Nixon) might not have been the President, it is not the case that he might not have been Nixon (though he might not have been *called* 'Nixon').

38 Frege 1988 [1892]: 47 note. Frege in a letter to Husserl of 24 May 1891 draws a diagram:

Satz sentence	*Eigenname* proper name	*Begriffswort* concept word
Sinn des Satzes *(Gedanke)* sense of the sentence (thought)	*Sinn des Eignennamens* sense of the proper name	*Sinn des Begriffsworts* sense of the concept word
Bedeutung des Satzes reference of the sentence	*Bedeutung des* *Eignennamens* reference of the proper name	*Bedeutung des* *Begriffsworts* reference of the concept word
(Wahrheitswerth) (truth-value)	*(Gegenstand)* (object)	*(Gegenstand der unter* *dem Begriff fällt)* (object falling under the concept)

He has previously distinguished *Begriffswort* (concept word) as *Gemeinname* (common name) (Frege, 1976, II: 94–98).

39 S'il n'y a d'effet d'idiome, d'effet de propriété absolue que dans un système de relations, de différences avec autre chose, avec quelque chose qui est proche ou non, à ce moment-là, le nom propre secret est tout de suite, structuralement et *a priori* inscrit dans un réseau qui le contamine de noms communs, de sorte que même ce nom propre secret serait impossible, du moins dans sa pureté.

(OA, 142)

if an idiom effect or an effect of absolute properness can arise only within a system of relations and differences with someting else that is either near or far, then the secret proper name is right away inscribed – structurally and a priori – in a network where it is contaminated by common names. Thus, even this secret proper name would be impossible, at least in a pure state.

(*EO*, 107)

40   For *mise en abyme* see Gasché 1994b and Dällenbach 1977.

41   'Des choses si particulières, *idiotes*, que ce sont toujours des exemples qui ne sont exemples de rien pour être trop exemplaires, exemples sans exemple de la singularité même, nécessité de l'arbitraire et de la contingence' (SéP, 91) ('Of things that are so particular, so idiotic, that they are always examples which are examples of nothing, being too exemplary, examples without example of singularity itself, the necessity of the arbitrary and the contingent') (SéP, 90).

42   And perhaps of Blanchot? Cf.

singular neutral names something which escapes from nomination, without even the noise of origin. We modestly, thoughtlessly, call it the thing. The thing, because, obviously, things belong to another order and are what is most familiar, what makes us live in an environment of things, which are, however, not transparent.

(Blanchot 1973: 102, trans. MRN)

43   'Ding' in German can mean thing, and 'bedingt' means 'conditioned'. 'Wir sind im strengsten Sinne des Wortes die Be-Dingten', 'we are in the strictest sense of the word the be-thinged/determined' (VA, 173, my translation).

44   Cf. Pöggeler 1959.

45   Pöggeler (1963: 145) quoting Heidegger:

Event, that means Being as the occurrence of a truth in particular circumstances, in a way that is not at our disposal, a truth which the thought of man needs for itself and so is 'identical' with it, which lets [us] see being in its Being historically in an each time particular way, and which thus tears open the 'difference' between Being and beings, which is the foundation for metaphysics' thought of being.

46   'C'est à la condition de ne pas chercher à dominer son oeuvre . . . que renonçant à tout maîtrise ou appropriation, j'aurai la chance et courrai le risque d'un événement' (SéP, 21) ('It is on the condition of not seeking to dominate his work . . . that renouncing any mastery or appropriation, I will have a chance and run the risk of an event') (SéP, 20).

47   Cf. Heidegger (ID, 25) where *Ereignis* ('event of appropriation') is used as a 'singulare tantum', as an uncountable singular event.

48   J'expose ici une souffrance: comment citer un texte, exemple dans une démonstration, si chaque texte est unique, exemple d'aucun autre jamais, signature inimitable par le signataire général et porteur du nom lui-même. Il y a pourtant une loi et une typologie de l'idiome et de là notre souffrance. Le drame qui agit et construit toute signature, c'est cette répétition insistante, inlassable, tendanciellement infinie de ce qui reste, chaque fois, irremplaçable.

(SéP, 21)

I expose a problem here: how to cite a text, an example in a demonstration, if every text is unique, the example of nothing other ever, a signature not to be imitated by the general signer and bearer himself. There is nonetheless a law and a typology of the idiom, whence our problem. The drama that activates and constructs every signature is this insistent, unwearying, potentially infinite repetition of something that remains, every time, irreplaceable.

(SéP, 20)

Cf.

La métonymie n'est pas l'erreur ou le mensonge, elle ne dit pas le faux. Et à la lettre, il n'y a par exemple pas de *punctum*. Ce qui rend toute énonciation possible, mais ne réduit en rien la souffrance; c'est même une source, la source de la souffrance; im-ponctuelle, illimitable.

(Psy, 302)

metonymy is no mistake or falsehood; it doesn't speak untruths. And to the letter, there is perhaps no *punctum* as such. What makes all utterances possible but doesn't reduce suffering in the least is actually a source, the un-punctual, illimitable source of suffering.

(*RB*, 293)

49   Il [the title, *Le Pré*, of a work by Ponge] ne fait la loi que depuis une violence d'avant la loi . . . en accumulant dans la puissance oraculaire du nom propre toutes les ressources des phrases tues, il fonde sa propre état, sa propre légitimité.

(Par, 231)

it only makes the law right from a violence before the law . . . in accumulating in the oracular power of the proper name the entire resource of mute sentences, it founds its own state, its own legitimacy.

(*Title*, 11)

And

L'histoire de la serviette-éponge, telle du moins que je la raconte de mon côté, voilà une fable, histoire au titre de fiction, simulacre et effet de langue (*fabula*) mais telle que par elle seule la chose en tant qu'autre et en tant qu'autre chose peut advenir dans l'allure d'un événement inappropriable (*Ereignis* en abîme).

(SéP, 103)

The story of the sponge-towel, at least as I tell it from my point of view, is indeed a fable, a story with the name of fiction, a simulacrum and effect of language (*fabula*), but such that only by means of it can the thing as other and as other thing come to pass with the allure of an inappropriable event (*Ereignis* in abyss).

(SéP, 102)

50 Note how Derrida murmurs against Ponge's explicitation of his ethical thrust (Sép, 53; 52). Cf. also ALT, 71–2, where Derrida argues that ethics as traditionally done has been too limited to certain forms of responsibility (*sujet, conscience, ego, liberté*, etc.) and seeks to widen the responsibility to questions which do not make regional assumptions. He goes on to point out that the hiatus between *law* which is general (and which creates ethics) and justice or the singularity of the other goes beyond what has traditionally been called ethics: 'Je dirais que l'ouverture, ou l'attente, une certaine soumission, une certaine fidélité à la venue, chaque fois, de l'autre singulier, a une dimension qui ne peut pas se laisser convenir dans ce qu'on appelle le domaine le l'éthique' (ALT, 71). He calls for a negotiation, a strategy (or a mediation, or a

composition, as *Signsponge* and 'The deaths of Roland Barthes' call the process) which would bring together the law and its axioms, and the irreducible singularity of the other. Once again, two of the problems which drive this book, of heterogeneity, and of localization, localization which accepts and effaces that heterogeneity by placing it, are raised, this time in ethical terms.

51 Summarized by a quotation from Ponge, 'Les hirondelles', on which Derrida comments: 'Mais c'est quand elles partent *de* nous qu'elle nous quittent sans retour, et quand elles ne partent pas *de* nous qu'elles nous restent le mieux attachées' (SéP, 135) ('But it is when they depart from us that they go away without coming back, and when they do not depart from us that they remain the most closely attached' (SéP, 134).

52 Cf. 'Like the Biblical text itself, writing for Duras bears in turn on the manner of a prophecy as illumination, to the presence as the heart of language and textuality of something, an object of experience, which cannot be described except as an interruption, as a cessation of discourse, as a moment of transgression or transcendence' (Hill 1989: 3, à propos writing and Duras).

53 Yet others pick up the subtitle of the volume 'Inventions de l'autre', cf. Psy, 163, where appears the phrase 'le nom de l'autre, faudrait-il l'inventer?', and also 198.

54 Kneale 1971: 600. This is in the context of a mild attack on Russell for attempting to excise any expression which presupposes acceptance of an existential proposition: all designations do. Literature in this perspective has to take rooms with the false, because it 'fails to designate anything' (sc. anything existing).

55 See Prior 1957: 28–31 for some of the existential implications of non-modal language.

56 The term has a strong recent genealogy: active in Freud's work, but also in that of the anthropologist Marcel Mauss, in theories of potlatch (the gift, or consumption, of all possessions in a struggle for mastery) and in the reintegrating gift system described by Lévi-Strauss, where the criminal turned out of the community, and whose property has been destroyed, is reintegrated by the gift of new possessions, a debt incurred towards him by the society which destroyed the old ones. Cf. C. M. Johnson 1996.

57 Otto Pöggeler (1959: 107) links the 'es gibt' to the 'event of appropriation' (*l'événement/Ereignis*):

> Being as the event of appropriation is neither an ultimate ground nor a highest being, but this is not so precisely because it is the 'granting' of beings [das Geben vom Seienden] because 'it grants' itself. The 'it grants' [es gibt] is not a 'ground for the world': neither is it the power over its 'granting': it is not God who 'creates' beings. Being as the event of appropriation gives beings into openness, and allows them to reveal themselves as the Being 'of' beings.

58 See Marion (1989) for an account of the relation between intuition and 'donation' in Husserl and Heidegger.

59 'Wissenschaft und Besinnung' in VA.

60 Heidegger, GA, I: 20 (1912). Cf. Ott 1988: 103, where Heidegger's criticism in 1917 of Husserl for merely accepting a theoretical and abstract notion of the object is related.

61 Cf. Geach and Stoothoff 1968.

62 Cf. Frege 1980, 'On concept and object' (specifically mentioned by Heidegger) – but also *Dialog mit Pünjer über Existenz*, in Frege 1969: 60–75 for a discussion of whether 'this table exists' has the same content as 'there are [es gibt] tables'.

63 Cf. also the passage added to '*Pas*' for its insertion in the book *Parages*.

Voilà une écriture, la plus risquée qui soit, soustrayant quelque chose à l'ordre du langage qu'elle y plie en retour avec une rigueur très douce et inflexible. [And then he adds in *Parages*] Mais qu'y soustraire ainsi? La 'pensée'? Une pensée 'hors la langue'? Il y aurait là de quoi scandaliser une certain modernité. C'est un risque à courir, le prix à payer pour penser autrement le 'hors la langue' 'de la pensée'.

(Par, 26)

This is writing of the most daring sort, removing something from the order of language, which it folds there in return, with a very gentle and inflexible rigour; [added] But what is being removed here? Thought? A thought 'outside language'? That would be enough to scandalize a certain modernity. That's a risk to be run, the price to pay for thinking about the 'outside language' of thought.

(Par, 26, my translation)

64 Cf. 'Envois' on Hegel's awareness of what the forbidding of (pictorial) representation portended, but which he erased by insertion into the dialectical process:

L'interprétation de cet interdit se trouve dérivée et réinscrite dans un procès plus vaste, de structure dialectique, et au cours duquel l'interdit ne constitue pas un événement absolu venu d'un tout autre qui déchirerait absolument ou du moins retournerait dissymétriquement la trame d'un procès dialectilisable.

(Psy, 140–1)

It comes about that the interpretation of this interdict is derived and reinscribed in a vaster process, dialectical in structure, and during which the interdict does not constitute an absolute event come from a wholly other, which would tear absolutely or at least would send back in dissymmetric fashion the workings of a dialectizable process.

(Psy, 140–1, my translation)

65 Cf. Marx's argument, where he shows that no production is possible without an instrument of production, which may be in the widest sense a mode of production, precisely a 'handed down' way of using the hand. There is, then, no production without stored up past labour, for there is always even in non-technical cultures 'the facility gathered together and concentrated in the hand of the savage by repeated practice' (1993: 85).

66 The English text has '*Epoche* of absolute knowledge', the French, '*époque*'.

67 Cf. Gasché 1994b; Evans 1992: 28.

68 'Schuldig, keiner Schuld bewußt' ('Guilty, conscious of no guilt'), Goethe, *Der Gott und die Bajadere*, quoted Heidegger, BT, §58.

69 The relation to Grelling's paradox is evident. The paradox was widely discussed by analytical philosophers in the 1950s. (In the paradox, an adjective is 'autological' if it can be applied to itself, 'heterological' if not. Is 'heterological' heterological? If yes, it can be applied to itself and so is autological.)

Chapter 4

1 This phrase, which has no neat translation, is used by Derrida on many occasions, usually in relation to the work of Maurice Blanchot.

2 Ritter 1976, article 'Negation, Negativität', quoting Spinoza.

3 Forman 1971. There is a close relation too between Heyting's intuitionistic calculus and one of the modal systems (S4).

4 Derrida is not suggesting that what is going on is the 'failure of language to succeed in *evoking*, *uttering* or *referring* to anything at all' (Rosen 1982: 149) by a determining of Being, but an un-determining of Being, not a failure but a movement on. Cf. the Richard paradox, where a finite number of words can define a decimal which was not included in the (infinite) set of decimals defined by that finite number of words; or Berry's paradox where 'the least integer not nameable in fewer than nineteen syllables' can act as a name for something, but which itself has only eighteen syllables.

5 Stern 1995. Cf. Heidegger, KPM, 49:

> Only if the letting stand against [gegenstehenlassen] of . . . is a holding oneself in the nothing can the representing allow a not-nothing [ein nicht-Nichts], i.e. something like a being if such a thing shows itself empirically, to be encountered instead of and within the nothing.

6 An exceeding of beings in their totality

> Being held out into the nothing – as Dasein is – on the ground of concealed anxiety makes man a lieutenant of the nothing. . . . Being held out into the nothing – as Dasein is – on the ground of concealed anxiety is its surpassing of beings as a whole. It is transcendence.
>
> (BW, 108; WM, 38)

7 WM, 40; BW, 110. Cf. Rosen 1982: 148, quoting Josef Simon. Simon's comment on Hegel would be, according to Rosen (145–6), either this linguistic assimilation of being and nothing, or else the Parmenidean fallacy of equating thinking 'nothing' and not thinking anything.

8 Heidegger, WM, 34.

9 Cf. Ott 1988. Heidegger had studied maths; he had written a review of recent trends in logic. He was familiar with at least the tendency of Russell's work on Leibniz – the thrust of *The Metaphysical Foundations of Logic* is to argue that for Leibniz, as for logic in general, ontology is primary, not, as Russell claimed, logic itself (poor Leibniz, according to Russell, having an unfortunate tendency to go off the logical rails into dubious ontology). Heidegger knew and quoted the work of the distinguished modal logician Oskar Becker.

10 Carnap 1931: 219–41, a work entitled 'The overcoming of metaphysics through logical analysis of language' (my translation). There are some curious though unsurprising points of contact between Carnap and Heidegger, notably their concern to go 'beyond metaphysics', and their disquiet with, in Carnap's case, the expunging, of the relation of subject–object: 'The given has no subject', cf. Williams 1981: 149.

11 Taubes 1971. A helpful survey of the problem in Parmenides, Hegel and Heidegger is in Tugendhat 1992.

12 The problem is whether negation is a logical function or whether it has ontological ties and is an indefinable element in judgement – cf. Rosen 1969; Hübener 1971; Frege 1971b.

13 Ritter 1976, article 'Negation'.

14 Cf. Dummett, FPL, 325:

> Frege expressly denies the existence of a distinction between affirmative and negative intrinsic to the thought expressed rather than to its linguistic expression. Which of the sentences, 'Christ is mortal' and 'Christ is immortal', expresses a negative thought? 'Christ is immortal' because it means 'Christ is not mortal'? Or

because it means 'Christ does not die'? Or 'Christ is mortal' because it means 'Christ does not live for ever'? or because it means 'At some time Christ is not alive'?

15 CP, 429; *PC*, 402; OG, 57; *OG*, 67; SéP, 71; SéP, 70). And:

> Mais pourquoi *cela* s'explique-t-il *dans des préfaces*? Quel est le statut de ce troisième terme qui n'est *simplement* comme *texte*, ni dans le philosophique, ni hors de lui, ni dans les marques ni dans la marche ni dans les marges du livre? qui n'est jamais relevé sans reste par la méthode dialectique? qui n'est ni une forme pure, tout-à-fait vide, puisqu'il *annonce* le chemin, et la production sémantique du concept, ni un contenu, un moment de sens, puisqu'il reste extérieur au logos et en alimente indéfiniment la critique, ne serait-ce que par l'écart entre la ratiocination et la rationalité, l'histoire empirique et l'histoire conceptuelle.
>
> (D, 21–2)

> But why is *all this* explained precisely *in prefaces*? What is the status of this third term which cannot simply, as a text, be either inside philosophy or outside it, neither in the markings, nor in the marchings, nor in the margins, of the book? This term that is never sublated by the dialectical method without leaving a remainder? That is neither a pure form, completely empty, since it *announces* the path and the semantic production of the concept, nor a content, a moment of meaning, since it remains external to the logos of which it indefinitely feeds the critique, if only through the gap between ratiocination and rationality, between empirical history and conceptual history?
>
> (*D*, 15–6)

It is also found in Foucault 1969: 74, 84, 93, 100.

16 The next sentence shows clearly the relation of this kind of negative to the Hegelian: 'c'est contre la réappropriation incessante de ce travail du simulacre dans une dialectique de type hégélien (qui va jusqu'à idéaliser et "sémantiser" cette valeur de *travail*)' (P, 59) ('against the unceasing reappropriation of this work of the simulacrum by a dialectics of the Hegelian type (which even idealizes and "semantizes" the value of *work*)') (*P*, 43). The following paragraphs have been developed from Hobson (1987).

17 And if one supposes that there are logical frameworks to these forms of negation (rather than traces of actual influence transmitted to thinkers in their syntax of argument), one could wonder whether Derrida's terms to be defined do not represent a ghostly, spooky, spoof version of von Wright's 'ultimate genera'.

18 Von Wright (1959: 7) is at this point protesting against the Russell trichotomy 'true/false/meaningless': 'the meaningful/meaningless distinction has been badly misused in modern philosophy and should, whenever possible, be abandoned in favour of more discriminating logical tools'. A point relevant to some dismissals of Derrida's work.

19 This is made very clear, for instance, in Kojève's lectures on Hegel, round the following passage (*Encyclopaedia*, §83):

> Dialectics has a positive result because it has a *specifically determined* (bestimmten) *content*, that is to say, because its result is not truly [wahrhaft] empty and abstract Nothingness [Nichts] but the Negation of certain specific determinations which are contained in that result.
>
> (Kojève 1947: 477, my translation)

20 Quoted Rosen 1982: 23.
21 Hyppolite 1946: 19–20. An understanding of the role of the notion of totality in Hegel's work is increased by observing the energetic use Kojève (1947: 505) makes of it:

> But dialectics shows us that Negativity (= Liberty) is only different from Nothingness to the extent that it is inserted in Totality (= historical synthesis, where the future is incorporated into the present through the intermediary of the past) and that the real is only Totality instead of being Identity to the extent that it implies its own negation.
>
> (my translation)

22 V. Descombes has expressed the relation of modern French philosophy to Hegel's tentacular system almost in terms of 'Hegel or how to get rid of him'. Derrida discusses in 'Violence and metaphysics' the way in which trying to think against Hegel may make a thinker paradoxically close to him (ED, 147; WD, 99).
23 M. Rosen 1982: 120.
24 Gasché 1994a: 183, 181.
25
> L'anneau est trop serré. N'abandonnons pas. Ce que je cherche à écrire – gl – ce n'est pas une structure quelconque, un système du signifiant ou du signifié, une thèse ou un roman . . . c'est ce qui passe, plus ou moins bien, par la stricture rythmé d'un anneau.
>
> (*Glas*, 125b)

> The annulus is too tight. Let us not give up. What I am trying to write – gl – is not just any structure whatever, a system of the signifier or the signified, a thesis or a novel . . . but what passes, more or less well, through the rhythmic strict-ure of an annulus.
>
> (*Glas*, 109b)

26 Freud's use of the telephone as metaphor:

> [The doctor] must turn his own unconscious like a receptive organ towards the transmitting unconscious of the patient. He must adjust himself to the patient as a telephone receiver is adjusted to the transmitting microphone. Just as the receiver converts back into sound waves the electric oscillations in the telephone line which were set up by sound waves, so the doctor's unconscious is able, from the derivatives of the unconscious which are communicated to him, to reconstruct the unconscious which has determined the patient's free associations.
>
> ('The dynamics of transference', 1912: 115)

27 Weber, 1984
28 Derrida links explicitly Freud's account of 'fort: da' not with BT, §69, as I have done, but with the contemporaneous and perhaps related account in Heidegger's *Kantbuch* of the spinning out of time as 'self-affection'.
29 It is in this part that there is, to my belief, the first occurrence of 'quasi transcendental', as an adjective for the 'privilege' of the drive for power.
30 It is worth noting that in the set-theoretical derivation of the natural numbers based on the work of Cantor, the null set starts the whole system in a sense, since it is by counting it that one arrives at the cardinal. Zero is defined on the set of things not identical with themselves (i.e not entering in that two-place relation). Such a set is

empty {0} and its cardinal is 0. The set which contains {0{0}} has cardinal 1, and so on (Kneale 1971: 465–7).

31 Note the strange cognates *route/road/rout* – all derived from *rupta*, broken off, *rout* referring to groups of transiting objects or animals, on the road.

32 Pokorny 1959, 922–3, with *schicken* as the factitive of *geschehen*. I owe this reference to Professor Sidney Allen.

33 The term is from Hofstaedter 1979.

34 A closely related passage, an imaginary conversation with Heidegger, urges against what might be Heidegger's position, that the postal principle is not a possibility-phase which occurs in the history of being, but works as a parasite within being (CP, 207; *PC*, 192).

35 B. Johnson 1977; Lacan's 'Séminaire sur la lettre volée' (on Poe's *The Purloined Letter*) in *Ecrits*, Derrida's 'Le facteur de la vérité' (the factor, the postman) in *The Post Card*. Part of this section has been published in Hobson 1982.

36 Johnson attempts to dissolve this mirror effect: 'The reflexivity between receiver and sender is . . . not an expression of symmetry in itself but only an evocation [*sic*.] of the interdependence of the two terms, of the question of symmetry as a problem in the transferential structure of all readings' (B. Johnson 1977: 503). But the uncertainty of her vocabulary reveals that this dissolution is not really possible.

37 Cf. Chomsky's proof that the Markov chain is an inadequate model for language, precisely because it cannot model any embedding effect (Chomsky 1957).

38 Cf. '[Deconstruction] becomes the Law. But the Law is guaranteed by a more powerful Law – the process has no end. This is why deconstruction is not a movement of transgression, of liberation, [though it has something of this effect]' (Beehive, 13).

39   Que se passe-t-il quand des actes ou des performance (discours ou écriture, analyse ou description etc) font partie des objets qu'ils désignent? Quand ils peuvent se donner en exemple de cela même dont ils parlent ou écrivent? On n'y gagne certainement pas une transparence auto-reflexive, au contraire. Le compte n'est plus possible, ni le compte-rendu, et les bords de l'ensemble ne sont alors ni fermés ni ouverts.

(CP, 417)

What happens when acts or performances (discourse or writing, analysis or description, etc.) are part of the objects they designate? When they can be given as examples of precisely that of which they speak or write? Certainly, one does not gain an auto-reflective transparency, on the contrary. A reckoning is no longer possible, nor is an account, and the borders of the set are then neither closed nor open.

(PC, 391)

40 Derrida has on several occasions criticized use of the term 'performative' if it implies 'logos' in the Genesis sense: a co-presence of word and deed.

41 The relation between Heidegger's Ungesagte and the Freudian unconscious is indicated by Derrida in *Envois*.

42 Derrida 1983b: 36–7.

43 Cavaillès (1947) had posed the problem of the relation between the constituted experience and the constituting subject in terms of level and hierarchy. Tracing the status of logic from Kant to Husserl, Cavaillès suggests that a question has been begged: the rules of logic are the rules for the use of our reason in general. They are the structure of our reason, and yet, in its definition, words like 'action' or 'power' are used which only have meaning, he argues, in relation to an actual consciousness. So that either an endless recursion develops: a logic is needed to give laws to the

consciousness which will reveal the laws of logic to the actual consciousness; or else logic will be revealed each time as a kind of event co-occurrent with an act of thought, and this will barely be a logic (the idea of form, he says, had provided a kind of escape route out of this dilemma, for Kant, as for Arnauld and Nicole in the *Logique de Port Royal*.) This is one of the principal problems of meta-logic: are the norms of thought a hierarchy, is there one overarching justification for them? For Kant 'the pure logic of tradition' was not one in any sense engendered by a transcendental consciousness (Cavaillès 1947: 59) whereas for Husserl 'the authority or logic has its foundation in its relation to life, developing as an internal necessity of the transcendental subjectivity' (*ibid.*: 58). Cavaillès, whose own thought-trajectory in this book relates Husserl to the great logical work of the first three decades of this century (Wittgenstein, Brouwer and Gödel), suggests that Husserl uses a principle of reducibility to homogenize or, rather, to bottom off hierarchies of different types of logical object (*ibid.*: 54, 56) (this would then be an equivalent of his assistant Becker's reduction principle for reiterated modalities). But Cavaillès adds that Gödel's work has shown that logic cannot contain its whole progeny, that a system of sufficient complexity will be 'non-saturatable' and subject to an endless series of extensions, the effect of whose structure may not be to contain what went before so much as to revise it (*ibid.*: 78). So that the intellectual acts which constitute intellectual objects are not each time of the same ilk, linked among themselves by the same deductive relations: 'the term of consciousness does not bring with it a univocity of application – no more than the thing does isolatable unity' (*ibid.*: 78, my translation). Logic will become a system of regulated extensions, but between entities which are not homogenous.

44 Derrida shows, through Herder's critique of Kant, that when the question of language is asked of a transcendental philosophy, it provokes a recursive search for prior or more powerful norms. So that the return to the 'actual facts' of language makes language valid both *de re* and *de jure*: 'un retour à la facticité comme droit du droit. C'est une réduction de la réduction donnant carrière à une discursivité infinie' (OG, 61 note) ('a return to facticity as the de jure character of the de jure itself. It is a reduction of the reduction and opens the way to an infinite discursiveness') (*OG*, 70 note, trans. mod.)

45 Blanchot proposes a set of substitutes:

> The *sacred* in relation to the *god*, *absence* in relation to *presence*, *writing* (taken here as a non-exemplary example) in relation to *word*, the *other* in relation to *me* (as well as to this Me which is someone else), *being* in relation to existence, and *difference* in relation to the *One*. The neuter . . . recognizes itself in or rather plays in each of these terms which have as a trait not to be easily conceptualizable and, perhaps, not to be because there is introduced with them a negative possibility of a type so particular that it couldn't be marked with a negation, no more than it could be affirmed.
>
> (Blanchot 1973: 103, my translation)

Cf. the passage quoted above from *Writing and Difference*, 33.

46 Derrida's more recent work on the sexual in Heidegger tends to show that exchange is an abstract rounding up (as in a sum) of movements to and fro which are never in equilibrium.

47 Derrida has developed this in his work on justice, and on the force of law.

48 'Inventions of the other' in this text is contrasted with Leibnizian invention, with an *ars inveniendi*, that is a calculation using the existing, to find what does not yet exist. Yet his probability calculus, his calculation of chance, rests on closure: certainty is 1, and probabilities are functions moving between 0 and 1. If one does not know what

certainty is, the calculation would be impossible; such a structure being the matrix for Leibniz' hope for social invention, for rational discussion of already available possibilities.

Chapter 5

1 Cf. the speculative origin of life in the work of the biologist Pattee (see Chapter 1), a result of a booting up, of a paradoxical constraint. (Here as elsewhere in Derrida, narrative and event are not chronologically distinct, there is not event first and narration after, though they are not coincident either: this failure of coincidence varies in kind in the different Derridean contexts)
2 Diderot's novel *Jacques le fataliste*, influenced by Sterne's *Tristram Shandy*, wittily examines the similarities between superstition and belief in determinism. Both pick on apparently trivial or marginal connections, according to Diderot.
3 'Random' is thought to be derived from words meaning 'uncontrolled rush'.
4 Cf.

> Quand la totalité du calculable est déjouée par une écriture dont on ne sait plus décider si elle calcule encore, et mieux et plus, ou si elle transcende l'ordre même et l'économie d'un calcul, voire d'un indécidable qui serait encore homogène au monde du calcul.
>
> (UG, 51)

> When the whole of the calculable is outplayed by a writing about which it is no longer possible to decide if it still calculates, calculates better and more, or if it transcends the very order of calculable economy, or even of an incalculable or an undecidable which would still be homogeneous with the world of calculation?
>
> (*TWFJ*, 157–8)

5 Levinas' view has in fact a complex time structure: thematization supposes synchronicity, because it is based on the copula, as the present tense of the verb 'être' (Psy, 171; 'At this very moment', 21), whereas 'mon ravissement au discours' ('my ravishment from the discourse'), which is what is plunged by discourse itself back into coherence and unity, is of another temporality, a kind of ecstasis beyond the present moment.
6 *Symploké*, 'weaving together', 'combination', Plato, *Sophist*, 259e *et seq.*, has been discussed by Gasché (1986).
7 Cette série ab-solue est *sans un seul noeud* mais noue une multiplicité de noeuds re-noués et qui ne re-nouent pas des fils mais des interruptions sans-fil laissant ouverte l'interruption entre les interruptions. Cette interruption n'est pas une coupure, elle ne relève pas d'une logique de la coupure, mais de la dé-stricturation ab-solue. C'est pourquoi l'ouverture de l'interruption n'est jamais pure.

> (Psy, 180)

> This ab-solute series is *without a single knot*, but ties a multiplicity of retied knots, and does not re-tie threads but the interruptions without thread, leaving open the interruptions between interruptions. This interruption is not a cut nor does it fall under a logic of the cut, but rather that of ab-solute de-stricturation. That is why the opening of interruption is never pure.
>
> ('At this very moment', 28–9)

8 Compare 'fractal objects' where nondifferentiable functions, functions with absolute breaks in their tangents, are given cohesion in the sense that they can be theorized and imagined.

9 Cf. 'You define the trace as an element which is phonologically null, but which marks the initial position (in the deep structure) of an element which has been either suppressed or displaced by a transformation' (Chomsky 1977: 168, my translation); where, of course, the notion of basis or level is crucial to make such a trace comprehensible. Cf. Manfred Frank's exposition of Saussure's *aposème*, which he is comparing to Derrida's 'restance non présente d'une marque différentielle' (Frank 1983: 511).

That interruption in language is a trace of God may be a religious version of the idea is suggested by Levinas' work: the Positive Infinite leaves traces of absence. Whereas in Blanchot's work, it is the *neuter*, neither one nor the other, which by effacing the exclusion of the middle allows the unknown as neither negative nor positive, cf. EI, 444; Blanchot 1973: 102.

10 The entire article on Levinas is placed, or almost so, between 'il aura obligé' and 'elle aura obligé', a future perfect which is the combined grammatical form of protention reaching forward, and retention turning back. This, in Heidegger's interpretation of Kant, allowed out of a form of intuition a formal object of intuition to develop. The avoidance of violent objectification 'volonté de maîtrise et de cohérence [où] on prétendrait échapper à la dissymétrie absolue' (Psy, 163), the negotiation, constant realigning and backing off, makes possible the approach to the incalculable – 'Cette *reprise* [= 'mending' as in the darning of socks] est même la condition pour que l'audelà de l'essence garde sa chance contre la couture enveloppante du thématique ou du dialectique' (Psy, 177) ('This *resumption* is even the condition upon which what is beyond essence may keep (garder) its chance against the enveloping seam of the thematical or dialectical') ('At this very moment', 26).

11 The account is to be found, for instance, in an unpublished lecture given in Cambridge in 1992 by the English philosopher Tom Baldwin, 'Intentionality as difference'.

12 'Le simple passage de l'intutition descriptive au langage, la simple mise en discours d'une donnée empirique ouvre le champ à la spéculation, donc aux prédilections' (CP, 406) ('The simple transition from descriptive intuition to language, the simple setting into discourse of an empirical given opens the field for speculation, and therefore for predilections') (*PC*, 381).

13 Cf. 'The concept (thus the whole language) is the instrument in this undertaking to institute the sure rule. Untiringly we build up the world so that the secret dissolution, the universal corruption that governs what is, might be forgotten to the benefit of this coherence of notions and objects' (Blanchot, EI, 46, trans. MRN).

14   S'inquiéter des concepts fondateurs de toute l'histoire de la philosophie, les déconstituer, [nb] ce n'est pas faire oeuvre de philologue ou d'historien classique de la philosophie. (C'est sans doute, malgré l'apparence, la manière la plus audacieuse d'esquisser un pas hors de la philosophie).

(ED, 416)

To concern oneself with the founding concepts of the entire history of philosophy, to deconstitute them, is not to undertake the work of the philologist or of the classic historian of philosophy. Despite appearances, it is probably the most daring way of making the beginning of a step outside of philosophy.

(*WD*, 284)

15 For a lively discussion with its feet firmly on the historical ground, see Hacking 1993.

16 Derrida suggests that the power behind the *resemblance* and the *rassemblement* is the sun, as centre, as source of light and as that which hides and reveals itself, and which is therefore the metaphor of metaphor (M, 319; *M*, 267).

17 There is an unflagged attack on Foucault for neglecting the weight of such historical sediment, and for indulging in an essentially linear if syncopated history, one which neglects the complex stratification of cultures (M, 274–5; *M*, 230–1). In contrast, Derrida seems to summarize the kind of history he himself is doing:

> ni étymologie ni origine pures, ni continuum homogène, ni synchronisme absolu ou intériorité simple d'une système à lui même. Cela implique qu'on critique *à la fois* le modèle de l'histoire transcendentale de la philosophie et celui des structures systématiques parfaitement closes sur leur agencement technique et synchronique (qu'on n'a jamais reconnu jusqu'ici que dans des corpus identifiés selon le 'nom propre' d'une signature.
>
> (M, 304)

> neither pure etymology nor pure origin, neither a homogenous continuum nor an absolute synchronism or a simple interiority of a system to itself. Which implies a *simultaneous* critique of the model of a transcendental history of philosophy and of the model of systematic structures perfectly closed over their technical and synchronic manipulation (which until now has been recognized only in bodies of work identified according to their 'proper name' of a signature).
>
> (*M*, 254–5)

18 It seems to me that the ontological status expressed by this quotation is that there are only actual objects and words, specific and thus individuated; modality, time or possibility, is a manner in which things happen (Prior and Fine 1977: 117)

19 Compare Dummett, FOP, 297, in relation to Frege's conviction that a piece of deductive reasoning is not necessarily a tautology, where it is shown à propos a pair of sentences closely related in meaning, but not identical in terms, that 'by analysing the content of the first member of any of our pairs, one could extract a concept which obtained explicit expression in the second member, but that the content itself remained unaltered'. In spite of the very different mode, and very different vocabulary, he and Derrida are concerned with viewing the new as more than a reshuffling of the already known.

20 This dissociation Derrida evokes, and indeed the whole matter of this chapter, should be compared to Putnam (1988), which was discovered too late to build into the argument.

21 This point is, for reasons which will become apparent, being made in terms of English discussions of relativism, cf. Williams 1981: 158.

22 C'est en ce sens que je voulais dire que la philosophie était la thèse de la traductibilité en un certain sens du concept de traduction, c'est-à-dire, la traduction comme transport, pas comme 'herméneia' active, poétique, productrice, transformatrice, mais transport du sens univoque, ou en tout cas d'une plurivocité maîtrisable, dans un autre élément linguistique.

> (OA, 185)

> When I said that philosophy was the thesis of translatability, I meant it not in the sense of translation as an active, poetic, productive, transformative 'hermeneia', but rather in the sense of the transport of a univocal meaning, or in any case of a controllable plurivocality, into another linguistic element.
>
> (*EO*, 140)

23 'Aucun de leurs noms n'étant un X conventionnel et arbitraire, l'attache historique ou généalogique (ne disons pas étymologique) qui lie le concept signifié à son signifiant (à la langue) n'est pas une contingence réductible' (M, 302) ('None of their names being a conventional and arbitrary X, the historical or genealogical (let us not say etymological) tie of the signified concept to its signifier (to language) is not a reducible contingency') (*M*, 253).

24 That Whorf's position is more complex than this is certain; in the present book I am leaving aside any attempt to establish more accurately what it was.

25 Though Derrida here does not comment on the use of the middle voice, as he will elsewhere, its havering between active and passive might be thought to re-express the curious co-implication of language and thought, word and concept.

26 Gadamer, with a much less differentiated view of Heidegger, seems to assimilate the latter's views to those of Benveniste:

> You can also see that the language group to which Greek belonged and out of which European thought has grown, had the sort of effect of preforming metaphysics. The Greek language, in that it distinguished its subject from its predicate, was predisposed to think of substance and accidents, so European thought was already through its linguistic prehistory put on its own fate, to develop metaphysics and logic and in the end modern science.
>
> (1983, 157)

27 Cf. Blanchot, EI, 377, quoting Nietzsche:

> I rather take the *I* itself as a construction of thought, in the same range as 'matter', 'thing', 'substance', 'individual', 'purpose', 'number' thus as a regulating fiction through which one can insert a kind of constancy, thus a kind of intelligibility in a world of becoming. Faith in grammar, in the linguistic subject, in the object has so far kept metaphysicians under the yoke; I declare that one must deny this faith.
>
> (trans. MRN)

The relation to Locke is evident – even to the examples.

28 These questions seem to me to be versions of, or perhaps rather the matrix for, modern discussions of relativism. Cf. Bernard Williams (1981) 'The truth in relativism'. He makes a distinction between notional options and real options in ethical cases. Precisely the linguistic version of the problem seems to show that this distinction is not really tenable: it leaves aside how understanding influences what we expect (and thus our ethical options – television proves a striking example of what I am talking about) in a way that is not conscious; it assumes that 'outlooks' are some kind of whole in a way that they are probably not. The divorce implied in Williams' discussion between understanding and living will not, it seems to me, do the work he wants it to do. There are extremely fine shadings of grades of understanding which surround everything we do. The argument that knowing another language opens other options for living *and* for understanding, an argument I believe to be correct, again makes the distinction between real and notional options hard to draw.

29 I omit here Williams' implied suggestion, in his last sentence, that there must thus be a flaw in this argument, since there is conflict between what leads to the assertion and the assertion itself.

30 Le silence des arcanes préhistoriques et des civilisations enfouies, l'ensevelissement des intentions perdues et des secrets gardés, l'illisibilité de l'inscription lapidaire

décèlent le sens transcendantal de la mort, en ce qui l'unit à l'absolu du droit intentionnel dans l'instance même de son échec.

(OG, 85)

The silence of prehistoric arcana and buried civilizations, the entombment of lost intentions and guarded secrets, and the illegibility of the lapidary inscription disclose the transcendental sense of death as what unites these things to the absolute privilege of intentionality in the very instance of its essential juridical failure.

(*OG*, 88)

31 Phenomenalists appear to have a parallel difficulty at the level of material objects. All statements about the material world are to be translated into statements about sense-data, and if the objects are unobservable, then into statements about the hypothetical sense data of hypothetical observers. But, as Williams points out, this translates as: 'Even if there were no empirical observers, if there were empirical data belonging to observers, then sense data would show that . . . ', which is hardly satisfactory (Williams 1981: 149).

32 Cf. Frank 1983: 492, who, comparing Derrida with the 'pragmatists', says that both hold language, as a system of signs and conventions about utterances, to be a transcendental principle; that it becomes one through a pre-language system of conditions of possibility which can no longer be characterized as transcendental (efficaciousness, individuality for Deleuze, interpretation for Peirce). The remark is illuminating but it appears to me to neglect the way the relation between transcendental and non-transcendental is constantly being resited by Derrida.

33 For the development in German philosophy of the relation between language and transcendentality see e.g. Apel 1973, for whom the transcendental comprehensibility of language proves the formation of an intersubjective consensus.

34 'What Husserl's investigation discloses is the corporal substructure of our relationship with things and with other Beings, and it seems difficult to "constitute" raw materials from the attitudes and operations of consciousness, which refer to another category, that of theory and ideation' (Merleau-Ponty 1968: 149, trans. MRN).

35 Precisely, 'quasi' suggests status; whereas 'simili' is showing how, when 'transcendental' is designed to exclude by closing the door, what is excluded comes back through the window as a 'simili-transcendental' (*Glas*, 272a; *Glas*, 245a)

36 Cf. von Wright 1996: §16: 'It cannot be taken for granted that the principles according to which sound reasoning proceeds are the same in all (types of) context. The "laws of logic" are not necessarily valid *semper et ubique.*'

37 'It may very well be the case that in the vast majority of the world's languages it is impossible for a speaker to assert the object's existence independent of either epistemic or deontic possibilities' (Lyons 1982: 112).

38 This is too cursory an account, neglecting much that is done from within 'logic' – some of the work of von Wright, the 'paraconsistent logic' of Newton da Costa, the recent book by Priest (1995), for instance.

39 *Sécurité* in the phrase *rupture de sécurité* (Par, 28), and *obstacle* (Par, 38), are both replaced by *barrage* which rhymes with *parage*, which continues tenuously the marine or aquatic vocabulary, and which refers to partition or hindrance of link.

40 The next section is a development of a section of Hobson 1992b.

41 Cf. Merleau-Ponty 1968: 82:

There is thus a dialectical absolute, which is only there in order to maintain at its place and in its relief the multiple, to oppose itself to the making absolute of relations. It is 'fluidified' in them, it is immanent to experience. An unstable position, by definition, and always threatened either by positivist thought or by negativist.

(my translation)

42 In this respect, as in his sense of the particularity of languages, Derrida can be compared to the eighteenth-century German philosopher of language and defender of poetry, J. G. Hamann.

43 The paragraph is full of submerged references: the other for whom the place must be left is named as Elijah (as in the feast of Elijah, which is Derrida's Jewish name; see Derrida 1991b).

44 In a sense, what one watches here is the development about an argument used of phenomena (there is first the appearance, then that divides between apppearance and what it is appearance of – see Heidegger, *Plato's Doctrine of Truth* [*Platons Lehre der Wahrheit*]).

45 Cf. Dummett, FOP, 302, and the process of 'decomposition':

The latter process does not purport to display the structure of the thought, in that sense of 'structure' in which a grasp of the thought depends upon an apprehension of its structure. Rather, it picks out a pattern common to that thought and a range of others, a perception of which is not required in order to grasp the thought. A recognition of this pattern yields a new concept which is not, in general, a constituent of the thought, though it is attained by regarding the thought as exemplifying that pattern.

Bibliography

Only works cited in the book appear in this bibliography.

Agamben, G. (1988) 'La Passion de la facticité', in *Heidegger: questions ouvertes*, Collège International de Philosophie, Paris: Osiris, 63–84.

Alféri, P. (1989) *Guillaume d'Ockham: le singulier*, Paris: Editions de Minuit.

Angelelli, A. (1967) *Studies on Gottlob Frege and Traditional Philosophy*, Dordrecht, Holland: D. Reidel.

Apel, K. O. (1973) 'Sprache als Thema und Medium der transcendentalen Reflexion zu Gegenwartsituation der Sprachphilosophie', in *Transformation der Philosophie, II*, Frankfurt am Main: Suhrkamp, 311–29.

Austin, J. L. (1962) *How to Do Things with Words*, Oxford: Clarendon Press.

Baldwin, T. (1992) 'Anglo Saxon platitudes?', *The Cambridge Review*, vol. 113, no. 2319.

Barthes, R. (1953) *Le Degré zéro de l'écriture*, Paris: Editions du Seuil.

——(1980) *La Chambre claire: note sur la photographie*, Paris: Cahiers du Cinema/Gallimard/Seuil [trans. R. Howard (1993) *Camera Lucida*, London: Vintage].

Becker, O. (1927) 'Mathematische Existenz: Untersuchungen zur Logik und Ontologie mathematischer Phänomene', in *Jahrbuch für Philosophie und phänomenologische Forschung*, vol. 8, Halle.

——(1930) 'Zur Logik der Modalitäten' (LM) in *Jahrbuch für Philosophie und phänomenologische Forschung*, vol. 11, Halle.

Bennington, G. (1988) 'Deconstruction and the philosophers (The Very Idea)', *Oxford Literary Review*, vol. 10, nos 1–2.

Bennington, G. and Derrida, J. (1991) *Jacques Derrida*, Paris: Editions du Seuil.

Bianchi, M. L. (1987) *Signatura rerum: segni, magia e conoscenza da Paracelso a Leibniz*, Rome: Edizioni dell'Ateneo.

Blanchot, M. (1969) *Entretien infini*, Paris: Gallimard. The dates given for the individual articles in this collection are from personal communication by Dr M. Holland.

——(1973) *Le Pas au-delà*, Paris: Gallimard.

Bowie, A. (1996) *Romanticism to Critical Theory: The Philosophy of German Literary Theory*, London: Routledge.

Cantor, G. (1932) *Gesammelte Abhandlungen*, Berlin: Julius Springer.

Carnap, R. (1931) [1932] 'Überwindung der Metaphysik', *Erkenntnis*, 218–41.

Cavaillès, J. (1947) *Sur la Logique et la théorie de la science*, Paris: Presses Universitaires de France.

Caveing, M. (1982) *Zénon d'Elée: prolegomène aux doctrines du continu*, Paris: Vrin.

Chaitin, G. J. (1971) 'Randomness and mathematical proof', *Scientific American*, April, 47–52.

Chomsky, N. (1957) *Syntactic Structures*, The Hague: Mouton.

——(1977) *Dialogues avec Mitsou Ronat*, Paris: Flammarion.

Critchley, S. (1992) *The Ethics of Deconstruction: Derrida and Levinas*, Oxford: Blackwell.

Dällenbach, L. (1977) *Le Récit spéculaire: essai sur la mise en abyme*, Paris: Editions du Seuil.

Davidson, D. (1984) *Inquiries into Truth and Interpretation*, Oxford: Clarendon Press.

Debru, C. (1977) *Analyse et représentation: de la méthodologie à la théorie de l'espace: Kant et Lambert*, Paris: Vrin.

Deleuze, G. (1968) *Différence et répétition*, Paris: Presses Universitaires de France.

Derrida, J. (1962) (2nd edn 1974a) *Introduction à 'L'Origine de la géométrie' de Husserl*, Paris: Presses Universitaires de France [trans. J. P. Leavey (1978) *Edmund Husserl's 'Origin of Geometry': An Introduction*, New York: Harvester Press].

——(1967a) *De la grammatologie*, Paris: Editions de Minuit [trans. G. C. Spivak (1974) *Of Grammatology*, Baltimore MD: Johns Hopkins University Press].

——(1967b) *L'Ecriture et la différence*, Paris: Editions du Seuil [trans. A. Bass (1978) *Writing and Difference*, London: Routledge & Kegan Paul].

——(1967c) *La Voix et le phénomène*, Paris: Presses Universitaires de France [trans. D. B. Allison (1973) *Speech and Phenomena*, Evanston IL: Northwestern University Press].

——(1972a) *La Dissémination*, Paris: Editions du Seuil [trans. B. Johnson (1981) *Dissemination*, London: Athlone Press].

——(1972b) *Marges de la philosophie*, Paris: Editions de Minuit [trans. A. Bass (1982) *Margins of Philosophy*, Brighton: Harvester Press].

——(1972c) *Positions*, Paris: Editions de Minuit [trans. A. Bass (1981) *Positions*, London: Athlone Press].

——(1973) 'L'Archéologie du frivole', in Condillac, *Essai sur l'origine des connaissances humaines*, Paris: Galilée.

——(1974) *Glas*, Paris: Galilée [trans. J. P. Leavey and R. Rand (1986) *Glas*, Lincoln NE: University of Nebraska Press].

——(1976a) 'Entre crochets: entretien avec Jacques Derrida, 1ère partie', *Digraphe*, 8, 97–114; and in *Points de suspension* (Derrida 1992).

——(1976b) *Epérons: les styles de Nietzsche*, a quadrilingual text in French, Italian, English and German, trans. S. Agosti, B. Harlow and R. Schwaderer, intro. 'Coup sur coup' by S. Agosti, Venice: Corbo e Fiore Editori.

——(1977) 'Ja, ou le faux-bond', *Digraphe*, 11, 37–81; and in *Points de suspension* (Derrida 1992).

——(1978) *La Vérité en peinture*, Paris: Aubier-Flammarion [trans. G. Bennington and I. McLeod (1987) *The Truth in Painting*, Chicago IL: University of Chicago Press].

——(1980) *La Carte postale: de Socrate à Freud et au-delà*, Paris: Aubier-Flammarion [trans. A. Bass (1987) *The Post Card: From Socrates to Freud and Beyond*, Chicago IL: University of Chicago Press].

——(1982a) *L'Oreille de l'autre: otobiographies, transferts, traductions: textes et débats avec Jacques Derrida*, ed. C. Lévesque and C. V. McDonald, Montréal: VLB Editions [trans. P. Kamuf and A. Ronell (1988) *The Ear of the Other: Otobiography, Transference, Translation: Texts and Discussions with Jacques Derrida*, Lincoln NE: University of Nebraska Press].

——(1982b) *Affranchissement du transfert et de la lettre*, colloque autour de la *Carte postale* de Jacques Derrida le 4 et 5 Avril 1981, ed. R. Major, Paris: Editions Confrontation.

——(1983a) 'Mes chances: au rendez-vous de quelques stéréophonies épicuriennes', *Tijdschrift voor Filosofie*, 45, 1, 3–40; 'My chances/Mes chances: A rendez-vous with some epicurean stereophonies', trans. I. E. Harvey and A. Ronell, in J. H. Smith and W. Kerrigan (eds) (1984) *Taking Chances: Derrida, Psychoanalysis and Literature*, Baltimore MD: Johns Hopkins University Press, 1–32.

——(1983b) 'The time of a thesis: punctuations', in A. Montefiore (ed.) *Philosophy in France Today*, Cambridge: Cambridge University Press, 34–50.

——(1983c) *D'un ton apocalyptique adopté naguère en philosophie*, Paris: Galilée; previously published in Ph. Lacoue-Labarthe and J.-L. Nancy (eds) *Les Fins de l'homme: à partir du travail de Jacques Derrida*, Paris: Galilée.

——(1984a) *Signéponge/Signsponge*, bilingual edn, trans. R. Rand, New York: Columbia University Press.

——(1984b) 'Women in the Beehive; a seminar with Jacques Derrida', *subjects/objects*, Providence RI, spring, 5–19; reprinted in A. Jardine and P. Smith (eds) (1987) *Men in Feminism*, New York and London: Methuen, 189–203.

——(1984c) *Otobiographies: l'enseignement de Nietzsche et la politique du nom propre*, Paris: Galilée; the first part trans. T. Keenan and T. Pepper as 'Declarations of independence', in *New Political Science*, 1986, summer, no. 15, 7–15.

——(1985) 'Préjugés: devant la loi', in *La Faculté de juger*, Paris: Editions de Minuit; the translation, by A. Ronell (1987) in *Kafka and the Contemporary Critical Performance: Centenary Readings*, Bloomington IN: Indiana University Press, is not complete.

——(1986a) *Parages*, Paris: Galilée; contains 'Pas', 10–116; parts trans. T. Conley (1981) 'Title (to be specified)', in *Sub-Stance* 31, 5–22; A. Ronell (1980) 'The law of genre', *Glyph*, 7, 55–81.

——(1986b) and Pierre-Jean Labarrière, *Altérités*, avec des études de Francis Guibal et Stanislas Breton, Paris: Editions Osiris.

——(1987a) 'Chôra', in *Poikilia: etudes offertes à Jean-Pierre Vernant*, Paris: Editions de l'EHESS.

——(1987b) *Psyché: inventions de l'autre*, Paris: Galilée [trans. C. Porter, 'Psyché: Inventions of the Other', in L. Waters and W. Godzich (eds) (1989) *Reading de Man Reading*, vol. 59, Theory and History of Literature, Minneapolis MN: University of Minnesota, 25–65; trans. P. Caws and M. A. Caws, 'Sending: on representation' (an incomplete trans. of 'Envoi') in *Social Research*, 49, 2, 294–326; trans. C. Porter and P. Lewis (1984) 'No apocalypse, not now (1982)', in *Diacritics*, 14, 2, 20–31; trans. P. A. Brault and M. Nass (1988) 'The deaths of Roland Barthes', in H. J. Silverman (ed) *Continental Philosophy I: Philosophy and Non-Philosophy Since Merleau-Ponty*, New York and London: Routledge, 259–97; trans. K. Frieden, 'How to avoid speaking; denials', in S. Budick and W. Iser (eds) (1989) *Languages of the Unsayable; the Play of Negativity in Literature and Literary Theory*, New York: Columbia University Press, 3–70; trans. Ruben Berezdivin, 'At this very moment in this work here I am', in R. Bernasconi and S. Critchley (eds) (1991) *Re-reading Levinas*, London: Athlone, 11–48].

——(1987c) *Ulysse gramophone: deux mots pour Joyce*, Paris: Galilée [trans. G. Bennington, 'Two words for Joyce', in D. Attridge and D. Ferrer (eds) (1984) *Post-Structuralist Joyce: Essays from the French*, Cambridge: Cambridge University Press; and trans. T. Kendall and S. Benstock, 'Ulysses Gramophone: Hear Say Yes in Joyce', in B. Benstock (ed.) (1988) *James Joyce: The Augmented Ninth*, Syracuse NY: Syracuse University Press].

——(1987d) *De l'esprit: Heidegger et la question*, Paris: Galilée.

——(1987e) *Feu la cendre*, Paris: 'bibliothèque des voix', Editions des Femmes; text and tape read by Derrida and Carole Bouquet.

——(1988) *Limited Inc.*, ed. G. Graff, Evanston IL: Northwestern University Press ['Limited Inc a b c...' was originally published in *Glyph* 1977, vol. 2, 1–79].

——(1990a) *Limited Inc.*, introduced and translated by E. Weber, Paris: Galilée.

——(1990b) *Le Problème de la Genèse dans la philosophie de Husserl*, Paris: Presses Universitaires de France.

——(1990c) *Du droit à la philosophie*, Paris: Galilée.

——(1990d) *Mémoires d'aveugle: l'autoportrait et autres ruines*, Paris: Réunion des Musées Nationaux [trans. P.-A. Brault and M. Naas (1993) *Memoirs of the Blind: The Self Portrait and Other Ruins*, Chicago IL: University of Chicago Press].

——(1991a) *Donner le temps: 1. la fausse monnaie*, Paris: Galilée [trans. P. Kamuf (1992) *Given Time: 1. Counterfeit Money*, Chicago IL: University of Chicago Press].

——(1991b) with G. P. Bennington, *Jacques Derrida*, Paris: Editions du Seuil.

——(1992) *Points de suspension: entretiens*, chosen and presented by E. Weber, Paris: Galilée.

——(1993a) *Khôra*, Paris: Galilée.

——(1993b) *Spectres de Marx: l'etat de la dette, le travail du deuil et la nouvelle internationale*, Paris: Galilée [trans. P. Kamuf (1994) *Specters of Marx: the State of the Debt, the Work of Mourning, and the New International*, with an introduction by B. Magnus and S. Cullenberg, New York and London: Routledge].

——(1994) *Force de loi*, Paris: Galilée [trans. M. Quaintance, 'Force of law', in D. Cornell, M. Rosenfeld and D. G. Carlson (eds) (1992) *Deconstruction and the Possibility of Justice*, New York and London: Routledge, 3–63].

——(1995) *Mal d'archive*, Paris: Galilée.

——(1996) *Apories*, Paris: Galilée.

Descartes, R. (1647) *Méditations métaphysiques*, in F. Alquié (ed.) *Oeuvres*, vol. II, Paris: Garnier.

Descombes, V. (1979) *Le Même et l'autre: quarante-cinq ans de philosophie française (1933–78)*, Paris: Editions de Minuit.

Dews, P. (1987) *Logics of Disintegration: PostStructuralist Thought and the Claims for Critical Theory*, London and New York: Verso.

Diderot, D. (1968–73) [1778–80] 'Jacques le fataliste et son maître', in Diderot, *Oeuvres complètes*, 15 vols, ed. R. Lewinter, Paris: Le Club Français du Livre, vol. 12.

Dummett, M. (1973) *Frege: The Philosophy of Language*, London: Duckworth.

——(1978) *Truth and Other Enigmas*, London: Duckworth.

——(1981) *The Interpretation of Frege's Philosophy*, London: Duckworth.

——(1993) *Origins of Analytical Philosophy*, London: Duckworth.

——(1996) [1991] *Frege and Other Philosophers*, Oxford: Oxford University Press.

Evans, G. (1992) [1982] *The Varieties of Reference*, ed. J. McDowell, Oxford: Clarendon Press.

Fenves, P. (1997) 'Marx, mourning, messianicity,' in H. De Vries and S. Weber (eds) *Violence, Identity and Self-Determination*, Stanford CA: Stanford University Press, 253–70.

Fish, S. E. (1981–2) 'With the compliments of the author: reflections on Austin and Derrida', *Critical Inquiry*, 8, 693–721.

Forman, P. (1971) 'Weimar culture, causality, and quantum theory, 1918–27: adaptation by German physicists and mathematicians to a hostile intellectual environment', in R. McCormmach (ed.) *Historical Studies in the Physical Sciences*, vol. 3, Philadelphia PA: University of Pennsylvania Press.

Foucault, M. (1961) *Folie et déraison: histoire de la folie à l'age classique*, Paris: Plion.

——(1969) *L'Archéologie du savoir*, Paris: Gallimard.

——(1972) 'Mon corps, ce papier ce feu', appendix to second edition of Foucault 1961, trans. G. P. Bennington, *Oxford Literary Review*, 1979, 4, 1, 9–28.

Fraenkel, A. (1966) *Set Theory and Logic*, Reading MA: Addison-Wesley.

Frank, M. (1972) *Das Problem 'Zeit' in der deutschen Romantik Zeitbewußtsein und Bewußtsein vone Zeitlichkeit in der Frühromantischen Philosophie und in Tiecks Dichtung*, Munich: Winckler Verlag.

——(1980) *Das Sagbare und das Unsagbare*, Frankfurt: Suhrkamp.

——(1983) *Was ist Neostrukturalismus?*, Frankfurt: Suhrkamp.

Frege, G. (1969) *Dialog mit Pünjer über Existenz*, in G. Gabriel, H. Hermes, F. Kambartel, C. Thiel and A. Veraort (eds) *Nachgelassene Schriften und wissenschaftlicher Briefwechsel*, 2 vols, Hamburg: Meiner, vol. I, 60–75.

——(1971a) *Der Gedanke [La Pensée]* [1918–19], in Imbert, C. L., ed. and trans. G. Frege (1971) *Ecrits logiques et philosophiques*, Paris: Editions du Seuil.

——(1971b) *die Verneinung [La Négation]*, in Imbert, C. L. ed. and trans. G. Frege (1971) *Ecrits logiques et philosophiques*, Paris: Editions du Seuil.

——(1976) *Nachgelassene Schriften und Wissenschaftlicher Briefwechsel*, vol. II, G. Gabriel, H. Hermes, F. Kambartel, C. Thiel and A. Veraaort (eds), Hamburg: Meiner.

——(1988) [1952] 'On concept and object' [1892], in P. Geach and M. Black eds and trans., *Translations from the Philosophical Writings of Gottlob Frege*, Oxford: Blackwell.

Freud, S. (1912) 'The dynamics of transference', in *Works*, ed. J. Strachey, standard edn, vol. 12, London: Hogarth Press.

Gadamer, H. G. (1977) *Philosophical Hermeneutics*, Berkeley CA: University of California Press (trans. by D. E. Linge of a selection from Gadamer, *Kleine Schriften*, [1976] 3 vols, Tübingen: Mohr).

——(1983) *Heideggers Wege: Studien zu Spätwerk*, Tübingen: Mohr.

Gasché, R. (1986) *The Tain of the Mirror*, Cambridge MA: Harvard University Press.

——(1994a) 'Strictly bonded', in *Inventions of Difference*, Cambridge MA and London: Harvard University Press, 171–98.

——(1994b) 'A relation called "literary": Derrida on Kafka's "Before the Law"', *ASCA Brief 2, Amsterdam School for Cultural Analysis, Theory and Interpretation*, Amsterdam: University of Amsterdam.

Geach, P. and Black, M. (eds) (1988) [1952] *Translations from the Philosophical Writings of Gottlob Frege*, Oxford: Blackwell.

Geach, P. and Stoothoff, R. H. (1968) 'What actually exists', *Proceedings of the Aristotelian Society*, vol. xlii (supplementary volume), 7–30.

Gellner, E. (1979) [1959] *Words and Things: An Examination of, and an Attack on, Linguistic Philosophy, With a Foreword by Bertrand Russell*, London: Routledge.

Genet, J. (1968) 'Ce qui est resté d'un Rembrandt déchiré en petits carrés bien réguliers et foutu aux chiottes', in *Oeuvres complètes*, vol. IV, Paris: Gallimard, 19–31.

——(1972) 'Une lettre de Jean Genet', in *Lettres françaises*, 29 March 1972, 14.

Göbel, W. (1984) *Reflektierende und Absolute Vernunft die: Aufgabe der Philosophie und ihre Losung in Kants Vernunftkritiken und Hegels Differenzschrift*, Bonn: Bouvier.

Godel, R. (1957) *Les Sources manuscrites du 'Cours de linguistique générale'*, Geneva: Droz.

Guéroult, M. (1977) [1931] 'Le Jugement de Hegel sur l'antithétique de la raison pure', reprinted in Guéroult, *Etudes de philosophie allemande*, Paris: Vrin, 125–48.

Hacking, I. (1993) 'On Kripke's and Goodman's uses of "Grue"', *Philosophy*, 68, 269–95.

Hegel, G. W. F. (1969) [1802–3] 'Über die wissenschaftlichen Behandlungsarten des Naturrechts', in *Hegel: Werke: Theorie-Werkausgabe*, vol. 2, Frankfurt: Suhrkamp.

——(1821) *Grundlinien der Philosophie des Rechts*, Berlin [trans. S. W. Dyde (1896) *The Philosophy of Right*, London].

——(1973) [1807] *Phänomenologie des Geistes*, Frankfurt: Suhrkamp [trans. A. V. Miller (1977) *The Phenomenology of Spirit*, Oxford: Oxford University Press].

Heidegger, M. (1929a) *Vom Wesen des Grundes*, Frankfurt [trans. T. Malick (1969) *The Essence of Reasons*, Evanston IL: Northwestern University Press].

——(1929b) *Kant und das Problem der Metaphysik*, Frankfurt: Vittorio Klostermann [trans. J. S. Churchill (1962) *Kant and the Problem of Metaphysics*, Bloomington IN: Indiana University Press; trans. and introduction by A. de Waelhens and W. Biemel, *Kant et le problème de la métaphysique*, Paris: Gallimard].

——(1931–2, 1940) *Platons Lehre der Wahrheit* [*Plato's Doctrine of Truth*] in *Gesamtausgabe*, vol. 9.

——(1935–6) 'Der Ursprung des Kunstwerkes', in *Holzwege* (1952), *Gesamtausgabe* (1977) vol. 5, Frankfurt: Vittorio Klostermann [trans. A. Hofstadter, 'The origin of the work of art', partially reproduced in D. F. Krell, (1977) *Basic Writings*, San Francisco CA: Harper & Row].

—— (1956) [1977] *Zur Seinsfrage*, Frankfurt: Vittorio Klostermann [trans. W. Klubach and J. T. Wilde (1958) *The Question of Being*, New Haven CT: College and University Press].

——(1957) [1982, 7th edn] *Identität und Differenz*, Pfullingen: Neske [trans. J. Stambaugh (1969) *Identity and Difference*, New York: Harper & Row].

——(1966) *Einführung in die Metaphysik*, Tübingen: Niemeyer [trans. R. Manheim (1987) [1959] *An Introduction to Metaphysics*, New Haven CT: Yale University Press].

——(1969) *Zur Sache des Denkens*, Tübingen: Niemeyer.

——(1975) *Die Grundprobleme der Phänomenologie*, Frankfurt: Vittorio Klostermann [trans. A. Hofstadter (1982) *The Basic Problems of Phenomenology*, Bloomington IN: Indiana University Press].

——(1977a) ed. D. F. Krell, *Martin Heidegger: Basic Writings*, San Francisco CA: Harper & Row.

——(1977b) [1952] 'Die Zeit der Weltbild', in *Holzwege* (1952) and *Gesamtausgabe* (1977) vol. 5, Frankfurt: Vittorio Klostermann [trans. W. Lovitt (1977) 'The age of the world picture', in *The Question Concerning Technology and other Essays*, New York: Harper & Row].

——(1978) *Metaphysische Anfangsgründe der Logik im Ausgang von Leibniz*, Frankfurt: Vittorio Klostermann [trans. M. Heim (1984) *The Metaphysical Foundations of Logic*, Bloomington IN: Indiana University Press].

——(1978–) *Gesamtausgabe* [collected works] Frankfurt: Vittorio Klostermann, in progress.

——(1979) [1927] *Sein und Zeit*, Tübingen: Niemeyer [trans. (1962) J. Macquarrie and E. Robinson, reprinted 1967, *Being and Time*, Oxford: Blackwell].

——(1985) [1954] *Vorträge und Aufsätze*, Pfullingen: Neske.

——(1986) [1929a] *Was ist Metaphysik?*, Frankfurt: Klostermann [trans. D. F. Krell (1977) *Martin Heidegger: Basic Writings*, San Francisco CA: Harper & Row].

Heinemann, F. 'The meaning of negation', *Proceedings of the Aristotelian Society*, new series, vol. 44, 127–52.

Hill, L. (1989) 'Marguerite Duras and the limits of fiction', *Paragraph*, 12, 12 March, 1–22.

Hobson, M. (1982) 'Deconstruction, empiricism and the postal services', *French Studies*, 290–314.

——(1986) 'History traces', in D. Attridge, G. P. Bennington and R. Young (eds) *Post-Structuralism and the Question of History*, Cambridge: Cambridge University Press, 101–15.

——(1987) 'Les négations de Derrida', in D. Kelley and I. Llasera (eds) *Cross-References*, Leeds: The Society for French Studies, 57–64.

——(1992) 'Opinio Regina Mundi?', *Cambridge Review*, 113, 92–102.

——(1992) 'The Unsaid of Plato's Cave: Heidegger and Derrida', *Journal of the Institute of Romance Studies*, 333–48.

——(1993) 'La logique et ses confins: le cas d'Oskar Becker', *Le Passage des frontières, autour du travail de Jacques Derrida* (Colloque de Cerisy, 1992) Paris: Galilée, 421–6.

Hofstaedter, D. (1979) *Gödel, Escher, Bach: An Eternal Gold Braid*, Harmondsworth: Penguin.

Hofstaedter, D. and Dennet, D. (eds) (1981) *The Mind's I Composed and Arranged by Douglas R. Hofstaedter and Daniel C. Dennett*, Brighton: Harvester; see Lem 1971.

Howells, C. (1993) 'Sartre et la deconstruction du sujet', in G. Idt (ed.) *Sartre: itinéraires, confrontations (Etudes Sartriennes 5)*, Paris: RTM, Université de Paris X.

Hübener, W. (1971) 'Die Logik der Negation als ontologisches Erkenntnismittel', in H. Weinrich (ed.) *Positionen des Negativität*, Munich: Fink, 105–40.

Husserl, E. (1900) *Logische Untersuchungen*, Halle: M. Niemeyer [trans. J. N. Findlay (1970) *Logical Investigations*, 2 vols, London: Routledge].

——(1913) *Ideen zu einer reinen Phänomenologie*, Halle: M. Niemeyer [trans. W. Boyce Gibson (1931) *Ideas*, London: George Allen & Unwin].

——(1959) *Husserl*, in *Cahiers de Royaumont* (philosophie no. III) Paris: Editions de Minuit.

Hyppolite, J. (1946) *Genèse et structure de la 'Phénoménologie de l'esprit' de Hegel*, Paris: Aubier Montaigne.

Imbert, C. L. (ed. and trans. G. Frege) (1971) , *Ecrits logiques et philosophiques*, Paris: Editions du Seuil.

Jakobson, R. (1971), 'Shifters, verbal categories and the Russian verb', in *Selected Writings*, vol. II, The Hague: Mouton, 130–147.

Johnson, B. (1977) 'The frame of reference: Poe, Lacan, Derrida', *Yale French Studies*, 55/6, 457–65.

Johnson, C. M. (1993) *System and Writing in the Philosophy of Jacques Derrida*, Cambridge: Cambridge University Press.

——(1996) 'La leçon de philosophie: de Derrida à Lévi-Strauss', in *Passions de la littérature: avec Jacques Derrida*, actes du colloque de Louvain, Paris: Galilée, 125–40.

——(1997) *Derrida: The Scene of Writing*, London: Phoenix.

Kafka, F. *Vor dem Gesetz*, in P. Raabe (ed.) (1991) *Sämtliche Erzählungen*, Frankfurt: Fischer Taschenbuch.

Kant, E. (1781, 2nd edn 1787) *Kritik der reinen Vernunft*, Riga [trans. N. Kemp Smith (1929) *Critique of Pure Reason*, London: Macmillan].

——(1783) *Prolegomena to Any future Metaphysics*, trans. P. G. Lucas (1953) Manchester: Manchester University Press.

Kant, E., Brandt, R., Mohr, G., Perrinjaquet, A., Seel, G. and Stark, W. (eds) (1988) *'Du sens interne': un texte inédit d'Immanuel Kant*, in *Cahiers* of the *Revue de Théologie et de Philosophie*, vol. 13.

Kemp Smith, N. (1923) (trans.) *Critique of Pure Reason*, London: Macmillan.

Kierkegaard, S. (1830) *The Concept of Irony, With Continual Reference to Socrates*, trans. E. H. and H. V. Hong (1989) Princeton NJ: Princeton University Press.

Kisiel, T. (1993) *The Genesis of Heidegger's* Being and Time, Berkeley CA and London: University of California Press.

Kneale, W. A. (1971) [1962] *The Development of Logic*, Oxford: Clarendon Press.

Kofman, S. (1974) *Quatre romans analytiques*, Paris: Galilée.

Kojève, A. (1947) [1968] *Introduction à la lecture de Hegel*, Paris: Gallimard.

Kripke, S. (1980) [1972] *Naming and Necessity*, Oxford: Blackwell.

——(1982) *Wittgenstein on Rules and Private Language: An Elementary Exposition*, Oxford: Blackwell.

Lacan, J. (1966) *Ecrits*, Paris: Editions du Seuil [trans. A. Sheridan (1977) *Ecrits: A Selection*, London: Tavistock].

Leavey, J. P. and Rand, R. (1986) *Glassary*, Lincoln NE: University of Nebraska Press.

Lem, S. (1971) 'Non serviam', in *A Perfect Vacuum*, trans. Michael Kandel, Harmondsworth: Penguin; reprinted in D. Hofstaedter and D. Dennett (eds) (1981) *The Mind's I Composed and Arranged by Douglas R. Hofstaedter and Daniel C. Dennett*, Brighton: Harvester.

Levinas, E. (1990) [1974] *Autrement qu'être ou au-delà de l'ssence*, Paris: Gallimard [trans. A. Lingis (1981) *Otherwise than Being: Or, Beyond Essence*, The Hague: Martinus Nijhoff].

Lloyd, G. E. R. (1990) *Demystifying Mentalities*, Cambridge: Cambridge University Press.

Long, A. A. and Sedley, D. N. (1987) *The Hellenistic Philosophers*, 2 vols, Cambridge: Cambridge University Press.

Lowe, E. (1987) 'The indexical fallacy in McTaggart's proof of the unreality of time', *Mind*, XCVI, 61–70.

Lyons, J. (1982) 'Deixis and subjectivity: *Loquor ergo sum?*', in R. J. Jarvella and W. Klein (eds) *Speech, Place and Action*, Chichester: Wiley.

——(1991) [1977] *Semantics*, 2 vols, Cambridge: Cambridge University Press.

Mall, R. A. (1973) *Experience and Reason: the Phenomenology of Husserl and its Relation to Hume's Philosophy*, The Hague: Martinus Nijhoff.

Marion, J. L. (1989) *Réduction et donation: recherches sur Husserl, Heidegger et la phénoménologie*, Paris: Presses Universitaires de France.

Marx, K. (1993) [1939] *Grundrisse*, London: Penguin.

Merleau-Ponty, M. (1968) *Résumés des cours, Collège de France 1952–60*, Paris: Gallimard.

Moore, A. W. (1990) *The Infinite*, London: Routledge.

Moriarty, M. (1991) *Roland Barthes*, Cambridge: Polity.

Mouffe, C. (1996) (ed.) *Deconstruction and Pragmatism*, London: Routledge.

Ott, H. (1988) *Martin Heidegger, Unterwegs zu Seiner Biographie*, Frankfurt and New York: Campus Verlag.

Owen, G. E. L. (1986) *Logic, Science and Dialectics: Collected Papers in Greek Philosophy*, ed. M. Nussbaum, London: Duckworth.

Panofsky, E. (1975) [1924–5, first version, in German] *La Perspective comme forme symbolique*, préface de M. Dalai Emiliani, trans. directed by G. Ballangé, Paris: Editions de Minuit.

Pascal, B. (1962) *Pensées*, Paris: Editions du Seuil, collection *Points*.

Pattee, H. H. (1971, paper given in 1968) 'Can life explain quantum mechanics?', in T. Bastin (ed.) *Quantum Theory and Beyond*, Cambridge: Cambridge University Press, 307–20.

Peddle, F. (1980) *Thought and Being: Hegel's Criticism of Kant's System of Cosmological Ideas*, Washington DC: University Press of America.

Petrosino, S. (1983) *Jacques Derrida e le Legge del Possibile*, Naples: Guida Editori.

Plato, *Theaetetus and Sophist*, Greek text with trans. by H. N. Fowler, Cambridge MA: Loeb/London: Harvard University Press.

Pöggeler, O. [1959] 'Being as appropriation', in M. Murray (ed.) (1978) *Heidegger and Modern Philosophy*,, New Haven CT and London: Yale University Press, 84–115.

——(1963) *Der Denkweg Martin Heideggers*, Pfüllingen: Neske.

Pokorny, I. (1959, 1969) *Indo-germanisches etymologisches Wörterbuch*, 2 vols, Berne and Munich: Francke Verlag.

Priest, G. (1995) *Beyond the Limits of Thought*, Cambridge: Cambridge University Press.

Prior, A. N. (1957) *Time and Modality*, Oxford: Clarendon Press.

Prior, A. N. and Fine, K. (1977) *Worlds, Times and Selves*, London: Duckworth.

Proust, J. (1991) Postscript, in J. Searle, *Pour reitérer les différences: réponse à Derrida*, (trans. of J. Searle, *Reiterating the Différences*), Paris: Editions de l'Eclat.

Putnam, H. (1988) *Representation and Reality*, Cambridge MA and London: MIT.

Ritter, J. (1976) *Historisches Wörterbuch der Philosophie*, Darmstadt: Wissenschaftliche Buchgesellschaft.

Riha, K. (1971) *Cross-Reading und Cross-Talking Zitat-Collage als Poetische und Satirische Technik*, Stuttgart: J. B. Metzlersche Verlagsbuchhandlung.

Rorty, R. (1991) *Essays on Heidegger and Others: Philosophical Papers*, vol. 2, Cambridge: Cambridge University Press.

Rose, M. A. (1979) *Parody/Meta-Fiction: An Analysis of Parody as a Critical Mirror to the Writing and Reception of Fiction*, London: Croom Helm.

Rosen, M. (1982) *Hegel's Dialectic and its Criticism*, Cambridge: Cambridge University Press.

Rosen, S. (1969) *Nihilism: A Philosophical Essay*, New Haven CT and London: Yale University Press.

Rousset, J. (1962) *Forme et signification: essais sur les structures littéraires de corneille à Claudel*, Paris: Corti.

Ruby, C. (1989) *Les Archipels de la différence: Foucault – Derrida – Deleuze – Lyotard*, Paris: Editions du Félin.

Russell, B., see Gellner, E.

Ryan, M. (1982) *Marxism and Deconstruction: A Critical Articulation*, Baltimore MD: Johns Hopkins University Press.

Sartre, J.-P. (1943) *L'Etre et le néant*, Paris: Gallimard.

——(1971) *L'Idiot de la famille; G. Flaubert de 1821 à 1857*, vol. I, Paris: Gallimard.

——(1972)'L'homme au magnétophone', in *Situations*, IX, Paris: Gallimard, 329–37; reprinted 1969, *Les Temps modernes*, no. 274.

——(1977) [1952] Preface to Stéphane Mallarmé, *Poésies*, Paris: Gallimard.

Saussure, F. de (1985) [1916] *Cours de linguistique générale*, publié par Charles Bally et Alber Séchehaye, avec la collaboration de Albert Riedlinger; édition critique préparée par Tullio di Mauro, postface de Louis-Jean Calvet, Paris: Payot [trans. R. Harris (1972) *Course in General Linguistics*, London: Duckworth].

Schmidt, J. (1985) *Maurice Merleau-Ponty: Between Phenomenology and Structuralism*, Basingstoke: Macmillan.

Schmitt, H.-J. (ed.) (1975) *Romantik I*, vol. 8 of O. F. Best and H-J. Schmitt (eds) *Die deutsche Literatur: Ein Abriß in Text und Darstellung*, Stuttgart: Reklam jun.

Searle, J. (1969) *Speech Acts*, Cambridge: Cambridge University Press.

Sherover, C. M. (1971) *Heidegger, Kant and Time*, Bloomington IN and London: Indiana University Press.

Skinner, Q. (1988) *Meaning and Context: Quentin Skinner and his Critics*, ed. J. Tully, Oxford: Polity Press and Blackwell.

Smith, N. K. (1984) [1918] *A Commentary to Kant's* Critique of Pure Reason, Atlantic Highlands NJ: Humanities Press/London and Basingstoke: Macmillan.

Sollers, P. (1968) *Nombres*, Paris: Editions du Seuil.

Staten, H. (1985) *Wittgenstein and Derrida*, Oxford: Blackwell.

Stern, J. P. (1995) *The Dear Purchase*, Cambridge: Cambridge University Press.

Szondi, P. (1964) *Satz und Gegensatz: sechs Essays*, Frankfurt: Insel.

Taubes, J. (1971) 'Vom Adverb "nichts" zum Substantiv "das Nichts": Überlegungen zu Heideggers Frage nach das Nichts', in H. Weinrich (ed.) *Positionen des Negativität*, Munich: Fink, 141–54.

Taylor, C. (1964) *The Explanation of Behaviour*, London: Routledge.

Tugendhat, E. (1965) [1970] *Der Wahrheitsbegriff bei Husserl und Heidegger*, Berlin: Walter de Gruyter.

——(1992) 'Das Sein und das Nichts' (1970) in E. Tugendhat, *Philosophische Aufsätze*, Frankfurt: Suhrkamp, 36–66.

Vernant, J.-P. and Vidal-Naquet, P. (1974) *Mythe et tragédie en Grèce antique*, Paris: Maspéro.

Weber, S. (1984) 'The debts of deconstruction and other, related assumptions', in J. S. Smith and W. Kerrigan (eds) *Taking Chances: Derrida, Psychoanalysis and Literature*, Baltimore MD and London: Johns Hopkins University Press, 33–65.

Williams, B. (1981) *Moral Luck*, Cambridge: Cambridge University Press.

Wittgenstein, L. (1961) *Tractatus Logico-Philosophicus*, trans. D. F. Pears and B. F. McGuiness, London: Routledge and Kegan Paul.

——(1967) [1984, 3rd edn 1989, first published in English 1967] 'Zu Heidegger', in B. F. Guinness (ed.) *Wittgenstein und der Wiener Kreis, Gespräche, aufgezeichnet von Friedrich Waismann*, Frankfurt: Suhrkamp, 68–9 [trans. and ed. M. Murray (1978) in *Heidegger and Modern Philosophy*, New Haven CT and London: Yale University Press, 80–1].

Wolff, M. (1981) *Der Begriff des Widerspruchs: eine Studie zur Dialektik Kants und Hegels*, Königstein: Hain.

Wright, G. H. von (1959) 'On the logic of negation', in *Commentationes Physico-Mathematicae*, XII, Helsinki-Helsingfors: Societas Scientiarum Fennica, 1–30.

——(1996) 'Truth-logics', in 'Six essays in philosophical logic', *Acta Philosophica Fennnica*, 60, 70–91, Helsinki: Societas Philosophica Fennica.

Name index

Subject index